I0760193

Representing the National Landscape in Irish Romanticism

Irish Studies
James MacKillop, *Series Editor*

Other titles in Irish Studies

Carmilla: A Critical Edition
Joseph Sheridan Le Fanu; Kathleen Costello-Sullivan, ed.

Collaborative Dubliners: Joyce in Dialogue
Vicki Mahaffey, ed.

The Irish Bridget: Irish Immigrant Women in Domestic Service in America, 1840–1930
Margaret Lynch-Brennan

Making Ireland Irish: Tourism and National Identity since the Irish Civil War
Eric G. E. Zuelow

Memory Ireland. Volume 1: *History and Modernity*; Volume 2: *Diaspora and Memory Practices*
Oona Frawley, ed.

The Midnight Court / Cúirt an Mheán Oiche: A Critical Edition
Brian Merriman; David Marcus, trans.

"Other People's Diasporas": Negotiating Race in Contemporary Irish and Irish American Culture
Sinéad Moynihan

The Second Coming of Paisley: Militant Fundamentalism and Ulster Politics
Richard Lawrence Jordan

Representing the National Landscape in Irish Romanticism

Julia M. Wright

Syracuse University Press

First Edition 2014

14 15 16 17 18 19 6 5 4 3 2 1

∞ The paper used in this publication meets the minimum requirements of the American National Standard for Information Sciences—Permanence of Paper for Printed Library Materials, ANSI Z39.48-1992.

For a listing of books published and distributed by Syracuse University Press, visit our website at www.SyracuseUniversityPress.syr.edu.

ISBN: 978-0-8156-3353-2 (cloth) 978-0-8156-5266-3 (e-book)

Library of Congress Cataloging-in-Publication Data

Wright, Julia M.
Representing the National Landscape in Irish Romanticism /
Julia M. Wright. — First edition.
pages cm. — (Irish Studies)
Includes bibliographical references and index.
ISBN 978-0-8156-3353-2 (cloth : alk. paper) — ISBN 978-0-8156-5266-3 (ebook)
1. English literature—Irish authors—History and criticism. 2. English literature—19th century—History and criticism. 3. National characteristics, Irish, in literature. 4. Romanticism—Ireland. I. Title.
PR8752.W76 2014
820.9'9417—dc23 2013050919

Manufactured in the United States of America

Contents

Acknowledgments

I would like to begin by thanking the Canada Research Chairs Program and the Social Sciences and Humanities Research Council of Canada for their generous support not only while I worked on this book, but also during the years before I even began: with the funding that they provided, I was able to spend months in archives, across the past fifteen years, reading countless volumes of poetry and myriad novels as well as prose nonfiction both weird and wonderful, and only occasionally ghastly. My gratitude goes as well to the British Library, where much of that reading was done: it not only offers a truly sublime collection of books but also provides a marvelous workspace and knowledgeable, graciously helpful staff. No less vital to my research were the staff at Dalhousie's Killam Memorial Library, especially those in Document Delivery, who twice astonished me by finding and delivering nineteenth-century books so rare that they are not available even in the British Library and I had to read them in the welcoming environment of the Reading Room for Dalhousie University Archives and Special Collections.

I am especially grateful to the anonymous readers of the manuscript for their detailed and generative responses and to everyone at Syracuse University Press who helped it through the long process of review and preparation for the press. An early version of chapter 6 appeared as "'The Policy of Geography': Cavour's *Considerations*, European Geopolitics, and Ireland in the 1840s," *Romanticism and Victorianism on the Net* 48 (Nov. 2007), and parts of chapters 1 and 3 were initially presented in my keynote at the 2008 Wordsworth Conference, which was subsequently published as "Outlaws or

Immigrants? Atlantic Exile and the Stateless Citizen in Irish Romanticism," *Wordsworth Circle* 40, no. 1 (Winter 2009): 36–44.

As I was drafting sections of this book, I benefitted enormously from the feedback of audience members at too many conferences to list here, but particularly worthy of mention are the two "United Islands" conferences (Queen's University, Belfast, 2008 and 2009), "Wild Irish Girls" (Chawton House Library, 2006), and "Romanticism and Evolution" (London, Ontario, 2011). Among those who have generously participated in lively exchanges about Irish literature from which I have learned inestimably—whether in person, over email, or, increasingly it seems, on Facebook—are Frederick Burwick, Andrew Carpenter, Claire Connolly, Susan Egenolf, Danine Farquharson, Sean Farrell, Ina Ferris, Luke Gibbons, Colleen Booker Halverson, Tina Morin, Mary Helen Thuente, John Waters, and a truly wonderful scholar who is much missed, the late Siobhán Kilfeather. I am grateful to every one of them not only for the substance of our conversations, but also for sharing their excitement about the material. My thanks as well to my ever collegial colleagues here at Dalhousie, and, finally, my daily and profound thanks for what Edmund Burke termed "good company, lively conversation, and the endearments of friendship," especially from Joel Faflak, the best of friends, and Jason Haslam, the best of all.

Introduction

> In her sun, in her soil, in her station, thrice blest,
> With back turn'd to Britain, her face to the West.
> —WILLIAM DRENNAN, "Erin" (written 1795)

The land has long been central to articulations of Irish nationality, from diasporic phrases such as "the auld sod" to myriad representations of rural Irishness and from various contested demarcations of territory, such as "beyond the pale," connoting Irish-ruled land beyond English occupation, to the Land Wars. But what of "the emerald isle"? I start here with the source of that popular phrase: William Drennan's song "Erin," written in the mid-1790s and published in the United Irishmen songbook *Paddy's Resource*. In the epigraph for this introduction, Drennan defines Ireland geographically: in terms of agricultural production ("sun" and "soil"), trade routes ("station"), and its proximity to the emerging postcolonial United States ("her face to the West"). Similarly, in the opening verse, Drennan invokes the biblical language of Genesis but does so not to represent the land as an affective object ("the auld sod"), the site of authentic Irishness, or even as governed or owned territory, but in terms of its value:

> When Erin first rose from the dark swelling flood,
> God bless'd the green island. He saw it was good:
> The Emerald of Europe, it sparkled, it shone,
> In the ring of the world the most precious stone![1]

He emphasizes this view still further in a note he added to the 1815 edition of the poem, twenty years after the song was written: claiming credit for coining the phrase "emerald isle," which appears later in the poem, Drennan writes that the epithet is "descriptive of [Ireland's] prime natural beauty, and its inestimable value."[2] While many scholars have noted the close connection between Irish national identity and the land in Irish literature,[3] Drennan's poem suggests a nationalist discourse that is based not on cultural identity, but on general notions of economic viability as the basis for sovereignty: the epithet "the emerald isle" has come to invoke images of verdant green, but in Drennan's poem and note it is an economic image key to claims for sovereignty. Pedro I of Brazil, in an 1822 letter to the *London Times*, draws on the same philosophical framework as Drennan in arguing for his country's independence: "Such a state of things loudly called for a prompt reform of the Government—a reform fully authorized by . . . the violated rights of a country . . . which nature has peculiarly favoured by its geographical and centrical position in the midst of the globe, by its vast ports and maritime stations, and by the natural riches of its soil."[4] Ireland's location, natural resources, and aesthetic value similarly constitute the ground of Ireland's claim to national independence for Drennan and many of his contemporaries. The land is neither insular nor affective, but nationally significant precisely because of the leading edge of what we now term globalization, including trade routes, production of goods for trade, and tourism. In this context, Ireland is necessarily understood in terms of its relationship to other nations—it is "the Emerald of Europe," on the edge of the transatlantic and part of "the ring of the world." It is this concertedly international Ireland that is the focus of this study.

The "Amazing Map": Ireland in International Perspective

Taking its cues from such representations of the land, this study therefore begins not with the question "what does the land mean to the nation?" but rather "what does the nation mean by 'land'?" It presses this question in part to break apart the rigid framework of a romantic nationalism, rooted in the eighteenth-century work of J. G. Herder and related thinkers, in which the people are bound to the land as an article of national faith. The emphasis in Irish history on reclaiming the land—from early colonization to the Land Wars and the Easter Rising—and on exile has led inevitably to an emphasis in Irish studies on the force of romantic nationalism in the establishment of the "folk" as the core of the nation's true identity: the land is "rural," and the people are fundamentally attached to it. In their introduction to the recent volume *Land and Landscape in Nineteenth-Century Ireland*, Úna Ní Bhroiméil and Glenn Hooper suggest that the essays in the collection "stress the human interaction with the land and focus on perception and memory and on the symbolism of land and landscape as key determinants for the formation of character, of self identity," so that "land and landscape are thus linked in a cultural code as critical signifiers of a specific Irish identity."[5] This valuable approach is significant to much discussion of Irish literature, but it roots the nation in individual and national character rather than in public formations, especially the people as they are expressed through a state that operates on the world stage to protect their interests. Seamus Deane has addressed this distinction in part: "ownership of the soil was interpreted by them as a national right; ownership of the land was an individual claim."[6] Moreover, historians have recently considered overlapping geographical frames for Ireland, including the British Isles archipelago, Europe, and the transatlantic.[7] More recently, Claire Connolly has offered fresh insights into the relationship between cartography, travel writing, and romantic-era Irish fiction.[8]

But I wish to stress the economic implications of Deane's point, which can easily be elided in an emphasis on the problem of representation as such. As Benedict Anderson suggests,

> nation-statehood was . . . central to the nineteenth- and twentieth-century nationalist projects that destroyed the huge, polyglot imperial dynastic realms inherited from the age of absolutism, and the even larger colonial-imperialist conglomerations that survived them. For it was felt to represent, with its characteristically republican institutions, a new-found alignment of imagined home and

> imagined home-owners, and to guarantee the stabilization of that alignment through the organized deployment of its political powers and economic resources.[9]

Anderson's all-important "and," supplementing the relationship between "home" and "home-owners" (Deane's "land" relation) through a recognition of "political powers and economic resources," speaks directly to my concern in this study. For the nation-state exists to organize bureaucratically not only the domestic space of the nation, but also its international relations—and those international relations are inextricably bound up with trade (both the how and the what), military concerns, notions of national rights, and ideas of cultural distinctiveness and cultural connections. As Anthony D. Smith puts it, "the 'core doctrine' of nationalism . . . encompasses not only the domain of politics, but those of society and culture as well; and it embraces both the cultural particularism of individual nations and the universal outlook of a 'world of nations,'" although "nationalists have often conducted themselves in such a way as to deny the basic idea . . . of a 'world of nations.'"[10]

Drennan reappears throughout the present study in part because he is not the latter sort of nationalist, but a nationalist who is insistently aware of "the universal outlook of a 'world of nations'"—"the ring of the world," as he puts it in "Erin." In one of his pamphlets against the proposed Act of Union (passed in 1800), which would formally incorporate Ireland within the British nation-state, Drennan, for instance, argues for "a law of nations, recognized and supported, as might cover the universality of *independent* countries, fulfilling their duties and asserting their rights, with its tutelary authority, defending the weakest from the most ambitious, and guaranteeing to all the full possession of their independence, under the ægis of a common power."[11] Drennan clearly follows the more expansive elements of this "core doctrine of nationalism" but is also "international" in the full sense of the original coinage of this term by Jeremy Bentham just a few years before Drennan's pamphlet was written: "The word international, it must be acknowledged, is a new one. . . . It is calculated to express, in a more significant way, the branch of law which goes commonly under the name of the law of nations."[12] In other words, the concept of the "international" relies upon a "law of nations" to regulate what Drennan terms "the universality of independent countries." The phrase "law of nations" is not used by Bentham and Drennan coincidentally but builds on eighteenth-century discussions of this problem, most notably English translations of Emer de Vattel's influential *Le droit des gens* (1758) as *The Law of Nations* (including a 1787 Dublin edition). Drennan, United Irishman, poet, physician, and pamphleteer, is thus drawing on a European discourse of international relations—what Smith terms "the universal outlook of a 'world of nations'"—in which all nations have rights, just as individuals have rights (derived from "nature" or "God"), and nations can cooperate for mutual benefit, just as individuals can. That participating in international relations was a nationalist aspiration for Ireland rather than a historical reality in the eighteenth and nineteenth centuries does not negate its significance to the imaginative writing of this period or the importance of the principle to the diverse body of Irish nationalist thought.

From United Irishmen ballads that claim common cause with Revolutionary France and the postcolonial United States to *The Nation*'s publishing of reports in the mid-1840s from around the world, including migrant reports from North America and accounts of British defeats in South Asia, Irish nationalist writing often explicitly draws on larger geographical networks that establish wide-ranging international comparisons. Various prose narratives suggest, for instance, that the abjection of Irish men through exile ironically allows the demonstration of their merits: Lady Morgan's novel *O'Donnel* (1814), for instance, has a character declare, "I have always heard . . . that an educated and travelled Irishman made the most finished gentleman in the world: unfortunately, however, these advantages are generally purchased at a melancholy price, for, [he is] driven by religious and political disqualification to other countries for education and employment."[13] A number of texts discussed here—from Robert Torrens's novel *Victim of Intolerance* (1814) to the anonymous and undated narrative *The Exile of Ireland!*—similarly offer a kind of colonial Grand Tour in which travel is a corrective but not a solution to colonial disempowerment, replacing political power with demonstrations of individual merit in a larger international arena. On broader terms, various Irish writers grappled with the place of Ireland in the larger world in a substantial literary tradition of grasping Ireland's significance and identity in transnational terms that define "land" in terms of aesthetics, geography, trade, and migration.

The Exile of Ireland! is a sixpence pamphlet or chapbook published in the early 1800s that promises to deliver "the Wonderful Adventures, and Extraordinary Escapes, of an Irish Rebel" and it replicates, or is the source of, some passages in another popular pamphlet printed in at least two editions, *The Life, Voyages, Travels, and Wonderful Adventures of Captain Winterfield . . . a Distinguished Rebel Chief in Ireland.*[14] The *Exile* offers under the guise of autobiography a pastiche of conventional sensational plots, from the straightforward adventure narrative of an impoverished Irish scion having to seek his fortune abroad to a captivity narrative in North America set against the backdrop of military conflict, a gothic romance of forbidden love and attempted elopement in Spain, and a broadly pro-government account of the 1798 Irish Uprising. The narrative thus relies on the mobility of Irishmen, moving back and forth across the Atlantic, a point stressed in the conclusion (not included in the *Winterfield* variation). "On being released from prison," where he was being held for his role in the Uprising, the Exile abandons Ireland for "Wales, till [he] should find a favourable opportunity of escaping to America," and then goes on a small tour of Wales that centers on a climb up, and then down, Mount Snowdon. From the top of Snowdon, the Exile writes,

> I could with pleasure contemplate the amazing map that was unfolded to my view. From hence may be distinctly seen Wicklow Hills in Ireland, the Isle of Man, Cumberland, Lancashire, Cheshire, Shropshire, and part of Scotland; all the counties of

> North Wales, the Isle of Anglesea; rivers, plains, woods, rocks, and mountains, six and twenty lakes, and two seas. It is doubtful whether there is another circular prospect so extensive in any part of the terraqueous globe. Who could take such a survey without feeling his spirits elevated in some proportion to the height? Who could behold so bountiful a display of nature without wonder and extacy?[15]

This sublime vision of a British Isles unified by the perspective from Snowdon seems to heal the rift between state and subject, reconciling the "Irish rebel" to a pan–British Isles homeland through an aesthetic experience that is allied with four-nations unity and romantic transcendence.[16] But this remarkable aesthetic moment is followed by a paragraph with more practical concerns:

> it became necessary to consider that this was no spot where we could properly make any lasting abode, and that the return would be attended with as much difficulty as the ascent. Having descended about two miles, we did not think it would be much amiss to enquire about an exhausted mine we saw at some distance. The mine I was informed was only copper; and happy was it for the Welsh, that their mines did not consist of choicer metals: had they been cursed with either gold or silver, foreign nations long since, in the name of the God of Peace, and under pretence of teaching them an immaculate religion, had laid waste their country, and murdered its inhabitants.[17]

The pragmatic aside about the impossibility of living at the top of Mount Snowdon is an evocative gesture, registering in this otherwise pro-British polemic a suspicion of the sustainability of this unifying vision, particularly amidst the wars for resources that the Exile recognizes informs the imperial project in which he has been variously entangled.

The "pleasure" of the harmonious vision of the four nations thus gives way to the recognition that this cannot be home (no "lasting abode") and that the peacefulness of the peak arises in part from a poverty that has protected the space from imperial predation. Juxtaposing an aesthetic, imaginatively unifying account with a geopolitical account that considers mineral resources in relation to imperial conflict, the "Exile of Ireland" pivots smoothly between the two registers in his account, one uplifting and the other very much tied to his "descent." The Exile then learns that he has passage to Lima, Peru, and leaves the British Isles permanently—for a country that was "cursed with . . . gold" and was "laid waste," as a highly popular play by Irish dramatist Richard Brinsley Sheridan had recently addressed.[18] Traveling between three continents while identifying himself with a homeland defined by economic decline and insurgency, the Exile himself figures Irish subjects' mobility as an effect of national crisis. He simultaneously demonstrates the motility of Irish depictions of the landscape: mixing aesthetic transcendence with mining and "four-nations" integration with imperial predation, the Exile's survey of the landscape registers both the multiple meanings of "land," and the difficulty of reconciling the aesthetic frisson of the view with the violent scramble for resources that lies at the foundation of the imperial project and a modern economy—as well as the impossibility of a "lasting abode" for an Irishman defined at the outset as exilic.

Such texts point to the geographical complexity of Ireland's position in relation to the British Isles in a period when the island of Britain, as Linda Colley has famously argued, became imaginatively and institutionally more unified, without ever voiding the "four-nations" problem.[19] Moreover, the growing importance of Continental and transatlantic connections to economic and cultural life positioned Ireland in relation to larger geopolitical spheres of action. As spheres of action, crucially, they provide a space for agency that breaks free of the determinations of the "natural" or historiography—just as the Exile leaves Snowdon and its mythic vision behind him. As Chenxi Tang suggests, in "the modern semantics of geographic space," "the geographic reality of society . . . is marked by a peculiar kind of spatiality imbued with human purposiveness and action."[20] Moreover, space, as we shall see in chapter 6, is potentially an answer to the imperial temporality that represented Ireland as backward, primitive, and stultified in opposition to a progressive and advanced metropole, reframing the debate over relative merit rather than simply inverting the dominant paradigm.

Romantic Nationalism on Land

The territorial focus of nationalism is perhaps one of its most widely familiar features, but the multiple and contested meanings of "land" are as various as the forms of nationalism. Herderian or romantic nationalism ties the folk to the land on "organic" terms, viewing national identity and allegiances as arising from and rooted in the hills, rivers, and fields of the homeland. Civic nationalism, focusing on the willed participation of free individuals in a shared state, coming out of Lockean liberalism and related trends in Enlightenment thought, does not ground identity in the natural space but arguably overlaps with emerging bureaucratic regimes (associated by Smith with the "neoclassical" roots of modern nationalism) that increasingly concerned themselves with the management and control of territory, a concern that shifted toward geographical resources as the Industrial Revolution took hold. Diasporic nationalism understands the land as absent origin, on terms drawn from romantic nationalism and, Anderson suggests, is a response itself not to an actual ground, but to the increasing mobility of populations and print cultures (as is evident in the Exile's narrative): "The nativeness of natives is always unmoored, its real significance hybrid and oxymoronic. It appears when Moors, heathens, Mohammedans, savages, Hindoos, and so forth are becoming obsolete, that is, not only when, in the proximity of real print-encounters, substantial numbers of Vietnamese read, write, and perhaps speak French but also when Czechs do the same with German and Jews with Hungarian. Nationalism's purities (and thus also cleansings) are set to emerge from exactly this hybridity."[21] Antiquarian nationalism views the land as the palimpsest of history, defined by the sites of historical events and the archaeological residues of the past. Cultural nationalism often allows space for viewing the land as affective object, its aesthetic pull undergirding national feeling via works of culture (poetry, paintings, tourism); it also has strong ties to romantic nationalism, arising philosophically from the work of Herder and its understanding of the land as a determinant of cultural identity (and affiliated with the folkloric movement that links Irish and German nationalism from the 1820s, particularly through the exchanges between the Irish folklorist Thomas Crofton Croker and Germany's Grimm brothers). These are all broad classifications, of course, and nationalist discourse in literature is rarely so neatly pigeonholed.

For Herder and other romantic nationalists, the landscape shapes the national character, and affection for it is foundational to that character. In a work first published in German in 1784–91 but translated and published in English in 1800, Herder critiques the emerging theory of races in proto-anthropology:

> For every nation is one people, having it's own national form, as well as it's own language: the climate, it is true, stamps on each it's mark, or spreads over it a slight veil, but not sufficient to destroy the original national character. . . . Complexions run into each other; forms follow the genetic character: and upon the whole, all are at last but shades of the same great picture, extending through all ages, and over all parts of the Earth. They belong not, therefore, so properly to systematic natural history, as to the physico-geographical history of man.[22]

Herder offers a model of one race, many nations—with "a slight veil" of modification through climate. Hence, he later elaborates on his idea of "a *physico-geographical history of the descent and diversification of our species* according to periods and climates," suggesting that nations are altered by migration to other climates and that nations' characters cannot be altered by cultural influence.[23] Nature trumps nurture. At the other extreme, writing half a century earlier, David Hume argued strenuously against climate as a cause of national character—a point the influential nationalist thinker Ernest

Renan would repeat at the end of the nineteenth century.[24] Working within a larger tradition of civic nationalism with roots in the writings of John Locke, Hume proposes instead that national character is a consequence of shared history and culture both within one nation and between adjacent nations: "Where several neighbouring nations have a very close communication together, either by policy, commerce, or travelling, they acquire a similitude of manners, proportioned to the communication."[25] Hume and Herder are opposed on a number of ideas central to nationalism, while agreeing on the legitimacy of national character as an area of inquiry. According to Hume, "The same set of manners will follow a nation, and adhere to them over the whole globe," but Herder contends, "Nature has not established her boundaries between remote lands in vain," pointing to "the history of conquests, as well as of commercial companies, and especially that of missions" as evidence that those who journey out of Europe "have degenerated both in body and mind" and "*even the european industry of less debauched colonies in other quarters of the Globe is not always able to avert the effect of climate.*"[26]

This is a significant difference for debates about imperialism. Hume's model negates biological causes for national character, and so it can allow the preservation of national character outside of the home nation and for the reshaping of indigenous national characters through imperial influence. Herder's model, despite its historical connection to racism and association of non-European spaces with degeneracy, makes empire a fool's game:

> O sons of Dedalus, emissaries of Fate, how many instruments are in your hands for conferring happiness on nations by humane and compassionate means! and how has a proud insolent love of gain led you almost every where into a different path! All new comers from a foreign land, who have submitted to naturalize themselves with the inhabitants, have not only enjoyed their love and friendship, but have ultimately found, that their mode of life was not altogether unsuitable to the climate: but how few such there are! how seldom does an european hear from the native of any country

> the praise, 'he is a rational man like us!' And does not Nature revenge every insult offered her? Where are the conquests, the factories, the invasions, of former times, when distant foreign lands were visited by a different race, for the sake of devastation or plunder! The still breath of climate has dissipated or consumed them, and it was not difficult for the natives to give the finishing stroke to the rootless tree.[27]

Hume and Herder, both available in English in the British Isles from 1800 forward, bracket the range of ideas on national character available to many of the authors discussed here, including opposing views on such apparently physical fundamentals as the role of climate and geography. This diversity is not just about the much discussed reversibility of nationalism, able to support fascism in some contexts and liberation movements in others. To accept the foundational role of climate, as in Herder, is to challenge the imperial project, at least the form of empire that relies on a centralized bureaucracy and cultural assimilation, while enforcing a view of national identity as biologically determined and therefore monolithic. To reject the role of climate in favor of largely cultural influences, as in Hume, is to make the imperial project feasible, looking forward to a uniform imperial culture that stretches across the globe, while facilitating a more diverse and fluid national identity. As Hume insists, "The manners of a people change very considerably from one age to another; either by great alterations in their government, by the mixtures of new people, or by that inconstancy, to which all human affairs are subject."[28] Romantic nationalism, via Herder, facilitates both anti-imperial agendas and the determinisms of national character—land determines biology, and biology is destiny. Enlightenment ideas of nationality, such as Hume's, argue for the viability of imperialism's assimiliationist project not just for the sake of imperialism as such but also because it clears space for diversity within the nation's borders and the possibility of cultural change, and establishes the importance of the nation's relationships to those beyond its borders and in various configurations that include but are not limited to the imperial.

This debate is not just an eighteenth-century one but also continues to shape discussions of nationalism, particularly through the tricky term *ethnicity* and the recognition that such categories are constituted relationally. As Joep Leerssen puts it, "*Ethnicity* here [in nationalism studies] means nothing more or less than the collective acceptance of a shared self-image,"[29] not the biologically determined category it denotes in other contexts. For Leerssen, this "self-image" is not genealogically derived but interculturally produced, as he argues for "national thought and nationalism . . . as the articulation and instrumentalization of collective self-images, derived from *an opposition against different, other nations*."[30] This is not an unusual stance in modern nationalism studies. In an early essay, Anthony D. Smith offers a less conflict-driven version in identifying "certain cultural ties and sentiments" as constitutive of "an 'ethnic substratum' of nationalism among the European populations after the Reformation," including "an association of the population with a particular geographical location, and *with a distinctive constellation of neighbours*."[31] But in recent years Smith has moved away from his earlier view that nationalism as an ideology was shaped by the confluence of two streams of thought, romanticism and neoclassicism. He has consequently rejected the work of E. J. Hobsbawm and Benedict Anderson (and to some extent, implicitly, Ernest Gellner, who argued for nationalism as an ideology that serves elite interests) as "social constructionis[m]":[32] "Nations, in these views, are the product of 'cultural work' on the part of elites; without that cultural work, without such elite narratives, the nation is unimaginable and incommunicable"; he continues, "constructionists . . . are unable to grasp and credit the emotional depth of loyalties to historical nations and nationalisms," and so he proposes instead an "ethnosymbolic approach" that "analyze[s] the rise of nations in terms of antecedent ethnic ties and popular formations."[33] Hovering behind much of Smith's recent work is the premise that emotion arises from populist conceptions, as he seeks to "bring the popular, emotional, and moral dimensions of national identity back into focus."[34]

From the perspective of cultural history, there are two problems with this aspect of Smith's recent arguments. First, the idea that "cultural work" by elites and popular culture are discrete entities fails to account for the circulation of cultures across such divides (Hume acknowledges this in his discussion of diversity within nations and the flow of culture across national borders). While Marxist cultural studies have generally supported a Gramscian concern about an elite propagating self-serving ideas through culture, the details of cultural history complicate such a picture: consider, for instance, United Irishmen ballads lampooning Edmund Burke's *Reflections on the Revolution in France* or the eighteenth-century recuperation of oral, popular culture for elite audiences through songbooks and antiquarian studies. The arrival of modern print culture, which Anderson connects to the rise of nationalism,[35] further stirred the cultural pot by making available to more and more readers not only the works of canonical (largely hegemonic) authors, but also relatively cheap translations of literatures in other languages, controversial political pamphlets, pornography, and a vast array of other materials that do not easily fit into a top-down and nationally insulated model of cultural distribution. Second, the identification of emotion with the popular and the formation of self-serving "narratives" with the elite risks repeating a centuries-old hegemonic model in which those with power are rational and reflective and those without power are emotional and unreflective: men versus women, upper class versus lower class, white versus nonwhite, colonizer versus colonized. Such an identification is, moreover, fundamentally incompatible with eighteenth-century theories of emotion in which quality of emotion is identified with greater civility and reason and hence is rooted in ideas of nation by elites around 1800 through such concepts as "national feeling."[36] Further, while Smith tries "to dispense with biological references," he still relies on terms such as "prior ethnic ties," "memories," and "inner worlds,"[37] which seem to reinstate virtually what Herder and later, after J. S. Blumenbach, racist biology sought to achieve: a determining identity that somehow precedes culture.

Even Leerssen looks for a noncultural ground: "In this book I want to . . . tak[e] as my starting point a return to the technical meaning of the *ethnie* . . . as a subjective community established by shared culture and historical memories."[38] How "historical memories" might be distinct from "culture" remains as mysterious, however, as Smith's "inner worlds." Leerssen departs from Smith in focusing on a more poststructuralist view of identity formation: "whereas Smith sought the root system of nationalism in 'the ethnic origins of nations,' I propose to locate it in a tradition of *ethnotypes*—commonplaces and stereotypes of how we identify, view and characterize others as opposed to ourselves."[39] This oppositional logic, key to Leerssen's exploration of European nationalisms, risks oversimplifying the complicated field in which nations are defined. While Hume argues for the influence of history, personalities (both striking individuals and overall patterns of tendencies), political system, and neighboring nations on "national character," a century later the Irish nationalist newspaper *The Nation* proposed a model rather close to Leerssen's: "Opposition has a tendency to force its object to concentration, for resistance long-continued grows into hard unflinching unyieldingness, else it is converted into obsequious compliance. This peculiarity in the characteristics of a nation breeds dislike in foreigners. Foreign antipathy begets domestic love of fatherland."[40] Hume includes such "Opposition" as a possibility as well but also contends that "where several neighbouring nations have a very close communication together, either by policy, commerce, or travelling, they acquire a similitude of manners, proportioned to the communication."[41]

The understanding of nationalism as negation, as a rejection of what is "Other," is closely allied with territorialism, the latter spatializing what the negation renders ideological: marking a boundary between inside and outside. But such isolationist ideas of the nation fail to take account of the ways in which nationalist discourse might also accommodate sameness and multiple international connections such as those noted by Hume or readily demonstrated through print culture, including links between Ireland and the postcolonial

United States, between the United States and France during the early years of the republic, between England and Italy during the struggle for Italian unification, or including, say, pan-European learning in ancient Greek and Latin literature. Trade routes, the circulation of print, political alliances, and migration—all contributed to cooperative nationalist projects based not just on opposition to "them," but also on an expansion of "us" and with commensurately fluid notions of territory. Going beyond Deane's distinction between "land" and "soil," we need to take into account, for instance, the myriad ways in which "land" was used to solidify national claims not merely to territory, but also to legitimacy. With the rise of the picturesque, the beauty of national landscapes was taken as a reflection of national merit; with the increasing pressures of the Industrial Revolution, the value of the land in mineral resources and in trade routes was taken as the foundation of national autonomy; and, through it all, the land was used as a redolent symbol of the nation's political condition, where the waste land signifies political predation and rich green fields a successful and harmonious society. Geography, in other words, is figuratively and variously entwined with politics in this body of literature, perhaps most directly in the emphasis on economics as a necessarily international concern.

Romantic Literature Aslant Romantic Nationalism

While the "four-nations" approach inaugurated by J. G. A. Pocock has yielded a great deal of important work in romanticism studies that takes a comparatist approach to the literatures of the British Isles—notably such recent volumes as Murray Pittock's *Scottish and Irish Romanticism* and David Duff and Catherine Jones's *Scotland, Ireland, and the Romantic Aesthetic*, and such key earlier works as Katie Trumpener's *Bardic Nationalism* and Ina Ferris's *Romantic National Tale and the Question of Ireland*—it is arguably difficult to compare what is still only just starting to come into view.[42] Romanticist scholarship on Irish literature of this period has generally addressed a relatively small body of texts cobbled together out of the Irish offshoots of revisions of the English canon in the fields of women's writing (Maria Edgeworth, Lady Morgan, Mary Tighe), satire (Thomas Moore), antiquarian work (Charlotte Brooke, Morgan, Moore), and the gothic (Charles Robert Maturin). While Stephen C. Behrendt has recently called for "reconcil[ing]" "Irish studies" and "British Romanticism studies,"[43] and though many of us have been working in both fields for some time, there is arguably a growing divide between them precisely because of the latter's limited canon. Though heavily weighted toward twentieth-century writing, Irish studies has never entirely lost sight of a larger canon of Irish writing from the previous century, a body of work kept in view first through modernist anthologies, such as Justin McCarthy's massive ten-volume collection (1904), and then through foundational bibliographies such as Patrick Rafroidi's (1980) and critical work such as the first chapter of Terence Brown's *Northern Voices* (1975) and a number of the volumes in publisher Colin Smythe's Irish Literary Studies book series in the 1980s.[44]

Compare the literary authors represented in the 2011 volume to which Behrendt's piece is the afterword, *Ireland and Romanticism: Publics, Nations, and Scenes of Cultural Production*, and those represented in Claire Connolly's 2006 essay "Irish Romanticism": the 2011 volume includes some authors that Connolly does not mention as well as many of the leading authors she does discuss, with significant weight on what we might call the field's "Big M's" (Moore, Morgan, Maturin, and James Clarence Mangan).[45] Among the major literary writers of the period discussed by Connolly but not in the 2011 volume are John and Michael Banim, J. J. Callanan, Thomas Crofton Croker, William Drennan, Gerald Griffin, Charles Lever, William Maginn, Richard Lalor Sheil, and Mary Tighe. I note this not to suggest that any book on Irish romanticism must cover the considerable number of writers invoked by that term—I hope we are well past such basic surveying work—but as an illustration of what is a very common asymmetry: Tighe only excepted, the authors on this list have been generally long recognized in Irish studies that look to the nineteenth century, but they as yet have not garnered much attention in romanticism studies. Look more closely at these authors and more broadly at the relevant criticism, and it is difficult not to notice that Irish romanticism studies allied with British romanticism studies has remained predominantly Protestant in fiction and Dublin-centered in all genres: in fiction, scholars have focused on Edgeworth, Maturin, and Morgan, all Protestant and the latter two based in Dublin (along with lesser-discussed novelists such as Dublin-raised Regina Maria Roche), not on the Catholic novelists the Banims and Griffin, from points south of Dublin; in scholarship on poetry, the Dubliner Moore eclipses all, with scant attention to the Cork writers Callanan and Maginn (and the folklorist Croker) or Belfast poets such as Drennan.[46]

This asymmetry adds to a prejudicial imbalance in much comparatist work that places a barely sketched Irish romanticism of a handful of partly known authors against a richly documented and detailed British romanticism, thus reinforcing, if only tacitly, the secondariness of Irish literature in general and of Irish romanticism in particular—sidelined as either derivative of or reactive to the English metropole. Irish topographical verse, for instance, is grasped in relation to British topographical models; the Irish national tale is discussed in the context of the romantic-era novel, largely in Britain and especially through the example of Sir Walter Scott's historical novels. Opening up the space of Irish literary influence to the transatlantic and other geographical arenas, as we shall see, can shed new light on the influences on, and the influence of, Irish writing in this period. My interest in representations of the land as a national problem thus not only seeks to go beyond the usual romantic-nationalist identification of an affective and determining relationship between citizen and landscape but also aims to contribute to the larger project, under way for decades,[47] of investigating a broader Irish literary tradition that functions diachronically and cross-generically as well as interacts synchronically, but not exclusively, with British material within generic bounds.

In this project, I do not aim to offer a comprehensive view of Irish romantic-era literary production, but to add to a growing body of scholarship on this rich and diverse field of inquiry. My focus here is a selection of texts from Irish literature in English produced during what has conventionally, if loosely, been termed the "romantic period"—texts that engage, in various ways, nonaffective understandings of land. As a consequence, many of the texts here fall outside the usual British-romantic canon of Irish literature: under the heading of poetry, for instance, there is scant Moore in my study, but lots on the Banims, Drennan, and Leslie as well as Preston, Edwards, Brooke, Orr, Kidd, McGee, and others. Further complicating efforts to define this era of Irish literary history, the romantic period itself is fuzzily defined, with the "Romantic Century" (1750–1850) gathering some momentum in British romantic studies, while Claire Connolly has taken the much shorter span of 1800–1830 to define an Irish romantic era, roughly from the United Irishmen Uprising (1798) to Catholic Emancipation (1829). In Irish studies in the 1980s, Rafroidi followed the then-common British romantic period dating of 1789–1850, but Norman Vance suggested dividing some Irish literature at 1798, contending that before that year "the heroic mode of Irish national literature in English was neo-classical; thereafter it was *Romantic*."[48] German romanticism is earlier, but American and French romanticisms are later, highlighting the difficulties of dating eras of literary history by ideas rather than by temporal benchmarks.[49] I would tentatively argue here for the broad heuristic value of two Irish romantic periods, one from roughly 1790 to 1829 and the other from 1830 to the middle of the century, perhaps as late as the 1860s. The early era is dominated by neoclassicism, sensibility, and related Enlightenment philosophies (Lockean political thought, for instance) and by the gothic, the literary shadow of the Enlightenment; both sensibility and the gothic come together in the rise of the national tale as a branch of historical fiction but are also traceable individually in prose and verse of the period. The later era is marked by the rise of romantic nationalism in the affective rooting of national identity to the land, including in a greater stress on rural populations, and in responding to romantic poets in England (especially William Wordsworth; see chapters 4 and 5). As this framework suggests, and is meant to stress, while Pittock's call to reverse the "den[ial] of national distinctions in literary history" has merit,[50] we need to separate Irish romanticism more clearly, at a conceptual level, from romantic nationalism. In most Irish national tales, the *volk* do not represent the nation—the aristocracy does. The national tale is romantic in many conventional respects—stressing the feeling individual, nostalgia for the past (whether national or individual), and the revivifying effects of the natural—but it is far from consistent with romantic nationalism. If nationalism does foster "the elevation of culture as the source of politics," as nationalism theorist Smith has argued of late-eighteenth-century developments,[51] that need not mean elevating politics as the source of culture.

Political forces' significance for literary materials are not ignored here, however. My period of focus is also bracketed historically by the transformation of Britain's westward empire after the Seven Years' War (1756–63), but before the American Revolution (1776–81), and the emergence in the early 1840s of Young Ireland in relation to both Young Europe and the romantic nationalism that would dominate the following decades.[52] Crucially for any discussion of literary representations of land in this period, the potato crop failed in 1845, the leading edge of what would become known as the Great Famine. With the Famine and the attendant intensification of emigration—as well as the physical traces left behind in empty fields, depopulated villages, not to mention the sick, dying, and grieving—the representation of the land changed radically, especially in the affect produced by the landscape and the literary depiction of exile.[53] More importantly for a literary study, this period exhibits certain continuities of literary concern and strategy, from the influence of Edmund Burke's *Enquiry* on landscape aesthetics and the gothic to the dominance of the national tale as a form through which to address the breach between land, people, and governance. More broadly, aesthetics across a range of literary forms, particularly in the wake of such Enlightenment treatises as Adam Smith's *Wealth of Nations* (1776) and Thomas R. Malthus's *Essay on the Principle of Population* (1798), were put under pressure by more pragmatic nationalist concerns about the economy, geographical resources, and trading routes. The period addressed here thus constitutes a broadly coherent moment in the literary and philosophical articulation of land and nation.

This study begins in chapter 1 with John Leslie's *Killarney* (1772) not only as a key forerunner of the national tale, a central genre for any discussion of the representation of nation and land in this era, but also as a synecdoche for many of the key issues in subsequent chapters. Addressing its use of geography to argue for Ireland's significance within Britain's new maritime empire and its use of landscape aesthetics and symbolism to resolve Irish insurgency, I suggest that the poem informs the national tale as it emerged in Irish fiction a generation later. Chapter 2 considers the gothic double of Killarney in its eastern counterpart, Glendalough, as it was depicted after 1790, especially in the wake of the 1798 Uprising. In particular, William Drennan's "Glendalloch" (written around 1802 and first published in 1806) transforms the site of antiquarian-inflected tourism into a marker for a national failure that is framed in the language of the gothic—a terror that paralyzes the national subject and so stalls the nation's development along the terms mandated by civic nationalism and whig historiography. Like *Killarney*, "Glendalloch" revises the literary field as writers thereafter associate the site with the "gloomy" and with crisis. Scholarship has addressed the larger history of Irish topographical poetry,[54] and both of these poems, along with other long poems such as William Hamilton Drummond's *Giant's Causeway* (1811), are part of an emerging canon of Irish topographical verse of the long eighteenth century. But my aim here is less to add to accounts of the genre than to consider the ways in which these particularly influential instances offer suggestive engagements with my central concerns here—namely the ways in which geographical discourse, politics, and landscape aesthetics are used to define visions of the nation. *Killarney*, as chapter 1 demonstrates, haunts the national tale for the first decades of the nineteenth century, and Drennan's poem was republished again and again in both volumes and periodicals in the nineteenth century.

Chapter 3 returns to the problem of the transatlantic not from the perspective of England's triumph in the Seven Years' War, but from that of the post-1776 radical transatlantic. Surveying a number of works by Irish nationalist poets who emigrated and journeyed to North America, I suggest that the problem of US slavery repeatedly troubles the republican ideal of the United States as the "land of Liberty" in Irish literature (a point historians have addressed), as different ideas of nationalism—especially civic and diasporic—also complicate accounts of migration. This difficulty is registered, I argue, in novels that focus on exiled United Irishmen leaders from the native aristocracy. Both Alicia Lefanu's *The Outlaw* (1823) and Morgan's *The O'Briens and the O'Flahertys* (1827), for instance, address the fundamental problem of a nation without a state: those who were understood in this period to be the natural rulers of society, well-educated men of high birth and strong patriotic feeling, cannot be citizens of—or, in exile, find solace in—another nation. In chapter 4, I turn to a problem rarely considered in studies of Irish literature: depictions of England in the Irish gothic. Scholars have unified the Irish gothic tradition as either rooted in the colonial experience and hence the Irish landscape or, more recently, as grounded in a rural, folk culture that provides distinctive supernatural tropes. English writers of this period tended to place gothic novels in Catholic continental Europe, tacitly or explicitly contributing to the vision of Protestant England as ordered and safe, as in Jane Austen's *Northanger Abbey*, completed in 1803, where the hero protests that gothic horrors are impossible in England, "where every man is surrounded by a neighborhood of voluntary spies, and where roads and newspapers lay everything open."[55] Irish writers, however, at least occasionally set such violence in the English mainland. In "Limerick Gloves," arguably Maria Edgeworth's most socially chaotic short story, the fear of Irish terrorism in rural England drives solid John Bulls into irrational behavior that can be checked only by careful policing. The Banims' "Church-Yard Watch" offers real domestic horrors to challenge the Wordsworthian pastoral representation of the English countryside. The Banims' poetry, moreover, offers an opportunity for framing the geographical concerns of this chapter and the preceding ones by staging through different poetic modes three different arenas: the larger globe, the British Isles, and a nativist, rural Ireland. Together, these texts offer varying Irish constructions of a gothic English landscape, fractured by its own terrors, whether of the colonial relation (as in Edgeworth's tale) or of its own national failures (as in the Banims' work).

Chapter 5 extends this consideration by examining Irish writers' varied engagement with the problem of the foreign in the context of gender. In the texts considered in this chapter, gender is mobilized to identify unsafely domiciled women with a nation that has precarious control over its land, offering civil war and domestic violence as correlates. These texts examine the ways in which the notion of the nation as family meets resistance at the borders of the private and public spheres when nationalist identifications divide rather than build on familial relationships. Building on chapter 1, which extends the history of the Irish national tale back to 1772, where it was, at its origin, tied to larger geopolitical frames, this chapter encourages a different revisiting of the national tale's focus on the home nation—one in which the national tale is not rooted in the writer's home, but rather in a wider discussion of the problems of nation building in relation to domestic communities. The romantic nationalism of Young Ireland, against this historical backdrop, appears to reassert nationalist mores by eliding the problem of gender in a focus on masculinist autonomy and imagination—a muscular Wordsworthianism that voids the complexity of the relations articulated in the national tale through the asymmetries of gender and of the divide between the public and the private. Chapter 6 examines Count Camille de Cavour's essay on Ireland to frame the ways in which these debates about nation and land intersect with debates about international relations writ large. Extending earlier chapters' discussion of spatial versus temporal trajectories for the nation, my discussion of Cavour's text draws on the distinction between cosmopolitanism's deterritorializing impetus—as the globe is co-opted into a narrative of the individual's bildungsroman—and a geopolitics that foregrounds the local on terms generative for anti-imperial arguments, as suggested by Drennan's elaboration of "the policy of geography" a century before the term *geopolitics* was coined. In the conclusion, I turn to romantic-era love elegies, an understudied body of work that cuts across sectarian, regional, and political divides in Ireland. These poems reveal a distinctively Irish interest in the Latin love elegy as a vehicle for expressing civic advancement through the social affections and classical education.

Representing the National Landscape in Irish Romanticism

1

The Maids of Killarney

Transatlantic Circulation and the Origins of the National Tale

But chief thou, CÆSAR! tho' 'tis yet unknown
What place in heav'n's high seats you'll call your own:
Whether, of lands protector, you supply
Fruits, and control the tempests of the sky,
Your mother's myrtle round your temples twin'd,
Hail'd with one voice great patron of mankind:
Or o'er the boundless seas you stretch your sway,
Sole God of all, who tempt the wat'ry way.
—VIRGIL, *Georgic I*

While with war's thunders conqu'ring CÆSAR awes
Euphrates' flood, to willing worlds give laws,
Aspiring to Heav'n's heights, in humble strains
I sung of cattle, trees, and cultur'd plains.
'Twas then I VIRGIL my sequester'd seat
Fixt at Parthenope's belov'd retreat . . .
—VIRGIL, *Georgic IV*

It is a critical commonplace that topographical poetry in the English tradition harks back to Virgil's agricultural poems, the *Georgics* of 29 BCE.[1] As the epigraphs to this chapter attest, however, these agricultural poems are deeply entwined with imperial discourse. Virgil's *Georgics* not only hail Caesar as an imperial figure never distant from the agricultural space of the poems but also locate their poet's origin in Parthenope—a Greek colony before Rome's ascendance in the Mediterranean. Karen O'Brien suggests of the English tradition that "later seventeenth- and eighteenth-century georgics subsumed the binary opposition of country and city within the larger imaginative structure of universal, peaceful empire."[2] The Irish tradition, though interlaced with the English tradition, necessarily departs from both this "binary opposition" and a simple insertion into "empire." For various political and economic reasons, industrialization and concomitant urbanization were less significant factors in Ireland, and it is rare to find the country/city divide that Raymond Williams influentially addressed in his examination of the English tradition.[3] As a colonial outlier, moreover, Ireland had a position in relation to empire that was complicated by a history of conflict and ongoing political disenfranchisement, complications that influence literary representations of the land. Irish georgic is, perhaps for these reasons, relatively rare and ploddingly didactic when it appears, as in, for instance, the anonymous *Mount Leinster* (1819).

Irish topographical verse, however, sometimes stresses the genre's georgic origins in order to reframe the imperial impetus of the English tradition. In his topographical poem "A Walk by the Bay of Dublin," published in 1850, Denis Florence MacCarthy describes his poetic speaker as one

> Whose heart unchill'd and whose impartial eye
> Dare to be just to scenes which round him lie!—
> With skilless hand he ventures to portray
> A sketch, Eblana, of thy beauteous bay,—
> Rival and twin of bright Parthenope![4]

By explicitly invoking the Virgilian origin of the genre while tracing Dublin back to the Roman era (through its Roman name "Eblana"), MacCarthy simultaneously identifies his poetic speaker with Virgil and Ireland with classical imperial history—with Parthenope, risen from a Greek colony to the home of Rome's epic poet. These five lines compactly demonstrate one of the ways in which the neoclassicism of topographical poetry in English could be co-opted to serve particular Irish themes. Here, the objective eye recognizes the epic significance of both the landscape and its poet—an epic import elaborated later in the poem through accounts of military leaders who resisted invasions of Ireland, shifting the imperial frame to center on Ireland.

As John Wilson Foster has discussed at some length in his essay on Irish topographical poetry, eighteenth-century Irish poets generally take their idea of the genre from an English tradition that famously begins with John Denham's "Cooper's Hill" (1642).[5] Foster suggests that "Ireland can lay slender claim to the first topographical poet. Denham was born in Dublin in 1615," but "the first genuinely Irish topographical poem" is "'Phoenix Park' (1718) by James Ward," a point echoed by Andrew Carpenter.[6] Ward's poem announces its literary debts in its opening lines, invoking both Denham's "Cooper's Hill" and Alexander Pope's "Windsor-Forest."[7] In the English tradition, topographical verse is the discursive vehicle by which the sociopolitical order is grounded in the landscape and in turn positions the viewing subject. Pope's "Windsor-Forest" is a conventional example, connecting the landscape mythologically and materially to Britain's imperial and mercantile future, a future that ensures the pastoral ease of the poetic speaker, who can enjoy "careless days" in an economically reassuring landscape:

> See Pan with flocks, with fruits Pomona crown'd,
> Here blushing Flora paints th'enamel'd ground,
> Here Ceres' gifts in waving prospect stand,
> And nodding tempt the joyful reaper's hand;
> Rich Industry sits smiling on the plains,
> And peace and plenty tell, a STUART reigns.[8]

This imperative to simultaneously order and naturalize the subject's relationship to the landscape offers Barthesian myth in the guise of description.[9] Similarly, one of the more famous examples of topographical verse in British romantic studies is Wordsworth's "Tintern

Abbey," a poem that insistently elides the industrialization of the river Wye and the poverty produced by a downturn in the local economy in order to establish an ideal natural space that is untouched by progress and urban sprawl.[10]

Irish poetry, however, often functions differently. Williams points to the idiosyncratic attention to "process" in Oliver Goldsmith's *Deserted Village* (as distinct from the more usual static juxtaposition of city and country) and notes in another connection that writers from the Celtic periphery show traces of the "colonial process"—"we can see the history happening, see it being made"—inviting us, if only implicitly, to see Goldsmith's vision of a changing landscape as a colonial one, notwithstanding Goldsmith's emigration from Ireland.[11] Around the same time as Williams, Carole Fabricant offered an evocatively similar argument about Jonathan Swift's work: "Consistently Swift transforms the concrete features of his environment into a symbolic depiction of his society and his stance towards it, so that physical details about the land and its dwellings invariably assume ideological dimensions. Journeying through his landscape, however, we find few if any traces of the flourishing garden community, at once edenic and civilized, which [Maynard] Mack locates at the center of Pope's vision."[12] Fabricant sums up the general position of topographical poetry in the eighteenth century and the specific English, conservative version of it and locates Swift in opposition to it. Swift, like later Irish poets, including MacCarthy, stresses the ideological work of topographical verse and in doing so unsettles its mythologizing aim to naturalize and authorize a particular perspective on the land and its administration. Hence, in Irish topographical verse, as I argue in this chapter and the next, the landscape registers the ongoing pressure of historical forces (economic, cultural, colonial) rather than, almost allegorically, solidifying a static framework.

Such fractures and shifts are also perceptible in English poems, but in many of the more canonical Irish poems of place there are overt attempts to relocate Ireland within a larger geography—and even geopolitics—that reconfigure the mythic mechanisms of order. Andrew Marvell's "Upon Appleton House," Ben Jonson's "To Penshurst," Pope's "Windsor-Forest"—all imagine the estate as an example of proper rule and order that might spread. Marvell's poem thus ends,

> 'Tis not, what once it was, the world,
> But a rude heap together hurled,
> All negligently overthrown,
> Gulfes, deserts, precipices, stone.
> Your lesser world contains the same,
> But in more decent order tame;
> You, heaven's center, Nature's lap,
> And paradise's only map.[13]

As Frans De Bruyn suggests of other English eighteenth-century topographical works, "the prospect survey performs a centripetal function, like a kaleidoscope that organizes colorful fragments into an intricate, coherent pattern."[14] Effective local rule through an estate owner or, in the wake of the Enlightenment, through an "impartial observer,"[15] produces a fecund and orderly world that is made evident through the agricultural resources that such poetry surveys:

> The lower land, that to the river bends,
> Thy sheep, thy bullocks, kine, and calves do feed:
> The middle grounds thy mares and horses breed.
> Each bank doth yield thee conies.[16]

As Foster describes the trajectory, "the eye became a physical instrument instead of being confused with the muse and fancy, . . . point of view became fixed and limited instead of omniscient, . . . perspective became physically credible instead of ideal and unrealistic, and . . . the poet became an observer instead of an omnipresent witness."[17] But repeatedly in Irish topographical poetry, as far back as Ward's "Phoenix Park," connections with Britain, tourism, and mobile populations (from the military to economic migrants) constitute an integral part of increasingly pragmatic surveys of a location's social, aesthetic, and economic merits. In much Irish verse, in short, order does not spread outward from a stable center; order, and the centralization that anchors it, come from spreading outward.

John Leslie's long poem *Killarney* (1772) is an illuminating example with which to begin a discussion of Irish topographical verse's distinctiveness because it uses classical and historical referencing to position Ireland within an imperial cartography and narrative, and it is arguably the most canonical eighteenth-century Irish topographical poem. *Killarney* is discussed in the two comprehensive essays on the subject of Irish poems of place: Foster's 1974 essay "The Topographical Tradition" and, at greater length, John Waters's 2001 essay "Topographical Poetry."[18] It is also the only poem that Luke Gibbons discusses in his compelling analysis of nonfiction prose about Killarney in the context of sectarianism and insurgency as well as, more broadly, "the key, constitutive role played by Killarney in the formation of Irish Romanticism and its attendant discourses in aesthetics, travel writing, antiquarianism, and cultural nationalism."[19] Leslie's *Killarney* offers a unique perspective on such discourses because of its efforts to organize Irish assimilation to British hegemony through a narrative of social progress that has as its terminus the specific goal of Ireland's participation in the British transatlantic, consolidated by the Treaty of Paris (1763) at the end of the Seven Years' War. It is also, as I argue at length here, a key forerunner of the national tale in its representation of Irish reconciliation to English rule through a marriage plot. Leslie's *Killarney* and some later Killarney poems understand that reconciliation in the larger context of a globalizing impetus, but the national tale, limited by the domestic concerns of the novel, narrows its representational gaze to the national and the local. The national tale hence retains key features of *Killarney*, notably the gendered trope for Irish subordination and plea for tourism, but without advancing its larger argument for Irish participation in British military power and Atlantic trade.

Putting Ireland on the Imperial Map

Killarney, with a seaport in Ireland's southwest, became significant as a poetic subject in the wake of the transatlantic Seven Years' War, though its geographical value had been noted much earlier. Sir James Ware remarks, in the midst of a learned discussion on the global distribution of the moose, "it is not to be conceived how *Ireland* should be supplied with this Creature, which is not a Native of any other Part of the Old World; of which *Ireland* is the last or most Western Part, and is the nearest of any Country to the most Eastern Parts of *New Canada*, *New England*, *Virginia*, *&c.*"[20] Joseph Atkinson's *Killarny* (c. 1769) is likely the first poem dedicated to describing the region, although Killarney is frequently mentioned in histories, tour guides, and antiquarian prose works in earlier decades, as Gibbons has demonstrated. Atkinson's poem is often cited as if it first appeared in 1798, the year in which Atkinson published a version of the poem under his own name,[21] but Atkinson mentions an earlier anonymous, undated, and shorter version in his 1798 dedication, almost certainly *Killarny* by "an Officer in the Army."[22] The British Library identifies this edition of the poem as from "1750?" but Atkinson was born in 1743, and he claimed that a shorter version of the poem was first published around 1769: in his dedication, dated December 1, 1797, he writes, "about half the Poem was written by me, and published without my name, nearly twenty-eight years since."[23] Then, in 1772, Leslie published *Killarney*, and soon Killarney was a conventional poetic subject: the long list of Killarney poems that followed includes Anna Maria Edwards's "The Princess of Killarney" (1787), Mary Tighe's Killarney sonnets (1811), Charles Hoyle's three-canto *Three Days at Killarney* (1828), and Hannah Maria Bourke's seven-canto poem *O'Donoghue, Prince of Killarney* (1830), along with rather dreadful attempts such as "Killarney" by S.T.C.D. in the first issue of the *Dublin University Magazine* (1833) ("On the right / The broad bright moon climbs slowly into sight") and turgid topographical catalogs by Patrick O'Kelly in 1791 and Michael MacCarthy in 1816.[24]

These texts collectively demonstrate a developing set of conventions for depicting Killarney, particularly through what are cited as the region's must-see features, including the two lakes, the mountains (especially the one called "Turk"), the eagle's aery, and the ruined abbey of Innisfallen, and conventional narratives such as a stag hunt and the myth of O'Donoghue's apparition. In the early nineteenth century, this long history of poetry about Killarney was extended into novels that engage the new tradition of the national tale, such as Robert Torrens's *The Victim of Intolerance; Or the Hermit of Killarney: A Catholic Tale* (1814), Patrick Brontë's *Maid of Killarney* (1818), and Regina Maria Roche's *The Tradition of the Castle; Or, Scenes in the Emerald Isle* (1824),[25] featuring the descendants of "O'Donaghue, lord, by descent, of the lakes, but known in after times by the title of king, and the remains of whose ancient castle still stand on the island of Ross, in the famous lakes of Killarney."[26] In his influential essay "Topographies of Terror," Gibbons focuses on the ways in which largely nonfiction prose depictions of Killarney in this same period, roughly 1750–1840, engage with sectarian politics and rural insurgency, what Leslie terms in *Phoenix Park* (1772) "the tumults of the north and south."[27] In *Killarney*, however, Leslie eschews the local to develop an argument that resituates Ireland globally, placing it at the center of British power while emptying it of Irish sovereignty and offering it up as a key geographical resource for British Atlantic trade.

In many respects, Leslie's *Killarney* is a conventional eighteenth-century topographical poem. The poem consists of 736 lines of heroic couplets that are typically neoclassical in comparing local topographical features to the elements of classical landscapes, invoking landscape painters such as Nicholas Poussin and Claude Lorraine, and generally drenching the text in classical allusions. As Foster notes, the poem is heavily indebted to the picturesque as well.[28] Leslie's poem is also very much indebted to English poet James Thomson's influential long poem *The Seasons*, particularly in absorbing its idea of "an empire won from nature by industry and cultivation."[29] But Leslie reframes this idea as Ireland's possible future rather than England's present: in *Killarney*, Ireland is rich in largely untapped agricultural, commercial, and military resources. Waters has suggestively argued that Leslie's *Killarney*—along with other Irish topographical poems, including William Drennan's "Glendalloch," which I discuss in the next chapter—involves "a formal dropping from description into history and narrative, that . . . [is] the most salient textual and narratological symptom in landscape poetry of the historical conditions of Irish land."[30] As we have already seen, however, this "formal dropping" is a feature of Irish topographical verse that Williams and Fabricant trace in eighteenth-century examples. The author of the poem *Mount Leinster*, noting that it is set in the site of "the first English invasion in the reign of Henry the Second," refers to this formal element explicitly, citing his or her decision to "give the poem a mixed character, both descriptive of the country and of the principal events that history records as connected with it, and occasionally diverging into subjects, that (as Sanco Pansa would say) were pat to my purpose."[31]

Leslie's poem is tightly structured, developing this "mixed character" by organizing space and time in order to identify progress with expanding geographical frames. *Killarney* traces the speaker's tour of the lakes of Killarney, and it is tacitly divided into three parts.[32] One surveys the lower lake and focuses on the Irish past (1–396); one provides the "sylvan tale," a love story, narrated while the speaker pauses between the two lakes (397–492); and the third describes the journey through the upper lake and is void of specifically Irish historical reference, focusing instead on imperial histories (493–736). As the poem progresses, its geographical range extends from the immediate region in the days of Donaghoe, a legendary king, to the British Isles in the Elizabethan period to the transatlantic arena of the Seven Years' War in the near present. The conflicts in these three timeframes are also extended from family circles to wider and wider networks: in antiquity, Donaghoe struggles with an insurgent son; in the sixteenth century, Elizabeth I "vanquish'd Desmond" (54), stressing relations between rulers in the British Isles; and the final section of the poem brings together classical references and contemporary military references to locate Ireland in the present as an adjunct of an imperial Britain that is the successor of the Roman Empire. The poem thus charts an increasingly global geopolitics in which the merits of Killarney lie precisely in its location within a transatlantic sphere that is emerging from imperial history. With the Seven Years' War over, moreover, commerce and tourism promise to supplant internecine conflict, Irish–English wars, and imprisonment and so make possible peace, trade, and mobility.

Leslie's known works, two long topographical poems published in 1772, make explicit reference to the North American part of the Seven Years' War. In *Killarney*, for instance, Leslie compares a "patient, active Band" with "Milesian blood" (605) and "brawny shoulders" to "such, by Wolfe inspir'd, that fearless strain'd / Up Abram's heights, and Quebeck's ramparts gain'd" (609–10), a reference to the Battle of the Plains of Abraham, a key British victory in the Seven Years' War. Similarly, in *Phoenix Park*, he celebrates "The Royal Hospital, and Military Nursery" near Dublin in linking General James Wolfe's victory on the Plains of Abraham to William III's at the Battle of the Boyne (1690):

> High o'er the vale, the soldier orphans play;
> Wide o'er the plain, the hoary veterans stray;
> There, mix'd with peaceful flocks, they fondly tell,
> How many a hero for his country fell;
> Recount the battles fought in regions far,
> By Anna's rival thunder bolts of war:
> They boast of Wolfe, of William, and the Boyne,
> And ancient laurels with the modern twine.[33]

This passage is followed by a military review that unites the populace in "Their mutual ardour, and their martial love," as "Ierne, and the God of War, approve."[34] In the previous passage, Leslie also closely echoes and updates the first Irish topographical poem, Ward's "Phoenix Park." Ward writes,

Where vet'ran Bands, discharg'd from War, retire,
Feeble their Limbs, extinct their martial Fire:
I hear methinks, I hear the gallant Train,
Recount the Wonders of each past Campaign:
Conquests, and Triumphs in my Bosom roll,
And *Britain*'s Glory fills my wid'ning Soul:
Here blest with Plenty, and maintain'd at Ease,
They boast th' Adventures of their youthful Days.[35]

Leslie builds on Ward's image of Ireland as a resting place for retired military men—rather than as a site of insurgency—while folding in current details to identify Ireland with a British imperial narrative that runs from 1690 to 1763, and from the Boyne to the St. Lawrence. Leslie's Ireland participates in "*Britain*'s Glory" as that country's empire expands from the British Isles to North America, a participation Leslie details in *Killarney*.

In broad terms, the survey of the lower lake is allied with the Irish past, historically running from the legendary "Donaghoe the great" (440) in the remote past to the Elizabethan period and then the defeat of James II in the late seventeenth century, though the poem's narrative does not follow historical chronology. The "sylvan tale" is presented as a story to pass the time as the speaker and his companions move between the lakes; its only historical reference is the retelling of the decline of the Donaghoe family by the heroine of the sylvan tale, "the Maid of Killarney," who is the last of the familial line, and it focuses on a boy-meets-girl, boy-marries-girl romance. The third part of the poem, dedicated descriptively to the upper lake, focuses on a present in which Britannia literally rules the waves. Describing the islands of the lake, the speaker declares,

Dodona's rival, tow'rs the Oaken-grove,
Sacred to Britain's Genius, and to Jove.
But Jove no longer speaks; those awful woods
Pour only Britain's thunder on the floods:
And see, when Nature first to Britain gave

The green domain, and charter of the wave,
From yon rude coast, she took the marble block,
And sketch'd her future navy in the rock;
Chisel'd the prow, and hull; then o'er the tide,
Reclin'd its sable, adamantine side,
Bade her black bulwarks distant Empires shake,
And fix'd their glorious model on her lake. (505–16)

The reference to "sketch[ing] her future navy in the rock" is footnoted, "Representing the hull of a man of war" (p. 74). This is a peculiar move, from a colonial standpoint, and not only because Leslie is strongly echoing Pope's "Windsor-Forest" in the third and fourth lines. Pope writes,

Thy trees, fair Windsor! now shall leave their woods,
And half thy forests rush into my floods,
Bear Britain's thunder.[36]

With the retention of Pope's eye rhyme (woods/floods) and the phrase "Britain's thunder," the island in Killarney figuratively replaces Windsor forest as the center of British imperial power. Moreover, British naval power is "sketch'd" on Irish rock by "Nature." Leslie "roots," and "routes," British maritime power, quite literally, in Ireland.[37] As the poem progresses, it charts an ever-widening gyre of time and space, transforming Ireland from the site of local insurgency into the center of Britain's Atlantic empire.

Transatlantic Ireland

This rerouting of British maritime power from the metropole to the west of Ireland is in part a response to the increasing importance of the transatlantic arena in the wake of the Seven Years' War, an international conflict that overlaps with the French and Indian War in North America (1754-63) and is usually dated 1756-63 in Europe and 1754–61 in North America. The transatlantic conflict consolidated and significantly expanded British power in North America: under the 1763 Treaty of Paris, France ceded almost all of its territory in Canada and east of the Mississippi in what would become the United States, while Spain ceded Florida, and Britain was the beneficiary in both cases. This was a watershed moment in the establishment of a global, and specifically a transatlantic, British Empire, and Irish literature for the following decades would wrestle with Ireland's position in that newly drawn Atlantic world. Kevin Whelan has recently argued for a "Green Atlantic" in the wake of the American Revolution and most work on the Irish America is similarly framed temporally,[38] but an Irish transatlantic sensibility appears much earlier in literature. There are of course frequent references in the historical and literary record to transportation and economic migration to North America throughout the eighteenth century, but such Atlantic transits are generally treated as exile rather than the production of a transatlantic community. Laurence Whyte writes, for instance, in "The Parting Cup" (1740), a suggestive forerunner to Goldsmith's *Deserted Village* (1770),

> The *Landlord* had his Rent well-pay'd,
> Nor had he any Cause to dread,
> His *Tenant* to give up his *Lease*,
> As now, too often, is the *Case*,
> Run in Arrear, or fly away
> To North or South *America*.
> . . . .
> The *Tenants* rack'd and sacrific'd,
> Whole *Colonies* to shun the Fate,
> Of being oppress'd at such a Rate
> By *Tyrants* who still raise their Rent,
> Sail'd to the Western Continent,
> Rather than live at home like slaves.[39]

Printed versions of Thomas Sheridan's popular farce *The Brave Irishman* conversely center on an Irish captain about to embark from

London to fight in Virginia in one of the conflicts leading up to the Seven Years' War: "By my Shoul, my Jewel, I am going over to Whirginny to beat the Frinch — They say they have driven our Countrymen out of their Plantaations; by my Shoul, my Jewel, if our Troops get vonse among them, we'll cut them all in Pieces, and then bring 'em over Prisoners of War besides."[40] "Countrymen" is likely an allusion to descendants of the Irish enslaved by Cromwell but freed as African slavery became significant in the Americas, many of them settling in the American colonies rather than attempt to make the long trip home, while the Irish captain himself enters the transatlantic circuit for the British military. There is other evidence of Irish diasporic community in the middle of the eighteenth century. For instance, an English pamphlet on Nova Scotia laments in 1756 that Halifax's "grand Vizier of the publick works," "educated in the heart of *Ireland*," is strongly biased toward hiring Irish workers and that "the common language spoke at *Halifax* is wild Irish."[41] This anonymous pamphlet marks anxieties about the ascendancy of English settlers, leveraging increasing international hostilities on the eve of the Seven Years' War to solicit greater economic and legislative support from the metropole, but it also suggests both significant Irish settlement and the cultural continuation of an "Irish" identity on the other side of the Atlantic that was recognized in print culture before the American Revolution.

As Carol Watts suggests, the Seven Years' War demanded a new "imagining" of "the state": "Such an imagining was immediately geopolitical, concerned with the metaphorical mastery of space. One consequence of winning the war was the need to make sense of an extraordinary extension of territorial boundaries that troubled the limits of the state understood as a delimited arena."[42] Watts does not consider Ireland in this context, but the effects of this reimagining can be traced in Irish literature. Leslie's *Killarney* in particular works to position Ireland as a future transatlantic hub while dispensing with Irish difference in the historical parts of the poem, merging Ireland into a militarily and economically functional British-defined transatlantic. Irish prosperity and advancement, on terms consistent with the "four-stages" model circulating in Scottish historiography (as I suggest later), are made possible through the nation's new access to the transatlantic flow of goods and military men.

Early in *Killarney*, Leslie introduces the southern coast of Ireland as the site of ports and harbors that are significant both to trade and to British military interests. As the speaker takes in the view from a mountaintop (a device echoed in *The Exile of Erin!*, discussed in the introduction), he laments,

> Now Kenmare's harbours spreading from the main,
> Invite the passing mariner in vain.
> Hard fate! shall thousands on Ierne's coast,
> Be still to Commerce and to Britain lost? (57–60)

Foster has noted this passage in terms of "the inability of Kenmare's harbours to attract foreign shipping," and Waters characterizes it as an "inattention to development of [Ireland's] maritime industry,"[43] but Leslie's point is rather more timely in a transatlantic context. According to the larger passage, the region has already established its military significance, as Leslie indicates in the lines that immediately follow:

> Copious and calm, lo! Bantry's lordly tide,
> For all Britannia's fleets a station wide;
> A Port secure, long since well known to fame,
> And signaliz'd with gallant Herbert's name.
> To Dingle far we stretch, and o'er the main,
> Once fatal to the naval pride of Spain;
> And where, in fruitless war, conflicting tides
> Dash foamy round the Skellig's marble sides;
> On to the Capes, where haughty Shannon roars,
> And drives th' Atlantick backward from his shores. (61–70)

This passage is heavily footnoted, two elaborating on the military references: one notes Arthur Herbert's involvement in defeating the French in Bantry Bay, and the other recalls that some ships of the Spanish Armada, including the provocatively named "Rosary of

1000 Tons," were lost along the coast (p. 64n.). Less than a decade after the end of the Seven Years' War, Leslie identifies the Irish coast as a key military asset in earlier defeats of France and Spain, Britain's major opponents in that war. In between these notes is another crucial footnote: Dingle, we are told, is "the most westerly port of Europe" (p. 64n.). In other words, we need to re-read what Foster terms "the inability of Kenmare's harbours to attract foreign shipping" as more specifically part of a failure to take advantage of the transformation of Ireland's strategic value in the wake of the Seven Years' War. Once a key military resource, it is now valuable for "Commerce," a natural launching-off point for new British transatlantic trade as "the most westerly port of Europe."

Irish ports, moreover, remain secure ports: "The friendly bosom of a neighb'ring creek; / Such as the grateful port, that tempest-toss'd, / The shatter'd Trojan found on Lybia's coast" (354–56). Through this simile, Leslie identifies the "grateful port" with the safe harbor that Aeneas found in Africa between leaving Troy and arriving in Italy to found Rome. Alluding to British nationalist efforts in the late eighteenth century to identify Britain's growing empire with the Roman Empire, Leslie uses this Virgilian simile to incorporate Ireland into the map and narrative of British empire building. Hence, the legendary Irish king, Donaghoe, prophesies of a time

> When more refin'd, the wide extended globe,
> Should change her face, and wear a brighter robe:
> When, freed from Gothick gloom, a star should rise
> To dissipate the mists in Western skies.
> . . . .
> When Ocean's vacant bosom should be spread,
> With forests wing'd, and Commerce lift her head. (271–74, 277–78)

The "star" is footnoted as "Learning" (p. 69n.), tying the development of transatlantic trade with Enlightenment advancement on terms consistent with the Enlightenment historiography I discuss later in this chapter: progress means commerce, and after 1763 that necessarily includes Atlantic trade. The "vacant bosom" and "Gothick gloom" are alike rationalizations of westward expansion, one invoking the myth of the West as depopulated and therefore available for settlement, and the other the rationalization of imperialism as a civilizing mission. Other eighteenth-century poets echo this vision of Killarney as a key site in transatlantic trade. Atkinson, for instance, writes in his 1798 expansion of *Killarney*,

> And from the cliffs with joyful wonder gaze;
> Thence to behold the vast Atlantic Main,
> Where Britain's fleets in martial triumph reign;
> Bid her rich commerce to each nation roll,
> And naval thunder roar from pole to pole.[44]

Closely echoing the Popean passage in Leslie's *Killarney* quoted earlier, Atkinson makes the same argument as Leslie for the importance of Killarney in Britain's new maritime empire—but he does not in his pre-Leslie version circa 1769.

As Waters has noted, Leslie's poem also makes a strong argument for tourism at Killarney,[45] but this too needs to be read in the context of Ireland's larger participation in the British Atlantic. In the midst of the "wide extended globe" passage, Leslie inserts a call for tourism in Ireland: "When curious Guests should travel far from home / To sail his lakes, and o'er his mountains roam" (275–76). The speaker later declares,

> Let the vain Traveller the praise resound
> Of distant realms, and rave of Classick ground;
> Let him o'er Continents delighted run,
> Or search the Isles, the fav'rites of the Sun;
> Let him of foreign wonders take the round,
> Unrival'd still Killarney will be found. (563–68)

Leslie's tourism, in conjunction with this emphasis on transatlantic trade and military activity, locates Killarney in the midst of a dynamic Atlantic that recalls recent transatlantic scholarship, such as Charles J. Withers's argument for "the Atlantic Enlightenment as a space of margins and flows."[46] The circa 1769 *Killarny* instead imagines the beauties of the place as a resource for keeping the Irish at home:

> Hibernia's sons, no more their isle shall leave,
> But thou, the tributes of their pride receive;
> To thee from foreign realms shall nations roam,
> And we soon glory in our Bath at home.[47]

These Irishmen "no more . . . shall leave" while other "nations roam," so that Ireland, but not the Irish, participates in transnational movement. But Leslie's Irishmen, deeply wedded to the new Atlantic, are always on the move: hunters chasing their prey (first birds, then a stag) as preparation for military deployment, a "humble hermit" walking toward "Retirement" (558, 557), and myriad other figures in motion populate Leslie's Killarney, including "the active Mind [that] / Flies all abroad, and scorns to be confin'd" (119–20). Potential recruits and tourists and, at the end, a solitary peasant walking home (719)—these are the inhabitants of Leslie's Ireland, themselves always already on the move. But to do so they must first be loosed of their traditional, local fealties.

Whither Donaghoe? Putting Sovereignty into the Past

Leslie draws closely on an Enlightenment historiography that posits "four stages" of economic development, particularly in his emphasis on "Commerce." The "four-stages theory" was a staple of Enlightenment economic thought. Maureen Harkin offers a useful overview:

> The general sensation of being at the apex of historical development which Hume evidences is made systematic in the writings of the Scottish Historical School of the 1750s to 1770s. This group, including Robertson, Ferguson, John Millar, Lord Kames, and Smith, developed and shared a series of theories about social

> development, key among them a notion of history as progress through four successive socioeconomic stages, each based on a specific mode of subsistence that determined government, property relations, and other institutions. According to the stadial thesis, human society had progressed—or, in the case of non-European societies, was still uncertainly progressing—from a miserable subsistence hunting and gathering in the age of barbarism (stage one), through the progressive accretions of property and the accompanying establishment and refinement of government in pastoralism (stage two) and agriculture (stage three), to emerge into an age of commerce characterized by the division of labor, the spread of manufacture and trade, and general prosperity.[48]

This historiographic model is closely followed in Leslie's poem. An early verse paragraph begins with the "sportive Youth" (99) who hunts for the "mark to win a sportsman's fame" (105) and ends with the death of his prey: "He wheels, he flutters, bounds and dies" (118). The next verse paragraph proceeds to the second stage, "Where, to his pendant flock, the goat-herd sings" (122). Then, after a verse paragraph describing wild plants in the region, Leslie turns to the transition to agriculture: "The splendid native of the mountain's side, / Now in the garden lifts its snowy pride" (148). This transition is still under way in Ireland, however, as "Nature and Art their diff'rent claims maintain, / Divide their empire, and alternate reign" (219–20). Commerce, moreover, as we have already seen, is withheld from Ireland but strongly associated with Britain: "shall thousands on Ierne's coast, / Be still to Commerce and to Britain lost?" (59–60). The rhetorical liberties that Leslie takes for the purposes of pursuing the four stages in *Killarney* are highlighted by the very different position he takes in *Phoenix Park*, where the speaker refers extensively to Irish industry, and specifically "the Linen manufacture," suggesting,

> 'Tis from the labours of the wheel and loom,
> Ierne's treasures, and her glories, come;
> For these, fair commerce all her sails unfurls,
> And the white staple wafts to distant worlds.[49]

But in *Killarney* Leslie makes only passing reference to manufacturing in order to firmly locate Ireland in the third stage and Britain in the fourth, thus participating in a larger discursive tradition of representing Ireland as economically backward in comparison to Britain, from Edmund Spenser's notorious *View of the Present State of Ireland* (c. 1596) and Richard Lawrence's *Interest of Ireland* (1682) forward to the romantic-era improvement fiction discussed by Helen O'Connell and the 1845 Cavour essay I discuss in chapter 6.[50] Read together, Leslie's 1772 long poems pursue the partitioning of Ireland: Dublin and "the Northern part of Ireland, the seat of the Linen manufacture" are already participating in modern commerce, but the west of Ireland, newly positioned to take advantage of Atlantic trade, remains in the third stage because its potential is as yet unrealized. (Historians have recently noted that Irish Atlantic trade was indeed significant in this period, but that is not Leslie's argument, which relies rhetorically on the virtual absence of Irish trade to make a case for Ireland's potential contribution to British empire.[51])

Much of the remainder of the opening third of *Killarney* is devoted to the natural beauty of the lakes in particular and of Ireland in general, particularly in terms of valuable plants—a common device in English topographical poetry as well as in many European accounts of soon to be colonized territories to which imperial traders need to be drawn. So "Ceres smiles" (22), the flora "perennial bloom" (142), and a wide variety of trees can provide valuable woods for English manufacture, offering such Edenic plenty that the speaker gives up after a fifty-line catalog:

> Can Flora's self recount the shrubs and flow'rs,
> That scent the shade, that clasp the rocky bow'rs?
> . . . .
> Wond'rous the cause! can human search explore,
> What vegetation lurks in ev'ry pore?
> What in the womb of diff'rent strata breeds?
> What fills the universe with genial feeds? (175–76, 178–81)

It is only after a lengthy introduction of Ireland as an Edenic cornucopia willing to participate as a subordinate in England's "freedom" and "commerce" that Leslie's poem more concertedly enters history, but in order to locate Ireland's native government firmly in the nation's past. That government survives only in a figurative and minor contribution to the valuable fecundity of the landscape through the ghost of Donaghoe, which broadly functions as a fertility spirit.

The description of the lower lake is interspersed with various historical accounts tied to the region. Leslie thus begins with the late sixteenth century, when Elizabeth I "crush'd Rebellion's head" (56), and then turns to naval battles near Killarney, praising British victories over the Spanish Armada and later over the French in Bantry Bay, a defeat of James II's forces in the months leading up to the Battle of the Boyne. Then, after a lengthy descriptive interlude, Leslie turns to the only narrative acknowledged in the summary "Argument": "*The mythology of* O DONAGHOE" (p. 62) (the name "Donaghoe" gets its Gaelic "O" only in the prose portions of the text), centrally the legendary king's apotheosis. Leslie insistently separates Donaghoe from the Irish present, introducing him through a building at odds with the natural scene enjoyed by the speaker:

> Once more the charms of Paradise appear,
> And all, but Eden's innocence, are here.
>
> In rival contrast, lo, th' expanded Isle
> Of Ross displays her military pile!
> Long since illustrious, and the royal seat,
> As Fame informs, of Donaghoe, the great. (235–40)

The narrative of Donaghoe, a philosopher-king with the gift of prophecy who is transformed into a fertility spirit (240–334), rewrites the Irish heroic past in nonmilitary terms. While the "sportive Youth" of the present (99) "learn[s] to dare / The roughest deeds, and steel [his] nerves for war" (107–8), and Donaghoe is introduced in connection to a "military pile" (238), the description of Donaghoe's rule avoids all reference to military matters. Instead, Donaghoe is introduced as a judge, after some general statements about the truth of "hoar Tradition" (242) and his belief "that crowns are giv'n, / To serve mankind" (248): "Impartial he dispens'd, (Law's surest guard) / Disgraceful punishment, and bright reward. / Lenient, yet just, he spar'd not even his own" (251–53)—that is, in imprisoning even his own son for treason (a much cited aspect of the Donaghoe legend).

As Waters briefly notes, "Leslie imbued Donaghoe with all the princely virtues of concern and mutual affection that were professed within eighteenth-century political theory as the best guarantee against loss of social authority."[52] Enlightenment thinkers from Anthony Ashley Cooper, third earl of Shaftesbury, to Immanuel Kant debated the value of reward and punishment, instead of moral judgment or a recognition of the public good, as the twin motivators of good behavior. Moreover, Hume, to take one leading example in this large and complex debate, supports the value of "the impartial administration of justice" and suggests, "We are, therefore, to look upon all the vast apparatus of our government, as having ultimately no other object or purpose but the distribution of justice, or, in other words, the support of the twelve judges. Kings and parliaments, fleets and armies, officers of the court and revenue, ambassadors, ministers, and privy-counsellors, are all subordinate in their end to this part of administration. Even the clergy, as their duty leads them to inculcate morality, may justly be thought, so far as regards this world, to have no other useful object of their institution."[53] In this essay, "On the Origin of Government," Hume is much concerned with the "progress of society," and he associates the dispensing of reward and punishment with the development of an abstract system of law that operates independently of the monarch's will. In Hume's trajectory, societies progress from having a "chieftain" as "arbiter of all differences," "till the farther progress of improvement procured the magistrate a revenue, and enabled him to bestow rewards . . . and to inflict punishments," but "the government which, in common appellation, receives the appellation of free, is that which admits of a partition of power among several members, whose united authority is no less, or is commonly greater than that of any monarch; but who, in the usual course of administration, must act by general and equal laws."[54] In Humean terms, Donaghoe's rule is primitive if ideal: there is one magistrate but no larger administration to ensure justice, and there are rewards and punishments but no regular system of law separate from the monarchy. Hence, Donaghoe's prison is the place "where, agreeable to O Donaghoe's polity, the disturbers of the State were confined" (p. 68n.), the term *polity* appearing in its now obsolete sense of "administration."[55] As in Leslie's invocation of the "four stages," the depiction of Donaghoe identifies Ireland with an idyllic but underdeveloped state. This identification is further elaborated by the legendary catastrophe in which internecine conflict rather than political difference is the basis for rebellion: Donaghoe is betrayed by his "Rebel son" and incarcerates him in his "Prison-isle" (254).

Donaghoe's association with the premodern condition of Ireland undergirds the ruler's central role in the narrative as a prophet who anticipates the arrival of modernity. The bulk of the Donaghoe passage recounts the British arrival of the fourth stage of economic development in connection with the transatlantic and the "wide extended globe" the fourth stage makes available:

> Chearful he sat, and in prophetic rhymes,
> Darkling, rehears'd the fate of future times:
> When more refin'd, the wide extended globe,
> Should change her face, and wear a brighter robe:
> When, freed from Gothic gloom, a star should rise
> To dissipate the mists in Western skies:
> When curious Guests should travel far from home
> To sail his lakes, and o'er his mountains roam:
> When Ocean's vacant bosom should be spread,
> With forests wing'd, and Commerce lift her head.[56] (269–78)

This British advancement informs Leslie's depiction of British rule in Ireland as the strong defending the weak (and less advanced):

When Freedom shou'd uprear her infant head,
And on Britannia's realms her blessings shed:
When, from a-far, shou'd come a mighty Friend
Her cause to second, and her rights defend. (283–86)

Leslie's footnote to "Friend" identifies this figure as "K. William the Third" (p. 69n.)—William of Orange, who defeated Catholic Irish forces at the Battle of the Boyne and is compared to General Wolfe in *Phoenix Park*. This is the "Friend" of Ireland who shall "her rights defend." Suggesting further the obvious ideological weight of these lines, Isaac Weld's description of the site includes more than two dozen lines of the poem as evidence of the Donaghoe legend: Weld marks one ellipsis but silently elides lines 271–90 and so removes entirely the "curious Guests" and "mighty Friend" passage, while omitting just two couplets from the rest of his long quotation of this section of Leslie's poem.[57] Weld thus obscures the politically controversial elements of Leslie's Donaghoe passage, retaining the myth of the ideal king who becomes a returning spirit even as he surgically excises Leslie's fiction of that king's welcome of Protestant, British rule.

At the end of the verse paragraph, Leslie reinforces the military implications by suggesting that Ireland will "find, whene'er distress'd, / A fort impregnable in Albion's breast" (289–90). (He makes a similar claim in *Phoenix Park*, representing Ireland as "Long time depress'd, distracted by her kings, / Till Albion o'er her stretch'd her healing wings."[58]) This prophecy thus contends that eighteenth-century Ireland, just a few years before the establishment of the Volunteers, is incapable of self-defense.[59] Donaghoe can prophesy the arrival of troops but not muster them; he can anticipate the arrival of "Learning" (p. 69n.) but not dispense it, even though "He read, he search'd all Nature's volume thro'" (262). Moreover, in this larger passage, under the legitimation of "divine prediction" (291), Leslie yokes together Britain, military might, "Learning," and "Commerce." This is Britain after the Seven Years' War: ruler of a "wide extended globe" that practices "Commerce" over "Ocean's vacant bosom" while planting troops across that globe. Leslie thus uses the Irish heroic past to identify that history not with political autonomy, but with a necessary, and necessarily past, stage of social progress. With a nod to Lockean political thought, he also solicits the consent of the people to advancement from their present state: "from his tongue divine prediction flow'd, / And firm belief, in ev'ry bosom glow'd" (291–92). At this moment of popular consent to the changes of the future, Leslie dispenses with his idealized Irish king. The next lines depict Donaghoe's death, as "Sudden he rose" and a lake "quick receiv'd him in a chrystal grave" (293–96), and then the famous apparition of Donaghoe that, as Gibbons notes, is "one of the most pervasive set pieces in descriptions of Killarney."[60]

Leslie delivers this set piece with a twist, however. While Leslie relies on music and thunder as aural background for the ghost of Donaghoe, features of various prose texts,[61] the emphasis in the passage is on the people's misrecognition of the spectral Donaghoe as their ruler:

> A Form all-glorious started from the wave,
> On graceful courser, by a princely train
> Of guards escorted o'er the glassy plain,
> 'Twas Donaghoe. . . .
> His subjects bend their sovereign to enfold,
> Restor'd, they fondly deem him, as their own,
> Seated immortal on his native throne. (316–19, 324–26)

This "native" sovereignty, however, is just "Expectance vain!" (327). This passage is all the more striking given the people's correct interpretation of Donaghoe's prophecy just a few lines earlier, as if the act of their "firm belief" in his prophecy brings to an end their power to effect their own government, ending not only the life of one Irish king but also the very practice of native rule. Donaghoe remains in the earlier economic stages of the pastoral and agricultural as part of a cycle of fecundity, and his apparition, as both Waters and Gibbons note, is associated with May Day rituals:

still the natives mourn
And annual supplicate his bless'd return.
Oft as he deigns a visit, they behold
Their flocks increase, their harvests wave with gold. (331–34)

Waters suggests that these last lines transform the political undertow of the Donaghoe passage: "Although this ends by deflating the vision to peasant superstition, its potency remains unsubsumed within Leslie's didacticism or within any recognizable generic, literary imperative."[62] There are, of course, echoes of pastoral elegy here and of western European fertility myths in the "mourn[ing]" for the absent king, whose return signals the rejuvenation of the landscape. But, more to my point, Leslie pursues the framing of Donaghoe within a past that is not only remembered through tradition but is also confined to the past in Enlightenment historiography, as an old-style magistrate in a pastoral and agricultural economy, without a bureaucracy, civil judiciary, or a standing army. The march of history anticipated by the prophecy, moreover, contextualizes Donaghoe's transformation from a king into a *genius loci*, an insistently local entity that cannot participate in the "wide extended globe" envisioned by his prophecy. The connection of his rising to local features, including "the glassy plain" (317), highlights his operation as a spirit of the place rather than its ruler. Leslie thus mobilizes a series of geographical and historiographical frames to contain Donaghoe's potential ideological weight as a benevolent and long-remembered Irish king. In Leslie's poetic vision, Donaghoe, as effective "native" government, is lost in the past, surviving only as a ghostly trace that is purely local, while history marches forward to an expansive British Atlantic from which a subordinated Ireland can benefit.

Two Nations, Two Lakes, and Many Maids: Leslie's *Killarney* and the National Tale

Over the past twenty years, we have become familiar in nineteenth-century Irish studies and studies of the romantic novel with the marriage trope for intercultural relations: a woman who represents an abjected people marries a man who represents the dominant group, masking a colonial power relation in the asymmetries of gender and appearing to move beyond violence and alienation to happy, naturalized reconciliation. The colonized, like women, are happy to admire and obey, and are simultaneously reassured that they will be protected. Robert Tracy famously dubbed the trope "the Glorvina solution," after the heroine of the originary national tale *The Wild Irish Girl* (1806) by Sydney Owenson (later Lady Morgan). Mary Louise Pratt has traced versions of this trope in eighteenth-century travel narratives, and the now considerable body of criticism on the national tale since foundational work by such scholars as Ina Ferris and Katie Trumpener has elaborated on its significance in relation to the novels of Morgan and Sir Walter Scott in particular.[63] But this trope operates beyond these prose genres and, in Irish literature at least, arguably finds its origin in Leslie's *Killarney*, particularly in the embedded narrative dubbed "a sylvan tale" (404). Leslie's tale centers on a woman called only "the Maid of Killarney" and offers an early instance of "the Glorvina solution," predating *The Wild Irish Girl* by more than thirty years. (Leslie's *Phoenix Park* also offers an early instance of what would become a nationalist figure for Ireland, popularized through Glorvina, of a woman wearing a "robe of snowy white, the zone of green" and carrying "the radiant symbol," "The harp."[64]) Leslie's "Maid of Killarney" makes apparent the ways in which the national tale not only adapts the colonial trope discussed by Pratt but also inserts it into a nationalist narrative of progress: marriage in these texts marks a transition to a new, more harmonious dispensation in which the "tumults"[65] that define the Irish past are firmly confined in the past, a feature that Scott takes up in *Waverley* (1814).

Most Killarney poems of this period are catalogs of particular scenes peppered by praise of some inhabitants, including the local aristocrat (typically the current Lord Kenmare),[66] like many patronage and topographical poems of the period. Leslie's *Killarney*, as we have seen, is organized into three parts: the first details the so-called "lower lake," while telling the story of "Donaghoe, the great," his son's rebellion, and other bits and pieces of Irish history up to about 1600; the third details the "upper lake" but is virtually void of Irish historical reference. The upward movement from the lower lake to the upper lake is paralleled in the political imagery, which locates Britain above Ireland through a series of images and narratives. Between the two lakes lies the "sylvan tale":

> We seek the shore, and intermit our course—.
> And here, ye Pow'rs, who range the silent grove,
> Watch o'er the haunt, and wild recess of love;
> Permit a rural Wand'rer to reveal
> The tender secrets of the sylvan tale. (400–404)

The first line, ending "intermit our course," is accompanied by a footnote: "In passing to the upper Lake, it is necessary to land, in order to force the boats against the stream, thro' the arches of an old bridge" (p. 72n.). The topographical feature figures the ways in which the "sylvan tale" is a narrative bridge between the two parts of the poem, one set in the lower lake and the other set in the upper lake—one set in Irish history and the other in a picturesque landscape in which the historical focus is imperial Britain.

In the verse paragraph that symbolically allies Desmond's subjection and the superficially innocent depictions of hunting and herding that identify Ireland with economic backwardness, Leslie anticipates the marriage trope of the "sylvan tale":

> The woods expand their umbrage o'er the deep,
> And with ambitious aim ascend the steep.
> Stage above stage, their vig'rous arms invade
> The tallest cliffs, and wrap them in the shade.
> Each in its own pre-eminence regains,
> The high dominion of the subject plains,
> Smiling beneath; such smiles the people wear,
> Happy in some paternal Monarch's care. (85–92)

The "four stages" subtext of the poem is here reinforced: the woods are advancing "Stage above stage," while those left behind on the plains are "Happy in some paternal Monarch's care." The implication is heightened by the contrast with the oft-cited passage in James Thomson's *Seasons* that Leslie is echoing:

> Majestic woods of every vigorous green,
> Stage above stage high waving o'er the hills,
> Or to the far horizon wide-diffused,
> A boundless deep immensity of shade.[67]

There is no "invad[ing]" in Thomson's version or "subject plains," even though Leslie closely echoes the wording of this influential English topographical work ("woods," "vig'rous," "Stage above stage," "shade," and so forth). Imagery of conquest furthers the suggestion that the "woods," so central in Pope's "Windsor-Forest" as the building materials for Britain's imperial fleet, are a metonym for England. The "subject plains," however, suggest Ireland, subjected to England by the "vanquish'd Desmond." This is the promise of "the Glorvina solution": a conquered people "Happy in some paternal Monarch's care." The originary national tale, *The Wild Irish Girl*, similarly ends with the insertion of its English hero, Horatio, into a "new English-patriarchal order" in which "Horatio is not only to become his father's surrogate [as manager of his Irish estate], but also a foster-father to the Irish."[68] To reinforce the suggestion, Leslie offers an image of embrace: "their vig'rous arms . . . wrap" the cliffs. With this linking verse paragraph, the depiction of three of Smith's four stages is explicitly politicized: Britain continues to ascend, "Stage above stage," and Ireland's aspirations are reduced to "Smiling beneath" British shelter and offering up Irish ports to British trade.

This gendering is reinforced in Donaghoe's prophecy in which there is a crucial symbolic shift regarding Donaghoe's assertion of his ownership over Killarney: "his lakes" and "his mountains" are visited by "Guests," but then the landscape is personified as a woman, "Ierne." This feminized Ireland needs William of Orange

"Her cause to second, and her rights defend" (286). This shift from land to be surveyed to female personification paves the way for the appearance of the Maid of Killarney as the poem's central symbol of the nation in need of masculine governance—governance needed precisely because the patriarchal dimension of native Irish politics has come to an end through Donaghoe's passage into prophecy and legend. The Maid is the last of the Donaghoe family line, her only surviving relative an aging father: she is unmoored and hence is wandering unprotected when the tourist finds her. By taking the king out of the equation, Leslie leaves Ireland's sovereignty ("Ierne"), conventionally figured as a woman, languishing without a mate, separated from history—and hence from the progress that is marked by Enlightenment historiography's "four stages."

The "sylvan tale" builds on these passages in the first part of the poem, including Donaghoe's abstraction of Ireland into a female personification and its association of that abstraction with the end of history and Irish kingship. Anticipating the national tale, the "sylvan tale" establishes the Maid of Killarney as an embodiment of the nation. She is not only Donaghoe's descendant but also closely connected to the natural world of the lakes: she exhibits "primeval innocence" (411), "the rural Loves sat smiling on her breast" (412), and her hair is "Like the loose tendrils of the curling vine" (414). With "native eloquence" (474), she tells the story of the Donaghoes' decline with much more succinctness than Leslie's speaker and as her own family history. The protective promise of the union is established through the hero, who virtuously controls his lust for the unchaperoned woman with a father near death and instead promises marriage: "He felt the fierce extreme of wild desire. / But Honour's feelings soon the flame repress'd, / And check'd each ruder purpose of his breast" (416–18); "Won by his virtue, to the nuptial band, / She look'd consent, and pledg'd it with her hand" (489–90). Given the political allegory that undergirds the tale, this is a resonant passage: the threat of rape is contained and erased by the tourist's "virtue," and it is that virtue that "wins" the Maid. More directly than any canonical national tale, Leslie's poem represents marriage as an alternative to violent domination.

This marriage, moreover, is tied to the trope of elevation so significant in the first part of the poem: the tourist "led her forth, / To higher scenes more suited to her worth" (491–92). The Maid, we are told, is a shepherdess (recalling again the poem's insistent identification of Ireland with economic backwardness), and she has been found in the shade that is wrapped by the conquering forest in the early lines—the advanced tourist can thus take her "to higher scenes." But her personal rise ends her family's larger fall. Like Glorvina's family in *The Wild Irish Girl*, the Donaghoe family has lost its wealth, status, and land. Like Glorvina, the Maid of Killarney has only one relative left—a father near death and with no son to inherit, a symbol of a native aristocracy that is on the verge of annihilation. And like Glorvina, she does not speak assent to the marriage that will save her from poverty and familial oblivion, but merely "look'd consent." (Of Glorvina's assent to her engagement to him, Horatio's father writes, "She was silent—she was obedient."[69]) Just as the tourist takes the Maid of Killarney "to higher scenes more suited to her worth," Horatio's father offers "to *raise* [Glorvina] to that rank in life, her birth, her virtues, and her talents merit."[70] While Waters laments the "generic incoherence of a narrative about the beauties of place that ends with the removal to 'higher' scenes,"[71] this upward displacement is perhaps precisely the point. The "tale" recounts a transition from one kind of narrative to another, from the public plot of kings to the domestic one of marriage: Irish history has come to an end through the last male descendant, as prophesied by its legendary king, leaving the female embodiment of the nation unanchored and waiting for the time, as in the lines of Donaghoe's prophecy, "When, from a-far, shou'd come a mighty Friend / Her cause to second, and her rights defend." The Maid's muteness reinforces this relegation of Ireland to the private space of the feminine, outside of history—just as it does in *The Wild Irish Girl*. After the "sylvan tale," there are no more references in Leslie's poem to Irish precolonial history or native rulers.

Anna Maria Edwards's "The Princess of Killarney, A Traditionary Tale" (1787) is in some senses a rewriting of this abjection. Like Glorvina and Leslie's Maid, Edwards's princess, Eilleen, is "the last / Of all her princely line," and, like them, she is located in an explicitly natural setting:

Conceal'd from view, her cottage stood,
  Upon a verdant green.
Though unadorn'd with sculpture fine,
  Here nature's sweets were found."[72]

Leslie's maid, for instance, is discovered when the tourist, "Unmindful of the vulgar scenes of art, / The love of Nature pressing on his heart" (407–8), leaves his group. Similarly, Morgan's Glorvina is not only located in various natural settings but also repeatedly described as natural and distinguished from the artificial: Horatio, for instance, describes her as "both *natural* and *national*" and writes, "*I* who, turning revoltingly from the hackneyed artifices of female depravity in that world where art for ever reigns, sought in the tenderness of secluded innocence and intelligent simplicity that heaven my soul had so long, so vainly panted to enjoy!"[73] This is, of course, conventional eighteenth-century privileging of nature over artifice, but here it serves to reinforce these heroines' identification with Irish land in particular. Edwards's description of Eilleen's father, moreover, echoes Leslie's of Donaghoe:

Lord of the Lake, her sire had reign'd,
  And Kerry's sceptre sway'd;
So just, his subjects love he gain'd,
  They willingly obey'd. (123)

Edwards's royal family includes, however, four sons in addition to Eilleen, the only daughter. The day of Eilleen's wedding, celebrated by "minstrels," "maidens," "Bards," and a "priest" (125), the British invade, "For faithless Britons only meant / To seize the fertile land" (127):

> No lib'ral motive warm'd their soul,
>   No gen'rous wish for fame;
> To tyrannize without controul,
>   Was all their hope and aim. (127)

After a detailed description of the battle, along with accounts of British infamy and Irish popular heroism and some allusion to the first colonization of Ireland by the English, Edwards turns to her plaintive conclusion: Eilleen, all of her family dead on the battlefield, goes to the British leader (he has a "haughty mien, and look severe" [133]) to ask only for the body of her husband and is refused:

> I know dissembling maid, thy art,
>   Disguis'd beneath that tear;
> I know the purpose of thy heart,
>   To raise rebellion here. (135)

Eilleen, like Leslie's Donaghoe, turns prophetic:

> The time will come, in future days,
>   When I shall be no more,
> That Heav'n on Britain's tyrant race,
>   Its vengeance hot shall pour!
> . . . .
> And wound your guilty Nation through,
>   And lay it on the ground;
> And measure out that dole to you,
>   Which all from you have found. (137)

Morgan's *The Wild Irish Girl* and Leslie's "sylvan tale" end with an anticipated marriage. Edwards, however, explores another resolution: in "The Princess of Killarney" Eilleen, married and immediately widowed, retires to Innisfallen to mourn until she dies an early death. Edwards's poem, then, revises the last-maid-of-a-royal-line figure not to move history forward through subordination to the modernizing English, but to commemorate grievous loss alone. This loss is a violation of Killarney's aesthetic properties:

Though ev'ry grove with music thrill'd,
  Though mildest zephyrs blew;
Her gentle heart with sorrow fill'd,
  No consolation knew. (122)

Edwards offers instead only another kind of aesthetic moment, as the last lines of the poem suggest,

Thus early lost was Eilleen fair,
  By all admired and lov'd;
Ev'n haughty Britons scarce cou'd hear
  Her hapless fate unmov'd. (140)

Eilleen, widowed on the eve of her marriage, does not enter into a (re)-productive arrangement with either the native or the invading rulers and becomes simply a sentimental object of narration—a haunting of the British by history, for the Irish have been annihilated.[74]

Brontë's 1818 moral tale *The Maid of Killarney* continues Leslie's argument and builds on the conventions that were already informing the overlapping traditions of the national tale and literary depictions of Killarney, but in terms of religious rather than commercial advancement, highlighting the sectarian context traced by Gibbons. Gibbons notes of a passage in Arthur Young's *Tour in Ireland* (1776–79),

> The mention here of the great Catholic magnate, Lord Kenmare, is salutary, for, as we shall see, anxiety about his estate management was not limited to the condition of his property, but also extended to his representative role as a figurehead of Catholic Ireland under the Penal Laws. . . . [Killarney's] canonical status as a Romantic

> emblem of Ireland was underwritten by a distinctly political subtext: the rehabilitation of the Catholic cause, under Lord Kenmare's stewardship, by liberal-minded Protestants or, more accurately, the assimilation of what was still seen as a refractory native culture into the civilizing discourse of the British Constitution.[75]

Leslie's *Killarney* also works to appropriate Kenmare as a Catholic that Protestants can live with: Gibbons remarks of pertinent passages in Leslie's poem, "Lord Kenmare's politics and religion were evidently considered more enlightened than the old Gaelic order and the 'monkish' superstitions of the Catholic natives."[76] The subtlety, even obliquity, of Leslie's efforts to position Kenmare as a Catholic leader with whom the British can negotiate is lost on Patrick Brontë forty years later. As agitation begins again for Catholic rights in Ireland, his maid is busily converting Killarney's Catholics to the Anglican faith.

The central pair in the tale are allegorically named: the traveling hero is Albion, a poetic name for Britain; the maid of Killarney, instead of being merely like the foliage near the lakes, is named "Flora," the same name given to the ultra-Scottish heroine of Scott's *Waverley*, and both Floras, like Glorvina and Leslie's personification of Ireland in *Phoenix Park*, play the harp. Like Leslie's Maid and her successors in Morgan's and Edwards's texts, Flora Loughlean is explicitly identified with the natural rather than the cultural: Brontë's maid "could not bear even the thought of art or affectation."[77] Like Leslie's tourist and Morgan's Horatio, Albion is a visitor who begins with picturesque scenes and then gets to know the local population; and, like Horatio, he receives letters that seek to guide his behavior. In *Maid of Killarney*, however, Brontë argues against Catholic Emancipation, gambling, dancing, the theater, novel reading, and women's education in general, offering in his "Maid of Killarney" a fairly focused counterexample to Glorvina. Glorvina is educated in terms that largely follow Mary Wollstonecraft's *Vindication of the Rights of Woman* (1792).[78] Conversely, Flora is praised, immediately after a detailed tour of the lakes, for her religious studies: "From six o'clock to eight, she generally read the Scriptures, and other books of a divine nature and tendency. At half past eight, she joined family prayer . . . and she concluded the day as she began it, with lively and spiritual exercises, full of heavenly enjoyment" (86–87). Catholic Emancipation is dismissed as useless, one of the characters contending, "it certainly could not benefit the Protestants, and I think it will add but little to the comfort of the Roman Catholics themselves. They already possess full liberty of conscience, are under the protection of the laws, and may all get as high in the scale of power and influence, as their giddy heads, and still giddier principles, will carry them" (35–36). The tour of the lakes, with the requisite stops at "the beautiful Island of Innisfallin," "the glassy Lake," and the "Eagle's Nest," is largely focused on general aesthetic remarks, such as this: "all around, romantic mountains raised their fantastic forms" (78, 81, 84, 78). But Flora interprets the scene to a different purpose: "In these romantic seasons, I have sometimes wished that a Church might be erected here; for surely no place is better calculated for inspiring the sublime feelings of devotion!" (78). Her devotion is then demonstrated by her father's alarm that she is unaware that she is being soaked by the spray from a waterfall as well as by her repetition of her dream later in the chapter (78–79, 82).

The resolution of the tale thus relies upon a different conversion of Albion. Instead of learning about the Irish past, like Morgan's Horatio and the readers of Leslie's *Killarney* and Edwards's "Princess," Brontë's character is converted to a deeper sense of religion by Flora's piety as part of the tale's larger critique of Catholic aspirations in Ireland. Like *The Wild Irish Girl*, however, the tale ends with a paternal statement of the new husband's right to rule. Horatio is told how to supervise the Irish effectively,[79] and Albion is advised on supervising his wife: "Differ but seldom in your opinions; but if at any time you cannot agree, the law of God and nature requires, that the husband should bear the rule. And above all things, my children, remember that you have immortal souls; and encourage each other in the great work of laying up treasure for them in heaven" (164–65). The symbol of the nation is thus not a residue of a lost past that can be integrated into a more peaceful future, like that imagined by Leslie's Donaghoe and within some national tales more broadly, but a sternly gendered subordination within a devout Protestant framework. Moreover, Flora's father, unlike the fathers of Leslie's Maid and Morgan's Glorvina, is healthy, an officer in the army instead of a disinherited Irish aristocrat, reinforcing the means by which such subordination must be effected outside of the domestic sphere.

Robert Torrens's novel *The Victim of Intolerance* is something of an answer to such uses of the marriage trope in Killarney texts, repeatedly responding to that tradition's positive topoi with realist and even gothic transformations, particularly in the final volume, as well as resurrecting Leslie's reference to rape. Torrens was interested in reform through political economy, and he is the only author considered in the present study who has serious economic credentials: among his early works on the subject are *An Essay on Money and Paper Currency* (1812), *An Essay on the External Corn Trade* (1815), and *A Letter to the Right Honourable the Earl of Liverpool on the State of the Agriculture of the United Kingdom* (1816).[80] The grandson of a Church of Ireland minister, he wrote a pamphlet in favor of Catholic Emancipation that rehearses some of the arguments in *The Victim of Intolerance* and identifies him on the title page, as does *Victim*, as a "Major in the Royal Marines."[81] The fourth volume of *The Victim of Intolerance*, in which the hero becomes an Irish rebel, was controversial, so much so that it is perhaps not surprising that it is almost universally absent from surviving editions of the novel in major research libraries (hence, *The Victim of Intolerance* is typically characterized in library catalogs and recent print sources as a three-volume novel).[82] It is unclear why exactly the volume was so thoroughly suppressed; a leading suspect is not the protagonist's rebellion, but a lengthy inset narrative by a United Irishman of the lower ranks. To summarize this narrative: the United Irishman's mother, from a Catholic family that had dwindled in social status with every generation because of anti-Catholic laws, married a Protestant, who abandoned her when she was pregnant and had their marriage annulled. An unwed mother in eighteenth-century Dublin, she turned to prostitution, gradually falling into the worst levels of the trade. Her son, once he is old enough, starts to poach in order to feed his mother and keep her off the streets. But Catholics are not allowed to carry arms, and so he must hide his poaching guns. Arrested, he refuses to tell the magistrate where his guns are. Arrested again, he again refuses and is locked up for such a long period that his mother, without his assistance as breadwinner, starves to death. So, when he is released, he goes to the magistrate's house and rapes the magistrate's daughter in front of the magistrate: "Before his face I violated his daughter. I told him who I was—I explained for what he had received this terrible retribution at my hands. I would have stabbed him on the spot; but I saw him writhe with remorse and agony, and refused to put a period to his pain. The knife which I flung from me on the floor, his distracted daughter plunged into her heart—I had a great revenge."[83] It is conventional in accounts of the 1798 Irish Uprising to represent rape as a sign of the other side's barbarism, usually as a threat or as off-stage violence. In the sensationalist pamphlet *The Exile of Erin!*, for instance, a woman captured by the United Irishmen is given to the narrator for his "own private gratification," and he instead becomes her protector; in Charles Hamilton Teeling's 1828 memoir of the Uprising, two women are captured by an informal force on the British side, and "brutal violence was offered, and every ruffian of his band invited to the hellish example. To the honour of a British officer, who commanded in the neighboring garrison, the wretched victims were rescued the following morning."[84] But this passage in Torrens's *The Victim of Intolerance* breaks contemporary norms by describing the violence and its effects in some detail—instead of Teeling's strangely passive construction, "brutal violence was offered," we have the active voice specifying the form of the violence: "I violated his daughter." The novel is also highly unusual in literature of the period in representing the rape of a woman as a vehicle by which one man can torture another, a substitution made more emphatic by the daughter's committing suicide with the knife that was brought to murder her father. Moreover, narratives of rape committed during the 1798 Uprising are generally propagandist, but this rapist is, until this point, part of a sentimental narrative, the dutiful son of a betrayed mother, with some rather chillingly graphic details about what such women were forced to. It is also made crystal clear that the rape is revenge for what has been done to his mother—abandoned by her Protestant husband, forced into nearly two decades of prostitution, and then starved to death, all because she is Catholic. The novel's protagonist, O'Connor, who has been established as a vision of intelligence, morality, and political acumen, validated by Frederick Russel, an Anglo-Irish member of Parliament, has this to say about the rapist's story: "The effects which the penal laws produced upon the Catholics, it is unnecessary to describe, and, from the re-action of moral causes their operation on the Protestants was scarcely less pernicious. All was anarchy and convulsion. The elements of civil union appeared to be destroyed, and, in the shock and chaos of contending principles, the social character of man was lost" (4:266–67). So, here, to add to *Waverley*, we have another 1814 response to the new genre of the national tale—a "Catholic tale" that understands Irish social ills in terms of a religious intolerance in which "the social character of man was lost," for Catholics and Protestants alike. Moreover, in Torrens's account, women's bodies bear the consequences of that failure rather than serving as the unproblematic vehicles of reconciliation through properly domestic narratives, such as the marriage plot of the more genteel national tales discussed by scholars to date.

The first three volumes are much less shocking. The novel opens with conventional Killarney features—the sublimity of the scene, the landmarks of Innisfallen (1:3–4), then Mucruss, the Turk, and Mangerton (1:6–7), then various ruins, and "the ghost of O'Donohough the Great" (1:16–17). Various Killarney texts focus on the last woman of the O'Donaghoe line and her aging father, a feature echoed in *The Wild Irish Girl*, and this text is no exception: O'Connor's mother is "the only child of O'Donaghoe," and O'Connor is "idolized by his maternal grandfather" (3:11), the "good old man" (3:11) who "became unconscious of his age, and seemed to enjoy a second youth" around his grandson (3:12). This grandfather, having served Spain, attempted to rejoin his Spanish regiment when the Seven Years' War broke out (3:15–16), grounding Torrens's novel in the military history so key to Leslie's poem and complicating its picture of Irish fealty to the British cause. Just as Leslie addresses trade and agricultural resources, so too does the political economist Torrens, including a substantial discussion of the impact of British policies on the Irish economy and the principles of political economy in general (2:158–85). His Ascendancy politician, Russel, remarks in the dispute, "Ireland . . . though possessed of every advantage of soil and situation, and containing the most dense and hardy population in Europe, has been so fettered and unnerved by a ruinous system of commercial restriction, that in wealth and prosperity, she has continued inferior to many countries, the natural resources of which have been comparatively few" (2:158–59).

Although Leslie has the "sylvan tale" mark the transition to the upper lake, "As one lov'd Image parts with farewel sweet, / Another, and another still we meet, / At length the channel gain" (395–97), Torrens chooses a less pastoral scene for his traveler, describing first "an unfathomable lake, formed in the crater of an exhausted volcano, and called Poul-an-Iffrin, or the *Hole of Hell*," and then depicting the crossing: "We had now arrived at the entrance of a narrow and winding passage, which I was told led to the Upper Lake. We all got out of the boat, which, thus lightened, was dragged up the rapid stream" (1:7–8). This gothic twist is anticipated at the outset, when the speaker—as yet unidentified or unnamed, like the speaker of a topographical poem—remarks that "heavy clouds rested on the adjacent hills, obscuring the prospect, and giving an aspect of gloom to the spot which imagination had represented as the abode of beauty" (1:2). He finds ruins that are gothic rather than picturesque: "The massive arch tottered to its fall; the lofty tower scattered its ruins in the dust. A yew tree grew in the area of the cloisters, and proudly flourishing amid the general decay, flung its funeral shadows on the scene. On every side mouldering and shattered coffins were piled around; human bones occupied the place where the altar had once stood[;] human sculls peeped through the rending walls, and with ghastly and horrid frowns seemed to interdict me from this abode of death" (1:14–15). Similarly, the ghost of O'Donaghoe, generally painted as benign, is here paired with "the howlings of infernal spirits" (1:17). Shortly thereafter, the narrator presents the story of the hermit of Killarney, who appears "spectarian" (1:18) and sleeps in a coffin (1:19) and "hover[s] on the verge of *Poul-an-Iffrin*" (1:19). He dramatically intervenes in a sectarian "riot" (1:23) precipitated by an Orange celebration in an area "chiefly Catholic" (1:22): "He rushed into the midst of the infuriated mob . . . assuaged their wrath, and prevailed on them to retire" (1:23).

The Victim of Intolerance, published the same year as Scott's *Waverley* (with which it was sometimes reviewed in periodicals), not only expands the gothic resonances of the national tale but also challenges the marriage trope by reversing the genders. Early in the text, the parallel between domestic and national harmony that undergirds the "Glorvina solution" is made explicit by the Protestant wife of O'Connor's Catholic friend O'Neil: "The regulations of a well-ordered family resemble the laws of a well-governed state, and redeem the partial restraint which they impose, by securing to all who conform to them a greater share of liberty, than could otherwise be obtained" (1:91). Her household follows this model in a well-ordered home with regular meals in which children are subject to "few and reasonable commands" (1:85–86) and their parents "enjoy[] perfect liberty of conscience" (1:104) so that religion does not divide the household. But this is a subplot early in the text, the ideal from which the hero's life departs because of the discrimination against Catholics in Ireland that he repeatedly laments: he tells Mrs. O'Neil, "The regulations of the society in which I live having injured instead of benefiting me, I have never learned to respect them" (1:92). In the central love plot that dominates the first three volumes of *The Victim of Intolerance*, the Catholic O'Connor cannot marry his ideal mate, the Protestant Julia Russel (a relation of Mrs. O'Neil), because he is legally, and hence politically, disadvantaged by his religion. In the second volume, Julia's father, Frederick Russel, "the lineal descendant of one of the English adventurers who, in the reign of Henry the second, came over to Ireland under Earl Strongbow" (2:1), gradually discovers O'Connor's personal merits, particularly as a thinker on politics, political economy, and religion, and says at the end of the volume, unaware that O'Connor is Catholic, "I wish I could call myself your father" (2:238). At the end of the third, precisely because O'Connor is a Catholic, Russel refuses his permission for O'Connor to marry his daughter. In a speech that suggestively inverts the concluding letter from the benevolent English father in *The Wild Irish Girl*, Russel declares,

> To marry you to Julia was my darling object. You became identified with all my schemes, and all the ambitious hopes which I had cherished for my son, were to you transferred. I predicted that you would ensure the political aggrandizement of my family, and that a son of mine should yet prevail in the senate, and influence the councils of the country. But to the fulfillment of all these hopes, your religion, I now find, is an insuperable bar. I am not a bigot—I am not intolerant,—I do not deny you my daughter, because you are a Catholic; but because, as such, you are excluded from political influence, and from all the situations which a son of mine should fill. (3:217–18)

In other words, revising the gender in Leslie's line, he cannot enter "higher scenes more suited to [his] worth" (*Killarney*, 492); women, such as Glorvina, Leslie's Maid, and Flora, can be elevated by marriage, but the dispossessed man cannot. O'Connor's feminization is completed by the echoing of phrasing between the conclusion, in which O'Connor is "excluded from political influence," and Russel's opinions on his daughter's education in the first half of the novel: "Julia was instructed in every exterior accomplishment which could heighten the effect of her personal charms; but she was a female, she could *never become of any political importance*, and it was therefore deemed superfluous to bestow much pains in the cultivation of her mind" (2:47–48, emphasis added; see also 2:88).

It is through O'Connor that Ireland can potentially become a player on the world stage: he is a successful soldier in the British army on the Continent but is coerced into leaving when he is required to renounce his religion and ends up a merchant "when, under an enlightened system of policy, his rank and fortune might have secured him a seat in the senate, and afforded him an opportunity of interposing in the affairs of the empire, and of exerting an influence on the destinies of Europe" (3:161). The third volume (and hence almost all surviving copies of the novel) ends with O'Connor turning from the father for a final glimpse of his beloved, "to take a last, last look, and feast on agony's excess," but he is denied even this: "She had vanished" (3:221). *The Wild Irish Girl* (ironically) imposes an assimilatory agenda on the final pages, leaving the final word to the English patriarch, who lectures his son on the proper management of the Irish. However, the censored version of Torrens's novel ends not with the silence of the beloved, but with her invisibility and the collapse of the hero into his friend's arms—stressing his feminization and disempowerment. As in Edwards's poem "The Princess of Killarney," conflict ends but without the promise of a (re)productive future. The absence of this promise is stressed in the largely lost fourth volume as all descends into violence, chaos, and sterility, and our erstwhile hero and embodiment of the Irish desire for civil and domestic peace becomes the auditor of a brutal rape narrative instead. And, as in Morgan's *The Missionary* (1811), the Catholic hero with the potential to lead a more civil society ends instead a self-tormented hermit.

As this brief survey of Killarney texts with marriages demonstrates, alongside the conventions of invoking O'Donaghoe, the two lakes, Innisfallen, and the eagle's aery are a number of different versions of Tracy's "Glorvina solution" in which the problems of Irish history are addressed through the marriage plot. Leslie's poem offers not only an early instance of the national tale's central concerns and the specific device of the marriage plot as national allegory (along with various features, especially the last child of a royal line who exhibits personal talents and affinities with the natural landscape), but also its conciliatory politics in which Ireland is offered up to Britain as a willing subordinate. Suggestively, however, the later texts, more remote from the sea changes of the Seven Years' War, obscure the larger geographical context in which Leslie's "sylvan tale" operates. The marriage of Leslie's Maid to a tourist, including her removal from her native region, is part of a larger strategy of subordinating, apotheosizing, and otherwise removing a native ruling class precisely to allow another kind of rule over Irish land so that Ireland can participate in a modernizing and globalizing circuit. Leslie does not imagine British rule in the final section of his poem, but a natural order in which Ireland's participation in the new Atlantic empire is uncoerced—what he terms, in another context in the poem, "rule, without controul" (689). But the national tale, stressing the domestic as the site of retreat from the violence and conflict of the political, takes the "sylvan tale" out of its larger transatlantic context and inserts it instead into a (hetero)normative space posited as universal rather than nationally or historically distinct, in effect undoing the specificities that Williams and Fabricant find in Irish topographical verse. The natural, national heroine who is the last of a native, royal line marries a traveler, ending a history of native–English conflict. Thus far, Leslie's "sylvan tale" and its role as a bridge between the Irish past and the Irish present and future are absorbed fully into the tradition of the national tale.

What is missing from the national tale is the third part of Leslie's poem, in which "rule, without controul" is extensively imagined in a posthistorical Killarney that is defined through spatial movement and relationships rather than temporality, as Leslie pursues a series of images of elevation, from the "Queen of the ocean" who "rises" "Phoenix-like" (517, 526, 525) to "the gleaming Torrent pours" (550), roving "Travellers" (563), "Passions, which, like pilgrims, roam" (571), hunters who "scale the steep" (606), the Eagle's Aery which "teach[es] aspiring Genius how to rise" (666), and so forth. In the poem's final lines, motion is nearly relentless, with only a brief "pause" (572) for respite. In the domestic scene of the penultimate paragraph, this motion spirals:

> The homeward Peasant stops, and hastes by turns,
> And his rude heart with strange emotion burns;
> His joyful, rosy offspring gather near,
> The wonders of his magick tale to hear,
> List'ning they glow; while each believes he sees
> More than he tells, and clings about his knees
> 'Till fir'd their little breasts, they break away,
> And round their Sire, in mimick gambols play. (719–26)

This is the only appearance of the Peasant, and he serves here to stress the constant flux even of motion—"stops, and hastes"—as well as to provide an emblem of the poem's purpose. Just as Leslie's *Killarney* as a whole seeks to insert Ireland into an active and mobile British Atlantic in which it will remain a satellite of Britain, the Peasant's tale launches the children into action that still centers on "their Sire" even though they no longer "cling" to him.

Gibbons traces in Killarney accounts a concern with the local, from Kenmare to local insurgency, and Leslie's *Killarney* contextualizes this local focus through a significant rethinking of Ireland's geographic potential after 1763. The picturesque and conventionally topographical passages in *Killarney* stress the region's resources for hunting and gathering, agriculture, and the pastoral; however, the military, touristic, and commercial references also serve to relocate the region within a transatlantic that can be leveraged to advance Ireland's economic and civic progress. Geography is the ground, so to speak, upon which Ireland's track along conventional historiographical narratives of progress (and concomitantly backwardness) can be redirected. As we shall see in chapter 6, the spatial trope of geography is elsewhere used in Irish writing to counter the temporal lockstep of Enlightenment historiography. The national tale, conversely, through its focus on plot and a resolution that is entrenched in the domestic, disables the cartographic potential of Leslie's romantic interlude. Nostalgia and antiquarianism instead haunt the progress imagined by the national tale, embedding the nation's distinctiveness in a permanently lost past through a relentless focus on the historiographical. The cartographic and the specificities of place fade from view in the cultural and political assimilation of the local to the metropole through the universalized space of the domestic, and with it is lost the potential of the spatial to counter or recontextualize the dominance of temporality.

2

"This Vale of Tears"

Glendalough and the Gothic

> The scene [at Glendalough] that met our view more resembled the infernal regions than the habitations of living men. It was a heap of blackened and smoking ruins, in the centre of which blazed a red and lurid flame: round this, a group of figures were warming themselves, worthy of the pencils that have delineated Conrad and Bertram. The bare brown mountains and rushing torrents that encompassed this desolate spot were in gloomy unison with the objects around, and presented an unvaried aspect of desolation, that pressed upon the shuddering heart the impossibility of escape.
>
> —ALICIA LEFANU, *The Outlaw*

If Killarney occupies a special place in the romanticization of Ireland, as Luke Gibbons suggests,[1] then Glendalough is arguably its gothic double. Both in the south of Ireland, Killarney on the southwest coast in Kerry and Glendalough to the east in Wicklow, the two sites combine some of Ireland's higher mountains with lakes denominated "upper" and "lower." Both are associated with insurgency as well, first Killarney and then Glendalough in the early nineteenth century: in 1806, for instance, John Carr adds to the usual descriptions of ancient ruins at Glendalough a new ruin left by the 1798 Uprising.[2] Gibbons argues that Killarney entered the literary imagination in tandem with Edmund Burke's influential treatise *A Philosophical Enquiry into the Origin of Our Ideas of the Sublime and Beautiful* (1757), as Burke's "distinction between the ameliorating civil effects of the beautiful and the disruptive power of the sublime, resonates through the allegedly spontaneous descriptions of Killarney."[3] In depictions of Glendalough, however, the sublime—rather than the picturesque or "beautiful"—dominates, its "disruptive power" both its medium and its message. Hence, while most of the Killarney texts discussed in chapter 1 focus on some kind of accommodation through marriage, in the major Glendalough poems death, rather than marriage, is the keynote, and the gothic is the defining mode.

William Drennan's poem "Glendalloch" has frequently been noted in passing and occasionally discussed in a few paragraphs, yet its full significance in Irish literary history has been largely left unwritten. Scholars usually cite the poem from Drennan's *Fugitive Pieces in Verse and Prose* (1815) or *Glendalloch, and Other Poems* (1859), but it appeared much earlier in *The Poetical Register, and Repository of Fugitive Poetry, for 1804* in 1806 and in the "modernizing" journal that Drennan helped to found, *Belfast Monthly Magazine*, in 1811.[4] (Drennan had published other poems from *Fugitive Pieces*, with minor variations, earlier in the *Register*, and made multiple contributions to each of the volumes for 1805, 1806–1807, and 1808–1809.) "Glendalloch" is also a foundational treatment of Glendalough, the first of a long line of poetic depictions of the site from Thomas Moore's "By that Lake whose Gloomy Shore" (1811) to Samuel Lover's comic retelling of Moore's lyric, *Saint Kevin: A Legend of Glendalough* (c. 1846), the anonymous *Glendalough, or The Seven Churches: A Didactic Poem* (1848), Edmund Armstrong's medievalizing "Glandalough: A Story of Wicklow" (published posthumously in 1877), and Dora Sigerson's "The Deer-Stone: A Legend of Glendalough" (also published posthumously, in 1919).[5] To these poems we can add, for instance, Lover's short story "King O'Toole and St. Kevin: A Legend of Glendalough" (1832), Dion Boucicault's play *Arrah-na-Pogue* (1862), and numerous paintings of the region, including a series of works by Irish artist Joseph Peacock, such as *The Patron (The Festival of St. Kevin at the Seven Churches, at Glendalough)* of 1813, known for its depiction of the festival crowd but which also features the tall, thin tower to the right and a large ruined building on the left of the painting's middleground.[6] Drennan's poem not only appeared before all of these other depictions of the site but also sets some of the key conventions. Lord Kenmare figures prominently in Killarney texts as a moderate Catholic, but there is no such ameliorative figure in these Glendalough poems, where the recurring character is instead the ascetic Saint Kevin, highlighting precolonial Catholicism on terms that, along with the "disruptive power of the sublime," in Gibbons's phrase, suggest resistance to the improving narratives that Gibbons traces in relation to Killarney. In Glendalough poetry, as in Drennan's poem specifically, violence leads to tragic conclusions that are rarely couched in recuperative terms. For instance, in Drennan's "Glendalloch," the opening and closing metaphor is of the landscape as a graveyard; Moore's lyric focuses on Saint Kevin killing the woman who loved him; and Sigerson's "The Deer-Stone" depicts the violent deaths of a young couple, one poisoned and the other committing suicide on discovering her, leaving their infant lying next to their "cold" bodies.[7]

But Drennan's poem is also a crucial early instance of Irish gothic, heretofore overlooked in part because of the emphasis in gothic scholarship on prose fiction examples, typically beginning with Charles Robert Maturin in the early 1820s, then John and Michael Banim, J. Sheridan LeFanu, and Bram Stoker, but recently taken into the late eighteenth century in an important essay by Siobhán Kilfeather and taken back even further by Jarlath Killeen.[8] The gothic, as has been widely discussed, is founded in part upon mid-1700s concepts of the sublime, particularly in relation to Burke's discussion of terror. Robert Miles has generatively argued that the gothic aesthetic marks an historical anxiety,[9] but its aesthetic is also dominated by excess—not the elevating excess of the sublime, but an excess that cannot be made productive. As David B. Morris suggests, "the Gothic novel pursues a version of the sublime utterly without transcendence. It is a vertiginous and plunging—not a soaring—sublime, which takes us deep within rather than far beyond the human sphere."[10] The gothic as a literary mode, in other words, is peculiarly focused on perpetuating crisis—a mood that must be sustained and propagated through the text rather than simply used as the means through which to achieve a more enlightened perspective.[11] In this regard, it is important, following Morris and other scholars, to move beyond the gothic novel as a literary genre that is characterized by a set of stylized literary devices, including supernatural figures (ghosts, demons), antique stony settings with underground components (castles, monasteries), maidens in distress and helpless heroes who cannot rescue them. Recent studies in Irish gothic, especially considerations of gothic works by Catholic writers, have yoked the gothic to the folkloric via the supernatural, a trend that Richard Haslam traces back to Seamus Deane's critical and creative work.[12] This scholarship addresses a key nineteenth-century revision of the Irish gothic, but it risks both returning us to a view of the gothic mode that has been contested since the 1980s—that is, of the gothic as a mish-mash of supernatural machinery—and resurrecting the gothic representation of rural Ireland in part through its association with folklore.

The folkloric in Irish gothic is a phenomenon arguably related to the emergence of folklore studies in the early nineteenth century to document oral culture and simultaneously mark the modern hegemony of print, and it is difficult to find in Irish gothic before the Grimm brothers' first attempts at accurate scholarly renditions of folktales. The Grimms published their German tales starting in the 1810s but also translated Thomas Crofton Croker's *Fairy Tales and Legends of the South of Ireland* (1825) in 1826. That J. G. Herder also played a role in the emergence of folklore studies suggests the degree to which the field posited, at its origin, a natural relationship between the "folk" and the nation.[13] As such, folklore emerges as a register of the national condition, and gothic renditions of folkloric elements carry particular ideological weight. For instance, in the (unremittingly mediocre) verse of *Glendalough, or The Seven Churches*, the gothic landscape of Glendalough is transmuted into a catalog of folkloric figures stripped of their larger narratives or cultural significance to appear simply as otherworldly. They are gothic horrors that reinforce the stereotype of the melancholy Irish, and they are explicitly opposed to the characters that populate the healthful and aesthetic works of the classical past:

On Ida's tops your Jove may bend
To admire his own rare handy work,
A moonsick wish Endymion tend,
The Muses haunt Parnassus' fork,
May Hebe pour youth's nectared urn,
Round the happy banquet laughter burn,
These in their own bright sunny lore
Draw down the wide essence they adore;
Ours, tear's traditionary fall,
The hereditary hag's shrill thrall;
Our fears down Poul-a-phooka's height
Shall dance the night-mare's goblin sprite;
By coy deceptive Leprachawn
Our unsubstantial grasp be drawn;
Us Fetch's glassy features strike.[14]

Subsequent lines add to the catalog of folkloric figures, including the Banshee, the Coach-a-bowre, and the Dullahan.[15] This list of folkloric horrors evinces no gothic mood but operates within a comparative cultural view in which the Irish national character is identified with "tear's traditionary fall" instead of with "bright sunny lore"; the folkloric here does not render these examples of the gothic mode distinctively Irish but paints Irish culture as distinctively gothic.

The gothic aesthetic is more recognizable as an aesthetic when it is grasped as a focus on that which exceeds the Enlightenment rationalization and management of perception. Morris, for instance, argues for the gothic novel's innovations on Burke's theory of terror, beginning with Horace Walpole's use of "exaggeration and repetition," stylistic devices that "lend[] a strangeness to terror" on terms commensurate with Sigmund Freud's idea of "the uncanny."[16] As Morris adds, moreover, the gothic is tied to a particular practice of "representation as a means of expressing and of evoking what cannot be represented. . . . In contrast to the eloquent silences favored by neoclassical writers on the sublime, Gothic sublimity explores a terror of the unspeakable, of the inconceivable, of the unnameable."[17] These stylistic features—though echoed in character and plot, as Morris demonstrates—are not necessarily yoked to narrative prose. In Drennan's "Glendalloch," the Burkean sublime is set alongside the sort of sublime invoked by Charles O'Conor in his advertisement to the revised 1753 edition of *Seasonable Thoughts Relating to Our Civil and Ecclesiastical Constitution*, where the sublime is part of a transformation that first improves "Habitudes of Mind" and then leads to a "*political Regeneration*" in which the Irish people can become "*wise* and *free*."[18] In other words, O'Conor locates the sublime in relation to personal and hence to national sovereignty, and, in echoing that aspect of O'Conor's thought, Drennan's "Glendalloch" remains a distinctive statement about the politics of the nation in the wake of the Act of Union of 1800.

What I would like to trace here are the ways in which Glendalough emerges in concert with the gothic aesthetic as a site through which to ponder Irish history (once again recalling the "mixed character" of topographical verse), and not merely through the conventions of graveyards and tyranny. This consideration of history also proceeds through an attention to the core of gothic prose and verse—namely, the subject in crisis and specifically the paralysis of the national subject by an unproductive terror.[19] Crucial to gothic scholarship, all the way back to Ann Radcliffe's important essay "On the Supernatural in Poetry," published in the *New Monthly Magazine* in 1826, are the early sections in part II of the *Enquiry* in which Burke brings pain and power into the discussion. He writes, "No passion so effectually robs the mind of all its powers of acting and reasoning as fear. For fear being an apprehension of pain or death, it operates in a manner that resembles actual pain"; further, "pain is always inflicted by a power in some way superior, because we never submit to pain willingly. So that strength, violence, pain, and terror, are ideas that rush in upon the mind together."[20] Similarly,

> [t]o make anything very terrible, obscurity seems in general to be necessary. When we know the full extent of any danger, when we can accustom our eyes to it, a great deal of the apprehension vanishes. Every one will be sensible of this, who considers how greatly night adds to our dread, in all cases of danger, and how much the notions of ghosts and goblins, of which none can form clear ideas, affect minds which give credit to the popular tales concerning such sorts of being. Those despotic governments, which are founded on the passions of men, and principally upon the passion of fear, keep their chief as much as may be from the public eye. The policy has been the same in many cases of religion.[21]

Burke lays out a gothic world of "despot[s]," "ghosts and goblins," gloom and pain, to consider the problem of fear—a "passion" that "robs the mind of all its powers of acting and reasoning" and is related to inequities of power.

Glendalough and Its History in Tourism

Gibbons finds touristic depictions of Killarney as early as 1735 and widespread by midcentury. Killarney was so distinctive for its popularity as an aesthetic site that Isaac Weld remarks in his preface to *Illustrations of the Scenery of Killarney and the Surrounding Country* (1807), "the following pages [are] descriptive of a part of the united kingdom, which, though confessedly interesting, has hitherto remained very imperfectly known. The lake of Killarney, however, has not wholly escaped notice: in every general account of Ireland its extraordinary beauty has been dwelt on; it has been the theme of the poet; and has afforded subjects for a variety of engravings."[22] It is comparatively much more difficult to find descriptions of Glendalough before the 1780s. The site appears regularly in the print record, but as the location of key historical figures, gradually giving way to larger considerations of the landscape's historical significance, particularly through an emphasis on the ruins. In 1739, for instance, an expanded edition of Sir James Ware's early seventeenth-century work "The History of the Bishops" makes passing reference to Glendalough's topography by way of explaining the place-name, but overall the landscape is inextricable from the ruins through which this work traces the history "Of the Bishops of Glendaloch":

> The Cathedral of *Glendaloch* was under the Invocation of the Apostles *Peter* and *Paul*; and both that and the Abby are seated about the middle of a long Valley surrounded with Mountains of an amazing height; from whence the Water falls over many Craggy Rocks and feeds the two Loughs and Rivers which run through the Vale below; in the pleasantest part of which may be seen the Ruins of many Churches or religious Houses built of Stone, the Windows and Doors whereof appear at this Day to have been adorned with a great Variety of curious Work. . . . There appear among the Ruins to have been many Stones and Crosses curiously carved with Figures and Inscriptions thereon in the *Irish* language. The celebrated Bed of St. *Keivin* stands on the South side of the Lough.[23]

The repetition of the terms "Ruins" and "curious," particularly in connection to "the *Irish* language," highlights the ways in which Glendalough enters touristic discourse as a remainder of a remote, and alien, past. Like the gothic fiction discussed by Morris, this work also pushes representation into the domain of the unrepresentable: both the twice-used term "curious" and the phrase "amazing height" leave the description oriented toward mood rather than vision, its suggestiveness extended by the unusual qualification "appear at this Day to have been adorned." It is this view of Glendalough—site of ancient Irish Catholicism, Saint Kevin, and ruins, aesthetically a mix of the picturesque, the sublime, and the simply incomprehensible ("appear . . . curiously carved")—that echoes down the decades of the eighteenth century, appearing in ecclesiastical and general histories of Ireland.

Then, in 1789, tourism arrives. Arthur Young's famous *Tour in Ireland* (1780) does not name Glendalough, though there are general references to the Wicklow mountains and nearby towns. But an expanded version of William Camden's *Britannia* (1586) by Richard Gough, published in 1789 to update Camden's "chorographical" work at a time when "the rage of travelling about Britain has become so contagious," offers a double-columned page on Glendalough, noting, for instance,

> The river *Avonmore* flows from these lakes, and running a course of 15 miles through steep banks, beautifully wooded, discharges itself into the sea at Arklow. The ruins of the abbey . . . are situated at the bottom of the vale surrounded by stupendous mountains, over whose craggs falls the water that feeds the loughs below. They consist of the church, at the east end of which is an arch of several short columns, the capitals adorned with grotesque figures in the Saxon style.[24]

Like the 1739 revision of Ware's "The History of the Bishops," the emphasis is on the unusualness of the ruins, with some suggestively close repetitions of phrasing between these two additions to Early Modern topographical texts: the expanded Ware reads, "Water falls over many Craggy Rocks," and the addition to Camden uses the phrase, "over whose craggs falls the water"; the Ware notes, "There appear among the Ruins to have been many Stones and Crosses curiously carved with Figures and Inscriptions thereon in the *Irish* language," while Gough's addition to Camden remarks, "Among the Ruins are many tombstones with crosses, figures and inscriptions in the Irish language."[25] Such echoes, which also appear in Drennan's text, as I discuss later, recall the gothic mode's investment in repetition as a stylistic device, noted by Morris. But here, amidst the "inscriptions in the Irish language," are also "grotesque figures in the Saxon style," suggesting a hybridity of origins. These descriptions of Glendalough, then, are quite different from contemporary accounts of Killarney: authors dwelt on "the splendours of the scenery" at Killarney, "The Masterpiece of Nature," as one 1750 account put it,[26] with only passing mention of ruins and local buildings still in use, but writers put Glendalough's ruins, especially their peculiarity, at the center of the site's importance.

In 1795, Jonathan Fisher published *The Scenery of Ireland*, focusing largely on the southeast but promising a subsequent volume on Killarney because of high demand—a volume that appeared as an appendix in 1796.[27] In a long passage on Killarney, Fisher writes,

> the southern shore forms a bold outline of mountains, which give dignity and character to the scene; they are wooded as much as nature would seem to permit, the back part rising with savage grandeur . . . [and] displaying their cloud-caped tops in all the variety which their height and the neighbourhood of the great Atlantic naturally forms.
>
> In tracing the south-side of the Lake, we first notice the mountain Glena, . . . [which] assumes a bolder aspect, from projecting rocks, which give the most picturesque appearance, by the masses of light and shade with which they variegate the scene.[28]

Fisher thus continues the trend that Gibbons discusses: Killarney is a natural wonder, sublime in some features and explicitly "picturesque" in others. As in John Leslie's depiction in *Killarney*, moreover, its transatlantic significance is not only noted but also integral to the landscape's power. Fisher closes his earlier volume, *The Scenery of Ireland*, with a description of Glendalough. Like the expansions of Ware and Camden, but very much unlike his description of Killarney in 1796, Fisher stresses not Glendalough's natural beauties, but its ruins: "advancing about one mile through this romantic scene, you discover that part of the Glen which contains the Churches, &c.— Here the eye is agreeably surprized with the Ruins of several antique buildings, standing in the middle of a flat and rather extensive vale, environed by lofty mountains, watered by two small but rapid rivers, and terminated on the west by two deep lakes, from whence it derives the name of Glendalough."[29] As Glendalough passes from historical treatises to tourism guides, the ruins remain integral parts of the aesthetic scene. Thus, the viewer is "agreeably surprized" not by a waterfall or magnificent prospect,[30] but by the ruins themselves. Moreover, descriptions of the ruins now recall the gothic architecture that helped to name and shape eighteenth-century gothic fiction: "curious," "grotesque" ecclesiastical buildings that Fisher specifies are vaulted, including a "stone vaulted crypt," a "great arch, curiously wrought, and ornamented with singular devises," "an arched gateway," and "a small Church . . . with vaulted stone roofs."[31] Glendalough's ruins are too early for architectural gothic proper, and there are of course kinds of vaulted roofs that are not gothic—my point is rather Fisher's emphasis on features consistent with gothic architecture as part of a larger tradition of representing the church ruins as "grotesque" or "curious." For if "the praise lavished on Killarney's scenic beauties was closely bound up with the 1757 publication of Edmund Burke's *Philosophical Enquiry into . . . the Sublime and Beautiful*,"[32] the aesthetic role of Glendalough's buildings was strongly allied with that *Enquiry*'s gothic interpreters, beginning most famously with the first gothic novel, Horace Walpole's *Castle of Otranto*.

Ina Ferris notes a tension in ruin discourse between "the meditative-aesthetic and the analytical-historical approach" (broadly, the personal and the political), approaches yoked to attempts "to stabilize the unstable site of the ruin," the space of struggle between nature and culture.[33] Ferris suggests that "the scene of colonial ruin," in contrast, "moves destruction rather than 'calm decay' into the foreground and unsettles such literary-philosophic projects," or, perhaps more aptly than "destruction," it "moves" what Sean Ryder terms "unrelieved trauma" to the fore.[34] Kevin Whelan, approaching the problem from a different disciplinary perspective but briefly quoting Drennan's "Glendalloch," views the English tradition as "harmonising" in contrast to an Irish one, in which ruins are viewed "as a traumatic tear in the fabric of time."[35] Fisher presents another option: his description of ruins at Glendalough is gothic not in noting the violence of their ruination (Ferris's "destruction rather than 'calm decay'" or the trauma that Whelan and Ryder invoke), but in stressing the inexplicable diversity of their decline, a refusal of Enlightenment historiography that goes beyond the general discomfiture posed by the ruin. In Fisher's account,

> Some of the buildings are nearly entire . . . and expressive of great antiquity; others partly standing and partly fallen, with various trees growing out of the walls, form a pictureseque effect in shading these precious reliques, while others are either wrapt up in masses of ivy, and other ever-greens, or mowed down by the all-levelling and unrelenting scythe of time.—When to these we add one of those slender round Towers, which we often find erected near our most ancient Ecclesiastical Buildings, and which are in a great measure peculiar to the antiquities of this kingdom, we may have a general though faint idea of the present appearance of the Seven Churches.[36]

A mix of undamaged remainders of "great antiquity" and picturesque ruins "partly standing and partly fallen," Fisher's description is gothic in its representation of the scene as not only unrepresentable ("a general though faint idea"), but also resistant to the history making that Raymond Williams finds in Oliver Goldsmith's *Deserted Village*. The "unrelenting scythe of time" yet leaves "some of the buildings . . . nearly entire," and the degree of decay for the round tower is not even addressed. Fisher cannot organize his touristic account of the scene on the terms demanded by its previous historical incarnations, combining in one short passage the two forms of ruin discourse discussed by Ferris; the picturesque intercedes between the "entire" buildings "of great antiquity" and the "most ancient" tower. Fisher thus refuses the historical project of such ruin discourse, neither offering violence-produced ruins nor, as Ferris puts it, "distinguish[ing] between ancient ruins like the famous round towers of Ireland . . . and more recent historical ruins."[37] Integrating different streams of ruin discourse with a post-Burkean landscape aesthetics, Fisher's Glendalough develops a gothic aesthetic in its very refusal of neoclassical generic order as well as in its invocations of the sublime and vaulted church architecture.[38] Killarney invites improvement, but Glendalough here, as in other writing about the area, resists entrance into the linearity of history upon which the very idea of improvement is founded.

Another substantial description of Glendalough published before Drennan's poem more explicitly lays out the political stakes of such gothic descriptions of the site: Edward Ledwich's *Antiquities of Ireland* (1790). Ledwich, praised by Fisher as an important antiquarian and discussed as such in recent scholarship,[39] cites Camden's work, though not its 1789 expansion, and generally follows contemporary practices of scholarly description. But Ledwich is no objective commentator, congratulating himself that "in a former part of these papers, the pretensions of the Irish to an original alphabet have been examined and rejected" and repeatedly condemning portions of Irish history and literature as beneath serious attention.[40] Oliver MacDonagh suggests that "modern Irish historiography was born in 1790 with the publication of the Revd Edward Ledwich's *Antiquities of Ireland.* Ostensibly, Ledwich wrote as an enlightenment man, bent on dissipating by eighteenth-century sunlight what he called the bardic fictions which had enveloped early Irish history. . . . His real target was rising papists . . . who had combined agitation for Catholic relief with attempts to preserve the traditional Gaelic culture."[41] Recent commentators on Ledwich's antinativist agenda include Clare O'Halloran, Leith Davis, Joseph Lennon, and Joep Leerssen, the latter grouping Ledwich among "narrow-minded and illiberal Celt-haters" and indexing Ledwich as such.[42] In the preface to *Antiquities of Ireland*, for instance, Ledwich refuses to treat "our [Irish] mythological history," saying that to do so would be to suggest his "ignorance of its fictitious origin, of the low estimation in which it is held by the learned"; later, he peppers his prose with snide volleys, such as "Leaving the absurd and idle figments of Irish history to those who are delighted with romance."[43] He makes clear his polemic aims:

> Some confidence in the cause I was engaged in, which appeared to me that of the truth, has probably inspired a temerity of expression and of censure, which on any other subject had better been restrained. I confess I have taken but little pains to correct this error, if it be such, because here truths were to be delivered in strong language; the numerous defenders of our bardic fictions and

> historical romances being ever on the watch, and ready to convert guarded expressions and modest diffidence into strong symptoms of a weak cause. Nor have I been sparing of ridicule; for who in his senses would so egregiously waste his precious moments, as to enter into a serious discussion and confutation of monstrous assertions, and puerile absurdities?[44]

Although my focus is gothic depictions of Glendalough rather than the heated antiquarian debates of the late eighteenth century, this context is relevant here because, while the expansion of Camden echoes the expansion of Ware, it is Ledwich who appears to be the origin of "gloomy" Glendalough.

Other descriptions of Glendalough are broadly sublime—water falling over crags, mountains, ruins, and so forth—but Ledwich veers into the Burkean list of terrors as nineteenth-century poets would do so persistently when writing of Glendalough. Ledwich begins his description of the site,

> From the earliest ages, Glendaloch seems to have been a favourite seat of superstition. The tribe of wild and ignorant savages who here first fixed their abode, deprived of the light of letters; unoccupied by any amusing or profitable employment, and wandering among human forms as uncivilized and barbarous as themselves, were a prey to melancholy thoughts and the basest passions. Their fears animated every rustling leaf and whispering gale, and invisible beings multiplied with the objects of their senses. . . .
>
> The gloomy vale, the dark cave, the thick forest and cloud-capt mountains were the chosen seats of these aerial spirits, and there they celebrated their nocturnal Orgies. These superstitious and idle fears could only be appeased by the bold claims of pagan priests to mystic and supernatural powers, equal to the protection of the terrified rustic and the taming the most obstinate Dæmon.[45]

The gothic emerges here to discredit indigenous Irish culture. Ledwich manages to hit many, if not most, of the sources of Burkean terror cataloged by Morris: "vast cataracts, raging storms, lofty towers, dark nights, ghosts and goblins, serpents, madmen; mountains, precipices, dazzling light; low, tremulous, intermittent sounds, such as moans, sighs or whispers; immense, gloomy buildings; tyranny, incarceration, torture."[46] This is the fully fledged gothic as the nightmare of the Enlightenment: a world without reason, discipline, or science. But I would characterize Ledwich's passage as gothic less for its invocation of "superstition" and the "supernatural" than for its use of the weighty terms "melancholy" and "gloomy"; the overall mood of the scene is a gothic one, where terror alternates with despair, and an unremitting darkness casts a pall over intellects as it does over scenes.[47]

It is in this gothic mood that this passage most anticipates Drennan's "Glendalloch" and later poems about the site. But this similarity is not just about mood, but also about Drennan's heretofore unnoted incorporation of phrases and ideas from Ledwich. The long passage from Ledwich quoted earlier, for instance, is closely echoed by Drennan's "Glendalloch" both in the general point and in the specific image of Glendalough as what Ledwich terms the "seat of superstition." Drennan writes,

> There Superstition chose her seat;
> Her vot'ries knew, with subtle art,
> Thro' wond'ring eyes to chain the heart;
> By terrors of the scene, to draw
> And tame the savage to their law,
> Then seat themselves on Nature's throne,
> And make her mighty spell their own.
> The charming sorc'ry of the place
> Gave Miracle a local grace;
> And, from the mountain-top sublime,
> The Genius of our changeful clime
> A sort of pleasing panic threw,
> Which felt each passing phantom true.[48]

Both Ledwich and Drennan also use the relatively rare "-och" spelling of the name "Glendalloch" (though Drennan's Ulster connections and education in Scotland might also account for his choice). Moreover, Drennan refers to "Tuathal" (9), and Ledwich gives an account of a twelfth-century "Laurence O'Toole, whose ancestors had founded and endowed the Abbey," and provides the Irish spelling "O'Tuathal."[49] Most definitively, in 1811 Drennan added a footnote to "Glendalloch," retained in the 1815 version cited here, in which he plagiarizes a sentence from Ledwich. Drennan's note indicates, after general praise for the county of Wicklow and without quotation marks or any other sign of citation, "This particular Glyn is surrounded on all sides, except to the East, by stupendous mountains, whose vast perpendicular height throws a gloom on the vale below, well suited to inspire religious dread and horror" (p. 139n.). Ledwich writes, "Glendaloch is surrounded on all sides, except to the East, by stupendous mountains, whose vast perpendicular height throws a gloom on the Vale below, well suited to inspire religious dread and horror."[50] In *Stranger in Ireland*, Carr repeats some of the language from this sentence as well: "the stupendous mountains . . . a few miserable cabins . . . the deep shade upon the valley, are all well calculated to inspire the imagination with religious dread and horror."[51] Such repetition of phrasing is not that unusual for the time, but I trace it here to establish Ledwich's influence over the gothic rendering of Glendalough. The key phrases taken up by both Carr and Drennan—namely, "stupendous mountains" and "inspire religious dread and horror"—focus on specifically gothic elements, such as imposing landscapes evocative of the sublime, anti-Catholicism, and intense emotional states arising from awe. Ledwich is also the earliest author I have found to associate Glendalough with the word "gloomy," also foregrounded in Moore's title "By that Lake Whose Gloomy Shore"; Drennan uses it four times in adjective or noun forms, and Armstrong's reference to the Seven Churches as "the Churches of the Gloomy Lakes" stresses it again.[52]

Whether these borrowings are meant as recognizable references to Ledwich is an unanswerable question, one complicated somewhat by the distribution of references over the early revision of the poem and the different discursive climates from Ledwich's diatribe in 1790 to Drennan's composition of the poem around 1802 to Drennan's addition of the footnote in 1811. What is clear, however, is Ledwich's influence on the discursive transformation of Glendalough from the site of picturesque ruins into a gothic symbol of predation and conflict, an influence traceable both in specific verbal echoes and in the continuation of Ledwich's general association of the site with uncontrolled and irrational behavior. That Fisher praises Ledwich's scholarship but avoids his gothic diatribe on early "superstition" is also worthy of note: Ledwich's description of Glendalough uses the devices of anti-Catholic gothic, whereas Fisher aestheticizes the gothic to strip the scene of the ideological weight it has in Ledwich's account. In Ledwich, sublimity is transposed from the natural scenery—the crags, the ivy that pulls down the buildings—to cultural error, nearly tipping a gothic aesthetic into mere allegory through an almost parodically gothic catalog of horrors. Fisher counters Ledwich's approach, but Drennan, I suggest, partly contests and partly adapts Ledwich in a more deeply gothic text whose central theme is neither invasion nor the sublime nor religious error, but that which runs through them all—disabling terror.

Drennan's "Glendalloch"

A poem of just over four hundred lines, "Glendalloch" was dated 1802 by Drennan and was likely composed then, particularly since Drennan refers to a poem of this name in his letters as early as 1803. Some scholars have briefly discussed "Glendalloch," often as a troubling poem that departs from recognizable literary traditions. Mary Helen Thuente finds it exceptional among United Irishmen verse for "reject[ing] armed rebellion," and Terence Brown anticipates much later reference to the poem by noting, "This is no romantic poem of place. . . . Rather it is a work dominated by an historical moral imagination."[53] Waters tacitly counters Brown's point by suggesting that the poem "promise[s], in its opening pages, to offer a Wordsworthian argument about the potential unity of self-consciousness and perception in an experience of the personified figure of Nature" but then falls "from place-poetry into narrative"—narrative that Waters associates with Walter Scott's poetry.[54] Waters's account is a suggestive one, particularly for directing our attention to the structuring of the poem's engagement with history and place, though the literary coordinates are somewhat anachronistic in light of the poem's composition around 1802 and publication as early as 1806.[55] Drennan's "Glendalloch" was in print before Wordsworth's *Poems in Two Volumes* (1807) began to solidify Wordsworth's poetic reputation and was likely composed before Scott published his first narrative long poem, *Lay of the Last Minstrel* (1805).[56] Norman Vance argues more compellingly for the poem's melding of "the already old-fashioned mode of eighteenth-century topographical poetry . . . with the melancholy commonplaces of the so-called 'graveyard poets,'" "but . . . only as a starting-point" for a "melancholy historical review."[57] Foster mentions Drennan in passing as both an Ulster contributor to an increasingly regionalized Irish tradition and a poet who "retain[s] the formulaic structure of the genre."[58] Gibbons locates the poem within an Irish tradition of ruin discussed by David Lloyd, in which "ruins were the result not of a clash between nature and culture, but between several opposing cultures, the debris of a history of invasions."[59] Ryder, building on other discussions of ruin by Gibbons, focuses on the opening lines of the poem, noting the ruins' significance in "a literal grave of national hopes and identity."[60] I have surveyed this rich body of scholarship not only to trace the recurring concerns in scholarly discussion of this canonical text, but also to note a striking feature of this body of scholarship. Though published years apart by important scholars in the field of Irish literary studies—Foster in 1974, Brown in 1975, Vance in 1990, Gibbons in 1991, Thuente in 1994, Waters in 2001, and Ryder in 2005—not one of these discussions cites any other reading of Drennan's work. What we have here is not a debate, each critic marshaling evidence to counter or expand previous positions, but a remarkable register of the simultaneous exemplarity and exceptionality of this poem in terms of highly conventionalized forms both specific to Irish literary traditions and constitutive of a larger anglophone body of writing—and a strange metonym for the poem's own account of cultural forgetting under the weight of historical concern.

As discussed in chapter 1, Leslie's *Killarney* uses the picturesque double lakes of Killarney to figure a transition from an Irish past marked by English–Irish military conflict (the lower lake) to an Anglo-Irish future in which Ireland profits as a site for English tourism and a port for transatlantic trade (the upper lake). In his second verse paragraph, Leslie explicitly distinguishes Killarney from landscapes that suggest the sublime, including features that were becoming associated with the gothic:

No Alpine horrors on their summits frown,
Nor Pride, dark-low'ring, on the vale looks down:
No massy fragments, pendant from on high,
With hideous ruin strike the aching eye.
The swelling Hills in vernant bloom elate,
Smile by their sides, th' attendants of their state.[61]

As Waters suggests, the second verse paragraph of Drennan's poem is "Wordsworthian,"[62] perhaps presciently so, but the first verse paragraph begins the poem within a gothic tradition that has well-established roots in the Graveyard School of poetry:

Th' enchantment of the place has bound
All Nature in a sleep profound;
And silence of the ev'ning hour
Hangs o'er GLENDALLOCH's hallow'd tow'r;
A mighty grave-stone, set by Time,
That, 'midst these ruins, stands sublime,
To point the else-forgotten heap,
Where princes and where prelates sleep;
Where Tuathal rests th' unnoted head,
And Keivin finds a softer bed:
"Sods of the soil" that verdant springs
Within the sepulchre of kings. (1–12)

Drennan's poem thus begins not with what has been "by Nature made" (14), but with key elements of the gothic that Leslie explicitly excludes from his picturesque scene: "enchantment," darkness, sublimity, remote history, and Catholic icons, from the "hallow'd tow'r" to "prelates" and Saint Kevin. Drennan's focus on the tower, moreover, makes emblematic the building that is, according to Fisher, the most distinctively Irish and ancient building at the site.

But, arguably, the poem's closest precursor is Goldsmith's *Deserted Village* (1770). Like that poem, "Glendalloch" has a generalized speaker commenting on social decline as he contemplates a desolated scene of previous habitation. The two poems also have broadly similar turns from light to darkness through political error.[63] Both poems also end on the power of education to remedy the social ills that have been cataloged, including greed, both using the rather peculiar term "self-dependent." Goldsmith writes,

> Aid slighted truth, with thy persuasive strain;
> Teach erring man to spurn the rage of gain;
> Teach him that states of native strength possest,
> Tho' very poor, may still be very blest;
> That trade's proud empire hastes to swift decay,
> As ocean sweeps the labour'd mole away;
> While self-dependent power can time defy,
> As rocks resist the billows and the sky. (425–32)

Drennan's speaker pleads,

> That Education, HERE, might stand,
> The harp of Orpheus in her hand,
> Of power t'infuse the social charm,
> With love of peace and order warm,
> The ruder passions all repress'd,
> And tam'd the tigers of the breast,
> By love of country and of kind,
> And magic of a master mind. (353–60)

But the speaker despairs that such remedy is possible, so Ireland is

> Lost—to the world and future fame,
> Remember'd only in a name,
> Once in the courts of Europe known
> To claim a self-dependent throne. (387–90)

Both poems, in other words, make similar arguments about the merits of learning, reinforced negatively in Drennan through his critique of the church's schooling and positively through Goldsmith's dwelling on the "little school" (198) at Auburn—and both poems connect learning to independence. This is crucial to the gothic framing of Drennan's poem.

Drennan was, as Vance notes, a man of the Enlightenment, and he had declared, just months before writing "Glendalloch," that he would not let "the principles of John Locke wither in [his] hand, or in [his] heart."[64] In *Essay Concerning Human Understanding*, Locke offers as the central definition of reason "that faculty whereby man is supposed to be distinguished from beasts" and contends that "in this then consists Freedom, (*viz.*) in our being able to act, or not to act, according as we shall chuse, or *will*."[65] O'Conor, working in the same Enlightenment tradition, thus remarks, "*Thinking* infers, and produces *Action*, good or bad."[66] These propositions are of course conventional, even fundamental, Enlightenment ideas, and they run through much of Drennan's corpus as well as in the passages quoted earlier. They are particularly relevant to my discussion here, however, because of Burke's definition of terror: "No passion so effectually robs the mind of all its powers of acting and reasoning as fear."[67] This is the gothic nightmare of Drennan's poem: a nation of individuals who can neither act nor reason, leading to a crisis of both individual and national sovereignty. Invasion, death, and religion are important subjects in "Glendalloch," as the body of criticism on the poem attests, but it is this nightmare of the (national) subject's paralysis that undergirds them all.

Drennan's poem begins by invoking the remote Irish past of saints and heroes in terms that strongly echo Thomas Gray's famous "Elegy Written in a Country Churchyard" and, as Vance notes, the Graveyard School in general.[68] Gray writes,

> Beneath those rugged elms, that yew-tree's shade,
> Where heaves the turf in many a mouldering heap,
> Each in his narrow cell for ever laid,
> The rude Forefathers of the hamlet sleep.[69]

Drennan, however, shifts the landscape from natural decay to the gothic ruin:

> A mighty grave-stone, set by Time,
> That, 'midst these ruins, stands sublime,
> To point the else-forgotten heap,
> Where princes and where prelates sleep. (5–8)

Despite the close echoes—including the repetition of Gray's rhyme "heap/sleep"—there is a key difference between the two texts that recalls Drennan's use of the term "self-dependent." "Princes and . . . prelates," not "forefathers," "sleep" beneath the decaying "heap," making the focus here not ancestry, but sovereignty. For what Drennan's poem mourns is not saints or heroes or national glory, but sovereignty itself. Sovereignty is gradually lost both to the Irish and to the nation as his poem progresses—and it is lost through the tipping of sublimity into terror.

The first third of Drennan's poem focuses on the druids, especially the long speech of the Arch-Druid and his assuaging of his audience's terror at the sight of an eclipse. As Vance notes, the Arch-Druid exhibits "a crisply optimistic Enlightenment vision,"[70] and he is relentlessly associated with light in the poem. He "issued forth to light," wears a "robe, of spotless white," and "Behind his head a crescent shone" (34, 33, 37)—all consistent with contemporary depictions of druid priests—and the light imagery is also extended to "the illumin'd throng" and "the light of song" (41, 42). It is the druidic intervention that makes Glendalough beautiful. In this section of the poem, Glendalough is represented as "a dreary dark abode" (21) through which the druids celebrate and invite the light:

> O! fountain of our sacred fire,
> To whom our kindred souls aspire,
> (Struck from the vast chaotic dark,
> As from these flints we strike the spark,)
> Thou Lord of Life and Light and Joy,
> Great to preserve, but not destroy,
> On us, thy favor'd offspring, shine! (117–23)

Light, in other words, is conjured by the druids who worship nature and the sun as a symbol of divinity. By contrast, the arrival of Christianity involves

> A priesthood of another hue;
> More like the raven than the dove,
> Tho' murm'ring much of faith and love.
> . . . .
> And shunn'd th' approach of cheerful light. (132–34, 138)

To establish the central symbolism and theme of the poem, Drennan interrupts the Arch-Druid's speech with an eclipse:

> But ah! what dim and dismal shade
> Casts this strange horror o'er the glade
> Causes e'en hearts of brutes to quake,
> And shudders o'er the stagnant lake?
> What demon, enemy of good,
> Rolls back on earth this night of blood? (59–64)

In distinction to later inhabitants, the Arch-Druid uses reason so effectively that he "the terrors of the croud repress'd, / And smooth'd their troubl'd wave to rest" (77–78).[71] After this lesson, the priest marks the end of the eclipse:

> it is not death
> That shadows yon bright orb of day:
> See! while I speak, the orient ray
> Breaks, sudden, thro' the darksome scene,
> And Heav'n regains its blue serene. (102–6)

The light, he says, will "grim Glendalloch teach to smile" (112). The Arch-Druid teaches a rational reading of the natural world and so diminishes his audience's fears, but then Christian missionaries pervert the perception of the landscape in order to elicit terror, as Drennan adapts Ledwich's screed about the "first inhabitants" of Glendalough to refer not to pagans, but rather to the first Christians there:

> Where Nature reign'd, in solemn state,
> There Superstition chose her seat;
> Her vot'ries knew, with subtle art,
> Thro' wond'ring eyes to chain the heart;
> By terrors of the scene, to draw,
> And tame the savage to their law. (141–46)

Drennan thus appropriates Ledwich's gothic language to rewrite that history of Ireland: instead of "first inhabitants" who are "savage" "pagans," Drennan's first inhabitants are rational British druids who are supplanted by Christian missionaries who terrorize instead of instruct. Ledwich, according to Clare O'Halloran, "attributed . . . alleged scholastic eminence, not to native Irish scholarship, but to the influence of British monks and clerics who had fled to Ireland in the sixth and seventh centuries to escape the censure of the Roman Pontiffs."[72] Drennan similarly imagines a British origin for Irish enlightenment but shifts it back a few centuries to a pre-Christian revolt against Rome rather than a church schism. Drennan thus secularizes the intellectual tradition and arguably turns Ledwich's anti-Catholicism, modified by what O'Halloran terms the antiquarian's "sense of ownership of Ireland's early Christian heritage,"[73] into a broader argument for more deist approaches.

These representations of perception are embedded within a larger discussion of the sublime and terror in which the former is depicted as part of a natural and national aesthetic and the latter as the disabling tool of those who seek power. In Drennan's argument, religious "terror" is a misappropriation of natural sublimity. The early Christian leaders

> seat themselves on Nature's throne,
> And make her mighty spell their own
> The charming sorc'ry of the place
> Gave Miracle a local grace;
> And, from the mountain-top sublime,
> The Genius of our changeful clime
> A sort of pleasing panic threw. (147–53)

The phrase "pleasing panic" clearly invokes the aesthetic terror of the sublime, as does "charming sorc'ry." But the suggestive phrase "pleasing panic" predates Burke's *Enquiry.* In the advertisement to the 1753 edition of *Seasonable Thoughts Relating to Our Civil and Ecclesiastical Constitution*, historian and Catholic pamphleteer O'Conor writes, "an Alteration, from *ill* to *better* Habitudes of Mind, (for *Thinking* infers, and produces *Action*, good or bad,) is a Sort of *political Regeneration*, which rendereth even our Dangers useful, by a Retrospect to the Sufferings we underwent; and affords the *pleasing Panic* of viewing the Precipices we escaped. Of all the People, at this Day, in *Europe*, those of *Ireland* appear, at present, the *best disposed*, and the *most forward*, to *think* and *act*, as becometh a *wise* and *free* People."[74] Ledwich challenges O'Conor's pro-national and sympathetically Catholic antiquarianism, but the advertisement is rather an argument for the integration of Catholics into the polity as a remedy for a range of social and political ills. In shifting the ground from Ledwichian gothic early in the poem to O'Conorite sublimity in its middle section, Drennan tacitly moves from sectarianism to the Enlightenment transcendence of such tribalisms. Particularly crucial to this transition is that O'Conor, coming out of the same Enlightenment context as Burke, makes a direct connection between sovereignty and the capacity to "think and act"—and positions sublimity, particularly as "pleasing Panic," within a transformational process that can improve the mind and hence achieve "*political Regeneration.*"

Drennan, echoing this argument of O'Conor's as well as using his phrase "pleasing panic," hence distinguishes between a sublimity that is "pleasing" and both natural and national ("The Genius of our changeful clime") and its gothic counterpart, the disabling "terrors" produced by manipulating the "scene" with "subtle art." It is the former, not the latter, that he connects to native literature:

E'en at a more enlighten'd hour
We feel this visionary pow'r;
And, when the meanest of his trade,
The ragged minstrel of the glade,
With air uncouth, and visage pale,
Pours forth the legendary tale,
The Genius, from his rock-built pile,
Awful, looks down, and checks our smile.
We listen—then a pleasing thrill
Creeps thro' our frame, and charms our will,
Till, fill'd with forms fantastic, wild,
We feign—and then become the child. (155–66)

In the "pleasing thrill," the auditors echo the aesthetic experience of the "mountain-top sublime"—that is, a "pleasing panic." This also of course relies on Burke's theorization of art's ability to produce sublime effects, and, indeed, an anonymous 1799 review compared Drennan and Burke at some length, suggesting "Dr. D. is certainly a disciple of the better days of Burke."[75] In "The Effects of Sympathy in the Distresses of Others" in *Enquiry*, Burke famously notes in a discussion of the power of fiction that "terror is a passion which always produces delight when it does not press too close."[76] In the final section of the *Enquiry*, Burke details at some length the greater power of words, suggesting "that eloquence and poetry are as capable, nay indeed much more capable of making deep and lively impressions than any other arts, and even than nature itself in very many cases," specifically invoking the supernatural as "ideas" that "have never been at all presented to the sense of men but by words . . . [and] have however a great influence over the passions."[77] Drennan is thus closely following Burke and O'Conor to contrast a faulty, terror-inducing appropriation of the natural sublime with a proper nativist engagement with "The Genius" of Ireland through both oral culture and the natural. Crucially, the auditors of these tales are not paralyzed by them, like the "savage" "tame[d]" to Christian "law": they are "charm[ed]" and "feign," but their aesthetic response is dominated by pleasure, the proper effect of the literary sublime and hence of elevation rather than paralysis.

This three-part distinction—between nature, literature, and a false (Christian) view of nature—is repeated a few lines later in a passage on the tree of knowledge:

> Knowledge, by a forg'd decree,
> Still stands an interdicted tree.
> —Majestic tree! that proudly waves
> Thy branching words, thy letter leaves;—
> Whether, with strength that time commands,
> An oak of ages, Homer stands,
> Or Milton, high-topt mountain pine,
> Aspiring to the light divine;
> Or laurel of perennial green,
> The Shakespeare of the living scene,—
> Whate'er thy form—in prose sublime,
> Or train'd by art, and prun'd by rhyme,
> All hail, thou priest-forbidden tree! (211–23)

Relying on a longstanding trope for literature, used, for instance, in the title of Ben Jonson's *Timber*, Drennan figures each of his key writers as a tree and represents the Tree of Knowledge itself as literature in general and then loops his image back to the natural by representing the tree as an element of divine creation: "God did the foodful blessing give, / That man might eat of it, and live" (225–26). The passage, and the poem's larger concern with natural tropes for learning, also find parallels in contemporary Irish writing. Another northern poet connected with the United Irishmen, James Orr, writes in 1804,

> If self-taught prodigies, once in an age,
> Make bold attempts, like *Shakespeare*, or like *Burns*,
> How wonderfully great had been their rage
> Had lore enlarged their intellectual urns?
> Driv'n from the Tree of Knowledge with a taste,
> Nature's poor nobles wander ev'ry waste;
> And ev'ry stream beholds, as on it flows,
> Some embryo genius near, whose blossom never blows.
>
> O IRELAND! O my country! strive to mend
> The noble ruins of neglected mind.[78]

In Drennan's poem, this natural bounty (including "prose sublime") is misappropriated by those who seek control:

> But they who have usurp'd his throne,
> To keep his Paradise their own,
> Have spread around a demon's breath,
> And named thee Upas, tree of death. (227–30)

In his 1789 poem *The Botanic Garden*, the English poet Erasmus Darwin writes of the Upas, "Fierce in dread silence on the blasted heath / Fell UPAS sits, the HYDRA-TREE of death."[79] Darwin's footnote explains, "There is a poison-tree in the island of Java, which is said by its effluvia to have depopulated the country for 12 or 14 miles round the place of its growth."[80] Drennan seems to be echoing Darwin here, especially in the later reference to "murder" "Flash'd thro the trees . . . and poison'd all the air," so that even the birds "Forsook the death-polluted ground" (245, 247–48, 252). But, like his near contemporary in England, William Blake, Drennan understands the Upas in relation to a failure of perception rather than as a symbol of the dangers of nature.[81] Drennan does not, like Wordsworth across the channel or Denis Florence MacCarthy a generation later in Dublin, envision personal consolation in the natural space but traces a tangled web of associations between nature as both an image for healthy and unhealthy forms of intellectual growth and an arena in which the intellect is tested: enlightened, educated perception feeds on the "Majestic tree" and sees a light-drenched, divine, and sublimely "pleasing" nature; flawed perception is an effect of "a demon's breath" and views nature as blighted, polluted, and, above all, paralytically terrifying.

The emphasis that nationalism scholars such as Benedict Anderson have placed on the affective and "imagined" solidarity forged by nationalism invites us to view this poem as a lament for the lost nation, but Ernest Gellner and especially Anthony D. Smith have also noted the educational dimensions of early nationalism. Education provides a means for personal development that both supports and symbolizes the nation's progress, suggests Smith—and so argues Drennan. In tracing the overlapping ideas of romanticism and neoclassicism as they are articulated in the "emergence" of popular nationalism in the late eighteenth century, Smith invokes the principle of "social regeneration through education," a phrase that suggestively echoes O'Conor's "political Regeneration": "Education here stands for more than mere enlightenment. It is a process of self-development, of drawing out of oneself hidden and suppressed potentialities, until full self-realisation has been attained. Such education is closely linked to the elevation of culture as the source of politics. Both neo-classicism and Romanticism turn to morality and culture, in a word, to Nature, against external artifice and political rules."[82] Smith's final sentence is easily mapped onto Drennan's argument: for "morality and culture" read the "pleasing panic" and "pleasing thrill" of the natural scene and the literature that emerges from it; for "external artifice and political rules" read the "subtle art" through which terror is exerted to "tame the savage." Hence, Drennan writes of the tree of literature, "Thy root is Truth, they stem is Pow'r, / And Virtue thy consummate flow'r. / Receive the circling nations' vows" (231–33). Education was not only a vital part of Drennan's political praxis—from his own education to his work helping to found the Belfast Academical Institution—but also pivotal to his articulation of emergent ideas of a civic nation.

The second invasion described in the poem reiterates Drennan's interest in the stultification of the mind. Here, the Christian priests are "More like the raven than the dove," and "The Dane his raven standard bore: / It rose amidst the whit'ning foam" (133, 236–37) (the Viking is also later figured as a raven [240]). This verse paragraph offers a gothic lexicon—"bleak," "gloomy om'nous," "midnight murder," "horrid glare," "terrifying sound" (235, 241, 244, 246, 251)—as well as the recurring raven that would so interest gothic American author Edgar Allan Poe a few years later. The period of Viking invasions is represented through relentless repetition, a cycle of native growth quashed by invasion, but the effects are specifically intellectual:

> Thus flow'd in flames, and blood, and tears,
> A lava of two hundred years;
> And tho' some seeds of science seen,
> Shot forth, in heart-enliv'ning green,
> To clothe the gaps of civil strife,
> And smooth a savage-temper'd life,
> Yet soon new torrents black'ning came,
> Wrapt the young growth in rolling flame,
> And, as it blasted, left behind
> Dark desolation of the mind. (263–72)

In other words, Drennan condemns invasion, but he does so centrally for invasion's negative effects on the Irish "mind"—again recalling Orr's lament for "The noble ruins of neglected mind." This paves the way for the next significant historical section, in which the deposed king of Leinster invites the English to Ireland in support of his own claims, a crucial step toward full-scale English colonization. Leinster's actions were often invoked as a symbol of the ways in which the Irish were failing themselves: Morgan, for instance, depicts him as merely the first of the Irish absentees, responsible for a chain of events that "have multiplied from age to age those possessors and deserters of the soil, who have drawn over 'the profits raised out of Ireland, and refunded nothing.'"[83] Critics have stressed the poem's depiction of invasion, but this crucial incursion is specifically represented as a failure to be "self-dependent": Ireland is, Drennan writes, "Self-conquer'd by domestic strife" (314).

The national losses detailed in the poem's closing lines are not military or legal, but cultural and educational. Between Viking invasions and the first English incursion, Drennan notes some advances in learning, but they are "blasted," leaving "behind, / Dark desolation of the mind" (271–72). Thus, his speaker expresses the dashed hope "That Education, HERE, might stand" (353) to the nation's benefit. He then goes on to note the river Avonmore in the region, and to invoke the "hope" for

> a Shakespeare's name
> To give *our* Avon deathless fame;
> So, from the savage barren heart,
> The streams of science and of art
> May spread their soft refreshing green,
> To vivify the moral scene. (367–72)

This need for renovation is elaborated at length in subsequent lines, marking the loss of "ancient records" and of young men who go to England for their educations—"To Cam or Isis glad to roam" (391, 397). The speaker's description of the Irish population at the end of the eighteenth century returns to Ledwich once again in the triple insult "Sordid, illiterate, and base" (394), concisely rendering Ledwich's condemnation of the region's inhabitants as "uncivilized and barbarous," "deprived of the light of letters," and "a prey to . . . the basest passions." Hence, while Drennan's poem does, as scholars have noted, offer a history of invasions, from the druid refugees to the English colonists, the larger trajectory of the poem is, in its details, concerned with a reversal of the very narrative described by Smith: the druids, who remained true to their faith and Nature, are the origin rather than the terminus of the Irish national narrative, as Ireland has undergone what we might call, revising Smith, "a process of self-*un*development." The invasions certainly contribute to this process but are represented as the consequence primarily of a failure to progress in reason and knowledge. Invasions do not make ruins in Drennan's poem; invasions are both the cause and the effect of ruined minds. As a consequence, most of the imagery of blighting in the poem has nothing to do with the ruins at Glendalloch. Knowledge is blighted, the landscape is blighted, and the nation is blighted, but not buildings: "Thy spark of independence dead; / Thy life of life, thy freedom, fled" (399–400), a reversal of the "political Regeneration" imagined by O'Conor.

The ruins at Glendalough are suggestively depicted as the residues of national consciousness rather than as the targets of destruction. Hence, in the opening lines, the round tower "stands sublime, / To point the else-forgotten heap, / Where princes and where prelates sleep" (6–8). At the poem's end, Ireland's "spark of independence dead," the round tower shall "point her tomb" (399, 406). The poem thus begins and ends with the surviving round tower marking the burial of images of sovereignty—princes and prelates at the start of the first millennium, but the "spark of independence" at the end of the Enlightenment eighteenth century. Whelan suggests of Irish ruins in general that "they historicise space and spatialise history, becoming topochrons—a single site that contains multiple times. Topochrons secrete laminated historical layers, thereby freeing place from the tyranny of the actual, untethering them from the linearity of history, the contingency of necessity. They therefore enable a form of counter-memory, which answers back to history."[84] Drennan's insistent repetition of "Here" (as well as "where" and "there") throughout the poem to ground different historical moments suggests such an overlaying, "Here" signifying the site of "multiple times." What is "Lost" in the poem is not history, but power, as political autonomy and national reputation:

> Lost—by thy chosen children sold;
> And conquer'd—not by steel, but gold:
> Lost—by a low and servile great
> . . . .
> Lost—to the world and future fame,
> Remember'd only in a name. (381–83, 387–88)

It is sovereignty that Drennan's poem elegizes—sovereignty in the full Enlightenment sense of the term for individuals and nations—and the indeterminate temporality of the ruins facilitates the round tower's double reference to past and present violations of popular, civic sovereignty.

Glendalough: Nativism and National Culture

Drennan's "Glendalloch," then, is no simply nationalist text, since it critiques both invaders and invaded, nor is it a straightforward ruin text in which the ruins are objects of contemplation or registers of colonial violence. MacDonagh notes, "After 1800 Protestant and unionist antiquarians and historians worked, almost without exception, to undermine romantic or glorious conceptions of pre-Norman or pre-Danish Ireland, while their nationalist and Catholic counterparts strove to sustain and develop them."[85] Drennan was Protestant but not unionist, writing a series of important essays against the Act of Union; his larger body of work suggests that he was pro-nativist and antisectarian in principle but critical of Catholicism historically. Vance argues that Drennan "was the most effective literary exponent of the radical nationalist possibilities within Irish Presbyterianism" and notes the paradox of Drennan's public support for a pan-sectarian nationalism and private expressions of anti-Catholic sentiment, including "scorn" for "the torpor and helpless passivity of priest-ridden Ireland."[86] But this ideological contradiction extended far beyond his letters and is most evident in "Glendalloch," perhaps most strikingly in its echoes of both the anti-Catholic demagogue Ledwich and the pro-Catholic polemicist O'Conor. Waters notes in his discussion of "Glendalloch" Drennan's "elaborately professed hatred of superstition, into which category he placed much of Catholic teaching."[87] On nativist subjects, Drennan was less complicated: his 1815 *Fugitive Pieces* includes poems that invoke the Irish-language tradition, including "Verses for Old Irish Melodies," "Translation from the Irish," and an "Epitaph" on the harp that the "Celt-hater" Ledwich contended was an English symbol given to Ireland because the Irish could surpass the English at nothing besides music.[88]

As I have already noted, Drennan clearly knew Ledwich's text and followed some of its elements, including the premise that the landscape at Glendalough itself could produce "religious dread and horror," but on the subject of history the two texts diverge significantly. Drennan writes, in the same footnote where he repeats Ledwich's sentence, "It is said to have been an asylum of the Druids, who fled from Roman tyranny. It was afterwards the refuge of the Monks, who established there a different religious rule, in which mind and body were bound to the same bondage of five years' silence, severe fasts, obedience unto death; and this lake became their dead sea" (p. 139n). Ledwich, however, contends that the origins of settlement in the area are Viking: referring to "the oldest structure at Glendaloch," he writes that it has "no traces of Saxon" or "christian" features and "may well be called an unique specimen of the early Danish style in this kingdom."[89] This contention echoes such earlier writers as Edmund Spenser, whose infamous *View of the Present State of Ireland* (1596) develops an etymology of "Tanist" to argue for a Danish origin for Irish political culture and hence connects the Irish to the quintessential figures of marauding barbarism, the Vikings. Ledwich then refuses to discuss the round towers (even though a tower figures prominently in each of his volume's illustrations of the scene) and mentions instead a coin as evidence of "the early Danish princes who had embraced Christianity," allowing him to segue to the "zealous and bigotted votaries" of Saint Kevin, who brought the saint's relics to Glendalloch: "all flocked to the shrine of the new Saint: a naked and barren wilderness was quickly filled with churches and good houses."[90] This is the Enlightenment Ledwich, insisting on clear genealogy in which invasions and peoples do not mix: first there were the Danes, and then the Catholics, and this genealogy is not to be muddled by any round towers unique to Ireland or traceable, as Joseph Lennon has noted in his discussion of other antiquarian texts of the period, to Asia.[91] Conversely, Drennan, after his brief historical overview, contrasts the bleak monks with the area's other residents: "Here, however, was the school of the West, an ark that preserved the remains of literature from the deluge of barbarism which overspread the rest of Europe. Here, the ancient Britons took refuge from the Saxons, and the native Irish from the incursions of the Danes" (p. 139n.). For Drennan, Glendalough is not the site of a Danish settlement, as Ledwich contends, but the place where the "native Irish" defended themselves from Danish invasion, part of a larger history of Glendalough as the site where knowledge and seekers of freedom can be saved, even as he traces an historical trajectory in which that potential is dashed.

In the context of Ledwich and other writers on Glendalough, then, Drennan's focus on ruins is consistent with a long-standing tradition of representation, and Drennan's use of gothic devices in particular is part of his direct but not always simply mimetic engagement with Ledwich. "Glendalloch" is unlike canonical British romantic topographical poetry (especially if we take Wordsworth as our guide), but its blending of different genres and focus on ruins is consistent with the Irish tradition, particularly contemporary innovations in descriptions of the site and the "mixed character" of Irish topographical verse. As in the expansions of Camden and Ware as well as Fisher, in Drennan's poem the ruins are integral to a scene that, like Killarney, mixes picturesque and sublime landscape features; also as in all of these texts, the historical, the national, the international, and the natural jostle for space in the description of the landscape.

Drennan uses this multifaceted scene to offer an historical account that focuses on early advances in learning when Ireland was a refuge for those Britons fleeing Roman rule, equating the druidic worship of the sun with Enlightenment in its eighteenth-century sense. If Ledwich is the first to offer an Enlightenment account of Irish history and uses the powerful tools of Enlightenment thought to abject the Irish past, Drennan uses those same tools to turn Ledwich partly on his head. The decline of the region begins, in Drennan's narrative, with the arrival of Christianity and then continues with subsequent waves of invasion as the poet offers a nationalist history of the region in which a natural, enlightened religion is supplanted and perverted by waves of invasion, including the arrival of Christianity, that bring darkness to the land. The anti-Catholic diatribe remains vicious and disruptive, but it is closely allied in Drennan's poem with the gothic inversion of a natural scene marked by unadulterated perception and enlightened reason—the foundations of the "self-dependent" subject that Drennan, at the end of the poem, does locate in the same Irish past as the early Catholic Church, again recalling O'Conor's writings on Catholicism. Drennan's problem in a nutshell is this: his argument suggests that religion has violated the natural relationship between subject and landscape that is the foundation of individual and national sovereignty ("self-dependent"), but his key source, the gothic style, and the dominance of Catholicism at the time of the Anglo-Norman conquest of Ireland—which, after all, was concluded under papal permission—tend toward a focus on, and heavy-handed demonization of, the Catholic Church.

But there is something highly peculiar in this poem that, to my knowledge, no critic has yet addressed. If there is an idealized epoch in this poem, it is the time of the druids at Glendalough. Anti-imperial and enlightened, seeking truth and the god in nature, the Arch-Druid directs the people toward reason and light, and away from superstition and fear. Thuente suggests, "Drennan's vision of Irish history in 'Glendalloch' and in several other poems presented early Ireland as a free, cultured, and happy land until invaded by the barbaric

English," and Waters notes that the leading druid is "of a long lost age, when early Britons had fled 'Nero's yoke' to the shelter of Ireland," and that the druid's speech "typif[ies] Drennan's . . . fixation with what has been corrupted or lost."[92] But there is something odd here, at least from the usual nationalist perspective. A note added later refers to the "native Irish," but in the poem proper the Britons are the *first* inhabitants of Glendalough. Nero ruled 54–68 AD, during Britain's occupation by Rome; Saint Kevin, as Ledwich notes, lived in the sixth century,[93] and seventeenth-century Irish historian Geoffrey Keating has the earliest king named Tuathal postdate Nero, ruling from 79 AD.[94] This chronology obviously poses problems for a reading of the poem as a lament for the destruction of Ireland under waves of invasion, with the English as the latest aggressors who preside over what Drennan terms in a footnote "the wreck of [Ireland's] legislative independence" (p. 139n.). The only light, education, and reason in Ireland are brought there by British refugees.

The larger argument of the poem is a typically Enlightenment one: Ireland should have been the repository of knowledge and place of learning, from this moment in first-century Ireland forward to the present, but was instead deflected into a gothic narrative of decline and intellectual darkness. But this knowledge is cosmopolitan—international. In the celebration of the Tree of Knowledge, it is Milton and Shakespeare, with Homer, who constitute the literary canon. For an Irish nationalist condemning invasions, this is another peculiar passage: there is no celebration of native literature, of the oft-invoked O'Carolan or even Goldsmith, whose *Deserted Village* is part of the poem's literary inheritance. This passage is also the most ahistorical portion of what is largely a historical survey, and it interrupts the precisely situated history of the tenth century, from the spread of Catholicism to the first Viking invasions (235ff.), followed by "two hundred years" (264) and Leinster's betrayal in the twelfth century. This passage, however, paves the way for the possible renewal of Ireland. Returning to the landscape with an emphatic "HERE" (353), echoing the poem's opening lines, Drennan writes,

> As from yon dull and stagnant lake
> The streams begin to live, and take
> Their course thro' Clara's wooded vale,
> Kiss'd by the health-inspiring gale,
> Heedless of wealth their banks may hold,
> They glide, neglectful of the gold,
> Yet seem to hope a Shakespeare's name
> To give *our* Avon deathless fame;
> So, from the savage barren heart,
> The streams of science and of art
> May spread their soft refreshing green,
> To vivify the moral scene. (361–72)

The central simile here clearly addresses the ways in which the pursuit of knowledge can revive what seems "stagnant" and move the nation forward, especially by reviving the all-important "moral scene," the nation's psychological and ethical health. But that intervening couplet adds a further dimension: "Yet seem to hope a Shakespeare's name / To give *our* Avon deathless fame." "Avon" is a convenient reference to a river named Avonmore in the area, and it occupies the middle of a simile that draws on images of sterility leading to revivification. This couplet seems to introduce Shakespeare as a third line of revival. Drennan is no cultural nationalist here, but very much a figure of the Scottish Enlightenment. He counteracts the "history of invasions" with another history of cultural transfer in which the ancient Britons brought enlightenment and the principle of freedom to Glendalough through a nature-oriented deism, and a return to that state requires "A Shakespeare's name" and the Tree of Knowledge, on which Homer, Milton, and Shakespeare are prominent. Leaping to the recent past, passing from Pope Adrian's support of Henry II's rule over Ireland (316) to "GRATTAN's energetic tongue" (378) in just sixty-two lines, Drennan offers a multinational origin and literature for Ireland: founded by freedom-loving Britons, with knowledge perpetuated and advanced through native minstrels and English poets and Greek epic.

It is this cosmopolitan ideal, not a nativist one, that is disrupted by the invasions that deflect Ireland's historical course into gothic decline. Drennan's nationalism is not cultural nationalism, but Lockean in idealizing citizens in a healthy relationship with both land and state, developing their minds through what is good rather than just through what is native, as well as allowing for migration through the theoretical transfer of political sovereignty from individuals to a chosen state. Such passages in the poem resituate the reading of it as a lament for invasions of Ireland by positioning it partly as a response to the "four-nations" problem and by offering a vision in which cultural exchange and migration can be celebrated while force and exploitation are just as loudly decried.

Glendalough and Killarney: Mixing Traditions

Later writers tend to stress Glendalough not as a place of refuge and potential renewal, but instead as a more insistently gothic site. Hidden from view, it is the site of insurgency and conspiracy. This tendency is perhaps most overt in Carr's *Stranger in Ireland*, where Glendalough is from the outset treated as a gothic interruption in an otherwise harmonious landscape: "At Rathdrum we took fresh horses and proceeded to Glendaloch (or Glendalough), or the Seven Churches. . . . The whole scene, soon after we quitted Rathdrum, became altered: one might have supposed that an ocean had separated Glendaloch from Avonmore. We found ourselves surrounded by vast mountains covered with brown heath, or more sable peat, whose hard and gloomy summits the rays of the sun, beginning to be obscured, shone upon without brightening: the whole was desolate, gloomy, and sublime."[95] Carr then introduces a ruined estate as a symbol of the destruction of rebellion: "we passed a dark avenue of trees, which led to the ruins of a mansion burnt in the rebellion: it stood at the foot of a mountain; some of the walls, blackened by smoke, remained. The garden was overrun with briars and brambles; not a solitary rose-tree was to be seen, and the plantation was a wilderness."[96] This ruin is not only part of a ruined landscape, no longer aesthetic or productive, but also the catalyst for the traveler's gothic musing:

> The vast and gloomy glen before us, in the year 1798, afforded shelter and concealment, for a short time, to a body of twenty-five thousand rebels under the command of Dwyer and Hoult. The ruins which we saw marked the residence of a family which, having excited the vengeance of those miserable and deluded beings, were obliged to fly for their lives. Imagination depicted the torches of the frantic mob shooting a frightful gleam through the trees; and now it beheld the crackling blaze of the devoted pile, reddening the sable scenery below, and the murky clouds above, until it sunk amidst the yell of the misguided incendiaries.[97]

Shifting back to direct description, Carr notes that "near this melancholy monument of insurrectional fury a barrack has been erected, for the purpose of preventing this place from again affording protection to rebels."[98] In this preamble to a more typical description of Glendalough, Carr insistently separates the region from both the framing geographical space and the contemporaneity of his narrative: Glendalough is a place apart, as if "an ocean had separated" it from adjacent regions, and is now well secured from the insurrectionary violence that has scarred one estate in its domain.

Carr's work clearly influenced Alicia Lefanu's *The Outlaw*, which echoes elements of Carr's description—from Hoult himself to the juxtaposition of gloom and fire—in the fantastic tale of one of the novel's more absurd characters:

> "Returning home from his lordship's, one night after dark, my horse missed his way, and tumbled over a precipice, down which we continued to roll, my horse and me, I know not how many fathoms, till at length we came to *terra firma*; but the scene that met our view more resembled the infernal regions than the habitations of living men. It was a heap of blackened and smoking ruins, in the centre of which blazed a red and lurid flame: round this, a group

of figures were warming themselves, worthy of the pencils that have delineated Conrad and Bertram. The bare brown mountains and rushing torrents that encompassed this desolate spot were in gloomy unison with the objects around, and presented an unvaried aspect of desolation, that pressed upon the shuddering heart the impossibility of escape. Having received no material injury, I now humbly approached one of the men—"

"In buckram?" asked the incorrigible Miss O'Reilly.

"No, in green—the true green of the united, but mistaken defenders of Erin. I approached one of these men, I say, who proved to be general Hoult. He would have had me condemned at once as a spy, by martial law; but, observing some expression of relenting in the countenances of his companions, I briefly told them the particulars of my lamentable story, and then addressed them in the words of Shakespeare's beautiful eulogium upon mercy in the Merchant of Venice. I had not gone through half of it before I had the satisfaction to see they had totally given up their inhuman purpose."[99]

Whelan usefully points out that antique ruins were often the sites of imagined rebel meeting points (and this is the case elsewhere in Lefanu's novel),[100] and here Lefanu, like Carr, connects the 1798 Uprising to still "smoking ruins" in Glendalough. The association of Glendalough with the 1798 Uprising continued into the 1860s and Boucicault's play *Arrah-na-Pogue*. Boucicault's focus on Glendalough tacitly identifies it as one of the key sites in the 1798 Irish Uprising; the play depicts at some length both romanticized Irish insurgents and inflexible British officers, the two groups put at risk by the trickster figure of an informant. Boucicault's play is comic in plot and tone, but Armstrong's "Glandalough" (1877) offers a more gothic treatment of Irish insurgency. In Armstrong's text, set early in the period of English colonial rule, the men of the area are bloodthirsty brutes who seek to kill the English intruders. The anonymous author of *Glendalough, or The Seven Churches* (1848) also situates the region in the context of earlier Irish insurgency, detailing the deforestation and building of a fort by the Cromwellite Edmund Ludlow as he "subdued the Kernes."[101] The same emphasis on what is hidden appears as well in Sigerson's "Legend of Glendalough," where vision is thematized in a poem about the murder of a young couple in the time of Saint Kevin.

As the nineteenth century progresses, then, Glendalough's association with the gothic becomes bifurcated. Drennan's poem, republished at least four times between 1806 and 1859, sustains the site's association with the flawed national subject and with international literary and migratory connections, even as works by Carr, Lefanu, Armstrong, and others depict it as the place of concealment for dangerous insurgents, a more baldly gothic site of straightforward political terror. Boucicault's *Arrah-na-Pogue* plays on both traditions, representing the rebels as talented in the arts of concealment (including the ability to elicit fears of their powers of concealment), while focusing on the rebel leader's transregional and international movements, necessitated by his political dislocation from his native role as leader of the Mac Couls. Beamish Mac Coul, with "the Ruins of St. Kevin's Abbey; the Round Tower; the Ruined Cemetery" in the background, lies to a government agent he has just robbed, warning him to be quiet as he walks home because "at every fifty paces there's a man stationed behind either a rock or a bush."[102] But shortly afterward he tells his fellow rebels, "In a few hours I shall be on the sea, bound for a foreign land; perhaps never again shall I hear your voices nor see my native hills. Oh, my own land! my own land! Bless every blade of grass upon your green cheeks! The clouds that hang over ye are the sighs of your exiled children, and your face is always wet with their tears. *Eirne meelish, Shlawn loth!* [Sweet Ireland, farewell!] Fare ye well! And you, dear Abbey of St. Kevin, around which the bones of my forefathers are laid."[103] Beamish Mac Coul uses the fiction of Glendalough as the site of hidden insurgency to terrorize the central villain of the play but draws affectively on a representation of the region that recalls Drennan's poem: Glendalough is a graveyard, and it is tied to native sovereignty as this speech is followed by "All" shouting, "The Mac Coul! the Mac Coul!" marking him as their ruler under native tradition, as explained later in the play.[104] (In a play that appeared during the rise of the Fenian movement, the reference to Finn MacCoul was arguably an incendiary one.)

But Glendalough also had its cultural afterlife in the mixing of its representations with those of Killarney. This chapter began with the suggestion that we consider Glendalough as the gothic double of Killarney, but this doubling is not simply a critical parallel that draws on the striking geophysical similarities I noted at the outset or on their comparable importance in Irish topographical verse. It is a connection forged in the interplay of the literary traditions depicting the two sites. The exchanges of material between writing on Killarney and Glendalough speak to an emergent Irish topographical tradition in which the landscape is the site on which sovereignty is contested. Other topographical poems discussed by both Waters and Foster in their key essays on the Irish topographical tradition are less concerned with sovereignty. For instance, William Hamilton Drummond's *The Giant's Causeway* (1811) contributes to the general Irish topographical project of establishing "native sublimity,"[105] but it builds awkwardly on the mutually informing interests of the antiquarian and the geologist, offering Ossianic myth for the region's geologic peculiarities before turning to its central concern, largely laid out in its long preface and book III of the verse, with debates over whether the earth's surface was formed by water or upheaval and fire. Drummond begins with an Ossianic frame to present the story that explains the name "Giant's Causeway":

> Cumhal's son, to Dalraida's coast,
> Led the tall squadrons of his Finnian host,
> Where his bold thought the wondrous plan designed,
> The proud conception of a giant mind,
> To bridge the ocean for the march of war.[106]

Subsequent pages depict the building of the bridge, and Drummond later proceeds to his theology-tinged scientific argument. His poem ends with a tribute to sovereignty, but that of the deity: "O thou, who rul'st o'er ocean, earth, and air, / Whose sov'reign power but willed, and all things were."[107] Drummond, a religious minister who tended to erase nationalist (Catholic) arguments in a universalizing theology, arguably does the same in his poem, praising the Ossianic only to bury it under science and (Protestant) Christian belief. This approach was not lost on his contemporaries: as Brown has noted, Drennan's *Belfast Monthly Magazine* published a negative review of Drummond's poem, complaining of "its breaches of literary tact, and the fact that the author refused to sign a petition on behalf of the [Catholic] Emancipation movement"[108] (a further complication of Drennan's stance on Catholicism).

But nationalism-inclined poets returned to Leslie and Drennan. Moore, for instance, echoes some details in Drennan's "Glendalloch" in the 1811 lyric from *Irish Melodies* that is set in Glendalough. The lyric begins, "By that Lake, whose gloomy shore / Sky-lark never warbles o'er,"[109] recalling Drennan's reference in "Glendalloch" to the absence of skylarks:

> Her song the lark began to raise,
> As she had seen the solar blaze;
> But, smote with terrifying sound,
> Forsook the death-polluted ground;
> And never since, these limits near,
> Was heard to hymn her vigil clear. (249–54)

But Moore focuses centrally on Saint Kevin's view of Glendalough as a refuge from the world: the saint "Dreams of heav'n, nor thinks that e'er / Woman's smile can haunt him there."[110] When his refuge is violated, "Sternly from his bed he starts, / And with rude, repulsive shock, / Hurls her from the beetling rock."[111] It is the last lines of the poem that are most suggestive, however: "Round the Lake light music stole; / And her ghost was seen to glide, / Smiling, o'er the fatal tide!"[112] The last two lines are clearly an ironic twist on the earlier reference to the saint thinking that no "Woman's smile can haunt him there," but Moore is also echoing Leslie's *Killarney*. Leslie, after representing Donaghoe's apparition flying "o'er the glassy plain" to the sound of music, has his speaker mimic the apparition's motion: "Thus far all happy, we serenely glide / Along the windings of the glassy tide."[113] Moore uses the same rhyme (glide/tide) as well as broadly repeats the leading features of Leslie's apparition.

In the footnote to his poem set in Killarney, "O'Donohue's Mistress," from a later number of the *Irish Melodies*, Moore refers directly to the myth: "For many years after his death, the spirit of this hero is supposed to have been seen in the morning of May-day, gliding over the lake on his favourite white horse, to the sound of sweet, unearthly music."[114] Moore's story of the saint's murder in his Glendalough poem has no known precedent, though it faintly echoes Drennan's depiction in "Glendalloch" of a priest who either tripped or committed suicide when he "slipt his foot on holy ground, / And plung'd into the lake profound" (191–92). Moore's invention, however, makes possible a gothic transposition of Killarney's apparition: instead of a peacefully dying king, a woman murdered; instead of an apparition that brings fertility and hope, a ghost that challenges religious authority and solitude. In the footnote to "O'Donohue's Mistress," Moore tells the story of a "young and beautiful girl" who falls in love with O'Donohue's May Day apparition "and at last, in a fit of insanity, on a May-morning threw herself into the lake."[115] Moore thus associates both Killarney and Glendalough with strikingly similar plots: a young woman whose unrequited love for an unattainable legendary male leader (one a prince, the other a saint) leads to her death in a lake. That it is a murder with misogynist overtones at Glendalloch and "a fit of insanity" leading to suicide in Killarney emblematizes the different uses to which these sites were put.

It is not only in Moore's corpus that the two topographical traditions mix. In Armstrong's "Glandalough" (1877), for instance, set early in the period of English colonial rule, the heroine, Eileen, is an ameliorating influence on her violent brothers and father, and falls in love with a chivalrous English knight in a romantic interlude similar to the "sylvan tale" in Leslie's *Killarney*—and her name is the same, with a slightly different spelling, as the protagonist of Anna Maria

Edwards's "Princess of Killarney" (1787). Armstrong's "Glandalough" quickly turns from a gothic setting to gothic action on terms that closely echo Edwards's poem. As in "Princess of Killarney," the English massacre the Irish, including the heroine's family, and she gives herself over to the church and mysticism:

> She lived in other worlds, and converse held
> With those loved spirits which had passed before
> From the tempestuous billows of our life,
> And beckoned her to follow. She had found
> A bliss far higher, a Heaven upon this earth.
> A nobler love than man's had breathed on her
> The spirit of comfort.[116]

Armstrong's poem itself acts to conceal Glendalough, following the gruesome depiction of the slaughter and the women mourning over the dead with a focus on Eileen and transcendence, as if Glendalough itself no longer exists, not even in the powerful tale that Edwards's text imagines at its close. As in Leslie's account of Donaghoe's apotheosis, native sovereignty passes from the earthly to the spiritual plane—it evaporates.

One might argue that the colonial situation precipitated a specific set of concerns about land in relation to ownership and political power as well as the subtheme of internal conflict (traced in Drennan's "Glendalloch," Drummond's *Giants' Causeway*, and the anonymous *Mount Leinster*, for instance). But there is more going on here through the citationality that I have, in part, traced in this and the preceding chapter. These writers' textual references are not exclusively to the Irish and English poets of the English topographical canon—Denham, Thomson, Cowper, Goldsmith—but also to a significant body of Irish writing about these sites, as in Leslie's echoes of Ward and Drennan's appropriation of Ledwich. A genealogy of Irish topographical verse is not my central concern here, but I do wish to stress that these citations and continuities are the traces of a specifically Irish literary history—not a list of Irish poets who write about Irish sites on topographical terms that overlap with the English tradition, but a series of poems that exhibit an awareness of and engagement with their precursors, both Irish and English. This Irish tradition is distinctive not only for its concern with sovereignty and allusions to Irish texts little known in England, but also for a number of other features. While canonical English topographical poetry often draws extensively on the agricultural concerns of Virgil's *Georgics*, dwelling on farmland, orchards, and pastures, and debating, as critics such as Kevis Goodman have noted,[117] the tastefulness of such matters in verse, there is little agricultural poetry in the canon of Irish poetry of the long eighteenth century. *Mount Leinster* is a relatively rare exception, dealing with practices for growing the potato and rural sports at some length, but even it focuses extensively on Irish history and especially on internal dissension and British misrule.[118] Scholars of English literature have argued that the georgic tradition in English verse "bur[ies] history," in Alan Liu's memorable phrase, but Irish topographical verse digs it up—even just to bury it again, as Leslie and Drummond did.[119] Moreover, while English topographical verse builds on the local in ways that elide empire and labor, Irish topographical verse is frequently international in scope, linking the local to the imperial and to transatlantic networks.

3

Transatlantic Movements

Exile and Migration

Emma will share my joy and woe,
If to a foreign clime I go;
 Still shall I hear, though far we part,
  The music of her mind,
 And echoes soft from Emma's heart
  My wand'ring sense shall bind;
Listen,—how plaintive, sad, and low,
When to a distant clime I go!

—WILLIAM DRENNAN,
"Verses for Old Irish Melodies" (1815)

The significant expansion of the Irish diaspora in the period covered by this study is a well-established historical fact. Political exiles, particularly in the 1790s and 1840s, added to a steady stream of economic exiles, culminating in the exodus precipitated by the Great Famine. These migrants fed developing British Isles settlements in North America as well as in Australia and elsewhere and, along with the devastating toll of famine and cholera in the 1840s and 1850s, emptied Ireland—notoriously, Ireland's population has still not returned to pre-Famine levels. The nationalist diasporic community that emerges in Irish American and Irish Canadian writing gives credence to Benedict Anderson's argument in "Long-Distance Nationalism" that modern nationalism emerges to compensate for the loss of the physical attachment to the land—ideology replaces material possession, representing exiles and emigrants as having an abstract and portable but no less deeply felt sense of national identity and community.[1] The idea of the Irish man (occasionally Irish woman) forced to depart, forever looking back to the land where he wishes to remain, is developed through a number of well-known poems of the late eighteenth and nineteenth centuries, from the anonymous "Exiled Irishman's Lamentation" and the controversial "Exile of Erin,"[2] to James Orr's "Banks of Larne," a number of Thomas Moore's lyrics in *Irish Melodies*, and William Allingham's "Winding Banks of Erne: Or, the Emigrant's Adieu to Ballyshanny," which begins,

> Adieu to Ballyshanny! where I was bred and born;
> Go where I may, I'll think of you, as sure as night and morn,
> The kindly spot, the friendly town, where every one is known,
> And not a face in all the place but partly seems my own;
> There's not a house or window, there's not a field or hill,
> But, east or west, in foreign lands, I'll recollect them still.
> I leave my warm heart with you, though my back I'm forced to
> turn—
> So adieu to Ballyshanny, and the winding banks of Erne.[3]

Allingham's poem uses the body to figure the emigrant's attachment to the lost homeland, not only "leaving [his] warm heart" in Ballyshanny, but also understanding community as physical identity: "not a face in all the place but partly seems my own." True to the principles of Herderian nationalism as well, the memory of the landscape is integral to the emigrant's ongoing attachment to Ballyshanny. Such poems understand the emigrant as remaining bodily and intellectually rooted in the homeland through biological identification as well as memory and emotional attachment. The poem does not, however, tell us where he is going. As is typical of such poems, the moment of departure is focused on the homeland rather than on the destination and the new attachments, difficulties, or possibilities migration might raise.

This is not exclusively the pattern of Irish exilic writing in this period, however, and my interest in the present chapter is in the literary representation of the problems of exile from two vantage points not considered in most of the best-known poems of exile: first, the exile's experience in the new land, in particular the ways in which migration is troubled by "long-distance nationalism"; second, the impact of such losses on Ireland. This chapter begins with two sections that consider poems by three diasporic writers—James Orr, Adam Kidd, and Thomas D'Arcy McGee—who are explicitly shaped by a sense of place in their North American destinations, often simultaneously exhibiting both Herderian nationalism's requirement of attachment to the homeland and more Lockean notions of commitment to the migrant's new nation. It concludes with a consideration of two 1820s novels, one by Alicia Lefanu and the other by Lady Morgan, which depict United Irish leaders in exile and represent the departure from the homeland as a double violation of nationalism—the nation's loss of its natural leaders and the leaders' loss of their natural place. Together, these literary texts illustrate some of the more troubled contours of ideas of national identity and the land, and especially the problem of citizenship in early-nineteenth-century Ireland. That is, what does it mean to self-identify as "Irish" while in exile from Ireland, to be Irish but not an Irish citizen, or, even more complexly, to be Irish by personal and political attachment but the citizen of another nation?

Such questions are posed against a complicated philosophical backdrop. Locke argues for the individual's sovereignty as the basis for national sovereignty: "Where-ever therefore any number of Men are so united into one Society, as to quit every one his Executive Power of the Law of Nature, and to resign it to the publick, there and there only is a *Political, or Civil Society.* And this is done where-ever any number of Men, in the state of Nature, enter into Society to make one People."[4] In Locke's argument, individuals cede their sovereignty to a sovereign state on terms that allow movement from one nation to another. The political focus on sovereignty and the rising importance of the land as the foundation of national identity set aside Locke's transferrable personal sovereignty in favor of a relationship between land and people through which sovereignty flowed. In broad terms, nationalism increasingly used the Herderian premises of the people's attachment to the land and the land as a source of a unique national identity to form the basis for the people's right to govern that land and themselves. Eighteenth-century notions of sovereignty derived from Locke were hence displaced, moving from individual will within a political framework to collective authenticity. Eighteenth-century Irish nationalists generally focused on the people's collective will on broadly Lockean terms, but their nineteenth-century successors increasingly invoked the land as the affective basis of political legitimacy. This shift gathered impetus in Ireland where land ownership was contested, culminating in the Land Wars of the late nineteenth century and eventually in the Easter Rising. At the same time, older, Hobbesian models of the nation as a body whose sovereignty flows from above, most explicitly in the pre-Enlightenment principle of the Divine Right of Kings, was sustained in the idea of a naturally ruling elite, the stewards of the nation. In turn-of-the-century Britain, these competing schools of thought break down into the tension between Reformers, on the one hand, who sought moderate change in the distribution of political power, and Spencean Radicals, on the other, who sought a redistribution of land as the basis of economic power and a restoration of natural right in the land. As radical as the United Irishmen were to a colonial regime, they were focused largely on reform; contestation over the land was not an issue for them as it was for more rural groups such as the Whiteboys, the Rockites, and others (including some dimensions of the United Irishmen Uprising at a popular level), further multiplying the significance of the land in relation to proliferating nationalist aims and paradigms.

These overlapping ideological constructions of the meaning of land to the nation and to its people make exile itself problematic. Anderson suggests in "Long-Distance Nationalism" that nationalism itself is a response to globalization, compensating for separation from the land through the idea of a nationality that is eminently portable, but the domestic politics at work in Ireland—concern over the loss of the proper ruling elite; agitation for the popular redistribution of land; the cultural, religious, and often linguistic divisions between the ruling class and the ruled—also inform the representation of migration and exile in Irish writing of this period. The recurring literary figures of the absentee landlord or the heroic Irishman who works in another nation's military, for instance, highlight the erosion of Ireland's "natural" elite. Exile is thus both an effect of and a trope for the disempowerment of the indigenous, Catholic ruling class. Similarly, the image of the United States as a successfully postcolonial nation, founded on radical principles, made transatlantic migration in particular a resonant vehicle for considerations of the ways in which exile and migration troubled Irish nationalist aims. The texts discussed here wrestle with these ideological problems rather than resolve them, depicting transatlantic exile not only as a subject of personal grief, as in the better-known lyrics and ballads, but also as a register of transatlantic politics, a differential space in which "here" is always tacitly juxtaposed with "there," while "here" and "there" remain themselves contested categories that authors seek to define and stabilize.

The Revolutionary Transatlantic

The political meaning of the transatlantic changed after 1776. John Leslie's 1772 image of Ireland as part of a circulatory British transatlantic, assimilated and meaningfully contributing to British maritime empire (see chapter 1), is traceable forward to the 1840s, as we shall see in chapter 6. But this geographical perspective was extensively countered by Irish nationalists after the American Revolution. In his famous speech to the Irish Parliament, the "Declaration of Right" delivered on April 19, 1780, Henry Grattan argued for the autonomy of that body under the king partly on the basis of a shift in transatlantic power after 1776: "England now smarts under the lesson of the American war; the doctrine of Imperial legislature she feels to be pernicious; the revenues and monopolies annexed to it she has found to be untenable; she lost the power to enforce it; her enemies are a host, pouring upon her from all quarters of the earth; her armies are dispersed; the sea is not hers. . . . [T]he balance of her fate is in the hands of Ireland; you are not only her last connection, you are the only nation in Europe that is not her enemy."[5] The expansive British transatlantic disappears as English power is confined once again to the British mainland, and Ireland becomes powerful not as a transatlantic port, but as England's last and closest ally. William Drennan would write two decades later in "Glendalloch,"

> O COUNTRY, gain'd but to be lost!
> Gain'd by a nation, rais'd, inspir'd,
> By eloquence and virtue fir'd,
> By trans-atlantic glory stung,
> By GRATTAN's energetic tongue
> By Parliament that felt its trust,
> By Britain—terrify'd, and just. ("Glendalloch" 374–80)

This is the myth of Grattan as the eloquent voice who calls the nation into being, almost performatively,[6] through his "Declaration of Right." I cite Drennan's lines here because they suggest that the specific transatlantic context of Grattan's arguments was still firmly in view for the next generation. What emerges from Grattan's speeches on this subject, including this one, is an insistence on the Irish right to trade with the United States and other corners of the British Empire independently of English governance—a sovereign right rather than a colonial favor.[7] On August 12, 1785, for instance, he referred to a 1779 free-trade agreement in a speech to the Irish Parliament: "By that you recovered your right to trade with every part of the world, whose ports were open to you, subject to your own unstipulated duties, the British plantations only excepted; by that you obtained the benefit of your insular situation, the benefit of your western situation."[8] Grattan, in broad terms, rewrites Leslie's kind of transatlantic so that Ireland has its own right to take advantage of its circulatory commercial potential, while England itself wanes as a military and commercial power in that sphere.

By the 1790s, Grattan's political heirs were offering a related view in which the "Old" world must be left behind for the sake of the "New," as part of a radical historiography in which the West is associated with progress and Enlightenment—a historiography visible in British radical texts such as Anna Letitia Barbauld's "Eighteen Hundred and Eleven" (1812),[9] but earlier a part of the iconography of United Irishmen literature. "Erin," that popular United Irishmen ballad by Drennan, is typical:

> In her sun, in her soil, in her station, thrice blest,
> With back turn'd to Britain, her face to the West,
> Erin stands proudly insular, on her steep shore,
> And strikes her high harp to the ocean's deep roar.[10]

"Her face to the West," personified Ireland turns toward the postrevolutionary United States. The transatlantic in this body of literature is less a network than a conduit, a passage to a modernity that lies in the New World. Hence, in James Porter's popular United Irishmen satire *Billy Bluff and 'Squire Firebrand* (1796), an "Angel," "the Genius of Ireland," appears out of the west while the ruling elite are "flying to the dark clouds that still hung over the East, which had now turned to the colour of clotted blood,"[11] orienting hope toward the Atlantic West and away from the ancien régimes of Britain and Europe to the east. In such Irish nationalist writing of the 1790s, transatlantic exchange is neither military nor economic, but political: a union of political radicals on terms that recall Revolutionary France's 1792 "Edict of Fraternity."

After the failed Irish Uprising of 1798, followed by the Act of Union of 1800, which abolished the Irish Parliament, it is the general population—not just soldiers, as in eighteenth-century depictions of Irish transatlantic agents from Leslie's *Killarney* to Thomas Sheridan's *Brave Irishman*—that enters into this transatlantic space as the postrevolutionary United States is imagined as the site of freedom for those who no longer hope to find it at home. Historians have dealt extensively with Irish thought and a radical transatlantic. There are substantial connections between American revolutionary thinkers and the United Irishmen, and much interesting work has been done on many of the United Irishmen who went into exile in the United States after the failed Uprising of 1798 to find there what they despaired of achieving at home as well as on the complications arising from the conflict between American racial politics and United Irish support of abolition.[12] But the popular view remained an identification of the United States with freedom. David Wilson quotes one migrant's letter: "Here is your old friend arrived in the land of Liberty."[13] In *The Exile of Ireland!* the narrator similarly presents his seduction into a military career: "My heart panted as he talked of liberty and America: the cause I considered as that of glory, and America as the field where the harvest was to be reaped."[14] Other examples abound. A poem on the conventional subject of the freedom a bird enjoys in contrast to the speaker's lack of "liberty" because of the "tyrant's thunders," for instance, is prefaced by the remark, "Written in 1798, while in a state of concealment. The writer succeeded in getting out to America afterwards."[15] Allegorical formulations such as those echoed here and developed in the examples from Drennan and Porter given earlier, where "West" (the United States) means "Liberty" and "East" (Britain and Europe) means tyranny, are complicated, however, in such works as James Orr's Ulster Scots poem "The Passengers," published in his only volume of poetry in 1804. In "The Passengers," Orr not only depicts a shipboard community that is broadly egalitarian and affective but also represents the Atlantic space itself as a contested one. The mobility that in Leslie's *Killarney* appears only via simplified circulatory routes appears in "The Passengers" thirty years later as one in which different directions and nations meander, and attitudes shift with the passengers' transition from sea to land.

Orr was exiled briefly to the United States for his part in the 1798 Uprising, and so it might be tempting to read "The Passengers" as an authentic account of the transatlantic passage.[16] But the poem offers a very different depiction of the voyage than that provided in Orr's "Song," subtitled "Composed on the Banks of Newfoundland," included in his 1804 *Poems, on Various Subjects* as well. "Song," despite its innocuous title, is almost gothic in its depiction of the voyage. Beyond the ship, the speaker sees whales as "Unwieldy huge monsters, as ugly as *malice*," the vestiges of wrecked ships, solitary birds, and "bitter rain"; inside the ship, "children are screaming," "dames faint o' thirst," the "mate's mad and drunk," and the ship itself is just "A huge floating lazar-house."[17] "The Passengers," conversely, depicts a largely trouble-free passage. "Song" stresses the sickness of those in the hold; however, "The Passengers" represents the sickness passing quickly, so that "Few heads were sair or dizzy" after "twathree days."[18] The "Song" has terrifying whales and "bitter rain," but the speaker of "The Passengers" remarks,

> A bonie sight I vow it was,
> To see on some lown e'nin',
> Th' immense, smooth, smilin' sea o' glass,
> Whare porpoises were stening' [leaping]. (91–94)

There is a short storm after this, but after two verses all is set right again: "'Tis calm again" (118). More strikingly, the "Banks of Newfoundland" are in this poem "Newfoun'lan's becalmin' banks," where the passengers can fish (136–39) and participate in a maritime ritual of either paying the crew "a shilling, or a shilling's worth of liquor" or, if they refuse, being "shave[d], without soap" (p. 215n.)—what Orr terms a "poll-tax."

Orr's "Song Composed on the Banks of Newfoundland" focuses on the trials and tribulations of a dangerous and at best uncomfortable voyage, while "The Passengers" centers on a national community in transition from Ireland to the United States. It departs from the general tone of Orr's verse, which Terence Brown describes as "sombre and gloomy," "express[ing] a more general sense of social and historic catastrophe."[19] Specifically, in "The Passengers," Orr imagines shipboard life as a radical ideal of community, affectively bound and generally well ordered, seeking safety in the postcolonial United States. The poem's epigraph is taken from Oliver Goldsmith's *Deserted Village*, but Orr's poem gives scant attention to the losses emigration poses for the home country. Instead, Orr stresses a wider community of emigrants that includes the "Comrades" (10) who leave Ballycarry together and will form a connection between those who remain in Ireland and those who are already in the United States: during the farewell scene, the narrator remarks, after a reference to emigrating families, "What *keep-sakes*, an' what news are sent! / What smacks, an' what embraces!" (41–42).

The function of the traveler as the purveyor of news appears elsewhere in Orr's verse. In his "Song" beginning "As smiling Larne," "The soldier absent long" "Arriv'd at home."[20] The first verse deals with the returning soldier's recognition of home through the landscape: "Each wonted prospect well he knows; / The lofty dome, the hoarse cascade, / The fane, the ford he us'd to wade."[21] But, once in the house, the focus is exclusively on the exchange of information, and the poem ends,

> They weep—the laugh—they pray—they swear;
> And much they tell, and much they hear:
> His friends throng in; but some lie low,
> The maids he priz'd their children shew;
> And oft they ask with fond concern,
> For soldiers far from gentle Larne.[22]

The "passengers" are similarly part of a larger network of communication necessitated by the breaking up of local communities and the forging of new ones.

The functionality of the migrant community on board the ship in "The Passengers" is established in myriad ways. The migrants demonstrate, for instance, a capacity for self-governance by establishing rules and an internal force to maintain them: "The guid auld rule, 'first come first ser't,' / Was urg't by men o' mettle" (86–87). When some youths fail to observe this rule, their elders drive them off (88–89). The Enlightenment emphasis on intellectual development and social activities is not lost either: the ship is busy with conversation, singing, storytelling, games, and reading (129–33). In "The Passengers," then, Orr relies less on the gothic and more on what we might broadly call a pastoral aesthetic translated into the Atlantic, and that more welcoming Atlantic is aligned with a shipboard community with its own system of governance, from an informal tax system to managed and renewable food resources, as well as a rich cultural life of largely communal practices (singing, games, storytelling). This representation has correlates in a wide range of Irish depictions of landscape (as well as much traditional British topographical verse), in which there is a strong figurative association between community and the health and beauty of the land itself, first in topographical poems such as Leslie's *Killarney* and then (negatively) in the Big House and gothic traditions of the Irish novel. We might think here, for instance, of those interludes in Lady Morgan's *The Wild Irish Girl* that focus on storytelling, songs, games, as well as community involvement in ensuring that the society remains nonviolent, as when Glorvina gently chastises a child for abusing a dog.[23]

Suggestively, it is precisely at the moment that the ship's "tax" system is explained that Orr introduces the political context in "The Passengers": "An English frigate heaves in view" with the threat that the Irish passengers will be "press[ed]" (forced into military service), and all the men dive for cover, "Like whitrats peepin' frae their hole, / Cried, 'is she British, wat ye, / Or French this day?'" (151–53). Instead, "'Twas but a brig frae Baltimore, / To Larne wi' lintseed steerin'" (154–55). Here, near the end of the poem, Orr represents the North Atlantic off the North American coast as a multinational space of both military and commercial shipping, with France and Britain defining the military routes and America and Ireland serving as the terminuses of an alternative and benign trading route. That the English frigate can be so variously nationalized is itself a register of transatlantic conflict in which ships were seized and repatriated during various military encounters. These two stanzas then put this tale of emigration and shipboard community into a transatlantic context in which the military and commercial are not cooperative, as in Leslie's poem thirty years earlier, but politicized and nationally distinct.

The American ship also marks the proximity of land, and the emigrants start to see "mountains, bushes" (159). They land at New

Castle, Delaware, and the community evaporates: the poem ends, "We mix't amang the Yankies, / An skail't [scattered], that day" (170–71). There is no sense in the poem, then, that the emigrants will transfer their community as a coherent whole from Ireland to the United States, as cultural nationalism would mandate; instead, the movement is toward a willed assimilation and integration, a Lockean transition in which personal sovereignty is transferred from one collective to another, from Ireland to the shipboard community to the United States. But, at the same time, that transfer is marked as a shift in ideological perspective necessitated by the new nation—a shift rooted in racism.

There are two references in the poem to diasporic peoples from Africa, so that the "Black Atlantic" defined by Paul Gilroy intersects with the poem's radical "transatlantic" space.[24] In the first reference, members of the African diaspora are invoked as powerful figures on board the ship who are, along with the other passengers, terrified by the brief storm:

> While blacks wha a' before them drave,
> Lye cheepin' like a chicken—
> 'What gart [makes] us play? or bouse like beasts?
> Or box in fairs with venom? (111–14)

This is a slight reference indeed and does little to clarify the status of these people on board the ship, but it certainly suggests that the storm serves in part as a metaphor for racialized exploitation—they are housed like beasts and forced to "box in fairs." Andrew M. Kaye builds on documentary and folkloric evidence to describe a slave–sports economy in this period in which slaves were put to work in boxing matches to their owners' profit and occasionally with freedom as their reward.[25] Such matches often took place in the context of social agricultural events,[26] recalling Orr's specification "in fairs." Kaye traces the ways in which this economy was transatlantically propelled: "planters returning from their transatlantic tours" encouraged boxing, and some boxers became so successful that

"African Americans are known to have sailed for England throughout the nineteenth century to earn their livings as boxers."[27] Orr, then, is invoking the storm as a trope for a racism that coerces African American men into a blood sport and treats them like animals (tacitly drawing a connection between these boxing matches and animal fights). The second reference to this diasporic group makes little literal sense in light of the first: as the passengers disembark, "Creatures wha ne'er had seen a black, / Fu' scar't took to their shankies [legs]" (167–68). As David Roediger suggests, it is a common "myth" of Irish arrival in the United States that Irish emigrants would see a black person for the first time upon arrival and be terrified, a myth that Roediger suggests had little historical foundation.[28] Here, that lack of historical credibility is highlighted by the proximity of the two passages in the poem.

There is a strange ideological as well as factual disconnect between these two passages on the African diaspora, one calling attention to racist exploitation and the second instead simply repeating a banal racism in which difference is feared, even as the narrative voice gently mocks the "Creatures" who frighten so easily. This shift in ideological perspective from ship to shore does however echo an ongoing problem for Irish articulations of this radical transatlantic: the United Irishmen and later nationalist movements explicitly supported abolition, but, as scholars have noted, in exile in the United States many of the movement's supporters became complicit in slavery to varying degrees as well as in the racism that underwrote it.[29] The problem of slavery in the United States led to an increasing emphasis on the forty-ninth parallel in Irish writing. Early-nineteenth-century texts use "America" loosely to refer to "North America": *The Exile of Erin!* notes, for instance, "we at length rejoiced to set our feet upon the vast continent of America. Our landing was about the distance of twenty-five miles north of Quebec,"[30] placing them clearly in Lower Canada. But the division within "America" intensified as the abolition movement expanded in both the United States and the British Isles, as we shall see in the work of Adam Kidd and Thomas D'Arcy McGee. In 1843, "the

Liberator" Daniel O'Connell famously declared to Irish Americans, "come out of such a land, or if you remain, and dare countenance the system of slavery that is supported there, we will recognize you as Irishmen no longer,"[31] and in that same year the Irish nationalist newspaper *The Nation* published an anonymous poem titled "A Voice from America" that, with almost Orwellian double-think, represents the antebellum United States as "sp[eaking] of freedom to the slave— / Of comfort to the crushed."[32] In these closing stanzas of "The Passengers," then, Orr broadly traces a common radical trajectory from a self-governing migrant community to its assimilation into a radical United States, but he also touches on complications in that idealized trajectory, starting early in the poem with a critique of the American Dream as a fantasy for fools:

> Ilk mammies pet conceits itsel'
> The makin' o' a Banker;
> They'll soon, tho', wiss to lieve at hame,
> An' dee [die] no worth a totam [spinning top]. (48–51)

The scission between an ideal radical Irishness and an integrated capitalist Americanness pivots on race, as Orr's "passengers" are transformed from radically minded abolitionists to stereotyping and stereotyped white immigrants in the United States.[33] They leave the radical-Irish community of the ship and "mix't amang the Yankies."

British North America versus the Radical United States

This anxiety over the articulation of "freedom" in a slave-owning nation continued through the following decades, particularly in the notable cases of the poetry of Adam Kidd in the early 1830s and of Thomas D'Arcy McGee in the 1840s and 1850s. Both authors published poetry that pursues a distinction between a more benign British North America and a deeply troubled United States—a distinction that Moore also articulated in relation to his brief visit to North America.[34] Kidd and McGee were alike permanent emigrants who had significant dealings with the power structures in Canada; both were explicit about their debts to Moore; and though Kidd was Protestant and McGee Catholic, they shared a similar Irish nationalism and sense of diaspora (to what degree this similarity was, for both, derived from Moore's poetry rather than from demographic affiliations is an interesting biographical question). What emerges from McGee's corpus in particular is a rhetorical complication in historians' attempts to identify the racial politics of Irish exiles in North America: his works' political position changes with the geographical location, recalling the emigrants in Orr's "Passengers" who change their politics as they move from ship to shore.

McGee, like Orr, immigrated to the United States in the wake of political tumult. Born in 1825 in Carlingford, his father an employee of the Coast Guard Service, he left for Boston in 1842 and began a successful career as a journalist in the northeastern United States, but he moved back to Dublin in 1845 to take a job with the *Freeman's Journal*. He was soon involved in the Young Ireland movement and writing for *The Nation* but was arrested in 1848 and returned to the United States soon after his release, eventually migrating to Canada, where he quickly rose in Canadian politics and became one of the Fathers of Confederation.[35] His biographer Wilson notes, "Comparing him to other Young Ireland writers, Samuel Ferguson declared that McGee was 'the greatest poet of them all,' ahead of Davis, Duffy, and James Clarence Mangan."[36] He published a dozen volumes, including poetry and works on Irish history. Much of McGee's later writing was directed against the Fenians, arguing that British North America was more open to Catholics than the United States. He was assassinated in 1868, and the attack was quickly attributed to the Fenians, though this conclusion is now widely disputed, and the evidence remains sketchy. Much less is known about his predecessor Adam Kidd. Kidd died, like so many other romantic poets, at a very young age. He was the son of a farmer from Tullynagee; he was born around 1802 and died in 1831, but even the year in which he arrived in Canada is unknown. By 1824, though, he was working in Quebec as a teacher and began publishing poetry in the periodical press. In 1830, he published his magnum opus, *The Huron Chief, and Other Poems*, and began work on a projected account of native Canadian culture, making him a particularly significant figure for discussions of early Canadian depictions of native peoples.[37]

Both poets were critical of US policies, especially toward non-white peoples. In "Freedom's Journey," published in *Canadian Ballads and Occasional Verses* (1858), McGee's personified figure Freedom travels south but finds no home there:

> She lodged 'neath many a gilded roof,
> They gave her praise in many a hall,
> Their kindness check'd the free reproof,
> Her heart dictated to let fall;
> She heard the Negro's helpless prayer,
> And felt her home could not be there.[38]

In the preface to his 1830 volume of verse, Kidd condemned the United States for its treatment of native peoples: "From the days of the American Revolution until this very hour, the poor Indians have been so cruelly treated, and driven from their homes and hunting-grounds, by the boasted freemen of the United States, that the MOHICANS, the NARAGANSETTS, the DELAWARES, and others, once powerful Tribes, have now become totally extinct—while the remaining Nations are daily dwindling away, and in a few years hence will scarcely leave a memorial to perpetuate their names, as the once mighty rulers of the vast American regions."[39] Both McGee and Kidd offer key contributions to the Irish-diasporic complication of the radical transatlantic by addressing the paradox inherent in the idealization of the United States as the "land of Liberty,"[40] emphatically so by juxtaposing racist practices with "Freedom" (McGee) and "boasted freemen" (Kidd).

This paradox extended to debate among Irish nationalists. Charles Gavan Duffy excoriates fellow nationalist John Mitchel for writing against him in the heated climate of the late 1840s, and for Mitchel's politics. Referring generally to Mitchel's statements on

"SLAVERY, SUICIDE, and RIBBON-LODGES" and thus invoking in part Mitchel's support of slavery in the United States, Duffy remarks, "I well remember the last of your 'doctrines,' which I declined to have 'expounded' through the *Nation*; it was a vehement protest against the emancipation of the Jews!"[41] Early in this pamphlet, Duffy also condemns Mitchel's failure to work with diasporic communities outside of Ireland: "After ruining, in a few weeks, your position in the United States, you are pleased to denounce me for mismanaging a great opportunity for the Irish cause. Returning from Van Diemen's Land with a broken *parole*, which makes the men you were proudest to call friends hang their heads when your name is mentioned, you venture to impeach me with a discreditable escape from the responsibilities of my position."[42] That diasporic community works effectively, in Duffy's account of his trials, to monitor other Irishmen: "the police spy who sought to betray me had to fly the American cities from dread of Irish vengeance, and died on the banks of the Mississippi with the arrow of an Indian in his breast."[43] Amidst competing representations of the United States—either as the site of slavery and the oppression of indigenous peoples or as the site of freedom or as the new home of a properly functioning diasporic community that can even pursue just retribution against Duffy's "police spy"—some writers shifted their stances from work to work, year to year, and audience to audience, complicating debates about the weight of individual cases on one side or the other of the historical debate over racism among Irish expatriates in the first half of the nineteenth century.

As a Canadian articulating a nascent Canadian identity, McGee condemned the United States for the exploitation of Irish workers, arguing that Fenianism merely distracted Irish expatriates from their economic powerlessness and from racism in general. Writing earlier from the American Northeast as an Irish emigrant, however, McGee had heralded the radical United States as the site of Freedom. In *Poems by Thomas D'Arcy McGee, Chiefly Written in America*, a "Supplement to the 'Nation'" (1854),[44] slavery is elided in general praise for the postcolonial United States. McGee thus writes, "Hail to the land whose wide domain / Rejoices under Freedom's reign, / Where neither right nor race is bann'd,"[45] ignoring slavery as thoroughly as the anonymous 1843 poem "A Voice from America" that "told of hearts that burned to right / Those wrongs the weak must bear— / Of hands to aid in freedom's fight."[46] In McGee's poem "Hail to the Land," the land, unoppressed, is healthy and verdant:

The land is worthy of its place
The vanguard of the human race—
Its rivers still refresh the sea,
As Truth does Time, unceasingly;
Its volum'd plains as open lie
As a saint's soul before God's eye;
Its broad based mountains firmly stand
Like Faith and Hope in their own land.
Heaven keep this soil, and may it bear
New worth and wealth to every year.[47]

In this collection of McGee's verse for the Dublin-printed newspaper *The Nation*, the United States is depicted as a key new site for a proud Irish diaspora that retains its Irish identity rather than merges with new nations (as in Orr's "Passengers"). In "A Salutation," the closing poem of the collection, McGee's speaker declares,

Hail to our Celtic brethren, wherever they may be,
In the far woods of Oregon, or o'er the Atlantic sea—
Whether they guard the banner of St. George in Indian vales,
Or spread beneath the nightless North experimental sails,
One in name, and in fame,
Are the sea-divided-Gaels.[48]

The "sea-divided-Gaels," whether serving England in India or North American settlement or "In Northern Spain and Brittany," retain their nationality, "Tho' fallen the state of Erin."[49] Similarly, in another poem in the same collection, a diasporic Irish community transplants entire their Catholic faith, the Irish language, and Irish literature, singling out nationalist writers O'Connell and Moore.[50] In his later work, however, McGee, though a politician with significant credentials in the field of nation building, prevaricates uneasily between a cultural nationalism that would bind Irish migrants inevitably to nostalgia and regret and a more Lockean model in which peace, prosperity, and successful citizenship can be found in a new land under a different regime.

Just four years after his supplement for *The Nation* was published, in a volume that includes a number of poems from *The Nation* collection, McGee located himself firmly within a Canadian nation and state. The title page of *Canadian Ballads, and Occasional Verses* (1858) announces McGee's status as an "M.P.P."—an elected member of Provincial Parliament in Canada. The volume is also dedicated "To Charles Gavan Duffy, M.P.P., Minister of Public Works and Land, Victoria, Australia, In Memory of Old Times."[51] Duffy, one of the founding editors of *The Nation*, had immigrated to Australia in 1855 and had quickly risen to government office. Both Duffy and McGee had been arrested in the wake of 1848 unrest in Ireland: McGee was released before trial, but Duffy was repeatedly brought to trial and eventually released after "more indictments were brought against [him] were sent to the Grand Juries by the crown, than ever were levelled for the same offence in the whole annals of British law."[52] McGee's *Canadian Ballads*, then, nods toward the irony of two Young Irelanders, charged for political dissent in Ireland, later rising high in the governments of British colonies. McGee's preface declares as well that the volume seeks to inaugurate a distinctively Canadian literature, as McGee characterizes his book as "an attempt to show . . . that by those who are blessed with the divine gift of poesy, many worthy themes may be found, without quitting their own country": "That we shall one day be a great northern nation, and develope within ourselves that best fruit of nationality, a new and lasting literature, is the firm belief, at least of those to whom this volume is mainly addressed."[53]

These jostling nationalisms, one rooted in Young Ireland and one emerging in Canada, shape the volume's division into the two sections anticipated by the title (recalling the divisions in the Banims' *Chaunt*, discussed in the next chapter): "Canadian Ballads" and "Occasional Verses." The first section deals primarily with Canadian subjects, celebrating the age of exploration with poems on Sebastian Cabot, Jacques Cartier, and Henry Hudson; on the diverse peoples of Canada (including implicitly Christian natives and happy French settlers); and on the opportunities of settlement. Benign, open, and prosperous, with visions of the Virgin Mary to assuage the harshness of the weather in "Our Ladye of the Snow," Canada is celebrated as the ideal destination for the nineteenth-century emigrant. The "Occasional Verses," however, return again and again to Irish subjects, including such poems as "Carolan the Blind," "Home-Sick Stanzas," "Kildare's Bard on Tournaments," and "'Twas Something Then to Be a Bard." *Canadian Ballads, and Occasional Verses* charts the uneasiness with which the migrant is transformed from Irish exile to Canadian and does so just six years before McGee would become instrumental in the formation of Canada out of most of the remaining colonies of British North America. And here, in his inauguration of a distinctively Canadian literature, he invokes slavery to depict the territories that would soon become "Canada" as better governed than those of the United States. In other words, slavery in "Freedom's Journey," the poem with which this section began, operates to serve early Canadian nationalism, but McGee's more positive representations of the United States appear in the context of Irish nationalist statements in which the United States is a symbol of the postcolonial: "the land where freedom first, / Through all the feudal fetters burst," the home of Franklin and Washington.[54]

In McGee's "Occasional" poems, however, the migrant is an exile. Hence, in "Home-Sick Stanzas" (first published under the more neutral title "Experience" in *Poems*), McGee begins, "Twice had I sailed the Atlantic o'er, / Twice dwelt an exile in the west," and laments, "I felt a weight where'er I went— / I felt a void within my brain. . . . My heart was in my own dear land."[55] The poem closes,

Where'er I turned, some emblem still,
  Roused consciousness upon my track;
Some hill was like an Irish hill,
  Some wild bird's whistle called me back;
A sea-bound ship bore off my peace,
  Between its white, cold wings of woe;
Oh, if I had but wings like these,
  Where my peace went I, too, would go.[56]

Recalling *The Nation*'s debts to Herderian nationalism (see chapter 5) in his emphasis on the natural elements of the Irish landscape—"an Irish hill" and the "wild bird's whistle"—McGee's poem structures homesickness as an attachment to the land itself, suggesting Anderson's argument in "Long-Distance Nationalism" that nationalism is a response to diasporic detachment. McGee's poem "To a Friend in Australia," included under "Canadian Ballads" and readily associated with Duffy because of the dedication, again emphasizes the Irish landscape (specifically the same part of Wicklow that includes Glendalough):

Oh! for one week amid the emerald fields,
  Where the Avoca sings the song of Moore;
Oh! for the odour the brown heather yields,
  To glad the Pilgrim's heart on Glenmalur.[57]

The "Canadian Ballads" work to create a Canadian tradition of exploration and settlement to which future migrants can add, but the "Occasional Verses" focus almost exclusively on the remote Irish past, locating Thomas D'Arcy McGee, MPP, within two national histories and two national landscapes that remain divided by an ocean.

Kidd's poetry of migration tends to focus on the North American landscape as a temporary refuge for Irish subjects. Most of these poems in Kidd's volume *Huron Chief* stress the moment of departure and ongoing attachment to the home landscape. "My Irish Home," for instance, traces the receding horizon as first the coast, then the "green-clad hills," and finally the "mountains high" disappear from the shipboard emigrant's view.[58] "The Hibernian Solitary" stresses the speaker's memory of happy childhood moments in the Irish landscape, closing with a lament for the loss of that landscape, "ruined all" as the speaker "shed[s] the big and parting tear."[59] In "Cathleen," however, the Irish exile is located explicitly within a North American setting: "Upon a lonely bank, against whose base / Saint Lawrence wildly heaves, she sat and wept."[60] The setting is the site not only of grief, but also of physical damage:

> A sun more fierce than ever yet has flung
> Its scorching beams upon her own green hills,
> Had marked her care-worn cheek with brownest hue,
> And tinged her brow with deep Canadian die. (172)

Kidd thus invokes Herderian assumptions about climate to represent Cathleen as a stranger in a strange land, her body marked by the alien space's climate, making her "a wreck" (173) on terms congruent with Herder's claim that migration causes "degenerat[ion]" (see my introduction). This physical violation is directly tied to a resistance to English rule:

> Her plaintive tale was such, as Erin's child,
> No matter where he strays to find a home,
> Might well divine.—But my pen, too oft,
> Has freely strayed from that allegiance,
> Which some may say it owes to England's king. (173)

This "stray[ing]," as a consequence, will end once Ireland is free, as the poem concludes,

> Oh, Cathleen! I can truly share thy grief,
> And fain would hope, that yet a brighter day
> May shine with all its wonted cheerfulness,
> And give to Erin's Isle what Heaven designed;—
> . . . .
> And when the shell of joy has once proclaimed

> *Loved Ireland free*, I'll cross the ocean wave,
> And to thy mountain-cot thyself restore. (174)

Cathleen's return is thus associated with a transition from a "fierce" sun that marks her body to a benign "cheerful" sun. Kidd's poem is unusual in the early nineteenth century for depicting a woman as an exile from colonial rule, driven from her "mountain-cot" by "England's king" and lamenting

> Her sad misfortune—that dark misfortune,
> Which thus had forced her from her native cot,
> And doomed her in a distant land to seek
> A scanty pittance from a hand unknown. (172)

Cathleen is easily connected both to the literary tradition of Cathleen ni Houlihan as a figure for Ireland and to the economic diaspora that drove many of the poorer Irish, women and men, to North America, where the living and working conditions were often very difficult. But Kidd stresses the political pressures while implicitly representing North America as an inadequate refuge on economic grounds. Moreover, he argues for the physical toll of migration through a "fierce" climate, representing migration as politically coerced and with an ongoing physical price that compounds the diasporic subject's grieving for the homeland.

Such poems collectively suggest the complicated implications of the growth of transatlantic travel, commerce, and conflict in the early nineteenth century during the rise of Herderian or romantic nationalism in Ireland. At stake here in part is the defining rubric of modernity. John Leslie's *Killarney* wishes only for commerce and participation in the new British Empire; later Irish nationalist authors, however, along with some British radicals, saw the United States as the center of a transatlantic modernity. But the growing emphasis of nationalism on the diasporic subject's longing for the homeland, alongside discomfort with the realities of racism in the

United States, undermine more positive images of the United States as a postcolonial haven for dispossessed Irish nationalists.

Aristocrats at Sea: The Problem of Citizenship in a Nation without a State

Many of the poems discussed in this chapter focus on subaltern exiles, motivated at least in part by economic necessity. In the 1820s, however, there was also a renewal of literary interest in the figure of the "wild geese"—Irish leaders forced into exile. For instance, in such texts as *The O'Briens and the O'Flahertys* and *Absenteeism*, both published in the mid-1820s, Lady Morgan depicts the colonial status of Ireland through the political alienation of aristocrats and landowners: the disenfranchisement of colonization produces diaspora among the upper ranks, just as economics put diasporic pressure on the lower classes. Morgan's concern is not general members of the populace, but rather ideal citizens of the sort that Anthony D. Smith associates with the neoclassical roots of nationalism:[61] men of rank, education, and a strong sense of civic duty. In her fourth novel *The Outlaw*, Alicia Lefanu, niece of her namesake, Alicia Sheridan Lefanu, the Dublin playwright and poet who mentored Morgan in the early years of her writing career, offers a particularly rich exploration of the impact that this kind of post-1798 diaspora in the United States had on Irish governance. It is a novel in which none of Ireland's patriarchs are functional: there is a bumbling schoolmaster with literary ambitions and a sycophantic reflex and, among the aristocrats, an unrepentant fop who leaves the management of his estate to his wife, a repentant fop who abandoned his wife and child and committed treason for love of an Italian spy, and the heroine's father, a leader in the United Irishmen, whose misguided patriotism, as the novel represents it, has repercussions on his family, servants, and the larger society for nearly twenty years. As the children of these men pay various prices for their fathers' failure to act as proper citizens, in a magisterial weaving of plots, the central mystery is revealed: the heroine's father is not dead, as she has been told, but in exile in the United States, his return under a general amnesty part of the novel's resolution. *The O'Briens* is in key respects almost a prequel to *The Outlaw*: Morgan traces the political crises and colonial machinations that drive her aristocratic patriot from Ireland's shores in 1798, and Lefanu imagines the impact of such exiles on those who remain behind from the vantage point of the next generation, roughly around the time of Waterloo.

Another complicating philosophical ground here is the definition of nationhood, and nationality, at the intersection of two contradictory discourses: on the one hand, what Smith has termed the neoclassical roots of nationalism in Enlightenment notions of universal education, bureaucratic centralization, and the march toward progress; on the other, romantic nationalism, in which identity is rooted in the past rather than a progressive future and in cultural distinctiveness rather than generalized enlightenment. As Smith has noted, nationalism as it developed after 1789 brings together shared values from these two discourses, including "the elevation of culture as the source of politics."[62] We might grasp Smith's two threads—the neoclassical and the romantic—in terms of the "nation-state." The neoclassical defines the state: civic-minded, well-educated individuals working within a bureaucracy to further progress. The romantic defines the nation as the mythic signified of which the state is the signifier,[63] especially in rendering the values and interests of the people as sufficiently homogeneous to be adequately grasped by a single state.

With the rise of Daniel O'Connell's movement for Catholic Emancipation in the 1820s, however, the ground shifted slightly. Grattan argued for the nation's trading rights, but O'Connell argued for an extension of the franchise—of citizenship—to the Catholic majority. As one early historian of the Catholic Association put it in 1829, "The code which stripped the Catholic of almost every civil right, could not altogether pluck from him the heart of a true citizen."[64] In other words, citizenship was imagined on terms other than the Lockean. Instead of transferring their individual sovereignty to a new nation-state (say, to the United States like Orr's "passengers" or to Canada like McGee's migrants), O'Connell's audiences were invited to assert their inherent citizenship, or at least the adult men in those audiences were. The problem of citizenship in Ireland in the 1820s was first and foremost a question of religion, and so articulations of citizenship complicated any democratic assumptions about the full extent of the wished-for franchise. O'Connell's argument for Catholic rights did not propose universal suffrage, and it was only after Catholic Emancipation that the franchise was slightly extended to include more ranks of society. In 1824–25, Morgan's series of essays on absenteeism, for instance, relies heavily on a hierarchical model in which what we might recognize as citizenship is markedly limited to a ruling elite. It is "the genuine and educated gentry of Ireland, her hereditary senators and native legislators" who "made up the larger portion of the reading public of her capital" at a time when the periodical press facilitates the effective functioning of the Habermasian public sphere; hence, "the permanent residence of the major part, of the wealth, the nobility, and above all, and more precious than all, of the EDUCATION of the country, produced these blessed effects, the greater good, the 'last best gift,' which congregated interests and intellects could bestow on a community, Public Spirit, fell like dew in the desert upon the renovating nation."[65] This is Morgan's account of the 1780s and 1790s as a period in which Ireland moved toward an effective nation-state through the return of absentees to an improving Ireland, the same period that she addresses in *The O'Briens and the O'Flahertys* (1827), where her protagonist is one member of the "genuine and educated gentry of Ireland" who becomes involved with the United Irishmen but then has to flee the country, ending up in exile as a mercenary in Napoleon's court.

The limits on Irish enfranchisement imposed by nostalgic emphases on the indigenous aristocracy would shadow Irish nationalism throughout the nineteenth century and arise in part from the contradictory discourses of neoclassicism and cultural nationalism in romantic-era Irish nationalism: Enlightenment discourses of the ideal civic subject are, as is well established, tied to the legitimation of the growing middle class in Britain, and it is easy to see the antiquarian basis of the desire for a native aristocracy to return to power as well as the attractiveness of both elitist models to readers made uneasy by populist uprisings over land rights, most notably in the period immediately before *The O'Briens*, *The Outlaw*, and *Absenteeism* appeared—the Agrarian Rebellion of 1821–24. Morgan combines these two models in her novel's protagonist, a well-educated, civic-minded aristocrat who admires Locke and rejects his antiquarian father's desire for a return to precolonial governance. Just as the "Glorvina solution" of *The Wild Irish Girl* appears to unite indigenous territorial right with the colonizer's political might by anticipating the marriage of Glorvina and Horatio,[66] Murrogh O'Brien in *The O'Briens and the O'Flahertys* apparently unites indigenous aristocratic right with neoclassicism's modernizing impetus through what it presents as civic merit. This problem, though, of indigenous right and intellectual merit continues to haunt explorations of the problem of an Irish nation without a state.

One particularly interesting exploration of this problem is Alicia Lefanu's *The Outlaw*, a full-length novel included with a shorter tale in a four-volume work, united by a slight frame narrative entitled *Tales of a Tourist* (1823). Even as *The Outlaw* deals extensively with aristocratic men who fail to act as patriots and fathers, it attributes those failures to a range of causes and juxtaposes them all with a woman's successful governance. Lefanu's heroine, Geraldine, is supposedly an orphan and, as the novel opens, she has just returned from school to the care of her father's brother and his wife, Sir Charles and Lady Louisa Southwell. The Southwells have a daughter who, like Sir Charles, is flighty and superficial: Sir Charles is a fop who strays from the marriage bed, and his daughter is excessively concerned with social status and fashion rather than with the substantial subjects of improvement, aesthetics, and literature that concern her cousin and her mother. Lady Louisa is a paragon of Wollstonecraftian virtue, tolerating her husband's waywardness while managing his estate, overseeing the establishment of a local school, and strategizing to improve the cousins' marriage prospects. Enter Montfort, his real name O'Melvyl, an expatriate returned to Ireland with a mysterious past but with a well-developed sensibility demonstrated by his preference for Geraldine over the fashionable Miss Southwell. From Geraldine's perspective, Montfort runs hot and cold throughout the novel, behavior explained not by his willingness to listen to rumors, like Jane Austen's Darcy, but by his being rather viciously blackmailed and occasionally confused by social proprieties, making him all the more tortured over his love of Geraldine. Entwined with the romance plot are a series of subplots, including the stories of Montfort's father, who was duped into abandoning his family and then made an invalid by a botched poisoning attempt by an Italian schemer; of Geraldine's still-living father; and of some minor characters. Lefanu also does much in the novel to invoke the literary milieu of pre-Waterloo Ireland: there are a number of references to Moore, and characters discuss the death of the poet Mary Tighe.[67]

Two main subplots interweave with the romance and flashbacks: one, almost entirely comic, deals with a bumbling schoolmaster-antiquarian named Pendennis who has a number of wayward children, including a cross-dressing prankster daughter and an equally bumbling son who becomes a religious demagogue (a device through which Lefanu satirizes Protestant conservatism). The Pendennis patriarch would be at home in the comic portions of Sir Walter Scott's *The Antiquary*, his cross-dressing prankster daughter uses a demonstration of a new-fangled shower-bath to dump a gallon of water onto the fashionable Miss Southwell, and the vaguely ridiculous Pendennis heir responds, with good intentions at least, to Miss Southwell's crying over some social embarrassment by shoving, uninvited, rather a lot of snuff up her nose. She wallops him in reply, so hard that he begins to bleed, and then Miss Southwell's maid lectures him on his idiocy and runs him out of the room. The incident is rather minor to the plot but exemplary of the general foolishness and ineffectuality of the men in Lefanu's novel (as well as one of the novel's best comic scenes). The other main subplot centers on Geraldine and is gothic rather than comic, involving mysterious appearances, strange coincidences, threats of confinement or abandonment, mistaken identity at a masked ball, and other conventional gothic devices, all directed toward the revelation, near the end of the novel, of the fate of Geraldine's parents. Her father, Gerald Fitz-Clare, had been a leader in the United Irishmen Uprising and was estranged from his family for doing so. He arranges to see Isabel, Geraldine's mother, one last time before fleeing the country, but they are betrayed by his confidant, Knowlan, who is responsible for some of the mysterious apparitions later encountered by Geraldine, and the military sweeps in: Isabel "beheld her husband, faint and covered with wounds, dragged away by two of the military. It was then that all courage forsook her; she dropped down insensible" (2:238–39), and, of course, she sentimentally dies, soon after handing over responsibility for her daughter to Lady Louisa, who disguises Geraldine's identity by giving her the patronym "Southwell." Louisa then arranges Gerald's escape, and he flees to the United States via France. In the novel's present, Louisa has been working with lawyers and writing letters to secure Gerald's pardon and hence his return.

It is Gerald's return that speaks most directly to my concerns here. It takes him three days of traveling to reach the Southwell family after his return to Ireland, but it is only in the family that his real return is identified: "[Lady Louisa] welcomed the stranger by his name—welcomed once more to his long-resigned native home the exiled Southwell Fitz-Clare.—'Your daughter,' she added, but, overcome by contending emotions, was unable to point out to him *which* was his daughter. . . . [T]he first glance at Geraldine's expressive face was sufficient to convince him *which* was the child he had been forced to abandon" (3:45–46). Home and family are thus entwined, his identity defined through a relationship that returns with the end of exile. In the same section, the narrator remarks, "Whatever imagination has pictured as venerable and majestic in an ancient Irish king, was realized in the noble aspect of Gerald Fitz-Clare" (3:47). This, then, is at least figuratively the return of the king as well as of the father. Nearly twenty years after Morgan, a close friend of the Lefanu family, published the first explicitly "national tale," *The Wild Irish Girl*, the implications here are fairly straightforward: the daughter, as in that earlier novel, is identified with the national landscape and the father with a line of Irish kings, their reunion here evoking the expectation of the reuniting of kingship and land. To reinforce the connection, the real name of Geraldine's suitor, O'Melvyl, is the same as that of the prince of Inismore, Glorvina's father, with a slightly different spelling. After spending a few days "in compliment to sir Charles and lady Louisa Southwell" (3:48), Gerald Fitz-Clare returns to his own estate in Wexford, one of the major scenes of the 1798 Uprising.

Here, Fitz-Clare is tied extensively to the landscape from which he was exiled: "With what mingled feelings did Gerald Fitz-Clare, after such a lengthened banishment, prepare to revisit the abodes of his forefathers!" (3:49–50). It is a land that Fitz-Clare, even after an exile of nearly twenty years, remembers in visual detail and through a cultural form strongly tied to Irish cultural nationalism in the period, music: "One great amusement to Mr. Fitz-Clare was, to point out to his daughter's notice every striking object in their demesne and neighbourhood; another of his pleasures was, to hear her voice and taste exerted on those native strains which he had long despaired ever to hear in his own country again" (3:51). Instead of a happy reunion with the site where Geraldine expects to marry Montfort, however, Lefanu paints a gothic scene and a traumatized ruler. The narrator begins, "Here I might describe the gloomy appearance of the vast, long-deserted mansion; the exclamations of mingled grief and joy of Katherine Lawless, who had followed her old master into the country; and the fine field that the irregular magnificence of the park and grounds seemed to promise for the future exercise of Geraldine's taste" (3:50). Moore's mournful *Irish Melodies* become a symbol of Fitz-Clare's nationalist malaise:

> Geraldine was singing, for her father, some of those touching native airs in which he took such a dangerous delight; she accompanied them with that simple harp which we have already once described. Fitz-Clare had pointed out the song, and she was obliged to give utterance to the strain.

"Yes, weep; and however my foes may condemn,
  THY tears shall efface their decree;
For Heaven can witness, though guilty to them,
  I have been but too faithful to thee." (3:52)

This is an early lyric in Moore's series, "When He Who Adores Thee," and it is associated with Robert Emmet, the leader in the ill-conceived 1803 Uprising—in other words, this lyric links Geraldine's father with the ineffectual and starry-eyed rebel of 1803. However, other details complicate this association. The most prominent leader of the United Irishmen by the 1820s was arguably Lord Edward Fitzgerald, an aristocratic hero admired by Byron, Moore, and others for fighting on the side of right rather than privilege—very much like Morgan's hero, Murrogh O'Brien. He also traveled extensively in North America, making him something of a transatlantic precursor to Fitz-Clare in Lefanu's novel. Fitzgerald was a member of the Geraldine family celebrated in Morgan's *Absenteeism* and at the outset of Moore's 1830 biography of Fitzgerald—and so are our heroine Geraldine and her father, Gerald Fitz-Clare. The narrator notes, "The Southwell family traced their descent, in the female line, from this powerful chieftain. He was one of the Geraldines of Munster, and bore, as a patronymic, *that* name, which has since, like some other appellations in Ireland, been transferred to the other sex" (1:229). Fitzgerald died of stab wounds received during his arrest in the course of the 1798 Rising, an historical point echoed by the stabbing of Gerald Fitz-Clare during his own arrest—and both the historical arrest and the fictional arrest are associated with betrayal. Fitzgerald was betrayed by a Catholic informer, Magan, after his friends were betrayed into custody by Fitzgerald's friend Thomas Reynolds; Fitz-Clare is betrayed by his associate Knowlan, who leads the military to Fitz-Clare's hiding place.

Lefanu's hero, Gerald Fitz-Clare, then, is doubly associated with historical leaders of nationalist uprisings: Robert Emmett, on the fringes of the 1798 Uprising and made famous by the failed 1803 Uprising, and Lord Edward Fitzgerald, noble and heroic to the end of the more effective 1798 Uprising. These two figures symbolize the entwining of neoclassical and cultural nationalisms: Emmett became a romantic figure, famous for delaying his capture just long enough to see his fiancée one last time and for a defiant speech from the dock asking that his grave be unmarked until Ireland was free; Fitzgerald was a man of the Enlightenment, singled out as a military leader early on for his interests in "all that related to the science of Military Construction" and "seeing war carried on upon a larger and more scientific scale."[68] Moore celebrated the young Fitzgerald as "wholly free of the follies and frailties of youth" so that "the pursuit of science, in which he eminently distinguished himself, seemed, at this time, the only object that at all divided his thoughts with that enthusiasm for Irish freedom."[69] Lefanu's paternal hero is divided by these two precursors, praised for his education but pitied for his misguided participation in the Uprising. He even repudiates the Uprising, agreeing with the narrator and Montfort in representing his support of the United Irishmen as "the madness of the hour" and the result of misplaced patriotism (3:53). On his return to his native landscape, he is stabbed by the man who had betrayed him to the military in 1798, and he dies a patriot, grateful he was "allowed to breathe his last in that cherished land for which he had tempted and endured so much" and using his last words to express a love of country: "And thou, my country! . . . first, latest object of my hope and love! may these, my children, live to see thee happy—to see thy woes redressed—thy welfare guarded—thy blessings multiplied, by friends more enlightened—not, oh, not more sincere, than *I* was!" (3:63–64).

The novel does not end with a renovated Irish (e)state, but instead with a revision of *The Wild Irish Girl*'s conclusion: following Glorvina's plot, Geraldine marries Montfort and finds a new father in her father-in-law, but where Morgan's heroine was penniless and marriage with the English heir the only means of restoring the land to the lineage of the Irish kings, Lefanu's novel ends with the woman as the property owner within an entirely Irish marital economy. The last lines of the novel read, "Become, by the death of her father, sole heiress to Fitz-Clare's restored estates, Geraldine values fortune principally as it enables her to make amends to her amiable husband for the more brilliant prospects he generously gave up for her sake, and finds, in the tender and increasing attachment of lord Beaudesert, the best consolation for the tears she still gives to the memory of Fitz-Clare" (3:88). Lefanu thus represents Fitz-Clare as a disruptive figure, an aristocrat who leads an uprising that perpetuates violence in the Irish landscape until the cycle is closed when Knowlan successfully causes Fitz-Clare's death nearly twenty years after his first attempt to murder him. The political and sexual intrigues of the novel's male characters fade away as the women inherit wealth and power: Geraldine runs her father's estate as Lady Southwell runs the estate of Geraldine's uncle, both of them guided by the principles of domestic improvement, education, and aesthetics. The novel seems to move toward Fitz-Clare's return from transatlantic exile as a reintegration of citizen and nation, a return of the king and a healing of the rift between the nation-state and patriots, but then its conclusion suggests rather that Fitz-Clare's exile and Knowlan's stalking of Geraldine are alike gothic hauntings of an Irish landscape that needs other measures (a tension between narrative momentum and concluding subtext that is also evident in *The Wild Irish Girl*). Domestic management is offered as a local solution to Ireland's social ills, one that need not concern itself with the affairs of the nation-state that so concerned Grattan and 1790s radicals and thus one that sidesteps the problem that Lefanu cannot resolve: what to do with an Irish patriot when there is no nation-state?

This is precisely the sort of governance that Morgan's heroine Beavoin O'Flaherty offers at a convent in *The O'Briens and the O'Flahertys*, published four years after Lefanu's novel. Both Morgan and Lefanu are drawing on a model of women's governance that can be traced back to the work of Frances Sheridan and the elder Alicia Lefanu's play *The Sons of Erin* (1812)[70] as well as forward to the inimitable Lady Knollys in J. Sheridan LeFanu's *Uncle Silas* (1864). More to the point here, in both novels the figure of the male patriot is disruptive because there is no legitimate state through which he can articulate his place: Murrogh O'Brien in *The*

O'Briens and the O'Flahertys flounders his way from conspiracy to conspiracy, repeatedly needing O'Flaherty to rescue him and ultimately direct him to leave Ireland. In an early moment in the novel, an O'Brien family motto appears on the banner of an "Irish Brigade," "composed of the *élite* of the youth of the capital and the university" but described by Morgan's narrator as a "band of boy-citizen-soldiers"; the novel's hero is its leader, returned from eight years "as a soldier of fortune" on "the continent."[71] "Boy-citizen-soldiers" participating in a mock military battle for a public audience, they can only play at citizenship, even though their leader has returned from eight years as a "soldier of fortune" working outside of Ireland. O'Brien's exposure to various political factions, his participation in the United Irishmen, whose central aim is "to obtain a complete constitutional reform in the legislature" (318), and his drafting of a pamphlet titled "The State of Ireland" (358)—all are legible as attempts to act like a legislator in a country that will not recognize him as such, "a legislator, with a musket on his shoulder and a sword by his side" (136), as one wag describes another character. O'Brien and Fitz-Clare have no place in colonial Ireland. Both return as patriots to Ireland, only to leave it again—O'Brien once again becoming a "soldier of fortune" on "the continent," and Fitz-Clare meeting the death laid out for him in 1798. The positive governance by Geraldine, Lady Southwell, and O'Flaherty operate as feminist critiques akin to that of Mary Shelley in another novel from the mid-1820s, *The Last Man*—grand political change is presented as meaningless without domestic security and local benevolence. But this critique proceeds in Morgan's and Lefanu's novels specifically in the absence of proper masculine governance. While Orr's emigrants in "The Passengers" can transfer their Lockean citizenship to the United States, the cultural-nationalist pull of the nation prevents such a transfer for either O'Brien or Fitz-Clare. The aristocrat belongs to the nation, and the nation to him. Geraldine worries that her father has formed other attachments in the United States, but he has instead only awaited the day of his return—his life suspended while he is away from Ireland.

If the Enlightenment imagined a synergetic relationship between well-educated, civic-minded men and a nation-state through which they expressed their collective sovereignty, a model that Morgan invokes in her series of essays, "Absenteeism," the transfer of Irish political sovereignty to the British Parliament in London marked a crisis to which much of the literature of the period responds. With no legislative power domiciled in Ireland, and with most adult men of property disenfranchised by their religion, writers could not fit Ireland into the emerging idea of the nation-state and hence of modernity itself. Leslie's and Grattan's efforts to solve the problem through economic modernization via the newly important trading space of the Atlantic give way to a conundrum for individuals, a choice between transatlantic exile or domestic disenfranchisement. Cultural nationalism, moreover, tends to make this choice more difficult for aristocrats: Orr's lower-class "passengers" can freely move to, even hope to become bankers in, the radical utopia of the United States, but in Ireland citizenship in the full political sense is not an option or even a pipe dream for them. For aristocrats whose hereditary rights have been curtailed or denied by the colonial dispensation, including their claim to the civic education that would prepare them on more modern terms for governance in a bureaucratic nation-state, colonial disenfranchisement creates an ongoing crisis of identity. Murrogh O'Brien and Gerald Fitz-Clare both inherit and have earned through reason and education the rights of citizenship, but there is no nation-state to which they can belong: O'Brien ends a mercenary on the continent, and Fitz-Clare a patriot who can do nothing for his country but waste away in grief and then die at the hands of an old enemy. Citizens of a nation that has no state, they belong nowhere.

4

From Terror to Terrorism

Gothic Movements in England

The category of the gothic has been suggestively engaged by a number of postcolonial critics in recent years to grasp Irish writers' depiction of the colonial situation and the racist representation of the Irish. This project has recently moved into a new stage of nationalist gothic studies, one that focuses on a body of work that is distinctively Irish because rooted in Catholic and folk traditions. Irish gothic has thus been conceptually, and controversially, divided on religious terms, between a Protestant gothic tradition read as, in Siobhán Kilfeather's pithy phrase, "an allegory of class guilt," and a "Catholic" Irish gothic that relies on other religious traditions and hence is rooted in the supernatural (broadly conceived) rather than in material threat.[1] Discussions of the Catholic gothic have been invaluable in opening up the gothic canon beyond the Dublin–Protestant focus I note in the introduction to include such important writers as John and Michael Banim. But this scholarship nevertheless keeps the Irish gothic yoked to cultural nationalism's assumption of a unique national culture that grows out of a unique history—and, tacitly if not explicitly, to the assumption that a "minor" nation's literature is about itself.[2] The traditional characterization of the Banims as witnesses to the truth of rural Catholic Ireland is thus translated into the realm of the gothic rather than, say, using the gothic's interest in the gap between perception and truth to challenge the identifications and determinisms that arise from conflating literary realism and history. This chapter seeks, in part, to add a third category to the discussion of Irish gothic literature—Irish gothic (by writers of various faiths) that is, to a significant degree, not about Ireland. This category helps to grasp the fuller complexity of the terms on which the Irish gothic writes back not only to the colonial dispensation, but also to English gothic literature as such. Earlier chapters are concerned with the circulatory routes that link Ireland to other geographical spaces, but this chapter and the next focus instead on the ways in which modes and genres understood as concertedly grounded in Ireland's colonial context and national space—that is, gothic literature and the national tale—push at those boundaries in significant ways and signal that dissidence most obviously through the choice of setting.

Much Irish gothic poetry and prose fiction, of course, is set at least in part in Ireland, including Regina Maria Roche's *Children of the Abbey* (1796); Charles Robert Maturin's *Melmoth the Wanderer* (1820); John Banim's "The Fetches" (1825), recently heralded as the forerunner of Irish Catholic Gothic;[3] J. Sheridan LeFanu's early tales; William Hamilton Maxwell's novels;[4] William Carleton's "Wildgoose Lodge"; and myriad others. W. J. McCormack includes a number of Morgan's Irish novels under this heading, along with further late-eighteenth-century examples.[5] But many other texts, including those on which this chapter focuses, are set partly or entirely in England: Maria Edgeworth's partly (parodically) gothic "Limerick Gloves" and the Banims' more straightforwardly gothic "Church-Yard Watch" and "Chaunt of the Cholera." To this partial list we can add important sections of Maturin's *Melmoth the Wanderer* (1820), LeFanu's later fiction (including his revised tales, such as *Uncle Silas* [1864], which transfer originally Irish plots to English settings), Oscar Wilde's *Picture of Dorian Gray* (1890), and Bram Stoker's *Dracula* (1897), to name just a few.

One of the ongoing concerns of studies of Irish gothic is the relationship of Irish gothic literature to English gothic, a relationship in which the Irish tradition is generally understood as belated or secondary, despite the remarkable success of Irish writers in this far-reaching mode—an exemplary instance of the ways in which Irish literature can be treated as "an offshoot of English writing that was routinely absorbed back into the mainstream of English literary production."[6] McCormack suggests that what "distinguishes [Irish gothic] from the school of Walpole is its pronounced lack of interest in the medieval period" as well as its tendency to "engage[] quite promiscuously with other literary subgenres."[7] I would like to suggest here, however, that another distinctiveness of Irish gothic lies in its use of English settings. For to locate gothic narratives in England is unusual in English gothic fiction before the sensation fiction of the 1860s brought home tales of domestic violence, mystery, and terror—and even then it did so partly through the work of "the Irish Wilkie Collins," J. Sheridan LeFanu.[8] (Indeed, it is arguable that it is Irish gothic that led the English gothic home to roost in the sensation fiction of the Victorian period.) The political gothic, such as William Godwin's *Caleb Williams* (1794), offers notable exceptions, but most of the leading English examples of the gothic novel—from Horace Walpole's *Castle of Otranto* (1764) to Ann Radcliffe's body of work and Matthew G. Lewis's *The Monk* in the 1790s and then to Mary Shelley's *Frankenstein* (1818)—use foreign settings. *Frankenstein* does stop off in Ireland for a few pages, but none of the others set foot in the British Isles. This is an obvious effect of the gothic's interest in otherworldly events, and the oft-noted anti-Catholic elements of English gothic led readily to settings in Catholic Europe.

For Irish gothic to locate itself in contemporary England is thus perhaps the most radical adaptation of English conventions, reversing the anti-Catholic gaze that demanded foreign settings and refusing English readers the comfort of thinking that such terror is remote from their world, a comfort to which Sir Walter Scott, to whom the Banims have been frequently compared because of their historical fiction,[9] drew explicit attention in 1819. Writing of "the English reader," Scott's fictional persona in *Ivanhoe* contends,

> If you describe to him a set of wild manners, and a state of primitive society existing in the Highlands of Scotland, he is much disposed to acquiesce in the truth of what is asserted. And reason good. If he be of the ordinary class of readers, he has either never seen those

> remote districts at all, or he has wandered through those desolate regions in the course of a summer tour, eating bad dinners, sleeping on truckle beds, stalking from desolation to desolation. . . . But the same worthy person, when placed in his own snug parlour, and surrounded by all the comforts of the Englishman's fireside, is not half so much disposed to believe that his own ancestors led a very different life from himself; that the shattered tower, which now forms a vista from his window, once held a baron who would have hung him up at his own door without any form of trial.[10]

It might be tempting to read this shift of setting simply as an effect of the Irish gothic's much-discussed concern with the colonial problem—an early instance of the "empire writ[ing] back," as a major postcolonial work puts it.[11] However, this approach fails to account for significant bodies of Irish writing that engage with the gothic to critique English structures on broader terms. Take, for instance, the canonical example of Maturin's *Melmoth the Wanderer*. In that novel, the demon is an Englishman, and a number of its grisly tales take place in England, as Maturin's novel works hard to collapse the self/Other divide on which English anti-Catholic gothic was based: false imprisonment, familial violence, and religious extremism are to be found in Protestant England and Catholic Europe alike. Moreover, other works of Irish gothic seem to have nothing to do with imperialism at all, including one of the stories discussed here, the Banims' "Church-Yard Watch." This tale also has scant interest in the position of Catholics in the British Isles—distinguishing it markedly from other, but yet not all, works by the Banims.

To explore this third category of Irish gothic, this chapter focuses first on two short stories that use the gothic to represent the "popular" classes, specifically rural and village lower-class populations, but in English settings. These texts also engage with popular literary forms. Edgeworth's "Limerick Gloves" appeared in the collection *Popular Tales*, explicitly directed in the preface, written by Edgeworth's father, to the newly literate lower classes, and the tale arguably inaugurated the popular detective fiction form decades before

Edgar Allan Poe. The Banims' "Church-Yard Watch" is similarly directed at a wide readership—indeed, it was credited with launching the brothers' popularity—and offers a proto-Dickensian glimpse of rural England. The final section of this chapter explores the regionalizing discriminations in the Banims' gothic, international tour de force "Chaunt of the Cholera" in relation to their depictions of different populations within Ireland in the poems they published with "Chaunt." All three works engage not with the gothic's medieval surface, but with the mode's abiding interest in modernity,[12] specifically the myth of English modernity that was used to motivate Irish cultural assimilation and targeted the "popular" classes in particular.

The Myth of Irish Terrorism and the Origins of the English Police: Maria Edgeworth's "Limerick Gloves"

In recent years, studies of Victorian England have traced the alignment of the migrant Irish poor, particularly in the wake of the Great Famine, with social disruption, an unruliness and poverty that mark the Other of English order and prosperity—a nationalist vision promulgated from Early Modern topographical verse to Victorian realist fiction. The classic study of this subject is Louis Perry Curtis's *Apes and Angels* (1971), but recent scholarship has stressed the degree to which the problem for English writers in the Victorian period was Irish immigration specifically.[13] Thomas Carlyle's much-read *Chartism* (1840) provides a particularly gothic elaboration of Irish migration: "Crowds of miserable Irish darken all our towns. . . . the uncivilized Irishman, not by his strength but the opposite of strength, drives out the Saxon native, takes possession in his room. There abides he, in his squalor and unreason, in his falsity and drunken violence, as the ready-made nucleus of degradation and disorder. . . . And yet these poor Celtiberian Irish brothers, what can *they* help it? They cannot stay at home, and starve. It is just and natural that they come hither as a curse to us."[14] As Mary Jean Corbett notes in her generative discussion of *Chartism* along with Elizabeth Gaskell's

North and South (1854–55) and Friedrich Engels's *Condition of the Working Class in England* (1845), the Irish in England were depicted through "a discourse that racializes Irish 'blood' as posing a threat to contaminate the English working classes through proximity and amalgamation."[15] Michael de Nie notes of the Fenian campaign in England, "In the immediate aftermath of events such as Manchester and Clerkenwell, some newspapers went beyond metaphors of sickness and madness," depicting the Irish as madmen in straitjackets or as "wild beasts, alike incapable of rational motives and devoid of human feeling."[16]

Here, I would like to consider earlier representations of Irish migration to England in the context of maintaining national order through conformity of language, religion, and law on English territory. The pre-Victorian focus on Irish migration to England as that of the upper classes (officers, aristocrats), typically single men, puts the emphasis on a problem of governance rather than of unruly subjects.[17] In this category, we can include, for instance, a series of plays by members of the Sheridan–Lefanu family, many of them Irish immigrants to England: Thomas Sheridan's *Brave Irishman* (c. 1750), Richard Brinsley Sheridan's *The Rivals* (1775) and *St. Patrick's Day* (1788), and Alicia Sheridan Lefanu's *Sons of Erin* (1812). As the nineteenth century began, however, the emphasis shifted toward men of less traditionally mobile classes. In "Limerick Gloves," the Irish migrants include an artisan, his elderly mother, and a field laborer. The broader breakdown of ties to place is highlighted by the tale's title: "Limerick gloves" are supposed to be made in Limerick, not rural England, and so the title acknowledges the deregionalization of luxury goods, and John Carr would note about the same time that "it was whispered to [him] that Limerick gloves are manufactured in Dublin also."[18]

Edgeworth published *Popular Tales* in 1804. Pitched at the newly literate "popular" classes, it offers a series of educational narratives in which stoic virtue and obedience are rewarded. Like most of her fiction, it is concerned with education, but unlike her novels it is centrally concerned with the education of the lower classes. Several narratives represent subalterns being rewarded for learning the right lessons, including loyalty to the already-benevolent upper echelons. In "Lame Jervas," for instance, a slave in the West Indies, an Indian prince, and a Cornish coalminer are each allowed greater freedom and wealth and, in response, protect those in the ranks above them. "Limerick Gloves," one of the stories in *Popular Tales*, is similarly concerned with validating benevolence and loyalty, but more than the other stories it stresses the dangers of excessive loyalty and its extension in national prejudice.

I want to locate "Limerick Gloves" within two overlapping contexts: one, the emergence of detective fiction in relation to growing interest in the use of policing to maintain public order in an increasingly mobile population; two, a shift from Early Modern anxieties about religious terrorism to more racialized than sectarian concerns about Irish terrorism on the English mainland. Through these two contexts, I suggest that Edgeworth's tale not only participates in the early emergence of detective fiction and public discourse about policing but also, at this very early moment in that literary history, identifies the Irish as a threat to English civil order because of "popular" problems of prejudice among the English and affective impulsiveness among the Irish. The discomfort with the absorption of Ireland into Britain with the 1800 Act of Union that Ina Ferris has noted and the fears of Irish immigrants that Corbett discusses become hyperbolized here as an anxiety about terrorists threatening the peace and order of the English countryside.

The standard critical narrative of the history of detective fiction asserts that the genre begins with Poe in the early 1840s, though with debts to earlier forms of crime fiction—among them, Godwin's 1794 novel *Caleb Williams*. This novel features a detective, a locked-room mystery of sorts, court scenes, and even a lurid text that harks back to Newgate fiction and forward to the popular pulp that consolidated the detective genre in the twentieth century: a halfpenny work entitled *The Most Wonderful and Surprising History and Miraculous Adventures of Caleb Williams*. "Limerick Gloves" features a series of mysteries, comments explicitly on emerging ideas of public policing, and plays an incompetent bumbling detective against a supremely rational and capable detective, anticipating Poe's Dupin and his narrator, Sir Arthur Conan Doyle's Holmes and his Watson, and myriad other detective pairs. Edgeworth's story narratively defers the solution of the mysteries until the master detective gathers the evidence, reestablishing social order by doing so, in the final paragraphs of the tale. It also registers a relatively overlooked element of detective fiction: the education of the reader in the protocols of detection, from reason and the maintenance of objectivity to forensic methods and criminal psychology. Moreover, in addressing the incapacity of the rural English to react rationally to Irish migrants, Edgeworth's tale also picks up on a key aspect of *Caleb Williams*'s contribution to detective fiction. As Caroline Reitz argues, Godwin's novel uncovers the ways in which ideas of policing emerged in concert with anxiety about imperial governance: Caleb is an early instance in the development of the rational detective who can justly impose order.[19] In "Limerick Gloves," rational detection can resolve English–Irish tensions and, as in *Caleb Williams*, the origins of those tensions lie in England.

In the tale, an Irish glove maker named Brian O'Neill has immigrated to a corner of rural England and is courting the daughter of the local tanner, Hill. Because of their anti-Irish prejudice, wild speculation, and hostility to their daughter's being courted by someone they consider beneath them socially, Mr. and Mrs. Hill convince themselves that a hole in the base of their town's cathedral was made by O'Neill as part of his plan to bomb the building. In the meantime, we see O'Neill helping out a local single-parent family that had recently lost its home to fire; the Hills' daughter, Phoebe, concludes on the basis of his benevolence that her parents' prejudices are ill-founded. To protect the cathedral, Mr. Hill, who is also churchwarden, rallies local support for his views and institutes a watch to guard the cathedral while they also hatch a plan to arrest the glove maker for debt. Hill buys a bill from one of O'Neill's creditors, calls it in during the evening when ready money is not available, and then has O'Neill arrested for debt. O'Neill's mother bails him out, so Mr.

Hill continues his plot against the glove maker, eventually going to a local con man, who is posing as a gypsy with the magical power of omniscience, to get confirmation of all of his suspicions about the glove maker. Hill then goes to the local magistrate to tell his tale of Irish terrorism: he holds O'Neill responsible for the loss of his guard dog, the destruction of his rick of oak bark, and the hole in the foundations of the cathedral where, he says, a bomb is to be placed, and the con man has confirmed all of this. The magistrate, a paragon of Enlightenment rationality, pulls apart Hill's evidence bit by bit, mocks him for taking the word of a con man, and then distills the actual evidence of the case through interrogations and a physical investigation of the cathedral. They discover that it was the con man who stole the dog; that the angry Irish fieldworkers, led by Paddy M'Cormack (acting out of loyalty to his countryman, O'Neill), had destroyed the rick of oak bark; and that rats had dug a hole in the foundations of the cathedral. With all explained and the con man arrested, Mr. Hill gives up his prejudice against the Irish, though the tale, as is common in Edgeworth's fiction, allows for the mocking of the lower-class Irish. Brian O'Neill is accepted as an equal; Paddy M'Cormack remains an outlandish character with peculiar habits, strange speech, and an unthinking loyalty that makes it easy for him to break the law, including by organizing his friends to strike in darkness against English property necessary for English industry.

So unfounded fears of a plot to blow up a rural cathedral in England cause the gossipy linking of various minor crimes in the neighborhood into a terrorist plot by an Irish glove maker recently arrived in the area, and vigilante action against the glove maker provokes vandalism by local Irish fieldworkers of a sort not unusual in eighteenth-century Irish agrarian unrest. As in so many of Edgeworth's tales, this action is classed: the artisanal classes, centrally the Irish glove maker O'Neill and the English tanner Hill, misunderstand each other because of national prejudice and cultural differences, particularly in the management of business affairs. The lower classes, including the English con man and the hot-headed Irish fieldworkers, compound these difficulties through criminal activity. The moral lesson is straightforward: prejudice leads to paranoia, eventually creating actual violence among the lower classes, while the calm light of reason among the upper echelons reveals much more ordinary crimes and so mollifies terror.

The most peculiar part of the tale is perhaps the plot device of an Irish terrorist plan to bomb a cathedral. In 1804, there was no historical precedent for an Irish bombing, let alone on the English mainland. Much later there were the Fenian attacks of the 1860s, including an attack on a police van and the infamous bombing of an English prison in which many bystanders were killed. But even the first historical bombing in Belfast, discussed by Kerby A. Miller, took place in 1816, a dozen years after Edgeworth's story was published.[20] The narrative's historical precedents lie in what Lady Morgan would call in 1827 "the bugbears of terrorism" (*O'Briens*, 88), a specifically sectarian anxiety about religious conspiracies that threaten political hegemony: the Gunpowder Plot, the Bye Plot, and other early-seventeenth-century religious plots made terrorism part of the cultural imaginary and tied it ineluctably, though not exclusively, to religious difference.[21] William Preston's rather bizarre four-canto poem *The Female Congress* (1779) reminds us that these differences could even be within Protestantism. This Church of Ireland poet, a lawyer and later a magistrate, personifies Methodism as a harlot who, at the end, drives a mob to arson:

> But *Methodism* sublime in air appear'd;
> A bloody standard to the mob she rear'd;
> Her red right hand a flaming firebrand bore,
> And Suicide had stain'd her robes with gore.
> Demoniac Frenzy clamour'd at her side,
> Despairing Anguish, and religious Pride.
> In peals of thunder to the croud she calls:
> "Raze, raze, my children! . . ."[22]

The Gunpowder Plot in particular is salient to Edgeworth's tale, as it led to longstanding fears of incendiary devices being placed underneath English institutional buildings. Citing Philip Anthony Brown's *The French Revolution in English History*, James Whitlark has noted, for instance, that "the Birmingham riot of 1789 came partly because the Dissenter Priestley had written about laying gunpowder under superstition—superstition being one of those catchwords for crypto Catholicism. His language, however, reminded Anglicans of the Roman Catholic terrorist Guy Fawkes, so the rioters assumed that the Dissenters would likewise try to bomb Parliament."[23] Edgeworth's tale was written in the wake of the Irish Uprising of 1798, a conflict led by a pan-sectarian organization with a leadership drawn from both Dissenting and Catholic traditions, recalling the cross-sectarian associations that stoked the flames of the Birmingham riot. The story is thus closely tied to its cultural moment and the sorts of panics that led J. J. Stockdale to warn his readers in 1810, "Oh Protestants, observe then, as you have done hitherto, towards your Catholic brethren, perfect tolerance, perfect charity:—but, always bear in mind the fable of the wolves and the sheep. *Remember never to give up your vigilance. Remember the massacre of St. Bartholemew*,"[24] referring to a sectarian massacre of Protestants in sixteenth-century France (represented, as we shall see in the next chapter, in early-nineteenth-century Irish fiction, including a novel by Morgan that appeared soon after Edgeworth's *Popular Tales*).

The religious basis for fears of terrorism in England is comparatively muted yet clearly present in Edgeworth's narrative. For instance, when Hill is trying to persuade his fellow townspeople that O'Neill is plotting to bomb the cathedral, "several of the club had laughed at this idea; others, who supposed that Mr. O'Neill was a Roman Catholic, and who had a confused notion that a Roman Catholic *must* be a very wicked dangerous being, thought that there might be a great deal in the churchwarden's suggestions."[25] That Hill is also a churchwarden and that the cathedral rather than a public, secular building is the target intensify the religious underpinnings of the narrative, which Edgeworth counters through a secular, rational discourse of public policing that investigates clues rather than follows prejudice and panic. But even as the story offers Enlightenment reason as the solution to sectarian violence, it transforms religious terrorism into Irish terrorism.

Edgeworth metonymically addresses the question of religion through superstition. Hill goes to Bampfylde the Second, king of the gypsies—actually, a con man—for confirmation of his suspicions about O'Neill. Visiting Bampfylde in a twig hut in the forest, Hill is instantly made ridiculous. He not only loses his wig as he enters the small hut but also has his pockets picked by Bampfylde's accomplice while he stands "speechless" at the con man's "sublime appearance" (197). Bampfylde is the one historical character of the tale: he was the subject of a popular sensationalist work called *An Apology for the Life of Bampfylde Moore Carew*, and reprinted in various versions throughout the rest of the eighteenth century. *Apology* bridges exoticist literature about the Romani people and post-Newgate sensationalist crime literature, and it is cited in a variety of literary works, from Edgeworth's tale to Mary Elizabeth Braddon's *Lady Audley's Secret* (1862).

Apart from a suggestive invocation of crime literature in Edgeworth's early contribution to detective fiction, recalling Godwin's incorporation of a pamphlet about Caleb Williams, the popularity of the *Apology* also speaks to an expectation that the readers of the tale will know precisely how foolish Mr. Hill is for being awestruck by Bampfylde. Bampfylde obviously plays him:

> "Do you know a dangerous Irishman, of the name of O'Neill; who has come, for purposes best known to himself, to settle at Hereford?"
>
> "Yes, we know him well."
>
> "Indeed! And what do you know of him?"
>
> "That he is a dangerous Irishman."
>
> "Right! And it was he, was it not, that made away with my dog Jowler, that used to guard the tan-yard?"
>
> "It was."
>
> "And who was it that pulled down, or caused to be pulled down, my rick of oak-bark?"

> "It was the person that you suspect."
>
> "And was it the person whom I suspect that made the hole under the foundation of our cathedral?"
>
> "The same, and no other."
>
> "And for what purpose did he make that hole?"
>
> "For a purpose that must not be named," replied the king of the gipsies; nodding his head in a mysterious manner. (197)

This is the full extent of Mr. Hill's investigation. Before this, he has orchestrated the arrest of O'Neill by calling in a debt early, set up a guard to watch the cathedral, and busied himself with convincing his fellow villagers of the conspiracy, but he has questioned no one and investigated no crime scene. Hill dutifully runs off to the magistrate the next day and informs him that he has saved the cathedral:

> "Our Hereford cathedral, Sir, would have been blown up—blown up from the foundation, if it had not been for me, Sir!"
>
> "Indeed, Mr. Churchwarden! And pray how, and by whom, was the cathedral to be blown up; and what was there diabolical in this ball?"
>
> Here Mr. Hill let Mr. Marshal into the whole history of his early dislike to O'Neill, and his shrewd suspicions of him the first moment he saw him in Hereford; related in the most prolix manner all that the reader knows already, and concluded by saying that, as he was now certain of his facts, he was come to swear examinations against this villainous Irishman, who, he hoped, would be speedily brought to justice, as he deserved. (198–99)

Marshal instantly turns to matters of facts and evidence, matters completely ignored by Hill, who has been guided only by his prejudices, his fears, and his superstitious faith in Bampfylde:

> "To justice he shall be brought, as he deserves," said Mr. Marshal; "but, before I write, and before you swear, will you have the goodness to inform me how you have made yourself as certain as you evidently are, of what you call your facts?"

> "Sir, that is a secret," replied our wise man, "which I shall trust to you alone;" and he whispered into Mr. Marshal's ear that his information came from Bampfylde the second, king of the gipsies.
>
> Mr. Marshal instantly burst into laughter; then composing himself said, "My good Sir, I am really glad that you have proceeded no farther in this business; and that no one in Hereford, besides myself, knows that you were on the point of swearing examinations against a man on the evidence of Bampfylde the second, king of the gipsies." (199)

A footnote is attached to Marshal's assessment of Bampfylde's "evidence." It is the only footnote in the 1804 edition of the story, and it cites Patrick Colquhoun's *Treatise on the Police of the Metropolis* of 1796, a key work in the early development of modern policing (199n.). Colquhoun's text appears to be a source for this section of the narrative, offering a case in which

> a person having property stolen from him, went to consult the conjuror respecting the thief; who having described something like the person of a man whom he suspected, his credulity and folly so far got the better of his reason and reflection, as to induce him upon the authority of this impostor *actually to charge his neighbour with a felony*, and to cause him to be apprehended. The Magistrate settled the matter by discharging the prisoner, reprimanding the accuser severely, and ordering the conjuror to be taken into custody *as a rogue and a vagabond.*[26]

In other words, the Bampfylde portion of Edgeworth's narrative not only displaces Catholic–Anglican hostility by reframing the central issue as the Enlightenment alternatives of reason and superstition but also ties the narrative firmly to Colquhoun's model for handling the crimes that result from a capitalist economy. The narrative of this case appears in chapter 7 of the *Treatise*, where Colquhoun deals with "*reasons . . . why forgeries and frauds must prevail in a certain degree, wherever the interchange of property is extensive.*"[27]

This concern with economic transactions recalls the central and material difficulty between Hill and O'Neill: O'Neill does not understand English business practices. O'Neill, according to the narrator, is only vulnerable through the bill used to set him up as a debtor because he has a laxity in business matters that is represented as distinctively Irish and foreign to practice in England:

> Our Irish hero had not that punctuality which English tradesmen usually observe in the payment of bills. . . . This want of punctuality in money transactions, and this mode of treating contracts as matters of favour and affection, might not have damned the fame of our hero in his own country, where such conduct is, alas! too common; but he was now in a kingdom where the manners and customs are so directly opposite that he could meet with no allowance for his national faults. It would be well for his countrymen if they were made, even by a few mortifications, somewhat sensible of this important difference in the habits of Irish and English traders, before they come to settle in England. (194)

In the narrator's view, the real problem in Hereford is not religious difference or Irish migration, but a failure to properly educate the Irish in the correct behavior for a capitalist economy: the solution thus lies in a magistrate who behaves as Colquhoun's magistrate behaves in the flawed capitalist economy of London. He dismisses superstition and sifts through the actual evidence, bringing the values of the Enlightenment to bear on capitalist disarray. It is this capitalist underpinning, however, that facilitates Edgeworth's rewriting of terrorism as cultural and national rather than religious, aligning Irishness simultaneously with the precapitalist, the premodern, and the religious terrorism of centuries earlier.

The tanner's circulation of his belief that O'Neill is a terrorist propels a number of other conflicts in the text that set the Irish immigrant community against their English neighbors, demonstrating the wider danger of the tanner's vigilante policing of his neighborhood. Edgeworth thus argues not only for the merits of reason over prejudice, but also for the necessity of public policing over the sort of informal policing practiced by the tanner and then common in England as well as pursued with tragic results in Ireland. Between "Limerick Gloves" and James Porter's famous United Irishman satire *Billy Bluff and the 'Squire*, there are considerable continuities in the missteps by which faulty conclusions are made about Irish insurgency. It is tempting to read Edgeworth's magistrate as an answer to Porter's paranoid and illogical squire, who accepts what he hears if it accords with his prejudices and juggles facts around until he reaches the conclusion that he is surrounded by conspiracy and insurgency. The magistrate instead tests testimony and applies logic to reveal the peacefulness of the region. Edgeworth's vision of public policing is also an extension of what Ria Omasreiter has discussed as Adam Smith's influence on Edgeworth's writing, particularly "the impartial spectator" as an "abstraction" of the "interests and judgments of the community."[28] Instead of rousing insurgency, this objective observer engenders order.

Edgeworth's story is thus an early instance of detection being used to address crimes that directly threaten the public interest and that are best investigated by those who are held accountable for serving that interest. Moreover, the tale was published in *Popular Tales*, a collection of narratives underaddressed in recent Edgeworth criticism, which has generally focused on her Irish novels rather than on her moralizing short fiction. The volume was published by radical printer Joseph Johnson and also widely available in circulating libraries, as well as pitched, in its preface and its title, at the masses.[29] These pedagogical tales often tie elements of the detective form to the popularization of scientific method as the means of establishing an orderly, rational public. Edgeworth's "Limerick Gloves" thus offers instruction in a number of arenas: through O'Neill, she demonstrates key principles of English business practices and what can go wrong if migrants are ignorant of them; through Hill, she warns against prejudice and superstition as productive of terror and crime; and through Marshal, she demonstrates proper rational methods for detecting crime and restoring social order, especially the careful (but not leading) interrogation of witnesses and investigation of the crime scenes. But even with this relatively benign educational agenda, Edgeworth's vandalizing fieldworkers and the bomb plot position Irish migration to England as the first cause of the need for such instruction—terror and rural violence are presented as the effects of lower-class geographical mobility.

Bampfylde crystallizes this dimension of the tale. A migratory thief posing as "Bampfylde Moore Carew, king of the gipsies" (196), he is the locus of the tale's mock-gothic elements: Edgeworth associates belief in Bampfylde's "supernatural skill" with the lower orders of Hereford's society, as "numbers of servant-maids and 'prentices went to consult him," and with the lesser intellects among the higher classes, as "it was whispered that he was resorted to, secretly, by some whose education might have taught them better sense," including Hill, who "revolved great designs in his secret soul" to consult Bampfylde (196). After having a confused dream about bombs and "oak-bark turned into mutton-steaks, after which his great dog Jowler was swimming," Hill interprets the dream as confirmation of the wisdom of his decision to go to Bampfylde (196). Bampfylde's first appearance in the narrative draws heavily, and ironically, on the language of the sublime: "[Hill] now beheld, by the light of some embers, the person of his gipsey majesty, to whose sublime appearance this dim light was so favourable that it struck a secret awe into our wise man's soul; and, forgetting Hereford cathedral, and oak-bark, and Limerick gloves, he stood for some seconds speechless" (197). All gothic terrors are revealed to be based on fraud or unruly imaginations, but the English experience of both sublimity and terror is traceable to an inability to properly judge migratory figures. Hence, even as Edgeworth associates the Irish with the failure to behave properly, she locates the origin of English gothic in the inability to analyze and respond properly to those not native to England—whether "gipsy" fortune tellers or Irish artisans. The focus of English gothic fiction on the remote past or continental Europe is thus reframed as an English incapacity to understand cultural difference.

Domestic Terror and the Banims' "Church-Yard Watch"

The Banim brothers are best known for a significant corpus of novels and tales set in Ireland that address in broadly realist terms the history and consequences of Ireland's status as an internal colony. While John Banim and Michael Banim wrote much individually, they also closely collaborated as "The O'Hara Family" on a number of novels and a collection of poetry as well as on other literary projects. The Banims were among the first of a new generation of Irish writers who came not from Dublin or Belfast, but from less urban areas of Ireland. Such writers were the product of a confluence of forces: the erosion of the Irish language in rural areas and so a shift to English letters; rising literacy rates among the lower classes and rural populations; and a nationalist movement that was explicitly grounded in cultural production. The Banims' "popularity" thus occupies the intersection of a variety of notions of the "popular" classes: the populace as the foundation of the nation and the arbiter of its legitimacy; the populace as the lower classes who became literate at this time; writers "popular" because they offered an opportunity to connect to an authentic but disappearing national past.

This national past is a highly problematic one, however. Posited as a "natural" ground, it was highly contested in its details, in part because it was a key element of an emergent nationalism predicated on the sovereignty of the people as a whole: thus, the popular culture was presented as the authentic national culture (in distinction to contemporary arguments that the elite culture was the best representation of national merit) and its disappearance as an erosion of national integrity. Such claims drew their philosophical support from a branch of nationalism inflected by concepts of the primitive. Writers from Friedrich Schiller to William Wordsworth asserted that rural peoples and children were the strongest link to a national origin in which the natural still held sway: as Schiller wrote, "They are what we were; they are what we should once again become. We were natural just as they, and our culture, by means of reason and freedom, should lead us back to nature."[30] In combination with the emergence of nationalism in the late eighteenth century as an ideology in which political sovereignty resides in the people rather than in the state and the people cohere through a shared culture, this primitivism facilitated critiques of the present nation based on the need to return to a prior, more authentic national culture—one sought through antiquarian scholarship in particular in the late eighteenth and early nineteenth centuries. In Ireland, an "internal colony" of Britain, this more authentic culture was implicitly valorized for being distinct from the British culture that purportedly dominated urban areas.

At the same time, however, anglicization was tied to the promise of modernity: economic prosperity, growing literacy rates, and, most crucially for Irish national aspirations, a population capable of sovereignty because sufficiently well educated to be self-governing and economically successful. This paradox is fundamentally a romantic one, often rationalized through a "national tale" in which national distinctiveness is preserved as an object of private study while the nation's public sphere moves forward into a more English modernity. Scott's *Waverley* is perhaps the widest-known example of this kind of narrative—as the highlanders disappear, they leave behind them artifacts that sit in the parlors of those reconciled to civil and economic progress on English terms—but it also appears in earlier Irish instances, including Morgan's *Wild Irish Girl*. Instead of seeing the Banims, William Carleton, and others as "native informants" (in Gayatri Spivak's phrase) on rural Irish culture, then, we need to see their body of work as an intervention into a larger debate about the value and nature of "true Irishness" in a colonial context complicated by Adam Smith's "four-stages" theory (see chapter 1). For even as antiquarians lauded the past for the naturalness of its culture, economic thought privileged progress and identified agrarian economies with social backwardness. A commercial—and increasingly an industrial—economy was the dominant sign of modernity.

As Helen O'Connell has argued, Cesar Otway and Carleton write of rural Ireland in order to mark its modernization through anglicization.[31] Englishness brings access to trade markets and thus the promise of full participation in a future that capitalism will make prosperous. However, the Englishness being lauded across the Irish Channel by Wordsworth and others was one that, like the Irishness the Banims were supposed to embody, was rooted in the rural people, the cultural past, and a language that was "natural" to its speakers—not the English modernity of commercialism, urban trading centers, and imperial expansion. Thus, a third notion of the primitive served British political interests by devaluing Irish national authenticity through the representation of the Irish as corrupted rather than "noble" savages and hence the increasing use of negative Irish stereotypes in popular English culture, especially depictions of the Irish as alcoholic or superstitious and, in the racist lexicon of the nineteenth century, apelike. Irish people were thus barred simultaneously from anglicizing progress (because too primitive) and from an authentic national origin (because of alcohol, false beliefs, or degeneracy), even as the writers of the Irish "improvement" school exhorted rural Irish people to conform to English modernity, and some English nationalists, such as Wordsworth, celebrated "low and rustic life" as purer examples of "the primary laws of our nature."[32]

The Banims were not generally of the "improvement" school. While Carleton was celebrating the spread of the English language in Ireland, the Banims were writing material that, though in English, was broadly critical of the British and the Anglo-Irish. In her analysis of John Banim's 1828 novel *The Anglo-Irish of the Nineteenth Century*, Ferris compellingly argues for Banim's attempt to revise the national tale in order to situate the Anglo-Irish as a group alienated both from Ireland and from England, a project also pursued by such contemporary writers as Regina Maria Roche in *Tradition of the Castle* (1824) and Morgan in *The O'Briens and the O'Flahertys* (1827) and echoed in work on the Anglo-Irish, Protestant gothic.[33] According to the *Library of the World's Best Literature*, the Banim brothers' 1838 collection *A Bit o' Writin' and Other Tales* was the one that made them famous. In the somewhat florid prose characteristic of the headnotes to works included in the *Library*, the headnote on the Banims rhapsodizes, "The minor chords of the soft music of the Gaelic English as it fell from the tongues of Irish lads and lasses, whether in note of sorrow or of sport, had already begun to touch with winsome tenderness the stolid Saxon hearts, when that idyl of their country's penal days, 'The Bit o' Writin',' was sent out from the O'Hara fireside. The almost instantaneous success and popularity of their first stories speedily broke down the anonymity of the Banims, and publishers became eager and gain-giving."[34] This is not the first indication of the Banims' reputation as painters of true Irishness. The second number of the *Dublin University Magazine*, after complaining that "Irishmen are described as little superior, in externals, to the orang-outangs of Madagascar," praises one of the Banims for "sketches of Irish character [that] bear with them a forcible evidence of reality."[35] Such claims anticipate much recent Banim criticism in stressing the Irishness of the Banims' writing, both in language and content, but the *Dublin University Magazine* complaint registers the exoticization of otherness that shadows such "realism." Hence, the *Library* characterizes *A Bit o' Writin' and Other Tales* as an "idyl of [Ireland's] penal days," the century and a half between the Treaty of Limerick and Catholic Emancipation in 1829, when the penal statutes were in force to oppress Catholics economically and politically—hardly "idyllic." The excerpt the *Library* selects from *A Bit o' Writin'* confirms this view of the Banims as "native informants" to an English audience receptive to the exoticization of the Irish.

However, the Banims also wrote material that eschewed realism and was set in England. John Banim, who lived in London for most of his adult life, published, for instance, a futuristic novel called *Revelations of the Dead-Alive* (1824), in which the narrator uses a trance to transport himself to 2023 London, where he discovers that women no longer wear stays and the moon has been colonized by balloon ship. Banim's central objective in the novel, however, is to critique 1820s English culture ("an age," a character remarks in the twenty-first century, "towards which we cannot rationally entertain much respect"), and his protagonist discovers early in the novel that no one reads William Wordsworth anymore, though Byron and

Moore are admired and "Lady Morgan is still known to us . . . as a female thinker of much force and imagination."[36] The story with which the third volume of the Banims' 1838 collection opens is similarly not Irish in setting or language; "The Church-Yard Watch" is, like *Revelations*, set in England and, like *Revelations*, has anti-Wordsworthian elements. And it draws on a mode, the gothic, that the satiric *Revelations* identifies with British writers. As a character remarks, "Horace Walpole's little crude tale is the first parent of all that wild legend in our language; that Lewis is its more fruitful propagator; and that Ann Radcliff is its first, and Mr. Campbell its last and most successful adaptor or modifier"—the joke here being that Scott's historical novels are in the twenty-first century not only attributed to the Scottish poet Thomas Campbell but also identified with the English gothic tradition of the previous century, exploding Scott's reputation in 1820s England.[37]

"The Church-Yard Watch" first appeared in the giftbook *Friendship's Offering* in 1832 and was republished in 1833 before appearing again in 1838.[38] The tale is set in an unspecified location in rural England and draws on conventional dialect transcriptions of rural English speech with a northern flavor: "I am put upon by one and t'other of you; ye sleep in comfort every night, and leave me to go a-watching, out o'doors, there, in all weathers, but stop a bit, my man, it shan't be this way much longer" (318). The traces of Anglo-Saxon are pronounced in such passages: *a-watching* is what the *Oxford English Dictionary* terms "a worn-down proclitic form of OE. preposition"; *ye* is a close derivative of the Old English pronoun; and *t'other* marks the dialect as northern English, *t'* being a regional contraction of *the*. This story is, moreover, not one that could be characterized as an "idyll." First published a few years before Charles Dickens's *Pickwick Papers*, the Banims' tale addresses the difficult social issues for which Dickens's fiction would become known—child labor, domestic violence, and alcoholism. While much of Dickens's work, like Wordsworth's, would align cities with the worst examples of such social problems, the Banims' tale finds all three in a small rural village. This village has only two landmarks: the graveyard and "the Tap," where the protagonist's stepfather gets drunk every night. Moreover, the tale is presented by ethnographic narrators who recall the folkloric collections of romantic-era Ireland, from Thomas Crofton Croker's *Fairy Legends and Traditions of the South of Ireland* (1825) to Samuel Lover's *Legends and Stories of Ireland* (1832), crucial to what Richard Haslam describes as a "distinctive feature of Irish Gothic—its recurrent incorporation of folklore."[39] But here the folklore and the ethnographic objects of study are English.

In "The Church-Yard Watch," the ethnographic narrators present a history of a middle-aged man who is responsible for watching the graveyard at night to protect the dead from grave robbers of the Burke and Hare sort. In the narrative present, he is a quietly oppressive force: "the ghastly sentinel of the dead," even "his own children feared or disliked him, and did not smile or whisper in his presence" (317). He is not, however, the villain of the piece, but its victim. At the outset, the narrators, who present themselves as investigators of rural life, note, "We have seen and spoken with such an unhappy being, who seemed to have lost, in the struggle which conquered nature's especial antipathy, (nature in a breast and mind like his, at least,) most of the other sympathies of his kind" (317). As a youth, however, "the ill-fated lad promised . . . to be of an open, kindly, intelligent character" (318). The bulk of the narrative serves to recount this struggle, one in which the Wordsworthian child of nature is cast into darkness by a domestic world of violence and alcoholism. This child, suggestively named "Will," is an unspecified age, but old enough that some of his peers are already laborers—he is considered too weak to work and is in many respects a forerunner of the "sensitive" invalid that would soon become a recurring figure in English fiction, from Emily Brontë's *Wuthering Heights* (1847) to Thomas Hughes's *Tom Brown's Schooldays* (1857) and Frances Hodgson Burnett's *The Secret Garden* (1909). Will's sensitivity is shocked into "nerveless insensibility" (317) when Will is forced by his stepfather, Hunks, to take over his job as the churchyard watch so that Hunks can continue to pocket the wages while spending his nights uninterrupted at the Tap. Two nights watching over the dead for his stepfather, and Will is permanently altered from "open" and "kindly" to "ill-fated" and "unhappy."

Will's early life alone is idyllic: "He was the only child of an affectionate and gentle-mannered father" (317), who gave him the dog that is Will's constant companion for the early part of the tale. Hunks complains that Will and his dog fail to work, being "down by the marshes . . . or gone a-nutting, or lying stretched in the sun, the two idlers together" (318). This passing reference to "nutting" would have been recognizable to the Banims' readers as a theme in a famous Wordsworth poem, "Nutting," now known for its treatment of violence and nature. Will, like the speaker of "Nutting," describes his experiences in the natural world on terms rather different from his stepfather's account of him as an "idler" and wanderer. In "Nutting," harvesting hazelnuts is presented as a violation of the natural world:

> Then up I rose,
> And dragged to earth both branch and bough, with crash
> And merciless ravage; and the shady nook
> Of hazels, and the green and mossy bower,
> Deformed and sullied, patiently gave up
> Their quiet being.[40]

In the Banims' tale, Will tells his mother, "I walk out sometimes by the river, and, listening to the noise of the water over the rocks, where it is shallow, and to the rustling of the trees as they nod in the twilight, voices and shrieks come around me—sometimes they break in my ears—and I have turned to see what thing it was that spoke, and thought some grey tree at my side had only just changed and become motionless, and seemed as if, a moment before, it had been something else, and had a tongue, and said the words that frightened me" (319–20). Beyond the general trope of articulate nature, there are close parallels here with Wordsworth's poem. While Will "listen[s] to the noise of the water over the rocks," for instance, Wordsworth's speaker listens to "fairy water-breaks" that "murmur on": "with my cheek on one of those green stones / That, fleeced with moss, beneath the shady trees . . . I heard the murmur and the murmuring sound."[41] But rather than the "murmuring sound" of "that sweet mood" that comforts Wordsworth's speaker,[42] Will hears "voices and shrieks" and "the words that frighten[] [him]."

This alteration is prefigured by an exchange of fathers. After Will's "affectionate" father died, "His mother wept a month, mourned three months more,—and was no longer a widow. Her second husband proved a surly fellow, who married her little fortune, rather than herself, as the means of keeping his quart pot filled, almost from morning to night, at the village Tap, where he played good-fellow and politician to the expressed admiration of all his companions" (317–18). This "surly fellow," Hunks, is the center of the tale's pervasive violence, and that violence is directed at those left behind by the "affectionate" father's death. Will, for instance, has a dog that he treasures as a gift from his dead father. The dog is the only figure in the tale who enjoys an uncomplicated romantic innocence: "His poor dumb companion—friend of his boyhood, and his father's gift—coiled himself up before the blaze, and prepared to surrender his senses to happy sleep, interspersed with dreams of all the sports he had enjoyed with his master that day" (318). Hunks repeatedly beats Will's dog, and, it is implied, Will's mother as well. When she tries to convince Hunks to release Will from the churchyard watch, he gives her "a fixed look, which, short as they had been one flesh, she had reason to understand and shrink at" (319). Moreover, the narrative indicates that even she is morally questionable, having married Hunks too soon after her first husband's death. The domestic scene only gets nastier, however, as Hunks becomes more enraged: "'Don't lay hands on him!' screamed the mother as he strode towards the boy—'what I have often told you, has come to pass, Master Hunks—you have killed him!'" (319).

Will turns to nature for escape but only finds the dead and other violent homes. Will tells his mother,

> You know the lone house all in ruins upon the hill—I fear it, mother, more than my tongue can tell you! I have been taken through it,

> in my dreams, in terrible company, and here I could describe to you its bleak apartments, one by one—its vaults, pitch dark, and half-filled with stones and rubbish, and choked up with weeds—its winding, creeping staircases, and its flapping windows—I know them all, though my feet never yet crossed its threshold!—Never, mother—though I have gone near it, to enter it, and see if what I had dreamt of it was true—and I went in the first light of the morning; but when close by the old door-way, the rustle of shrubs and weeds startled me, and I thought—but sure *that* was fancy—that some one called me in by name—and then I turned and raced down the hill, never looking back till I came to the meadow ground where cows and sheep are always grazing, and heard the dogs barking in the town, and voices of the children at play! (320)

I have quoted this passage at length because of its insistent shaping of the haunted space as a gothic shadow of the rural. The gothic house, in ruins, with "winding staircases," "flapping windows," mysterious "rustl[ing]," and a voice "calling [him] in by name" is juxtaposed with the happy pastoral vision of a meadow with grazing animals and "voices of the children at play." But Will also contrasts two views of the house: one in his dreams, where he is "in terrible company," and one "in the first light of morning," when he is startled by sounds that he "fanc[ies]" were "some one call[ing] [him] in by name." These spectral perceptions mark the child's sensitivity to the dead. He tells his mother that he has dreamed of the dead since he was four years old and complains, "they used to come in such crowds around my cradle!" (319). Will occupies a liminal space between dream and reality, between solitude and "terrible company"—an invalid who sees the living and the dead, an abused child who finds horror where he should find comfort.

The world of "The Church-Yard Watch," then, is one of Wordsworthian rural innocence derailed by a violent figure—Hunks, the churchyard watch, nasty drunk, and abusive father figure. Will bears the brunt of the shock of the turn from pastoral idyll to gothic nightmare. "The Church-Yard Watch" traces the history of a child who fails to mature into the more adult perspective represented by Wordsworth's male protagonists and so fails to enjoy the natural harmonies that restore the mind after stress in much romantic literature. He is thus defined not by his return to nature and its soothing "murmurs," but by the repetition of his return first to the violent home and then to the churchyard where the dead lie; he matures without growing, and he survives without healing. While Will finds some joy among the dead, who play with rather than threaten him, this structure of repetition is bleakly summarized by the opening lines about the adult Will, who produces the same response in his own children that his stepfather elicited from him.

Not surprisingly given his supernatural ability (or delusion), Will is terrified by Hunks's idea to force him to take the churchyard watch in his place. The Banims spare their readers the depiction of the boy's fright during his first night as the watch, providing only a sketchy account that ends, "He had a pause from agony, then a struggle for departing reason, and then he was at rest" (322). Just as he faints when confronted with Hunks's violence in the scene where it is made clear that his mother is a battered wife, he faints a second time when confronted with the nightly horror of being the churchyard watch—one tropes the other, as the sensitive boy's only recourse in the face of his own powerlessness and fear is to lose all sensibility and faint. The story closes with an extensive description of his second night in the churchyard. It begins,

> The imaginary whispers he had heard the previous night—small, cautious whispers—came round him again; first, from a distance, then, nearer and nearer. At last he shaped them into words—"Let us walk," they said—"though he watches us, he fears us." *He*!—'twas strange to hear the dim dead speak to a living man, of himself! the maniac laughed again at the fancy, and replied to them:—
>
> "Ay, come! appear! I give leave for it. Ye are about in crowds, I know, not yet daring to take up your old bodies till I please; but up with them!—Graves, split on, and yield me my subjects! for am I not king of the church-yard? Obey me! ay, now your mouths

> gape—and what a yawning!—are ye musical, too?—a jubilee of groans! out with it, in the name of Death!—blast it about like giants carousing! (322)

The Banims do not rely on supernatural motifs here but make the boy's terrors a clear consequence of his more daily dread: it is "imaginary whispers" that he "shape[s] into words" and then knits into his own fantasy of power. In the churchyard, he is not the boy who cannot protect himself, his mother, or his dog from his stepfather's violence; he is "king of the church-yard," echoing his mother's pet name for him when they are alone, "my king" (318). The graveyard reinstantiates in limited ways the safety and solitude of the domestic space without the disruptive figure of Hunks—Will is the only living male within the churchyard's boundaries, and so he is king.

Will then invites the dead to rise up from their graves and dance in a passage evocative of G. A. Bürger's "Leonore," already available in English in a number of translations before James Clarence Mangan offered two different translations not long after this Banim story's publication. It is not a simple dance, but a carnivalesque inversion that reveals sexual scandals and transgressions of class: "They'll dance anon. Minuets, at least. Why they begin already!—and what partners!—a tall, genteel young officer takes out our village witch of the wield—she that died at Christmas—and our last rector smirks to a girl of fifteen—ha! ha! yon tattered little fellow is a radical, making a leg to the old duchess!—music! music!" (322). This vision of the dead does not level all but mixes high with low and transgresses the boundaries of polite behavior, so that the rector can "smirk[] to a girl of fifteen." In the boy's "fancy," he is not a part of the natural world, but the ruler of the dead—the dead who, like the battered boy-king, play with inversions of power. The boy's vision is not just a strangely happy one, however. Bruce Willis's character in the movie that turns upon the same plot device, *The Sixth Sense* (1999, M. Night Shyamalan), has to learn to see himself among the dead that haunt the child, but the Banims' protagonist is shocked by a different kind of recognition. He stops in the middle of calling to the dead to dance and interjects, "but what face is here?" The narrator continues, "it was the vision of a child's face, which he believed he caught staring at him through the glass of his watch-box—the face of an only brother who had died young. The wretch's laughter changed into tears and low wailings. By the time that his mother came to seek him, just at day-break, he was, however, again laughing; but in such a state as to frighten mirth from her heart and lips till the day she died" (322). Confronted with an image of innocence that has died young, the boy is shocked into an insensibility that permanently alienates him from those in the village, even his doting mother. His inability to face his dead brother also resonates with his mother's failure to mourn her first husband in her haste to remarry. This is a child who cannot inhabit the Wordsworthian ideal because he is shadowed by domestic terror, and he cannot enter fully into a gothic narrative in which he is "king of the church-yard" because he is also haunted by the grief that Wordsworth's "We Are Seven" wishes away through obstinate childhood innocence:

> "Seven boys and girls are we;
> Two of us in the church-yard lie,
> Beneath the church-yard tree."
>
> "You run about, my little Maid,
> Your limbs they are alive;
> If two are in the church-yard laid,
> Then ye are only five."
>
> "Their graves are green, they may be seen,"
> The little Maid replied, . . .
> And there upon the ground I sit,
> I sit and sing to them.[43]

In the Banims' tale, however, innocence is a stark reminder of all that has been lost—of what is not possible in an English village where a wife-beating drunk terrorizes a child into watching a grave-yard all night.

Will remains a figure caught between two versions of rural English life, the Wordsworthian ideal of rural innocence where children do not understand death, fathers do not interfere, and mothers send off their boys to play, and the more darkly realist view of a small village in which alcoholism generates exploitation and violence, children do work at ghastly jobs, fathers can be oppressive forces, and mothers can be victims of domestic violence. The tension between the two views is figured through a ubiquitous haunting that constantly disrupts the pleasures of nature for Will, turning nature's "murmurs" into "shrieks" and the innocent child into an "unhappy being" who frightens his own children. Rather than an "idyll" of Irish distinctiveness in the face of Anglo-Irish misrule, then, this gothic tale by the Banim brothers pointedly undercuts both anti-Irish stereotypes of the Irish as distinctively alcoholic and superstitious and English myths of rural bliss and nuclear families by projecting the gothic back to the metropole from whence it came. Instead of an Ireland "haunted by history," in Tom Dunne's phrase,[44] the Banims present an England haunted by domestic violence, alcoholism, and the economic exploitation of children—by what it projects onto other nations through the gothic. English modernity is revealed to be hollow, looking backward to watch over the dead without knowing how to mourn them.

Gothic Europe, Romantic Ireland: The Banims' Poetry and the Locations of Ireland

The Banims' volume *Chaunt of the Cholera; Songs for Ireland* (1831) was published just a year before the tale "The Church-Yard Watch" appeared in an annual. As Thomas D'Arcy McGee would later do in *Canadian Ballads, and Occasional Verses* (see chapter 3), the Banims formally divide their volume of verse on geographic terms. The gothic poem "Chaunt of the Cholera" opens the volume and is followed by a preface to the next section "Songs for Ireland," a collection of songs consistent in style and theme with nationalist ballads from the 1790s.[45] The preface to this second section divides the songs into two groups: under the heading "Songs for Ireland," the Banims include fourteen songs that convey "feelings that have been," obliquely referring to nationalist fervor that the Banims suggest has been superseded by Catholic Emancipation (1829); under the heading "Irish Peasants' Songs" is a group of seven poems, a "first attempt to throw into verse the peculiar phraseology, and occasionally the words, of the Irish peasantry, when they try to speak English."[46] The volume's three parts frame three different geographical arenas: "Chaunt" takes a global view in order to situate Ireland as a nongothic space on the margins of a gothic Europe that is corrupted by tyranny and imperialism and so stalked by Death in the form of Cholera; the pre-Emancipation songs represent Ireland largely in the terms of romance, inhabited by heroic patriots who fight for the nation, but locate that Ireland firmly in the past; the "Irish Peasants' Songs" narrow the geographic view to rural Ireland to document a waning Catholic, Irish-speaking culture. The last group, then, participates in a growing body of ethnographic discourse focused on rural, Gaelic-speaking Ireland, the nostalgic shadow of the improvement discourse that was charting an anglicized future. "Chaunt of the Cholera," however, is set neither in a pre-Emancipation heroic past nor in a primitive rural present but imagines an apocalyptic near-future grounded in current events.

In "Chaunt of the Cholera," disease stalks the land like the biblical plagues of Egypt to punish and frighten tyrants, and like Noah's flood it will winnow humanity down to the humble few:

To chasten, by Destroying!
    To spare not! till a few,
Alone, be left, in tremblings,
    Earth's people to renew,
And to cry—"There *is* a Godhead!
    And man his anger braved!
And to raise a race to fear Him
    We, lonely-ones, are saved!"[47]

A war between Russia and the Ottoman Empire (1828–29) and Russia's suppression of the Polish uprising in the months before the volume's publication are noted in the early stanzas of the poem. But the central event of "Chaunt" is the devastating cholera pandemic of 1826–37, an event still unfolding when the poem was published. The cholera outbreak began in India but spread over the next few years to the Ural Mountains, Iran (Persia), Moscow and its environs, Poland, Germany, and the Arabian Peninsula. By the fall of 1831, it had spread to England and Wales, but it would not hit Ireland until the year after the Banims' "Chaunt" was published. Countries in both the Old World and the New World were ravaged, revealing the network of trade, migration, and imperial routes that now cross-connected the regions of the globe. As Alan Bewell notes, the medical journal *The Lancet* understood as early as 1831 that the spread of cholera was connected to "British troop movements" and to other imperial military invasions, such as "a Cossack detachment from Koursk . . . march[ing] on Poland."[48] "In delineating the 'geographical history' of the pandemic, therefore, [*The Lancet*] is also mapping the contact lines of empire,"[49] as do the Banims in dramatic terms by personifying the disease as a Death-like figure who sings of his own imperial travels.

The emphasis of the poem on movement reinforces the central figure of conquest as a spreading disease. While Herder and Hume disagree on the ability of national subjects to thrive outside of their homeland (see my introduction), the Banims invoke the identification of people with the land at the outset in their depiction of disease's transgression of national boundaries:

> From *my proper clime* and subjects,
> In my hot and swarthy East,
> North and Westward I am coming
> For a conquest and a feast. (1–4, emphasis added)

While Cholera travels "North and Westward," the Russian czar journeys south and east: "And in my East he sought them [slaves], / From his frozen Baltic shore" (11–12). The parallel is made explicit with the second stanza's concluding couplet, "Ho, ho! my brother-tyrant, / Am I less a Czar than you?" (15–16). The refrain, "As from land to land I go" (50, 82, 146), is limited by the borders of France and Ireland:

Not yet appear my foot-prints
    On the ocean-kingdom's strand—
Not yet my fiend-wing's rustle
    Is heard in Gallia's land;—
All ye unshackled people!
    Hold bravely what ye've won—
With Freedom exorcise me,
    Until my race be run! (65–72)

The "ocean-kingdom" is likely Ireland, still free of the epidemic, and "Gallia's land" is France. There is also an oblique reference to the United States: "Ho! on a land more Western / Observing her [Freedom] I've stood" (73–74). The Banims thus revisit the post-1789 radical connections between Ireland, France, and the United States. Cholera would not hit France hard, or Ireland and the United States at all, until 1832, after the poem was published. Hence, the Banims offer a transatlantic trio of radical nations that are in 1830–31 free from disease. The poem makes this healthful state a symbol and effect of their support of liberty, for Cholera will "kill for Freedom, / When Freedom wars with Might!" (23–24). Conversely, Cholera does address in detail the other regions that were hit in the cholera outbreak, including Russia, Poland, and key transport rivers in Germany (Spree and the Danube), while threatening to terrorize the whole globe: "ye are cringing, / All Earth, to measure Me!" (89–90).

In "Songs for Ireland," however, the scope is not global but concertedly focused on English–Irish conflicts. The first "Song" draws on the longstanding trope of Ireland and Britain as sister islands: "'Twas fate call'd up, from laboring earth, / Us, Island-Sister, at a birth, / Sisterhood between us dooming."[50] The central problem is articulated in the first verse:

From me, engaged, at your own will,
To share your lot of good or ill,
The joy or grief, the shame or glory,
Of your fortunes and your story—
        Sister! no! no!
For a lot so high and brave
You cannot choose a willing slave,
And Slave I *will* not be![51]

Obliquely referring to the Act of Union through the marital trope so often used to denote it ("engaged, at your own will"), the Banims' speaker refuses the subordination it entrenched. Subsequent poems deal with Catholic abjection. In "The Irish Soldier," for instance, the hero is

                scorn'd of those
Who safely slept while he faced their foes
Irish soldier, soldier bold,
In your native land you now are told
'Twas traitor-blood on that field you lost,
For you call'd on the saints, and your brow you cross'd![52]

The next poem, "The Irish Mother to Her Child," represents a healthy baby boy, "Except, my boy, the answering mark of where the fetter is!":

Oh! many a weary hundred years his sires that fetter wore,
And he has worn it since the day that him his mother bore;
And now, my son, it waits on you, the moment you are born,
The old hereditary badge of suffering and scorn![53]

A later, more militant song has its speaker declare, "Come North-men,—come Normans,—come Devils! / We gave them our Sparth to the chine!" with a footnote indicating that the Sparth is "the formidable weapon described by Spenser, a blow from which—dealt by an arm to match—used, in his time, to cleave a rider in two halves, from the skull to his saddle!"[54] Acknowledging the violence of the poem, the authors add another footnote: "Of course the verses do not at all apply at present: they may, however, stand as a true record of former feelings, now calmed down by judicious conciliation" or Emancipation.[55] The final "Song" of this section is addressed explicitly to England by both Protestants and Catholics: "Here we are, Mr. Bull, your Orange and Green."[56] These poems collectively work to represent Irish Catholics as violently oppressed for centuries, implicitly and sometimes explicitly by "Mr. Bull" or the "Sister-Island." With babies born in figurative fetters, sons whose fathers have been executed after degradation ("they dragg'd him by [his] door"), and priests who rally "brother-Irishmen" for Irish liberty,[57] the "Songs for Ireland" not only echo United Irishmen ballads of the 1790s (particularly the "Song" that ends "We are—we *are* United!")[58] but also revise the pan-sectarianism of that movement to identify nationalism with Catholicism and colonialism with religious intolerance—while at the same time assuaging concerns about popular insurrection by locating nationalist violence, as with the Sparth, in the past.

The poems in the section "Irish Peasants' Songs" repeat these political concerns but shift the language and the positions of the speakers. Most of the "Peasants' Songs" incorporate Irish words or dialect-sensitive transcriptions: "Sassenach," "ma bouchelleen-bawn," "Soggarth aroon," "ould," "darlent," "praty-crop," and so forth.[59] Instead of professional soldiers, as implied in "The Irish Soldier," the poems are explicitly directed at agricultural workers:

Our fathers' fields we long have till'd,
    Despised and stricken down.[60]

            the sojer [soldier] grand,
    A hireling for his pay, boys,
Or we, the tillers of God's land,
    Unarm'd, but free, that day, boys![61]

This reference to unarmed rural men's contribution to national renovation appears in other poems, most explicitly in "The Peasants' Unarmed Police."

The three sections in this volume thus rehearse distinct geographical spheres for situating Ireland: the radical transatlantic, the British Isles colonial dyad, and a still Gaelic rural Ireland. All three geographical arenas are used to launch critiques of the imperial project, but the degree of success in challenging imperial rule is suggestively tied to the class of the protagonists. Cholera, with the power of a czar, devastates imperial countries, leaving alone only the lands of freedom. The soldiers of the section "Songs for Ireland" are successful and optimistic, from the "Irish soldier, soldier brave" who "fought on" to the Sparth-wielding soldiers who defeated "Northmen" and "Normans."[62] The overall ethos is that of the "Song" set to the tune of "The Minstrel Boy":

> warn'd at last, in our strength we stand
>   Crying out, with one deep chorus,
> For requital to this outraged land—
>   Land of our love, that bore us![63]

The poems in the section "Peasants' Songs," however, seek to mollify lower-class insurgency. The first lyric of the section depicts the peasants, after being "Forsaken, wrong'd, and spurn'd," "shrieking to the night . . . broke / On him and his—for blood!" before a disembodied voice calms them:

> The *Sassenach*'s frown no longer fear,
>   And dry your wretched eyes;
> For friends, with power *his* power to quell,
>   Are thinking now of you.[64]

And though "He goaded you to guilt," "your revenge shall turn away, / And blood no more be spilt!"[65]

The two sections also differ in the treatment of land. In "Songs for Ireland," metaphors that connect the land to family predominate: "Land of love, that bore us," "Island-Sister," "the land / In which my fathers' graves / Were hollow'd by a despot hand," "Humble brethren of our soil," and so on.[66] In "Irish Peasants' Songs," conversely, the land is insistently material and associated with work and agriculture: "Our fathers' fields we long have till'd"; "we, the tillers of God's land"; "So we watch the land"; "A nate young crop / Meantime did pop / Up through ould Erin."[67] The distinction between land and soil noted by Deane here emerges as a classed distinction rather than a referential one in that the "peasants" are associated with insurgency and agriculture, while the soldiers, priests, and unclassed figures of "Songs for Ireland" are associated with the familial tropes of nationalism to which I turn in the next chapter.[68]

These same class distinctions within rural Ireland are pursued in John Banim's story "The Fetches," the tale Haslam has recently identified with the origins of Catholic gothic.[69] There, the narrator, with an almost Edgeworthian comic tone, mocks folk belief and repeatedly pathologizes both reading and interest in folk traditions. Framed as a story based on authentic materials (anticipating J. Sheridan Lefanu's premise of the Purcell papers and the Banims' "Church-Yard Watch") and hence itself folkloric, the tale begins with the starry-eyed student Tresham and the woman he is courting, "whose almost childish thoughts, fretted with the common superstitions of her own country, were fearfully pleased to meet, under the borrowed name of philosophy, a downright system suited to her wildest daydreams; and she listened in awe and terror that admitted everything."[70] One character protests of an essay on fetches, "The object of the entire paper is to prove the re-appearance on earth of the dead; and history, biography, and anecdote—nay, Scripture itself—are all quoted to support the now childish belief" (225–26). This "childish belief" is traced to a common source: "Under the immediate tutelage of his [Larry's] mother, in whose cabin Tresham, when a sickly child, had also received the elements of his present absurdity, Larry, from his cradle, was a firm believer in supernatural agency" (233). And so the peasant mother is the origin of the superstitions of both her son and the more upper-class Tresham, who is driven to illness after he "went a ghost-hunting" (267) and receives the following medical instruction: "no books; no stewing of any kind; and, least of all, over the German fairy tales" (268). "The Fetches" identifies folk belief with the primitive and the unhealthy, representing it as "childish" and productive of sickness. As in "Songs for Ireland," in "The Fetches" John Banim seems to mock the rural Catholic population for whom he and his brother have been deemed to speak, drawing a complicated line between nationalist aspiration and modernity in which progress, if not on English terms, still requires the putting away of "childish belief" in favor of science and reason.

As the texts discussed in this chapter demonstrate, Irish deployments of the gothic are not always domestically directed or focused on English–Irish colonial relations, nor are they necessarily about Ireland itself. Moreover, as I noted at the outset, Irish gothic has been largely understood as a belated tradition coming out of English gothic,[71] but these texts rewrite rather than follow that dominant tradition. Histories of detective fiction need to take Edgeworth's "Limerick Gloves" into account as a key intervention in the genre by a then-popular and widely read writer. And the Banims' "Church-Yard Watch" revises "the country and the city" motif discussed so famously by Raymond Williams, challenging both Wordsworth's idealization of the rural over the previous three decades and the soon-to-appear complementary Dickensian laments that corruption and social decline are generated in urban spaces. *Chaunt of the Cholera*, published shortly before the full emergence of cultural nationalism in Ireland and the concomitant idealization of the peasantry, works to idealize Ireland on the international stage while discriminating between its different classes within its borders, tying genre to demographics on terms that reinstate solidifying ethnographic accounts of "popular" culture and anticipating, for instance, William Carleton's ethnographic rendering of "primitive" rural Ireland in his published autobiography. Together, such texts extend the picture of Irish gothic not only into other settings, especially England, but also into noncolonial concerns, including more complex anxieties about the "popular" classes and the nature of "popular" culture. If, as McCormack notes, there is scant medievalism in Irish gothic, it is in part perhaps because the country/city divide of nineteenth-century Ireland proceeded on ethnographic terms, making the rural itself a mystical remnant of a remote past through the emergence of folkloric studies in the 1820s as well as the site of agrarian insurgency that was mythologized through folk figures such as Captain Rock. The "country" in Ireland is less pastoral than otherworldly, in part because of the colonial discourse that demonized the native Irish, as Luke Gibbons has pointed out,[72] but also in part because of class and regional divisions that persistently complicate any homogenizing ideas of nation and national culture in nineteenth-century Ireland.

5

Foreign Landscapes and the Domestication of the National Subject

> Oh, but this butterfly! It fled the cloister's gloom. Poor insect! how natural! Unwittingly I pursued its devious flight. Its rich wings of purple and gold, expanded to every gale, glittered to every sun-beam. It revelled in such variety of bliss, so free, so wild, so uncontrol[l]ed, that I sighed, and wished to be a butterfly.
>
> —LADY MORGAN, *The Novice of Saint Dominick* (1805)

> I pushed open the casement, and, without waiting to look behind me, I ran with my utmost speed, scarcely feeling the ground under me.
>
> —J. SHERIDAN LEFANU, "A Passage in the Secret History of an Irish Countess" (1838)

As Benedict Anderson suggests in his essay "Long-Distance Nationalism," "The nativeness of natives is always unmoored, its real significance hybrid and oxymoronic,"[1] a belated effect of globalization and the circulation of languages, cultures, and bodies across the borders that nationalism would entrench. For instance, in 1825 William Maginn, living in England and about to move to France, contended in a Scottish periodical that songs circulated in England as Irish were not actually Irish, citing as evidence his own authority as a native ("us Irish people"), especially on the subject of Irish idiom:

"I must protest that I never heard the word 'joy' so used in Ireland by anybody, and yet it is a standing expression put into our mouths by every writer of Irish characters."[2] Later, he notes the use of the name "Bailie" in a song and asks, "What part of the world does that name belong to?" and concludes that "the author of the Irish Wedding . . . is a Scot."[3] Maginn roots national identity in cultural knowledge, especially language use, which allows him to maintain his own Irishness from outside of Ireland on the basis of that knowledge.

Maginn's essay appeared as Herderian nationalism, and especially its emphasis on the connection between people and land, was becoming increasingly significant in the wake of the folkloric project that proceeded in part from exchanges between German and Irish romanticism (such as those between the Grimms and Thomas Crofton Croker in the mid-1820s), and in the wake of a growing diaspora. The relationship between Herderian nationalism and diaspora is traceable, for instance, in the pages of *The Nation*, where reports from globally dispersed Irish correspondents jostle for space with a positive racial discourse of Irishness. Hence, one early issue of *The Nation* comments under the title "National Character,"

> It is only the Celts, who yielded their solemn woodlands, clear flowing rivers, and wide domains, to the barbarian Goths—it is the Celts alone who can tell why those patriarchal titles were conferred on the hills of Europe by the "world's gray fathers." Those military brigands who slaughtered, devastated, or enslaved us, knew not why the graphic and poetic genius of the ancient primitive ancestors of Europe coined their beautiful epithets, or crowned the towering cliffs with descriptive appellatives to last them for ever. It was reserved for the gentle and yielding Celt to come from the caves and howling wilds to which truculent, victorious barbarism relegated him—'twas for him to point to the hills, and, like the Hebrew seer in the Assyrian's presence, interpret the words which time had only chiselled deeper. He has done so; every mountain has vindicated his claims to primogeniture, despite the malignant grin of envious incredulity; and they who were sceptics in other times, are now believers.[4]

Simultaneously tying "the Celts" to an essential national character and to a fundamental relationship with the land, such passages ground identity not only in biology, but also in the landscape itself. Drawing on similar premises, Thomas Davis praises the publication of Charles Gavan Duffy's *Ballad Poetry of Ireland* (1843):

> Worse than meeting unclean beds, or drenching mists, or Cockney opinions, was it to have to take the mountains with a book of Scottish ballads. They were glorious to be sure, but they were not ours, they had not the brown of the climate on their cheek, they spoke of places far, and ways which are not our country's ways, and hopes which were not Ireland's, and their tongue was not that we first made sport and love with. Yet how mountaineer without ballads, any more than without a shillelagh? No; we took the Scots ballads, and felt our souls rubbing away with envy and alienage amid their attention; but now, Brighid be praised! we can have all Irish thoughts on Irish hills, true to them as the music, or the wind, or the sky.[5]

Davis defines ballads as more than key to the project of "the constitution of an idea of Irishness which could 'contain and represent the races of Ireland,'" as David Lloyd puts it.[6] Like those articulated in the essay "National Character," the views in Davis's text are insistently Herderian in their assumptions, tying the national subject and national literature so closely to the national landscape as to find soul destroying any disruption of that nationalist trinity.

Hence, Denis Florence MacCarthy's "A Walk by the Bay of Dublin" (written around 1842), part of the same Young Ireland literary movement as Davis's essay and "National Character," narrates (as discussed more fully later) the landscape's soul-healing properties. But such articulations of a Herderian nationalism that roots itself in the landscape are tacitly gendered, assuming a masculine subject, virile and mobile, secure outside of the domestic sphere and establishing his ownership by traversing challenging landscapes. More like Robert Burns than William Wordsworth, this ideal figure simultaneously evokes primitivist notions of a hardy masculinity and an uncontaminated national culture and so is not "degenerated both in body and mind" by leaving the national habitat.[7] Writing of Young Ireland and "the spirit of the nation," Lloyd suggests that, through the figure of a national spirit, "the individual represents the nation"—an idea that he elaborates through John Mitchel's construction of this role for himself and for James Clarence Mangan.[8] Lloyd writes, "The figure of the martyr, his identity totally immersed in the spirit of the nation, forms the ideal paradigm of the individual's relation to the nation," but as much as "the spirit of the nation . . . theoretically encompasses all classes," just as the ballads sought to "contain and represent the races of Ireland," it does not transcend gender.[9] In the context of Lloyd's martyr or Davis's balladic hiker, Lloyd's crucial use of the word *represent* (and his use of the singular masculine *his*) highlights the ways in which nationalist aspirations mandate a representative qualified, on nineteenth-century political terms, to act as such—an adult male and tacitly one of some means, especially in education.

What, however, of the nation's women? In a group of texts associated with the Sheridan–Lefanu coterie—Lady Morgan, Mary Tighe, and Charlotte Brooke, all part of Alicia Sheridan Lefanu's Dublin circle; poet and novelist Alicia Lefanu; and, in a later generation, Alicia Sheridan Lefanu's grandson, novelist Joseph Sheridan LeFanu—this question is addressed by focusing not on the reintegration of a (male) national subject with the national landscape, but on the unmooring of women from secured domestic spheres. In key examples by Morgan and Alicia Lefanu of what I term the "outsider national tale," the heroines' unrootedness operates as a key trope for national crisis. This trope is extended in early texts by J. S. LeFanu that appropriate the English gothic's originary Walpolean interest in an illegitimate ruling class that threatens unmarried women, but with a cannier attention to gender and nation that exhibits significant debts to the national tale. LeFanu's texts refuse the national tale's nominal resolutions, instead propelling their heroines into unending flight. And then, as we shall see, Denis Florence MacCarthy writes women out of the equation in order to reinstate a masculine representative of the nation—sovereign and autonomous, tied only to the land and the nation's history.

The Outsider National Tale: Morgan's *Novice of Saint Dominick*

In the Irish national tales and the Killarney verse discussed in chapter 1, women are allied with the land, but also with older forms of sovereignty, particularly through the Maid of Killarney motif traceable from John Leslie's *Killarney* to Morgan's *Wild Irish Girl* and novels of the 1810s. Marriage tropes an end to that figure's political autonomy and hence sovereignty as well as, concomitantly, the acceptance of a new regime of the "stranger" rather than the patriot. Attention to the national tale has tended to focus on novels set in the authors' home country and centrally on narratives in which colonizer and colonized are united through marriage: *The Wild Irish Girl* and Walter Scott's *Waverley* are hence leading examples of the subgenre, with some space cleared, albeit controversially, for Maria Edgeworth's *Castle Rackrent* (1800), a novel that collapses familial decline into a few years through a series of very short marriages. However, the term *national tale* was used more broadly in early-nineteenth-century fiction, including as the subtitle to Morgan's last Irish novel, *The O'Briens and the O'Flahertys: A National Tale* (1827), where the romance involves two colonial abjects, both descended from the native Irish aristocracy, well educated, and nationalist, one a soldier of fortune and the other the leader of a convent. Miranda Burgess has pointed out the diverse literary roots of the national tale, while yet retaining demographics as a determining frame (and a focus on prose genres). She argues that the national tale works to reappropriate "metropolitan" accounts of Ireland, so that "Irish national tales in particular insisted on the complex, ancient and continuing history of Ireland and its inhabitants, while documenting the fractures caused by transnational conflict and metropolitan control."[10] This is a valuable articulation of key features of now canonical national tales, but there is a degree to which postcolonial readings have privileged—and hence made canonical—national tales that conform to this colonial concern of "transnational conflict and metropolitan control" or, more specifically, what Ian Duncan has termed "the national tale's plotting of Anglo-British Union."[11] *The Wild Irish Girl* centers on an ancient family dispossessed by colonization, but *The O'Briens* traces internecine conflicts, especially an ancient feud between the O'Briens and the O'Flahertys as well as Murrogh O'Brien's alienation from his antiquarian father. The oppressors are the Anglo-Irish elite, some of whom are converts from Catholicism or actively mask their Irish accents, and one would be hard-pressed to find any English characters in the novel or any other clear evidence of "metropolitan control." Moreover, focusing on Irish novels about Ireland and Scottish novels about Scotland risks conflating the biography of the author with the structure of a genre, reinscribing the very identity politics with which the national tale often wrestles.

The national tale can be grasped more comprehensively—and, given its varied manifestations in the period, more accurately—as a narrative form that addresses the irreducibility of history to national myth. Such a definition of the genre clears space for the national tale's well-established connection to the historical novel, the gothic, and the imagining of the nation through the novel so central to what literary critics have taken from Anderson's *Imagined Communities*. This definition also acknowledges the ways in which the national tale is often ironic, despairing of a national solution to the messiness of history, as in *The O'Briens*' relentless attention to the various waves of settlement and invasion that complicate ownership of the land itself, or mourning the end of a culture that it has worked to idealize, as in both *The Wild Irish Girl* and *Waverley*. It also leaves room for national tales set in colonial contexts without requiring that they have that setting, for these narratives are "national" novels, not colonial ones.

Focusing on the problem of nationhood opens up the canon of novels considerably and provides further context for the familiar Irish novels about Ireland's colonial status. I would like to propose here a subgenre I term "outsider national tales"—that is, national tales about nations of which the author is not a member. Novels that fall into this category include English novels about Irish civil conflict, perhaps most famously William Godwin's *Mandeville* (1817) and Caroline Lamb's *Glenarvon* (1816), and British Isles novels about French civil conflict, including Lady Morgan's (then still Sydney Owenson) *The Novice of Saint Dominick* (1805), Charles Robert Maturin's *The Albigenses* (1824), Scott's *Quentin Durward* (1823), and Alicia Lefanu's *Henry the Fourth of France* (1826). With the exception of Lamb's work, all of these novels are set in more remote historical periods than Morgan's Irish national tales and are thus reminders of the national tale's coincident rise with historical fiction, but all share with the canon of national tales a focus on wide-ranging civil conflict, many on civil wars in particular. I do not call attention to these remoter histories to negate the importance of the 1798 Uprising and the 1800 Act of Union as key impetuses for the national tale's interrogation of the meaning of the nation-state after the French and American Revolutions. These novels' focus on civil conflict, however, does remind us that, although the 1798 Uprising is legible as a nationalist effort to overthrow a colonial government, the length of colonial rule in Ireland made it in part a civil war, a point stressed in some contemporary poetic treatments.

Mary Tighe, part of the same literary circle as Morgan in the early years of the nineteenth century, makes only one explicit reference to 1798 in her published verse. In a long ballad on sectarian violence during the Uprising, "Bryan Byrne, of Glenmalure," the narrator is Byrne's Anglo-Irish Protestant father-in-law, who tells a soldier of his daughter's marriage to the Catholic Byrne, of his pride in his son-in-law, and then of the murder of his three sons. He then reaches the climax of the tale: Byrne is killed by a mob seeking revenge for the deaths of the three Protestants, shouting, "let not one escape who owns / The faith of Rome."[12] Such texts complicate any easy understanding of sectarianism in eighteenth-century Ireland as a conflict between the Anglo-Irish Ascendancy and the Catholic, largely dispossessed majority; settlement and conversions over centuries meant that Protestants could be found at all levels of society, and intermarriage between Protestants and Catholics was a regular occurrence. Morgan was herself the product of such a union—her father was Catholic and her mother Anglican—and interfaith couples appear in literature from Tighe's poem to Maturin's *Melmoth the Wanderer* to the parents of Alicia Lefanu's protagonist in *Leolin Abbey* (1819) and the idealized couple, the O'Neils, in Robert Torrens's "Catholic Tale" *Victim of Intolerance* (see chapter 1).

Of the outsider national tales I have mentioned, three focus on religious wars in France: *The Novice of Saint Dominick* (1805), the novel that launched Morgan's career in advance of the more spectacularly successful *Wild Irish Girl*; and, nearly twenty years later, Maturin's *The Albigenses* (1824) and Alicia Lefanu's *Henry the Fourth of France* (1826). Lefanu's novel is particularly close to Morgan's: both stage a suspicion of romance while relying on various devices associated with that literary mode; both deal with the Huguenot conflict about the time of Henry of Navarre's accession to the French throne as Henry IV; and both display strong sympathy for the Huguenot side. There are more specific echoes as well. Both, for instance, focus on heroines caught up in the civil conflict and given opportunities to cross-dress as a minstrel: Morgan's Imogen takes up the disguise repeatedly, despite some feminine embarrassment, and an older woman sanctions her choice as one commonly used by women in times of war,[13] while Lefanu's more conventionally virtuous Rose is horrified and refuses when her uncle suggests such a disguise. The novels are modally distinct, for reasons traceable to literary chronology. Morgan's novel, published in 1805, is deeply rooted in the sentimental tradition and focuses on the heroine's ethical education, in line with eighteenth-century models, but Lefanu's 1826 novel, published after most of Scott's Waverley novels, is more dense in historical referencing, with pauses from the romance plot to describe activity in the royal court, and Lefanu takes her heroines' virtues for granted—as well as repeatedly invokes Scott. Despite such differences in mode and literary moment, both novels raise similar questions about gender and nation in the context of civil and religious violence. Given the authors' participation in the same literary group and close echoes between their heroines (as well as Lefanu's echoes of Morgan's *The Wild Irish Girl* in *The Outlaw* [see chapter 3]), the later novel may be in part a response to the former.[14]

In Morgan's *The Novice of Saint Dominick*, the travels and travails of the heroine, Imogen, give her various opportunities to discuss the nature of nationhood and civil conflict. For instance, late in the first volume, Imogen meets a "maniac" amidst some picturesque ruins:

> "This is all the benefit we derive from civil war," added the woman.
>
> "This was not then an accidental fire?" demanded Imogen.
>
> "No, no!" said the woman wildly; "I had one son fighting for the king and the other for the League; two fine youths! What business had they to meddle with party? They were happy and laborious, and dear to each other; but their brotherly love turned to deadly hatred, and—see, stranger! that withered spot is stained with the blood of my younger son, drawn by his elder brother, because he refused to change his religion and his party!" (1:326)

In such passages, *Novice* draws on a wider discourse about civil war, specifically one that voids a founding simile of modern nationalism: as Anthony Smith notes, "the metaphor of the family is indispensable to nationalism. The nation is depicted as one great family, the members as brothers and sisters of the motherland or fatherland, speaking their mother tongue."[15] Civil war thus finds its corollary in this scene in fratricide and the fracturing of the mother's tongue—the mother only "rave[s]" or speaks "wildly," no longer capable of coherent (and cohering) speech, like the traumatized mother in Tighe's "Bryan Byrne."[16] However, as Smith notes as well, the force of nationalism is such that "the family of the nation overrides and replaces the individual's family."[17] Highlighting a fracture not only in the nation but also in the ideology of nationalism itself, such accounts of civil conflict foreground nationalism's violation of the family's priority in discourses of sensibility and domesticity. The marriage plot of the most canonical national tales assuages this violation by reconciling not only colonizer and colonized, but also nation and family, healing its own metaphorical crisis in order to forestall the perpetuation of trauma envisioned in this scene in *Novice* and the general plot of "Bryan Byrne"—a perpetuation that scars the land itself in "that withered spot" and the ruins that the "maniac" is contextualizing for Imogen. More broadly, in *Novice* the civil conflict unmoors the heroine, disconnecting her from home, family, and even (as she cross-dresses for a time) gender. Her father puts his country first and his daughter second, leaving her not as a representative of the nation, like Glorvina or the Maids of Killarney (see chapter 1), but rather as a dramatization of the gothic consequences of such nationalist fanaticism: a heroine perpetually in flight. The novel's national and domestic breaches are healed only by the heroine's return to her native soil and then by a marriage that reunites her family and a neighboring family, synecdochally healing the breach in the nation.

Imogen's position at the outset of the novel foreshadows her father's abdication of parental responsibility for the sake of national duty: a foundling raised in a convent, she has no home, no family, and no patronym. In the novel's opening chapters, she is under the patronage of a woman, the religious-minded Lady Magdelaine, but only for a brief period before returning to the convent to take orders. While at Lady Magdelaine's, she falls in love with a minstrel, also apparently at the mercy of the powerful, and then she decides to flee. Lady Magdelaine is the first of a long line in Morgan's fiction of religious bigots who neglect the suffering of those around them. On discovering that her patroness will endow the convent with a large sum, Imogen declares, "The Order of St. Dominick is the most opulent in France, and the serfs on the skirts of the forest de Montmorell, the most wretched; oppressed by famine, by all the horrors of civil war, they languish in misery and want, while safety and abundance reign in the convent of Saint Dominick. Let then, madam, those wretches, who look up to you for assistance, feel the bounty it were the mockery of religion to bestow on those who, professing poverty, revel in opulence" (1:218). Many of Imogen's early declarations, most of them soliloquized, are of this sort: contemplations of the failure of sociopolitical structures to meet humanely the needs of the population. Unwilling to submit herself to these flawed structures, centrally the convent, she dons the disguise of a minstrel and flees. She arranges to have some accompaniment but is separated early on from her chaperones. Much of the novel's opening volume follows her as she meanders through the chaos of the French countryside at a time of civil war.

Cross-dressing allows her to enter into the action in a way that no woman, let alone novice, could, her "minstrel's garb . . . a passport every where" (1:275). But her disguise also calls attention to the omnipresent sexual danger for a woman outside of a secured domestic space. As a consequence, although she flees the conventional gothic plot of being trapped in a convent, she enters a series of other gothic plots. Before the second volume is half over, despite cross-dressing to protect her virtue, she has been captured three times, first by bandits who rob her, then by Catholic soldiers who think she might be a spy, and then by Huguenot forces who find her on the battlefield. Even when she is reunited with her long-lost father, she is not safe because he is not at their home, but in the field as a military commander on the Catholic "rebel" side. He tells her, "It is indeed true, a father's arms are a child's best asylum: yet the uncertain and hazardous situation in which I am now placed, renders that asylum of doubtful continuance; and a residence in a camp is as little consonant to female delicacy, as it is unsafe and incommodious" (2:75). In part, "it is unsafe" because the at first overjoyed father still places his familial obligations second, warning her, "in the breast of a man of honour, no private claims, or selfish feelings, can oppose themselves to the duty he owes society; and . . . the affections of the father must still be subservient to the soldier's duties" (2:76). The overall plot, then, particularly of the first volume, pursues Imogen as a bodily register of the nation's inability to know itself as a coherent and stable polity: divided by political factions and sectarianism, corrupted by Italian schemers and foreign mercenaries, France as a nation is as insecure as the cross-dressing, sexually threatened, and mostly nameless Imogen.

Imogen is insistently a register of the national crisis rather than a stable national icon like her successor Glorvina in *The Wild Irish Girl.* During Imogen's second capture, the narrator comments, "Those scenes, so novel and so striking, would have interested the mind, and pleased the picturesque fancy of Imogen, had she been a spectatress under any other circumstances; but wholly overcome by the situation in which she found herself, the danger to which she was exposed, and the fatigue she had undergone; every faculty was blunted, and her mind acknowledged no sentiment, no emotion, but what terror and amazement awakened" (1:352). Here is the same problem that so concerned William Drennan in his poem "Glendalloch": the paralysis of the faculties by terror (see chapter 2). And, as in "Glendalloch," the terror here is produced by a nation that no longer knows itself, a nation in a state of civil war—"Self-conquer'd by domestic strife," as Drennan puts it.[18] This second capture is followed by the first transformation of Imogen's identity: the soldiers take her to the Count de St. Dorval, who is instinctively "paternal" toward her at the end of the first volume and revealed to be her father early in the second (2:9-12). Of course, true to the romance mode that the novel follows, she looks and sounds just like her mother and has a distinctive birthmark, all contributing to her decisive recognition by her father and his closest servants.

She is then given an account of her family history, including the marriage of her Protestant mother and Catholic father, composed mainly of letters between her parents, the representatives of two long-neighboring families recently divided by "the heresies of Luther" (2:24). The second letter from her father to her mother begins, "You are right, madam, the soul is of no sect, no party: it is, as you say, our passions and our prejudices, which give rise to our religious and political distinctions" (2:32). The parents are caught in a Romeo-and-Juliet plot: Lady Julia de Ribemont is engaged by her family to someone else but is in love with St. Dorval, and the two elope (2:40). This elopement throws both families into turmoil, and St. Dorval writes to "his best and only friend" (2:48), De Sorville, "That I have stolen a portionless wife from the family of Montargis, you tell me, is not the main object of my father's implacable resentment; but that in wedding a Hugonot, this unfortunate union may give birth to a race of heretics, whose apostacy shall cast an indelible stain on the uncontaminated faith of the house of St. Dorval, and forfeit the religious as well as the political principles of their ancestors, incessantly harrows his mind, and aggravates resentment beyond the power of reconciliation" (2:41–42). St. Dorval's father dies, leaving him little but his title, "count," and explicitly dispossessing him of his land; but the named heir is de Sorville, and he returns the land to St. Dorval (2:50–51). But while St. Dorval is away dealing with his inheritance, his daughter is kidnapped, and his wife dies of exhaustion and a "delerious fever" (2:61) in her agitation over the loss of her child. As in the scene with the maniac, nationalist ideology overturns familial affections, driving a wedge between the lovers' families, then between the lovers and their families, and then between the new familial trio of St. Dorval, Julia, and Imogen.

Conversely, the novel presents a nationalism that is grasped through tropes of idealized familial feelings. De Sorville, the voice of moral authority in the novel (though his role as such is somewhat complicated by his willingness to marry Imogen, who is half his age), defines the true patriot as one "who opposes his individual exertions to the arm of oppression, to the threat of invasion, to the power of tyranny, whether foreign or domestic; who on the altar of public weal offers up the sacrifice of his private views and interest; who looks on the land which gave him birth as his parent, and on her children as his brethren; who holds to the mirror of recollection the past splendour and dauntless virtues of her ancient state, and opposes the glorious reflection to the feeble efforts of modern degeneracy" (3:46). Alternatively, the failed patriot contracts his geographic vision to his own plot of land and his familial vision to the dead. When St. Dorval, Imogen's father, defends his participation in the Catholic League as "a cause for which in ages back my ancestors bled in the fields of Palestine" (3:49), De Sorville replies, "My dear count, we too often take up our religious and political opinions by inheritance, and defend them as we should our estates, merely because they descend to us from our forefathers: but to cherish a prejudice because it is antiquated, or was the governing principle of our ancestors, must lead to everlasting error, and stop the progressive influence of all that tends to wisdom, knowledge, or happiness" (3:49–50). There is a fine distinction in De Sorville's remarks, where the "virtues of her ancient state" are the object of nationalist nostalgia, even as the "opinions" and "governing principle" of "our forefathers" and "our ancestors" are dismissed as "antiquated." As in Smith's account of nationalism, nation trumps family: the "ancient state" has virtues worthy of remembrance, but one's familial connections in that past do not. This is also a suggestive critique of Edmund Burke's arguments in *Reflections on the Revolution in France*, especially his praise for "wise ancestors"[19] in his analysis of more recent French civil upheaval. Locating virtue and national sustenance in the state rather than in "forefathers," De Sorville offers a more public and institutional history of the nation in which family remains only as a trope for a larger sense of community.

Morgan also connects these older forms of patriotism to the paradox discussed by Marlon B. Ross in relation to English nationalism in this period: the priority of the estate and of the empire that is needed to maintain it.[20] De Sorville continues, "Oh, my lord! had your brave and illustrious ancestors dared to have thought for themselves, they would not have united themselves to that assassinating band, who, under the sanction of religion, spread horror and desolation through the finest countries of Europe and Asia; a lawless banditti, who raised the standard of murder and oppression under the command of barbarity and fanaticism" (3:53). De Sorville thus attempts to shift the ground of St. Dorval's nationalism from a cultural heritage tied to aristocratic property and imperial aggression toward an iconic "land" and "state" in which the idea of family is extended to the people as a whole and in which history is public, not familial and private.

After her father's death and her engagement to De Sorville, Imogen travels a great deal in France and Italy before her fall: she amasses debts for luxury items that she cannot afford, putting her creditors in financial crisis, and has to sell off her possessions to pay them, and then she is the subject of a pamphlet that elaborates on her trials to turn them into scandalous intrigues in which she is depicted as a profligate woman marked by "inconstancy" (4:261), "the most finished and artful adventuress ever registered in the annals of imposition" (4:262). She flees Paris and travels to her family estate: welcomed by "her tenantry and vassals" (4:293), she "endeavour[s] to form a new code of laws, and become the legislature of her little dominion, encouraging industry, rewarding merit, promoting private felicity and public good," and becoming a model of "taste and prudence" (4:294). Imogen is thus the first Morgan heroine to become an admirable governor at a local but public level, a figure that Morgan would develop through all of her national tales. But Imogen's fall also registers the perils of being a woman without a home and family. Like the protagonist of Mary Hays's *Victim of Prejudice* (1799) and myriad other texts of the period, such a woman has no one to guarantee her virtue and so her public reputation. It is home, in the guise of her family estate, that restores Imogen—even as, ironically, she echoes De Sorville's description of the failed patriot in contracting her vision to her own family estates. After her return, "All looked upon her as the guardian genius of the soil" (4:296), and she is finally in the iconic position awarded to Glorvina throughout *The Wild Irish Girl* and to the Maid of Killarney in various texts.

In the final pages of the novel, all her trials are ended, and Imogen marries the man she has loved since the beginning of the novel. Her time on her familial estate thus restores her to herself, and especially to the virtues that she claims that she lost through her rearing as an unnamed orphan in a convent: "that abandonment of social prudence, that neglect of domestic duty" (4:349) are now presented as the spur to her adventures. She is also returned to the amorous narrative that undergirds the romance, gaining an ideal husband. In other words, her unanchored state, at loose in a civil conflict, is resolved on traditional gender terms: the heroine is removed from the public sphere and acts properly in the private one, albeit an expansive private sphere in which she is an effective manager of her family lands. This domestic stability is echoed on the national stage:

> Never was there a period in the historic records of France more congenial by its political situation to the peace, the happiness of social and domestic enjoyment, than that when after a three months residence at Paris the duke and duchess de Beauvilliers [Imogen and her husband] returned to the land of their forefathers, accompanied by their inestimable friend de Sorville. The sword of civil war deposited with the volume of sectarian controversy on the altar of concord and religious toleration, confidence, peace, and affluence, shed their rich blessings on every side.
>
> The laborious husbandman anticipated in full and happy security to reap the fruits of his toil, and to enjoy the produce of that grain which the devastation of civil warfare had so often blasted in the germ. (4:393)

This reinstatement of a conservative gender narrative—of a woman who must be safely ensconced in a home with a father and then husband—and of a stable polity is thus doubly rooted in the soil. Moreover, the "forefathers" are heralded here not for their principles, faith, or politics, as Burke and Imogen's father would have it, but simply for their land. Returning the heroine to the ground of nationality, so to speak, heals the breaches of faction.

Moreover, the marriage plot works, as in the better-known national tales, to solve more local territorial problems. Imogen marries the Baron de Montargis, the scion of her mother's family, enemies of her father's family:

> The family de Montargis embraced the heresies of Luther in the reign of Henry the Second. The counts de St. Dorval, at the same period, were active in their endeavours to check the innovation the schismatic spirit of the age was gradually introducing into the immutable system of their ancestors' holy faith. In a later day the barons de Montargis united with Catherine de Medicis, and afterwards

> with Henry of Navarre, in suppressing the League and crushing the house of Lorraine: the counts de St. Dorval in promoting the measures of the League and supporting the duke of Guise. Thus religious distinction and political faction seemed united in their endeavours to sharpen the asperity of family feuds; but it remained for that passion, which should be the great solvent of every rancorous sentiment, to hurl the arrow of defiance at every hope of reconcilement; and love completed that structure of discord, of which hereditary, religious and political hatred had laid the foundation. (2:24–26)

Here, then, in a novel published a year before *The Wild Irish Girl*, is a marriage that heals political divisions, including religious ones, and that is presented as the forerunner of national peace and nation building. Moreover, in this outsider national tale the marriage plot is not so clearly unequal as it is in many national tales set in Ireland or Scotland: Catholicism is the religion of established power for most of the novel and on such terms is frequently critiqued by Imogen, and the Huguenots are associated with an emergent modernity that transcends religious divisions. Imogen's marriage to the Huguenot de Montargis instead of to the Catholic de Sorville, who, we are repeatedly told, is too old for her, marks the union of France to modernity rather than a reconciliation between colonizer and colonized, and offers an early glimpse of some of Morgan's developing and complicated ideas on Catholicism.

Alicia Lefanu, the niece of Morgan's mentor Alicia Sheridan Lefanu, returns to Morgan's subject matter two decades later in *Henry the Fourth of France*. Lefanu's novel is more concertedly historical than Morgan's, with whole chapters given over to historical exposition. Morgan's novel focuses on Imogen and her development against the backdrop of sixteenth-century France, but Lefanu's offers a trio of key female figures: the foster sisters Rose and Blanche and their dark opposite, Henry III's dangerous mother, Catherine de Medici. Catherine is the gothic inversion of the benevolent women rulers of the Lefanu coterie: "The arts which Catherine practised were only an epitome of the system followed in France by women of all classes. To the deserved praise to which, as excelling in the virtues peculiar to their sex, they might justly have aspired, they preferred the dangerous honour of influencing public measures by their eloquence or their charms."[21] Catherine is not merely domestically improper, but religously so: she terrifies Rose as "a sorceress!" (2:65), and a late part of the novel depicts Catherine's obsession with Nostradamus. The queen's improper femininity is contrasted with the proper masculinity of Henry of Navarre, marked by God to be the ruler of France: "Providence, who watched over the safety of the hero who was destined, as Henry the Fourth, to be one day the glory and delight of France, enabled Henry of Navarre to elude all these great and pressing dangers" (1:46). The civil conflict is explicitly attributed to Catherine, and Henry of Navarre is depicted as the unwilling participant in a conflict he would end. Hence, in one telling scene, Catherine

> asked him if all the pains she had taken were to be productive of no advantage—she whose motto was peace, and who made it the great object of her life to preserve or to obtain it?
>
> The king, who had repeatedly suffered by her Machiavelian policy, was quite revolted by her hypocrisy.—"*Vive Dieu*, madame!" he exclaimed, with unwonted hastiness; "it is not *I* that bring on the miseries of civil war—it is not *I* that prevent you at Fontainebleau from sleeping quietly in your beds; but truly you, who, with incessant intrigues and plots, prevent me from ever having a good night's rest in mine. You are the enchantress that live but in the whirlwind, and would expire in a calm." (2:217–18)

This improper femininity not only provokes uncharacteristic "hastiness" in Henry of Navarre but also more broadly shatters proper familial relations: "Then was the struggle, the deadly strife of civil war; the unnatural conflict, in which not only the father might fight against the son, the brother against the brother, and the dearest relations of life be violently rent asunder, by those very hands that, in happier times, would have rejoiced to draw their sacred bands the closest" (2:146). Lefanu thus draws on the same lexicon as Tighe and Morgan in representing civil war as a public violation of the domestic sphere. If nationalism exerts its rhetorical force so that "the family of the nation overrides and replaces the individual's family,"[22] civil war is the vehicle of a counterargument that lingers on the violation of the individual's undefended family.

Lefanu, however, does not simply follow the marriage plot of the national tale. Instead of one heroine, she has two who are raised as the daughters of Raoul de Chastelar, a Catholic follower of the Huguenot cause, and who have very different endings: Blanche marries Henry of Lorraine, ruler of the region in which she grew up; Rose, of more humble birth, mourning Conrad the Wonderful, the man she loved, "proposed to devote herself . . . to the monastic life, but . . . died at the close of her noviciate" (4:226). Conrad's mother was Catholic and his father Lutheran; Conrad was raised in his father's faith, and his sister in his mother's, and it is to her convent that Rose retires at the end of the novel. Lefanu's novel, in other words, stays fairly insistently within a multifaith space. But her novel nevertheless works to use marriage to reconcile religious and political conflicts: Blanche's marriage to Henry of Lorraine is explicitly offered as a means of healing the rift between the Guise and Coligny families (4:18–20), a rift that dates back to the St. Bartholomew's Day Massacre, an event that haunts the novel. The massacre becomes in Lefanu's novel the cornerstone of national myth making:

> "But do you believe it?" said Rose, inquiringly.
>
> "Believe what?"
>
> "That the massacre of St. Barthélemi ever happened?"
>
> "Alas! Rose, how can it be doubted?"
>
> "*I* cannot conceive how persons could destroy multitudes of their countrymen for holding a different faith from themselves."
>
> "That is because, my dearest Rose, you turn away your eyes from the real truths of life, to your uncle's fabled tales of fancy and romance." (1:75)

The familial ground asserted as a value in Morgan's novel is here revealed as "fancy and romance": nation is not family, and the massacre proved it.

The traumatic significance of the massacre is introduced early in the novel through Raoul, a noble retired soldier and a Catholic, who observes two days of mourning: "the anniversaries of the death of his wife, and that of the massacre of la Saint Barthélemi," where "the second was a day of more austere observance, and passed by the sire de Chastelar in absolute solitude, and clothed in penitentiary sackcloth" (1:71). Later, just before giving his daughters his account of the massacre, Raoul declares, "Oh, St. Barthélemi! day matchless and unparalleled in the annals of blood and crime! when will the hideous phantoms that your memory awakens leave him who escaped you, and who was yet your victim, a moment of repose!" (1:181). The recognition scene in *Novice* involves the father's recovery of his long-lost daughter, but in *Henry* it centers on the recognition of Blanche as the daughter not of Raoul, as she had always been told, but of a couple who died in the massacre. Raoul, explaining the cause of Blanche's scar, tells her that after a wedding the "minions of the duke of Guise—French and Italian assassins" (2:10)—attacked the Huguenots, killing Coligny in front of Raoul (2:11): "At this moment the great bell of the palace tolled. It was the morning of the twenty-fourth of August—of the festival of St. Barthélemi; the streets resounded with the sudden and horrible cry of—'Kill, kill, massacre the Hugonots!" (2: 12–13). In his account, Raoul tries to save Coligny's daughter Louise, the woman he loved but who had married another man, and finds her with her child, catatonic by her husband's dead body (2:18); she then asks him to take the child and drops dead, after insisting she would not leave her husband (2:20). Raoul then discovers a "wound inflicted by the assassins on the left side of the infant's neck," a blow meant for the mother, and he muses, "thus had the child nearly saved her parent; but grief had snapped the strings of life, and the victim [Louise] expired without a blow—without a wound" (2:21). This child is Blanche, revealed to be Coligny's granddaughter.

The originary trauma that propels the action of Morgan's novel is a personal one tied to religious fanaticism: a Catholic servant kidnaps Imogen and gives her, under the guise of an orphan, to the Order of St. Dominick to ensure that she is raised in that faith, thus leading to her mother's death and to her own improper upbringing. In Lefanu's novel, the originary trauma is a political one: the St. Bartholomew's Day Massacre. Both are revealed through long narrative accounts by paternal figures who provide the heroine's childhood history, prompted by visual markers, centrally Blanche's scar and Imogen's birthmark. In both novels, political and sectarian conflict is resolved through marriage: Blanche marries a scion of the family that murdered her grandfather and father, and Imogen marries into her mother's alienated family. Following the general outlines of the national tale, then, these depictions of French civil war call attention to the relationship between nationalism and the trope of family, including the utility of marriage as a vehicle of reconciliation, but without invoking colonial situations. Moreover, given both authors' interests in depicting contemporary Ireland, these novels are also salutary reminders that, the canonical national tale notwithstanding, political conflict in Ireland was often understood as internecine rather than colonial.

The Drunk in the Parlor and the Madwoman in the Attic: LeFanu's Early Contributions to the *Dublin University Magazine*

In the 1830s, J. Sheridan LeFanu, a cousin of Alicia Lefanu and grandson of Morgan's mentor Alicia Sheridan Lefanu, follows these earlier texts from the Lefanu–Sheridan circle in focusing on the perils of national instability through the figure of the woman who is not safely at home, particularly in two early gothic tales, "A Passage in the Secret History of an Irish Countess" (1838) and "A Chapter in the History of a Tyrone Family" (1839). Both tales depict Irish heiresses who journey from troubled paternal homes to more troubled homes and become entangled in plots that share a number of features: domestic violence, patriarchal duplicity, the prospect of forced marriage, and threats first to the heroine's wealth and social status and even to her life itself. These two texts were published first in the *Dublin University Magazine* (originally the *Dublin University Review and Quarterly Magazine*), a quarterly founded in 1833 with nationalist but not explicitly political leanings, anticipating Young Ireland in praising Irish letters and the Irish past, but with the key difference that contributors made no arguments for the Repeal of the Act of Union. Both stories appeared there as part of a series of tales that LeFanu fictively framed as the "Purcell Papers" and also had considerable afterlife in nineteenth-century literature: "Passage" was rewritten at least twice by LeFanu, first as "The Murdered Cousin" (1851) and then as one of his best-known novels, *Uncle Silas* (1864); elements of "Chapter" were later reworked into *The Wyvern Mystery* (1869), and the story has long been considered a possible source for Charlotte Brontë's *Jane Eyre* (1847). In their first incarnations, these tales exhibit an engagement with the conventions of the national tale, focusing on Irish aristocratic women and marriage plots, though gone awry with a gothic twist.

In her last Irish novel, *The O'Briens and the O'Flahertys*, Morgan allies "insecurity of property" with "all the bugbears of terrorism" via their shared grounding in sectarian political conflict.[23] "Five hundred years of successive forfeitures," her narrator insists, destabilizes both sides of the religious divide: "Down to the middle of the last century, a feeling of insecurity in all classes prevailed through this anomalous condition of things. . . . The small but ascendant party of protestants, scarcely less harassed than the victims of their own oppression, suffered through their fears of the disabilities they had themselves imposed; and largely participated in the insecurity of property, which they had inflicted on their catholic opponents."[24] This anxiety is so disruptive, the narrator continues, "that at one epoch, the government had ordered the Irish bar not to defend the revived claims of an Irish noble of the old caste," and then turns to a depiction of a Dubliner fussing, "'We shall have the papists . . . rummaging out old claims, and proving their rights to all the landed property of the country; and his Majesty's protestant subjects of Ireland will have nothing to expect but poverty and persecution, the overthrow of the church, the murders of forty-one, the massacre of St. Bartholomew'"—a list summed up as "all the bugbears of terrorism."[25] Morgan's analysis is salient here because of LeFanu's interest in the Protestant beneficiaries of such "forfeitures" and because of both the English and the Irish romantic-era gothic's interest in illicit seizures of property, from the first explicitly gothic tale, Walpole's *Castle of Otranto: A Gothic Story* (1764), to Ann Radcliffe's threatened heiresses in the 1790s to Irish instances such as Edgeworth's *Castle Rackrent* (1800) and Maturin's *Melmoth the Wanderer* (1820). That Morgan's *O'Briens* is explicitly "a national tale" and arguments have been put forward for *Castle Rackrent* as one are even more salient to my point here.[26] The "Glorvina solution" is specifically a solution to a gothic problem—namely, the need to authorize what remains marked as the illicit seizure of property (recalling, too, the dispossession of Imogen's father in *Novice*) and to assuage the gothic anxieties that such instabilities produce.

The gothic mode and the national tale not only overlap in their shared concern with the tale of "forgotten history"[27] but are also conceptually yoked together in Irish writing. Gary Kelly includes one of Morgan's novels in a set of gothic novels,[28] and gothic elements are easy to trace in her texts: the ruins and evocative rural singers in *Wild Irish Girl*; the mysterious nun and the hanged man who yet lives, the mark of the rope on his neck, to help the hero in *The O'Briens and the O'Flahertys*; the Inquisition and love-struck monk and priestess in *The Missionary* (1811). This interpenetration of the national tale and the gothic extends to Morgan's inheritors: recent work on the Catholic gothic as a heretofore overlooked tradition within Irish gothic has highlighted the work of the Banims, for instance, whom Ferris and Burgess have discussed in relation to the national tale.[29] It is in *The O'Briens and the O'Flahertys* that gothic topoi get their fullest play in a national tale, however, from the focus on dispossession in the opening chapters to the mysterious nun and her many masquerades, the conspiracies in Ireland and later in France, and the attempted assassination of Napoleon with which the novel closes, but especially through the male hero's inability to secure political or any other kind of power. Although the form lingered for a few more years, the *O'Briens* arguably ends the national tale, at least in its Irish manifestations—the novel's despair and refusal of a solution, in effect, forcing the national tale to confront the gothic forces it seeks to deny. The marriage trope remains in the *O'Briens*, but it is explicitly divorced from any national allegory: the Protestant, aristocratic hero marries the Catholic nun from a warring family, recalling closely the leading couple in Morgan's first national tale, *The Novice of St. Dominick*, but instead of returning to the homeland, like Imogen and her mate, they end the novel in exile. Such texts reveal the ways in which the Irish national tale not only allegorically resolves sectarian conflict but also symbolically entwines religious traditions in ways that complicate the conventional binaries of the anti-Catholicism in the English gothic (see chapter 4).

A decade after Morgan published *The O'Briens*, LeFanu extended the implications of the national tale by turning even the marriage trope against itself. W. J. McCormack identifies LeFanu's story "A Passage in the Secret History of an Irish Countess" as "the first of the [*Purcell*] *Papers* in which confiscator Williamites are portrayed,"[30] and "A Chapter in the History of a Tyrone Family" draws insistently on the long-standing Irish gothic motif of Protestants in a strange (Catholic) land. Margot Gayle Backus has argued that children are sacrificed in nineteenth-century Anglo-Irish gothic to maintain colonial control in the face of such insecurity, but both of these early LeFanu tales concertedly critique this pattern.[31] These tales instead share an interest in women's domestic and financial vulnerability in late-romantic-era Ireland, allied with features that Alison Milbank notes in her discussion of *Uncle Silas* to associate LeFanu with "the female gothic"; and, as McCormack notes, they also mark a shift in "'Protestant' tales" from "a nervous interest in the supernatural" to "domestic interiors and explicitly criminal offences."[32] But these two stories also deal directly with the quite literal problem that Morgan outlines: the legitimacy of Irish landowners. The violence of Protestant Ascendancy is mirrored in the domestic violence committed by the patriarchs in both tales: in "Chapter," the heroine's husband, Glenfallen, beats the woman who claims to be his true wife and contributes to her execution by perjuring himself in court; in "Passage," the heroine's uncle Arthur is a thief and a murderer who plots to kill the protagonist for her money. Their estates are depicted on terms that highlight these patriarchs' failure to be social leaders and property managers and that echo the heroines' fathers' similar failures on their estates. Outside of the domestic pairing, then, which is clearly amenable to feminist readings, these tales represent the moral and hence political inadequacy of the men who control the land, and the women, of early nineteenth-century Ireland. Moreover, in a suggestive variation on the international unions of the national tale, both of these illegitimate landowners are associated with aging, foreign women: the woman who claims to be Glenfallen's first wife is a "poor, blind Dutch woman," and Arthur's "*chere amie*" is "a tall, raw-boned, ill-looking, elderly Frenchwoman."[33]

Margaret, the heroine of "Passage," lost her mother in infancy (502) and was raised by a father whose "treatment of [her], though uniformly kind, flowed less from affection and tenderness, than from a sense of obligation and duty" (503). Margaret's father, concerned that his brother, Arthur, carries the taint of suspicion of murder as well as a reputation as a dissolute gambler, makes out a will that stipulates that on his death Margaret will become his sole heir, but under the guardianship of Arthur, and that Arthur will inherit Margaret's wealth if she dies childless: "my father desired, by making it the direct, apparent interest of Sir Arthur that I should die without issue, while at the same time he placed me wholly in his power, to prove to the world, how great and unshaken was his confidence in his brother's innocence and honour" (506). Margaret's first view of Arthur's house stresses not only gothic decline, but also a pattern of "neglect" that suggests Arthur is anything but a capable steward:

> there was an air of neglect and decay about the spot, which amounted almost to desolation, the symptoms of this increased in number as we approached the building itself, near which the

> ground had been originally more artificially and carefully cultivated than elsewhere, and whose neglect consequently more immediately and strikingly betrayed itself. As we proceeded, the road wound near the beds of what had been formerly two fish-ponds, which were now nothing more than stagnant swamps, overgrown with rank weeds, and here and there encroached upon by the straggling underwood; the avenue itself was much broken; and in many places the stones were almost concealed by grass and nettles. . . . [T]o add to the general air of dilapidation, some huge trunks were lying scattered through the venerable old trees. (506)

This is only about a third of an extended passage that bears comparison to other accounts of Irish landlord neglect, including Edgeworth's *Castle Rackrent* and the opening chapter of Maturin's *Melmoth the Wanderer*, and it hammers repeatedly at this one note: Arthur is not taking care of his estate. By contrast, Arthur, a "reformed rake" (507), takes great care with his personal appearance: "his dress . . . was, however, handsome, and by no means carelessly put on; but what completed the singularity of his appearance was his uncut, white hair, which hung in long, but not at all neglected curls" (508).

Pressured to marry her less foppish but no less malevolent cousin Edward, Margaret recognizes her uncle's motivation, telling Arthur that he is "attempting thus to trick and frighten me into a marriage which he knows to be revolting to me, and which is sought by him only as a means for securing himself whatever property is mine" (511), exposing the national tale's marriage plot as both manipulative and driven by the desire to "secur[e] . . . property." Finally, father and son develop a plot in which Edward will pretend to travel to France but then remove a window frame to enter Margaret's room and kill her. He kills his sister by mistake, and Margaret manages to slip out of her room while they are disposing of the body. She tries to get to "the parlour windows [that] opened on the park" but finds the French woman—"fast asleep, having probably drank deeply"—in the room, which also shows signs of a disorderly drinking party (517). Unlike later LeFanu heroines who are much more gently Victorian,

Margaret pauses to consider slashing the woman's throat (518) but instead resigns herself to God's protection. She "noiselessly withdrew the bars, and unclosed the shutters—[and] pushed open the casement," exits the house, and then starts to run: "I ran with my utmost speed, scarcely feeling the ground under me, down the avenue, taking care to keep upon the grass which bordered it. I did not for a moment slack my speed . . . [T]here was not a bush or a bramble to shelter me" (518). Her dash across the estate revisits in reverse a number of the elements described in her original arrival—the grass-covered avenue, the old trees, and the lack of foliage—as she unwinds her uncle's hold on her by transgressing the boundaries of domesticity in which she had been contained first by her father and then by her uncle. After running for some time, she recounts, "I ran through the village, in which all was silent as the grave, until my progress was arrested by the hoarse voice of a sentinel, who cried, 'Who goes there?' I felt that I was now safe. I turned in the direction of the voice, and fell fainting at the soldier's feet. When I came to myself, I was sitting in a miserable hovel, surrounded by strange faces, all bespeaking curiosity and compassion. Many soldiers were in it also: indeed, as I afterwards found, it was employed as a guard-room by a detachment of troops quartered for that night in the town" (518). This home serendipitously provides Margaret with a patriarchal refuge: the masculine state appears to protect her after paternal domestic authority fails, twice. The soldiers return to her uncle's house to find the men gone but later capture "the Frenchwoman," who confirms that Arthur is guilty of the murder of which he was originally suspected.

In its depiction of rural Ireland, Margaret's arrival at the village is however a striking scene. Arthur's dilapidated estate is here paired with a village "silent as the grave," where "a miserable hovel" is the best that can be offered to billetted troops (518). Arthur's house is remarkably insecure, with removable window frames, easily dislodged bars, and drunk, unchaste servants, but the village is "safe" precisely because it is guarded by soldiers rather than by the men of "powerful and wealthy families" (502)—by professionals rather than by aristocrats. The only other measure of safety Margaret finds is in her faith: "the God who has conducted me thus far through the valley of the shadow of death, will not abandon me now" (518). LeFanu's tale thus departs from the general outlines of the gothic, including Irish gothic, both in representing safe harbor and in identifying it with civic institutions. Margaret is safe with soldiers and the Irish public but is not safe in a domestic space corrupted by Frenchness. In this respect, the tale picks up on depictions of military chivalry in accounts of the 1798 Irish Uprising as well as on positive depictions of the Volunteers in the 1780s and 1790s, even while representing Ireland as disorderly and impoverished because of corruption within the aristocracy. The rural Irish, despite having "strange faces," a phrase suggesting little contact between the Big House and the village, show Margaret "compassion" where her father could not show her "affection" or "tenderness." The instability of the aristocracy is anticipated by the story's opening lines about Margaret: "the Countess D——. She is no more—she long since died, a childless and a widowed wife, and, as her letter sadly predicts, none survive to whom the publication of this narrative can prove 'injurious, or even painful.' Strange! two powerful and wealthy families, that in which she was born, and that into which she had married, have ceased to be—they are utterly extinct" (502). "A Passage in the Secret History of an Irish Countess," then, marks the passing of "the history of Irish families" (502) and the transition—metaphorized in Margaret's flight—from an aristocratic to a modern nation-state, from patriarchal defense to a public militia. Like the various Maids of Killarney, Margaret ends her family line and, with it, Irish native aristocracy. Modernity is here exemplified not by a restoration of indigenous right to those with power, as in the national tale's "Glorvina solution," but by the presence of the military, who clear the land of foreign and disruptive elements. The marriage plot is the threat that drives the heroine into the modern nation-state rather than the modernizing solution to nationalist divisions that it is in national tales.

"A Chapter in the History of a Tyrone Family," published a year after "Passage," revisits the same plot of a daughter with emotionally cold parents who arrives at a strange estate to find her life threatened. "Chapter," moreover, also includes the familiar marriage trope of the national tale, as the heroine is married to the morally questionable landowner, Glenfallen, early in the text. According to Fanny's mother, Glenfallen seeks the marriage because of "the antiquity and high reputation of [their] family" (404); Glenfallen's family, conversely, has "influence" that Fanny's mother desires to access (404). In discussing his estate, Glenfallen reinforces the implications of the distinctions between the two families, telling Fanny, "I have no taste for antiquity. . . . Indeed I do not recollect that I was even so romantic as to overcome my aversion to rats and rheumatism, those faithful attendants upon *your* noble relics of feudalism" (407). In other words, Fanny's family is old Irish, and Glenfallen's is one of the newer families settled after Cromwell, if not specifically after William III. The first marriage of the tale weds Fanny's elder sister to an Englishman, recalling the cross-national unions of the domestic national tale, including Morgan's *The Wild Irish Girl*; the second marries Fanny to a powerful Ascendancy man, recalling the marriages used to heal internal national breaches, as in Morgan's other national tales, *Novice* and *O'Briens*.

In contrast to Arthur's estate, marked by myriad signs of decay, Glenfallen's estate "had nothing whatever of the gloom of decay about it" (406). Moreover, the local people appear only at the end of "Passage" in the "strange faces" that surround the terrified Margaret, but they appear, albeit remotely, fairly early in "Chapter": "in the distance a group of dairy maids were plying their task, which they accompanied with snatches of Irish songs which, mellowed by the distance, floated not unpleasingly to the ear," and Fanny remarks, "As I looked upon this scene . . . a feeling of tranquillity and happiness came upon me, which I have never experienced in so strong a degree" (407). Having just traveled from Tyrone to "a southern county" (406), Fanny has moved from the predominantly Protestant north to the old Catholic, Gaelic south and finds it both aesthetic and anaesthetic, "picturesque" (406) and "tranquil" (407). Even "old Martha" is a source of aesthetic comfort to Fanny: "A hale, good-humoured, erect, old woman was Martha, and an agreeable contrast to the grim, decrepid hag, which my fancy had conjured up, as the depository of all the horrible tales in which I doubted not this old place was most fruitful" (407). This soothing scene is disrupted by the madwoman of the attic, the Dutch Flora Van-Kemp, who, as Victor Sage notes, suggests an association with Protestantism and, of course, the Dutch William of Orange, who haunts Irish political symbolism.[34] Instead of "horrible tales," Fanny finds a blind woman in her room one day who thinks she, not Fanny, is Lady Glenfallen:

> "I say, madam," I repeated, approaching her, that I might be more distinctly heard, "that I am Lady Glenfallen."
>
> "It's a lie, you trull!" cried she, in an accent which made me start, and, at the same time, springing forward, she seized me in her grasp and shook me violently, repeating, "it's a lie, it's a lie!" with a rapidity and vehemence which swelled every vein of her face; the violence of her action, and the fury which convulsed her face, effectually terrified me, and disengaging myself from her grasp, I screamed as loud as I could for help; the blind woman continued to pour out a torrent of abuse upon me, foaming at the mouth with rage, and impotently shaking her clenched fists towards me. (410)

Glenfallen intervenes and calls the woman a "demon" "out of her mind" (410). Her effect on Fanny is the precise inverse of the "tranquil[lity]" produced by the scenes and sounds that greeted her arrival: "This occurrence, so startling and unpleasant, so involved in mystery, and giving rise to so many painful surmises, afforded me no very agreeable food for rumination" (410). "[N]either English nor Irish" (414), Van-Kemp precipitates a precise contrast between an aesthetic and peaceful Gaelic pastoral and a violent Protestant domesticity akin to the violent home in John and Michael Banim's "The Church-Yard Watch." That violence is perpetrated both by and upon the body of the Dutchwoman, who physically threatens Fanny and is herself beaten, Martha and Fanny believe, by Glenfallen: "I had reason to think," writes Fanny, "that Lord Glenfallen wreaked his vengeance upon [Van-Kemp] . . . with a violence which was not satisfied with mere words, for old Martha . . . told me that she feared her master had ill used the poor, blind Dutch woman, for that she had heard her scream as if the very life were leaving her" (413).

The connection of violence to foreignness is further developed as the tale progresses. Glenfallen offers Fanny a choice between "Cahergillagh or France" (411), but Fanny finds a national space inhabited by the foreign only slightly less threatening than an entirely foreign space:

> as to accompanying him in the continental tour so suddenly determined upon, I felt that it would be a hazard too great to encounter; for at Cahergillagh I had always the consciousness to sustain me, that if his temper at any time led him into violent or unwarrantable treatment of me, I had a remedy within reach, in the protection and support of my own family, from all useful and effective communication with whom, if once in France, I should be entirely debarred. As to remaining at Cahergillagh in solitude, and for aught I knew, exposed to hidden dangers, it appeared to me scarcely less objectionable than the former proposition. (411)

As in Morgan's *Novice*, the heroine's insecurity registers a larger crisis in which national order breaks down. Margaret can rely on the army, but Fanny can only stay in Ireland and hope to communicate with her family in the remote north. Arthur is malicious, but Glenfallen, the man who wields wealth and national influence, is simply mad.

At the end of the tale, Glenfallen tells Fanny he "shall have a special messenger before two days have passed" as a letter addressed "To the Archangel Gabriel in heaven" lies on his desk (419)—Gabriel being the archangel understood in Christian tradition as the messenger of God and so implicitly the "special messenger" for whom Glenfallen waits. He expects to receive proof of "the necessity of [his] conduct" (418). That Gabriel is the messenger of the Annunciation and the interpreter of a prophetic vision with strong political overtones in the biblical book of Daniel makes the choice even more suggestive, presenting Glenfallen as falling into religious mania as he searches for an authority to legitimize his position. His other witness is Van-Kemp, who, he tells Fanny, is in the next room—the room where he later dies, either via suicide or through the unnatural vengeance of the ghostly Van-Kemp. McCormack suggests of LeFanu's *Purcell Papers*, "Solitude is the destiny which the central figures face, and in some cases the result is self-destruction, suicide, the absolute but purely formal escape from solitude" that may have larger implications as a comment on "men who share a common history."[35] But McCormack's central example is "the last heir of Castle Connor[,] [who] was finally a representative figure absorbed into a dying landscape."[36] In "Chapter," the death of Glenfallen and even the undecideability of whether he commits suicide are tied to the erasure of Irish history itself by Fanny's remark, "All, then, was over; I was never to learn the history in whose termination I had been so deeply and so tragically involved" (420). Like Anna Edwards's Killarney Princess and Alicia Lefanu's Rose, Fanny turns from the perilous world of history to the security of religion: "I directed my thoughts and my hopes to that place where there is no more sin, nor danger, nor sorrow" (420). Like Margaret, she ends "childless," the last of her "antiqu[e]" family line.

"Chapter" is also suggestive given recent discussions of Catholic gothic. "Passage" is Radcliffean in focusing on criminal men who pose sexual and other bodily threats to an orphaned woman, but "Chapter" has clear supernatural elements: the ghostly carriage that presages the death of Fanny's sister; the dropping black curtain that announces a death in the Glenfallen family, resonant with the "fetch" that appears in texts from Alicia Lefanu's *Strathallan* (1816) to the text that Haslam has suggested originates "Irish Catholic Gothic," John Banim's "The Fetches" (1825);[37] and Glenfallen's supernatural communion with a dead woman and an archangel. Reading these supernatural elements and Van-Kemp's role allegorically, along the lines of national tales, "Chapter" resituates the purported modernity of the Ascendancy as one that works violently, on the one hand, to contain an insurgent Orangeism with which it was formerly allied and now seeks to repudiate and, on the other, to repress a pervasive affiliation with the *volk*, through fetches and Catholicism, that it cannot manage or fully comprehend. Fanny's sister's marriage to an Englishman, moreover, produces not transnational harmony, but a trauma that is supernaturally figured, intensifying the story's Catholic gothic underpinnings. On seeing the ghostly carriage that marks her sister's death, Fanny writes, the family was "more panic-struck than I can describe. . . . [and] it produced a strong and lasting effect upon my spirits, and indeed, I am inclined to think, upon my character" (402). Julian Moynahan has pointed to the colonial order as the source of terror in gothic fiction,[38] but here the union of English and Irish aristocrats produces that terror—an ongoing trauma among the older aristocratic order. Glenfallen's madness is at a symbolic level the inevitable result of his insistence to Fanny that he is a modern man, his refusal to see the residual national order and its cultural forces in the Catholic gothic he dismisses as antiquated detritus.

In these two influential tales of LeFanu's early career, then, anxieties over nation formation are reproduced domestically, as in the national tale—the threat of the foreign becomes the dangerous foreign woman, and internecine conflicts are played out in troubled marriages. In LeFanu's tales, the larger geographical connections of Ireland are collapsed into the space of the home, the land beyond its walls a symbolic register of the home itself rather than a terrain to be mapped or surveyed. As in a number of national tales, these narratives also mark a break in history, but they do so not through the patriarchal erasure of the woman's name through marriage, as "the Glorvina solution" requires, but through childlessness, thus refusing the national tale's vague anticipation of a reproductive futurity.[39] These short tales, then, write the failure of the national tale through the collapse of romance into the gothic—marriages are coerced, women are childless, the Big House is the site of hidden violence, and aristocratic families, both "antique" and Ascendancy, pass into history, leaving only isolation and trauma in their wake. Although LeFanu is often associated with the articulation of Ascendancy anxieties, these tales of domestic violence—including the Ascendancy Glenfallen's brutal beating of the Dutch woman Van-Kemp—give a sharp turn to the allegory of the national tale, resurrecting the violence of the colonial relation, evident in Leslie's *Killarney*, that the romance of the national tale would obscure.

Masculinist Patriotism and MacCarthy's "A Walk by the Bay of Dublin"

Even though near-contemporary writers such as Morgan, Alicia Lefanu, and J. Sheridan LeFanu complicate the gendered tropes of nationhood and reconciliation, the Young Ireland poets of the 1840s often seem to solve the problem by writing women entirely out of the equation, returning to the iconic female figures of United Irishmen discourse and the Irish-language tradition—beautiful Erin, mother Ireland, and proud Hibernia. In doing so, they pursue instead more complicated articulations of the patriot's relationship to the landscape as a problem of masculinity. If the national tale emerges in Ireland as a response to the Act of Union, its marital unions figuring the political union of Ireland and Britain, then Young Ireland poetry more explicitly emerges as a response to the Repeal movement to reverse the Act of Union. Instead of imagining domestic reconciliation through romantic marriage, this poetry tends to stress the renovation of the masculine subject on terms that echo the vision of an Ireland ready—through education, national feeling, and sheer force of will—to be sovereign again. The "individual represents the nation," as Lloyd suggests, but it is specifically a male individual, with all the sovereign power and virility that nineteenth-century thought attached to masculinity.

Among these Young Ireland poets, Denis Florence MacCarthy was a prominent figure, heralded as the heir to Thomas Moore by the 1850s, although he has largely since dropped from the view of literary history. He was a regular contributor to the nationalist periodical *The Nation* in its heyday as well as to the less emphatically political *Dublin University Magazine* with which LeFanu was so closely involved. With literary and social connections to such key figures as Davis, James Clarence Mangan, and Samuel Ferguson, MacCarthy was both popularly and historically at the center of midcentury articulations of cultural nationalism and was hailed as "our national poet" in Irish print of the final decades of the nineteenth century. He also made key contributions to the topographical tradition, specifically in "Afghanistan" and "A Walk by the Bay of Dublin," dated 1842 and published in his volume *Ballads, Poems, and Lyrics* (1850), reorienting an anglocentric geopolitics on terms that revalue the spaces devalued by the British Empire. Lloyd points to MacCarthy's *Book of Irish Ballads*, one of the first volumes the poet published, as evidence of MacCarthy's "belief that contact with the Irish spirit, which a knowledge of ballads provides, will give back a distinctive character to an Irish literature which must perforce be written in English,"[40] but MacCarthy's larger corpus is less domestically focused. In addition to volumes of original verse, he also established a reputation as a leading translator of Pedro Calderón de la Barca's plays through six published volumes between 1848 and 1873. He acknowledged his debts both to English poet P. B. Shelley with *Shelley's Early Life* (1872), a biography centrally concerned with recovering Shelley's interest in Ireland and his Irish pamphlets in particular, and to Moore with the elegiac poem *The Centenary of Moore* (1880). His work was also heavily indebted to William Wordsworth, and the *Dublin University Magazine*, a journal to which MacCarthy was a leading contributor, echoed dismissals of Moore in comparing MacCarthy's work unfavorably to that more Wordsworthian Victorian poet Matthew Arnold.[41]

Contemporaries of MacCarthy recognized the complexity of his literary reach. A review excerpted in an advertisement for *Ballads, Poems, and Lyrics* remarks, "But though we have said that Mr. M'Carthy is a national poet, it does not follow that his poems consist of nothing but Irish traditions."[42] In "A Walk by the Bay of Dublin," MacCarthy positions the speaker as emotionally connected to and even dependent on the landscape on terms congruent with such 1798 English poems as Samuel Taylor Coleridge's "Fears in Solitude" and Wordsworth's "Tintern Abbey." The former, for instance, is framed by the speaker's apostrophe to "A small and silent dell," "a quiet spirit-healing nook" that is itself within "O dear Britain! O my

Mother Isle!" where "by nature's quietness / And solitary musings, all [his] heart is softened."[43] MacCarthy writes of his own "spirit-healing" landscape,

When grief or pain, despondency or care,
Fell on my heart, and worked their ruin there,
One quiet walk along thy silent shore,
One look at thee, and all my grief was o'er![44]

The English Lake Poets invoke their "Mother Isle" and English "Nature"[45] as unproblematic sources of spiritual renewal, but MacCarthy functions within the perspective of the Young Ireland movement of the 1840s, which viewed education and the renovation of the arts as necessary precursors to such national pride. Wordsworth does argue in "Tintern Abbey" for the benefits of a maturer vision in the engagement with rural England, but nature is itself a stable ground from which even the child and untutored "Friend" can benefit, if not to the same extent as the poet. For Young Ireland poets, conversely, nature is not inadequately perceived, but rather *mis*perceived because of a false education that has taught Irish (male) poets to value other nations. As a consequence, artistic representations of the landscape were hailed as the means by which to counter a false, colonial privileging of foreign landscapes over Irish scenes. In Mangan's "The Lovely Land" (1846), for instance, the speaker praises a painting as an Italian landscape in the style of Nicholas Poussin, only to recognize at the end of the poem that it is an Irish landscape by Irish painter Daniel Maclise:

Shame to me, my own, my sire-land,
   Not to know thy soil and skies!
   Shame, that through Maclise's eyes
I first see thee, Ireland!

No! No land doth rank above thee
   Or for loveliness or worth!

So shall I, from this day forth,
Ever sing and love thee![46]

Shame is transferred from a colonial embarrassment over the Irish landscape to the national subject, who has so far internalized colonial abjection as to fail to recognize his own native scenes—an extension of the arguments that Davis puts forward in his essay on ballads and in *The Nation* in general. As Lloyd notes, moreover, Mangan's poem invokes "the Irish pillar tower" on terms resonant with MacCarthy's best-known poem, "The Pillar Towers of Ireland," part of a larger tradition in which "the apparently remote past of these towers [is] a metaphor for the continuity of Ireland's history," a key aspect of Young Ireland's project.[47]

Like "The Lovely Land," MacCarthy's topographical "A Walk by the Bay of Dublin" opens with a complaint about "tourists" and "travelled poets" (3, 1) and offers instead

One who, yet free from fashion's freezing zone,
Admires not every country but—his own!—
Whose heart unchill'd and whose impartial eye
Dare to be just to scenes which round him lie! (15–18)

MacCarthy appropriates Wordsworth's and Coleridge's construction of a private and healing relationship with the natural space but adapts it to the specifically nationalist project of vindicating Ireland by suggesting that the "impartial eye," untainted by colonial abjection, will recognize the beauty of the Irish landscape and so celebrate it. This is a recurring topos in Irish topographical verse, from Leslie's *Killarney* to the anonymous *Mount Leinster*:

Bards for Sicilian scenes their harps have strung,
Shall Erin's fruitful fields remain unsung?
No; fired by you, new numbers wake the soul,
And ope a fair Arcadia at the pole![48]

As in "The Living Land," another MacCarthy poem from the same 1850 volume, the nation needs "Sons who have eyes and hearts to prize / The worth of a Living Land!"[49] The healing of the national subject is thus not simply a matter of a return to nature, of a Wordsworthian revisiting, but also requires the speaker's renewed and renewing recognition of the aesthetic value of Ireland's landscape as integral to Ireland's merit as a nation. MacCarthy's "Walk" closes, "Oh! shame if then I acted not my part, / And gave not back to thee my ever-grateful heart!" (106–7), anticipating (given the presented composition date of 1842) Mangan's use of "shame" in the same context—to mark the national subject who fails to appreciate the Irish landscape as aesthetic object.

Revaluing the landscape, setting aside colonial abjection and the metropole's cultural hegemony, is a keynote of 1840s Young Ireland topographical verse before the Famine, when poetic constructions of the landscape were still naively embedded in the narrative of progress discussed by Christopher Morash and traced back to Leslie's *Killarney* in the present study. The Famine "constituted" not only an "assault on the idea of progress" that could be grasped only through the tropes of apocalypse, as Morash suggests,[50] but also a violation of the principles of nationalism: through famine, the land ceases to function both on Enlightenment terms as economic resource and ground for advancement through the "four stages" invoked by Leslie and on Herderian terms as a register and guarantor of the people's bodily health. According to Herder, human beings are adapted to be healthy in their native land: "The californian, on the verge of the earth, in his barren country, exposed as he is to want, and amid the vicissitudes of his climate, complains not of heat or cold, eludes the force of hunger, though with the utmost difficulty, and enjoys happiness in his native land. . . . [T]hese poor creatures are healthy: . . . well made, straight, and active."[51] Famine in Herder's account prompts national transformation: "But as men are not firmly rooted plants, the calamities of famine, earthquakes, war, and the like, must in time remove them from their place to some other more or less different.

And though they might adhere to the manners of their forefathers with an obstinacy almost equal to the instinct of the brute, and even apply to their new mountains, rivers, towns, and establishments, the names of their primitive land; it would be impossible for them, to remain eternally the same in every respect, under any considerable alteration of soil and climate."[52] This was part of the nationalist crisis of the Famine. The land was no longer "the same" and so no longer safe, propelling survivors into diaspora and a cultural nationalism in which identity is loosed from the soil—a racialized Irishness that is as biologically determined as Herderian thought would contend, but eminently portable, traveling with the diaspora rather than being left behind through geographical dislocation and cultural transformation, as Anderson traces in "Long-Distance Nationalism." Published post-Famine but dated pre-Famine, MacCarthy's topographical poem "Walk" is a nostalgic return to the "well made, straight, and active" national subject, a native physically attuned to his native land and so finding health in his connection to it.

In MacCarthy's "Walk," the landscape is, as in *Killarney* and "Glendalloch," the site of historical erasure. But MacCarthy recoups the landscape as the site of Wordsworthian consolation by blending narrative with scenery, time with space, to create wholeness again through a process akin to what Elizabeth Fay terms the Wordsworthian process of "self-composition."[53] Fay poses two crucial questions pertinent here: "How do we think about, and then how do we represent, the kinds of intersections that arise when temporal and spatial trajectories array themselves in and against the aesthetic? And further, how does this kind of terrain embed the performative as a mode of becoming?"[54] For Wordsworth, as Fay argues, the answer lies in circuits of collaboration and centrally the domestic understood through "the French republican rhetoric of a utopian family-nation,"[55] but this "utopian" paradigm was unavailable in Ireland. The national tale ties it to the romance of an ending (often even locating the wedding itself outside the space of the narrative) and cannot go further, and it is striking how few major Irish poets address lyrics to the siblings that Fay identifies with this "new utopian relation."[56]

Moore's Epistle II, "To Miss M—e," in *Epistles, Odes, and Other Poems* (1806), addressed to the poet's sister, is a rare exception. MacCarthy hence solves the problem without either the "maiden" or the sibling figure analyzed by Fay.

In "Walk," MacCarthy begins by collapsing different epochs into a single space, first through a personal focus that he quickly extends to a wider historical view:

Oft have I paced and traversed o'er and o'er
Marino's woods and Moynealta's shore,—
Both classic spots, both worthy of the bay,—
The one of old, the other of to-day. (42–45)

He elaborates on this historical view by connecting Brian Boru, as the victor over Viking interlopers, with the first earl of Charlemont, who led the nationalist militia, the "Irish Volunteers," in the late eighteenth century. The repetition of "Here" during a seven-line survey of these two historical moments separated by a thousand years repeatedly grounds the larger sweep of history in a single space (as well as closely echoes Drennan's "Glendalloch," where the same device is used to similar effect):

Here aged Brian taught the Danish horde,
The offended justice of a patriot's sword.
Here too, when nigh a thousand years had roll'd
. . . .
Brian lived in Charlemont once more!
. . . .
Here did the patriot take his well-earned rest. (46–48, 51, 53)

Framed by a reference to patriots, this passage elides the shifting fortunes of Irish history by creating a single continuity: patriot heroes who are "here," and "here" with the Young Ireland poet. But MacCarthy adds to this abstracted historical continuity an attention to the immediate physicality of "here": "But not alone the lore of vanish'd days / Gilds this sweet spot with its reflected rays / Here nature sports in most indulgent mood" (54–56), introducing a survey of the natural elements of the landscape. Both national narrative and the visual aesthetics of the natural scene "Gild[] this sweet spot." This conflation of national "lore" with natural beauty marks the appropriation of the English Lake Poets' transcendent poetic memory for the Irish "spirit of the nation," in which "The individual represents the nation": both MacCarthy and his English counterparts herald the healing power of memory and the affect of nature, with the crucial difference that Wordsworth's and Coleridge's speakers typically remember their own pasts in the natural world but MacCarthy's speaker remembers the nation's past.[57] "Here" MacCarthy's speaker merges the personal, the national, and the natural in a transcendent wholeness.

The next verse paragraph extends the implications of this passage on Irish history and the capacity of narrative to replace what is missing from the landscape—to paper over the cracks, so to speak, in the topographical order that English literature typically idealizes and Irish topographical poetry often cannot find. Residues of history left on the landscape compensate for the loss of other markers commemorated in historical narrative:

> What tho' no giant oaks adorn the scene,
> As fond tradition tells there once had been;
> . . . .
> Still it is rich in many a charm and grace,
> Which age revives and time cannot efface;
> Rich in the relics which its glens retain
> The druid altar and the ruined fane. (75–76, 80–83)

Ruins were generally allied with loss and mortality, and especially colonial violence in the Irish ruins discussed by Ferris, Ryder, and others.[58] The representation of ruins as "relics," however, stresses their function as remainders of a precolonial past—and as a means of accessing that past instead of mourning what has intervened. Recalling Drennan's "Glendalloch," in which the tower is used to mark national decline, ruin in "Walk" is associated with the effects of colonial abjection, but, more hopefully than in Drennan's poem, ruination can be reversed:

> When grief or pain, despondency or care,
> Fell on my heart, and worked my ruin there,
> One quiet walk along thy silent shore,
> One look at thee, and all my grief was o'er!" (96–99)

These complicated compensatory moves combine natural elements, archaeological remainders, and historical narrative to restore a sense of wholeness to the landscape, which in the closing verse paragraph in turn restores the speaker's sense of personal wholeness. Again, time and space—"a quiet walk" and "one look"—combine to compensate for "ruin," but ruination of the "heart" rather than the land.

This marshaling of completeness by combining remainders—in narrative, in nature, and in architectural ruins—is echoed in a larger progress throughout the poem and constitutes a striking revision of the ruin motif traceable in English and Continental European discourse. The first verse paragraph is written in the third person, shifting from "them" to "one" in changing the focus from the failed travelers to the more successful speaker:

> While travelled poets pen their polished rhymes
> In praise of distant lands and southern climes,—
> While tourists tell of gorgeous realms afar,
> How bless'd by heaven—how beautiful they are!—
> While every scene but moderately fair,
> Shines on their page, as if all heaven were there!
> . . . .
> One who, yet free from fashion's freezing zone,
> Admires not every country but—his own!—
> Whose heart unchill'd and whose impartial eye
> Dare to be just to scenes which round him lie!—
> With skilless hand he ventures to portray
> A sketch, Eblana, of thy beauteous bay. (1–6, 15–20)

The second verse paragraph treats the speaker not as a grammatical subject, but only as the possessor of aesthetic vision: "what a vision bursts upon my sight" (26); "my raptured eyes survey" (28). The word *I*, despite the poem's debts to Wordsworth, master of the "egotistical sublime" (in Keats's famous slur), does not appear until the opening line of the third verse paragraph, "Oft have I paced" (42), constituting the narrative "I" not only in walking, but also in the repetition of that walking in the past. In other words, the speaker of the poem is an agent insofar as he is constituted through his walk through the landscape. MacCarthy reverses Wordsworthian alignments, speaking of the poet in the third person and of the active walker in the landscape in the first person. The next verse paragraph radically shifts the perspective again to the first-person plural: "Now let us ascend" (68). The shifting use of pronouns, then, first separates the speaker as object of the narrative gaze from a group of touristic writers and then gives him vision through the landscape, granting him agency only in his physical engagement with that landscape—which is then combined with others who also participate, like him, in a walk through the landscape, as "Now let us ascend." This language not only anticipates the closing lines' resolution of the speaker's traumas by using the landscape to revive his grammatical agency but also suggests that agency—individual and collective—comes through activity in the landscape itself. The first use of "I" is in the phrase, "Oft have I paced"; the first use of the plural first person is in the invitation "let us ascend" the mountain; and "one quiet walk" is part of the recipe for healing the grief-stricken subject. The poem is not only a Wordsworthian walk through a landscape; it thematizes such walks as the reconstitution of the specifically national subject. The speaker walks himself into agency, but it is an agency rooted aesthetically in the topographical: "Here those who love to view a noble scene, / Tho' vast, distinct,—sublime, but still serene,— / Here may they rest, and feast their dazzled sight" (87–89).

The patriot needs not only to have aesthetic regard for the land but also to rehearse national memory as he walks through it. But this subject is specifically a male patriot, celebrating "his own" "country" (16) and pondering a history of male patriotism, from Brian Boru to his eighteenth-century avatar, Charlemont. The female gender is reserved in MacCarthy's poem for the personification of the land, representing three hills as "Three Sisters" and closely echoing Coleridge's "Fears in Solitude" in representing the land as mother: "Like a fond mother watching o'er her child, / Thus hast thou ever on my footsteps smiled" (104–5). Hence, MacCarthy's poem appropriates the English association of land with the female body, but without the Irish dimension of sovereignty, using that landscape and its remainders to reenergize instead the virile patriot and empower him to "act" his "part" (106). At the level of gender, then, the poem posits a feminine land through which the male patriot is spurred to national fervor and hence action, recalling United Irishmen ballads more than topographical verse.[59] In Drennan's "Erin," the titular personification of Ireland commands,

Let my sons, like the leaves of their shamrock, unite,
A partition of sects from one footstalk of right;
Give each his full share of this earth
. . . .
Arm of Erin! prove strong.[60]

The elegiac "Edward" offers a less militant version:

What plaintive sounds strike on my ear!
They're Erin's deep ton'd piteous groans,
Her harp attun'd to sorrow drear,
In broken numbers join her moans.
In doleful groups around her stand,
Her manly sons (her greatest pride),
In mourning deep.[61]

In his poem on the death of Davis, "The Living Land," MacCarthy also represents the land as both female and the ground of male action:

A Living Land such as Nature plann'd,
    When she hollowed our harbours deep . . .
Oh! it was not to slaves she gave these waves,
    But to sons of a Living Land![62]

Again note MacCarthy's resonant use of pronouns: Nature has created Ireland, but it does not belong to her. They are "our harbours," he writes, and "she gave these waves" "to *sons*." In MacCarthy's volume *Ballads, Poems, and Lyrics*, there is a peculiar emphasis on women who are subordinate to men, from the depiction of a mother in "The Sick Youth" who "only lives" for her son to a description of a beloved in "Contentment": "Fix'd on my face were her innocent glances."[63] But in his nationalist poems there is a more specifically recurring depiction of the national "Land" as both feminine and granted to male patriots on terms that can restore such men to full agency. MacCarthy's "Walk" thus programmatically follows the pre-Famine forms of cultural nationalism that center on the figure of the male patriot, but it does so by rooting that patriot's identity, health, and grammatical agency in his physical engagement with the landscape on terms that are consonant with Herder.

The outsider national tales by Morgan and Lefanu put pressure on nationalism's easy appropriation of familial tropes by focusing on civil conflicts and the families shattered by them, and LeFanu's best-known early tales from the *Dublin University Magazine* bring that violence directly into the home. MacCarthy's virile patriot, however, is completely protected from violence, a spectator of history as well as the "sublime" ("Walk," 88) scene that together heal him. Looking inward, MacCarthy's speaker finds a romantic transcendence that separates him from the vicissitudes of history. Moreover, as LeFanu uses the figure of the foreign woman to suggest the corruption of the proper domestic and national sphere, MacCarthy, even as he embraces foreign literature, condemns foreign travel by associating it with the artificiality condemned by Wordsworth's preface to the *Lyrical Ballads*: "travelled poets pen their polished rhymes," "in learned rhyme and prose," "While every scene but moderately fair, / Shines on their page, as if all heaven were there!" ("Walk" 1, 11, 5–6). MacCarthy's ideal poet, however, has an "impartial eye" and "Skilless hand," and he "Dare[s] to be just" (17, 19, 18). Invoking authenticity, objectivity, and justness as he details the "sublime," MacCarthy claims a properly masculine style like that being entrenched in a British Victorian aesthetics indebted to Wordsworth, but within a specifically Irish set of concerns about national memory and agency.[64]

6

Geopolitics from Drennan to Cavour

Locating Ireland in a Changing Europe

> 'Tis true! the vast Atlantic tide
> Has scoop'd thy harbours deep, and wide,
> Bold to protect, and prompt to save,
> From fury of the Western wave:
> And Shannon points to Europe's trade.
>
> —WILLIAM DRENNAN, "To Ireland" (1815)

As the foregoing chapters suggest, there was considerable debate in Irish literature about the place of Ireland both in the British Isles and in a wider global field, and specifically interest in Ireland's international relationships. While this chapter focuses on nonfiction prose, it does so to continue earlier chapters' exploration of this debate and thus the terms on which Ireland was imaginatively positioned. In particular, my interest here is in the ways in which imagining the nation as a space—as we have seen in topographical verse, accounts of transatlantic travel and migration, settings and landscape descriptions in fiction—can complicate the narrative emphasis of nationalism by, for instance, juxtaposing different temporalities within one space, as in John Leslie's *Killarney* and William Drennan's "Glendalloch," or representing the space at a moment of transformation, as in national tales or Denis Florence MacCarthy's "Walk." In this vein, *Considerations on the Present State and Future Prospects of Ireland* (1845), an English translation of a French essay by the Italian politician Count Camille de Cavour, accepts the legitimacy of past Irish grievances but insists that Britain is a liberalizing power that functions as a globally stabilizing force and so must be protected from Irish disturbances which are only local in importance. In doing so, it counters emerging arguments for national independence, using geopolitics, an extension in some respects of Herderian thought, as the basis for containing national aspirations as merely local phenomena.

In *Considerations*, Irish aspirations to national sovereignty are insistently distinguished from, and represented as insignificant in relation to, a universal history in which the British Empire leads the globe toward modernity and liberalism. Cavour's strategy is not typical by any means, but it does serve to register the ways in which universal history and geopolitics sanction opposing views of global relations and the foundations of sovereignty, further contextualizing the preceding chapters' interest in the interrelations of narrative (history, progress) and place (landscape, routes), as in Irish topographical poetry's "mixed character."[1] In this chapter, I first situate the *Considerations* within a larger European political landscape in which nationalism was frequently understood in an international context and geopolitics shifted with international treaty and political perspective. Then, I turn to the *Considerations* as a specific elaboration of the interdependence of the categories of geopolitics and universal history, of national and international, and of Ireland and Britain. Finally, I offer a preliminary exploration of the ways in which geopolitics and universal history might be grasped as countervailing frameworks for addressing questions of nation and empire in nineteenth-century Europe; in this, I draw particularly on Drennan's elaboration of what he termed—anticipating by more than a century the 1904 coining of the term *geopolitics*—"the policy of geography."

Island, Archipelago, Transatlantic: From the Napoleonic Wars to Young Ireland

In his first *Letter to the Right Honorable William Pitt* (1799), addressing the current prime minister of Britain, William Drennan, the author of the poem "Glendalloch," explicitly draws on geographical models.[2] British–Irish relations, for Drennan, must be considered in the context of the British war with France and contemporary fears of an invasion of England. By 1799, Napoleon had already entered Milan, seized Malta from the British, and conquered Egypt. Drennan writes,

> plans of the two great contending European powers . . . are turned entirely into a military direction, and they are endeavouring, with rival celerity, to mold, or rather to hammer, whatever is malleable in surrounding countries, not into instruments of peace, but into weapons of war. No country so great as to be safe within the wind of this commotion, none so small as not to be instigated, seduced or terrified, into this perilous, but to them profitless, contest. France wishes to assimilate abroad. Britain hastens to consolidate at home. The strength which the one acquires by expansion, the other strives to get by consolidation, by compressing all its parts closer to a common centre, by making its own centre the centre of the whole system. (8)

This is a suggestive model of European geopolitics: France is centrifugal and Britain is centripetal, and "surrounding countries" are the material on which these two forces act. Drennan's model is Eurocentric in this instance, tacitly ignoring British imperial expansion outside of Europe in the late eighteenth century, but it might arguably be extended to consider that expansion as adding further centers of British power under which regions were consolidated centripetally. Hence, suggests Drennan, "this is the purpose of the Union—*not* to give speed to the plough, or add wings to the shuttle—but to concentrate the military force of the empire, and to organize the country so as best to favor the action of the military machine; to make an arsenal here, a post there, and an advanced redoubt of the whole island" (8–9). Ireland, in other words, is subjected in order to create an attractive military target that will draw off French forces and so protect Britain from invasion. Pitt, he argues, is "conscious that as France has got all by land, and England has all by sea, there is no point of contact for the contending powers, but at his own home, or *here*, resolves at all hazards it shall be *here*, if any where, and provisionally places the Irish nation in the hollow square of the British militia" (28) (in such passages he echoes the insistent "here" of "Glendalloch"). This view of the military map is part of the basis for Drennan's comparison, in *A Second Letter to the Right Honorable William Pitt*, of Pitt to Louis Lazare Hoche and John Joseph Amable Humbert,[3] both French leaders of failed attempts to invade Ireland—Hoche in 1796 and Humbert in 1798. Drennan's *Letters* understand the motivation for Union not in terms of religious intolerance, imperial aggression, or poor government strategy for dominating Ireland, but rather as a "policy of geography"—an attempt to defend Britain from France by reconfiguring the military map.

In 1772, Leslie addressed Ireland's transatlantic importance in the wake of the Seven Years' War (1756–63) and its entrenchment of an Atlantic British Empire, but Ireland's geographical significance changed again in 1814 with the Battle of Waterloo. With Napoleon's defeat, France was no longer such a significant threat to British national security, and Ireland's strategic importance to Britain's military defense arguably diminished accordingly. This military reframing was not simply a matter of France's defeat, but also of the impact of the treaty that followed. The standard historical reading is straightforward: the Congress of Vienna, with the task of forging a European treaty to restore the old order in the wake of Napoleon's defeat, reinstated the pre-Napoleonic empires, with some adjustments and often at France's expense. This was seen in part as a way of quashing a rising "liberalism" in Europe that was fueling movements for nationalism and democratizing reform. Britain itself made no territorial gains in Europe but further established its naval power through the Congress, effectively developing part of the infrastructure necessary to build the Victorian empire. As Paul W. Schroeder has argued, the Congress of Vienna sandwiched three lesser empires—Prussia, Austria, and France—between the two most powerful empires, Britain and Russia.[4] As the *Times* put it in 1831, "The modern policy of Europe—that is to say, the policy suggested by a more comprehensive view of international interests, drawn from a more extended and matured experience than that of former ages—has had for its acknowledged object to maintain an equilibrium among the several Powers."[5] Before Waterloo, Ireland occupied a militarily strategic position, particularly, as Drennan suggests, during the Anglo-French conflicts in the wake of the French Revolution and Napoleon's rise to power (not least the attempted plans to land French forces in Ireland as part of a larger strategy against Britain). After Waterloo, Ireland was adjacent to a world power that was significantly more secure than it was in the 1790s, when mutinies compromised national security, the American war was only recently over, and Napoleon was marching across Europe. (The mutinies at Spithead and the Nore, motivated by sympathy for Revolutionary France and a concomitant resistance to the poor treatment of low-ranking sailors, left large sections of the English coast undefended for months during the Napoleonic wars.[6]) The Congress also reentrenched Austrian power in Italy, leading Giuseppe Mazzini to found the Young Italy movement in the early 1830s and then to encourage its duplication in a range of other Young Europe movements. These Young Europe groups were nationalist in their privileging of language and territory, rather than empire or treaty, as the foundation of political identity. Young Italy launched failed uprisings in 1834 and 1844 and was then supplanted by the more successful Italian Risorgimento, which brought together Cavour, Mazzini, and Giuseppe Garibaldi.

Meanwhile, in 1840s Ireland, Young Ireland splintered from Daniel O'Connell's movement to Repeal the Act of Union, in part because of a difference over religion. The Young Irelanders were generally pan-sectarian and favored liberal ideas of education, but O'Connell supported Catholic state education. Young Ireland was associated with *The Nation* newspaper, a weekly publication whose contributors included poets James Clarence Mangan, Thomas Davis, Speranza Wilde, Denis Florence MacCarthy, and Thomas D'Arcy McGee and which, as we have seen in previous chapters, published pieces congruent with Herderian or romantic nationalism. On

October 15, 1842, its inaugural editorial, titled "The Nation," made the newspaper's nationalist aims clear: "our pages will be always open to fair discussion, we hope to reflect the popular mind, and gather the popular suffrage, within our columns upon this and all other questions of National politics."[7] Within months, the newspaper enjoyed tremendous circulation, and R. F. Foster suggests that "the readership [of *The Nation*] was possibly 250,000 by 1843."[8] While focused on Repeal and an emerging cultural nationalism, *The Nation* was also, from its first issue, concertedly international. In the 1840s, the newspaper regularly featured accounts of military engagements around the globe, including the First Anglo-Afghan War (1839–42), and reports from the Irish diaspora, particularly in the United States. The literature of *The Nation*'s contributors in the 1840s and 1850s was similarly international in sweep, including alongside a large body of writing about Ireland such internationally themed works as Jane Wilde's *Ugo Bassi: A Tale of the Italian Revolution* (1857), MacCarthy's "Afghanistan," McGee's poems about Irish migration to North America (see chapter 3), Davis's essay arguing for Prussia's system of education as a model for Ireland, and Mangan's influential *German Anthology* (1845). Ireland was, however, notoriously rejected by Italian nationalists, who did not view Ireland as a national cause qualified to join Young Poland, Young Italy, and Young Germany in Young Europe: without a language distinct from its oppressors', Ireland was deemed ineligible to join the "Young" club even though "Young Ireland" stuck as a name for part of the Repeal movement, and its writers continued to laud Italian nationalist activity.[9]

In the early 1840s, against this backdrop of inter-European imperial competition while various national groups fought for political autonomy within Europe and debated the precise qualifications for nationhood, Cavour wrote an essay on Ireland's Repeal movement, in particular O'Connell's branch of it. The essay, *Considérations sur l'état actuel de l'Irlande et sur son avenir*, was published in French in a Swiss periodical in 1843 and 1844, then translated into English by the anonymous "A Friend to Ireland," and printed in London in 1845 as *Considerations on the Present State and Future Prospects of Ireland.*[10] It was translated again in 1868 by William Ballantyne Hodgson as *Thoughts on Ireland: Its Present and Its Future.*[11] The work is usually passed over briefly, if mentioned at all, in Cavour scholarship, perhaps because it has little explicitly to do with Italy and predates Cavour's active period in the Risorgimento, recalling the same biases that marginalize Irish literature that is not about Ireland. Nicholas Mansergh summarizes the 1868 translation, and Harry W. Rudman hints at its political significance in the British Isles,[12] joining a number of scholars who note that the essay "was quoted in the House of Commons and has twice been translated into English."[13] These two translations, however, had a decades-long impact in the British Isles on discussions of "the Irish question," even being cited in a legal analysis of the financial ramifications of the establishment of the Irish Free State in 1922.[14]

But the striking timing of these two translations has apparently not been noted. The first translation appeared in 1845, in the wake of Thomas Carlyle's *Chartism* (1839), where English unrest was attributed to misrule in Ireland,[15] and as the Repeal movement gathered considerable momentum (meanwhile, beyond the British Isles, Britain was licking its wounds after a stunning military failure in Afghanistan, detailed in early issues of *The Nation*, and continental Europe teetered toward the Revolutions of 1848). The second translation appeared in 1868, just months after a minor uprising in Ireland and agitation over the second Reform Bill, but, more saliently, in the wake of a wide-ranging series of actions by Fenians that amounted to a transatlantic campaign against Britain. The Fenians invaded Canada in 1866 and made two notorious attempts to release Irish prisoners in England: in September 1867, they attacked a police van carrying two men; in December 1867, they bombed Clerkenwell Prison in an attack in which bystanders were killed. In 1868, this international group of Irish nationalists was held responsible for the assassination of *Nation* poet and Irish Canadian politician Thomas D'Arcy McGee. Hodgson explicitly invokes Fenianism as one of the spurs to his translation (while euphemistically referring to the Famine and the exodus from Ireland that it propelled as mere "emigration"): "in spite of a vast amount of emigration,—in spite of the National School system,—in spite of all legislative measures,—Irish discontent has, after another quarter of a century, burst forth in armed Fenianism."[16] These two English translations of Cavour's essay, then, appeared at times of rising tensions over Irish insurgency, British national security, and the viability of the empire, situating the English circulation of Cavour's essay within larger attempts to quell Irish nationalism and defend British ascendancy.

Cavour's *Considerations*: From History to Geopolitics

All references here are to the 1845 translation because my interest in this essay is the use of the translation as a volley in Repeal politics after the rise of *The Nation* and before the major crises of the late 1840s, centrally the Famine. This 138-page translation reviews the history of Irish grievances, the Repeal movement, economic ties between England and Ireland, and other factors related to the question of Ireland's place in the Union with Britain in order to accept the errors of the past but argue ultimately that Ireland will gain much from political and economic ties with Britain. The translation is itself geopolitically positioned: "A Friend to Ireland" suggests in a short preface, "The opinions of an intelligent foreigner on Irish affairs can never be a matter of indifference to this country" (iii). The European public, however, does not enjoy the same status Cavour has as an "intelligent foreigner," and the translated text dismisses foreign opinion in general "on Irish affairs" (1–5). Hence, in the opening paragraphs of the 1845 translation, the European press is depicted as unbalanced, even sensationalist, in its reporting on Ireland's Repeal movement:

> The singular state of Ireland has attracted throughout Europe the attention of all who take any interest in politics. . . . The newspapers, those faithful interpreters of whatever is uppermost in the public mind, make Ireland one of their constant themes for discussion. Usually so laconic with respect to the affairs of England, they

> at once open their columns to the reports of the most insignificant meetings in favour of the Repeal of the Union; and we are regularly informed of the minutest details of the great trial which O'Connell and his associates are at present undergoing. (1–2)

This interest in the condition of Ireland is politically but diversely motivated:

> It must be admitted, that public opinion on the Continent is not, in general, favourable to England. . . . From Petersburg to Madrid, in Germany as in Italy, the enemies of human progress, and the partizans of political revolutions, alike consider England as their most formidable adversary. The former charge her with being the focus whence all revolutions emanate—the certain refuge—the citadel, as it were, of propagandists and levellers. The latter, on the contrary, with more reason perhaps, look upon the English aristocracy as the cornerstone of the European social edifice, and as the greatest obstacle to their democratic views. (2–3)

The translation is thus positioned as an attempt to reshape international debate on Ireland, framing "intelligent" responses as ones sympathetic to the current British administration while condemning as biased or "unintelligent" responses that favor Irish independence: for instance, bias is clear in those "men who care the least for liberty and toleration [and] are heard every day exclaiming against English tyranny, and the melancholy lot of the Irish Catholics; whilst these same persons can find no word of pity for members of their own church in Poland, who are victims of the religious persecution of the Emperor of Prussia" (4). This lament is followed by the dire warning, "It is important to sift to the uttermost the real causes of this demonstration in favour of Ireland, for the purpose of guarding against the influence they may exert on the mode in which the events of that country and their probable consequences should be appreciated. Any mistake in this respect would be fatal" (5). *Considerations* thus opens with the position that European support for Irish nationalism is misguided, hypocritical, and dangerous, while the essay as a whole works to inoculate Europe (from the politically neutral site of Switzerland) from such perilous opinions.

My focus is the first English translation and its domestic circulation, but it is important to note as well that Cavour was participating in an attempt to solicit international opinion in favor of Italian nationalist policy. Britain would eventually become instrumental in the establishment of a sovereign Italian state, and its Protestantism (as well as competition with other European empires) made it in some senses an inevitable ally because one of the main stumbling blocks to Italian unification and independence was the existence of the Papal States, an autonomous region governed by the pope in virtually monarchical terms (there was, for instance, no constitution until the pope issued one in early 1848 in response to rising political agitation from nationalists and republicans). In the face of nationalist-republican insurgency, including the assassination of his prime minister, the pope was forced to flee Rome in disguise in late 1848 and only returned in 1850 with French military support. If Catholic nations were to be expected to support the pope's territorial claims in Italy, it is not too surprising that the nationalists were reaching out to the most powerful non-Catholic empire in Europe—Britain. Moreover, while we are wont to paint the evils of the British Empire, it is salutary to recall that other European empires, including Russia and Austria, were more directly repressive, not least against their own citizens, than the British government. Austria banned the works of Lady Morgan, for instance, but Britain never suppressed her work and eventually gave her a literary pension. Depicting the British government as the vanguard of European liberalism, then, made some sense, even though historians have represented Cavour in particular, and the Risorgimento leadership in general, as "anglophile."[17] They have also noted in relation to the *Considerations* "the popular belief that [Cavour] was more interested in money-making and in business for its own sake than in the cause of national freedom."[18] But the specifics of Italy's situation and British politics suggest strategic reasons for an alignment with British interests to foster British support. Indeed, Britain would prove a valuable ally. It provided important military support in the months leading up to Italian unification in 1861, including a naval escort for Garibaldi's troops in 1860 as they moved from Sicily to the Italian mainland. In other words, Cavour's essay and its translation are geopolitical in context as well as in content: the *Considerations* solicits international support for British and Italian domestic aims as the global arrangements, and reactionary politics, consolidated by the Congress of Vienna began to crumble.

In the preface and notes, the "Friend to Ireland" who translated Cavour's essay into English is less concerned with the Italian problem than with taking domestic advantage of Cavour's argument for Britain as a liberal power that functions as a globally stabilizing force. Acknowledging the violence of British rule in the past, the translated essay proposes that slow and cautious reform is the best solution to Ireland's social and economic ills and that such reform is possible only under the supervision of an 1840s British government that is, unlike its less enlightened predecessors, liberal and orderly. It locates Britain's political leadership in a progressive trajectory that decisively separates the present from the past:

> In reviewing the history of so much misery and of such long-continued oppression, one is involuntarily led to pass a severe judgement upon the nation which has been, if not the author of it, at least its accomplice, and to call them to account even in these later times for the barbarity of which their fathers were guilty. . . . When, however, the generous emotions of indignation are tempered by the calm judgement of reason, one is forced to admit that the English, from the time of William III. and of Queen Anne, are not so culpable as they would appear to us, judging them as we now do with the superior light of the nineteenth century. In persecuting the Catholics, in heaping on their heads vexation after vexation, for the purpose of rendering the exercise of their religion humiliating and difficult, the politicians of those times were not conscious of the crime they were committing against mankind. They did no more than follow opinions of their day; they applied with rigorous fidelity the doctrines of intolerance, which at that time in Europe no one dared openly to dispute. (12–13)

Progress is now accomplished: "If we compare the effect these cruelties and persecutions produce on us, the offspring of the nineteenth century, with the effect produced by them on the most enlightened and civilised men of the preceding age, we cannot withhold our meed of praise for the great progress which has been going on in the moral judgements of the world" (14). Strangely echoing Protestant jeremiads, the *Considerations* then transfers guilt for Ireland's condition from Britain to a Providence that is using Ireland to move the world forward: "Providence did not permit that these salutary measures should take place at that time. She destined Ireland to become, after a long course of misery, a never-failing source of anxiety and trouble to her oppressors; for the purpose, as it should seem, of furnishing a great lesson to the world, and teaching nations, however powerful, that the crimes and errors which they commit will, sooner or later, recoil on themselves" (19–20). Throughout the first sections of the essay, British wrongs and Irish "misery" are acknowledged only to be set aside for and by universal history—as here, where the essay suggests that Britain makes great strides forward while Ireland remains subordinate both to Britain and to a guiding hand that uses it as "a great lesson to the world."

Conversely, Daniel O'Connell, Irish member of Parliament and leader of the movement that achieved Catholic Emancipation in 1829, is synecdochally collapsed with the entire Repeal movement and nationalist leadership in Ireland, and he is depicted as too mercurial to supervise the complex process of wide-ranging reform. O'Connell is represented as changing his politics from one moment to the next: "in the midst of these apparent contradictions, perfect consistency is observable in O'Connell's views. Employing a thousand different means which he knows how to multiply, and vary to infinity according to the exigencies of the moment, he ever follows the same objects,—the political restoration of his co-religionists and of his country. Out of consideration for the consistency of his principle of action, history will forgive his repeated changes, and the very opposite judgements he has passed on the same measure and the same men" (51–52). If, however, the Irish were to follow the liberal (and so implicitly postsectarian) British instead of the Catholic-focused O'Connell and to accept the claim that reform is necessarily slow, progress would be within their grasp:

> The peaceable and orderly conduct of the Irish ever since the formation of the Melbourne ministry, bears ample testimony to the progress which that people has made in the path of true civilisation. Government had only to evince its good intentions towards them, and to show that their convictions would be respected, and their national feelings not offended, for that same people, so turbulent and so restive, to evince at once respect for the laws, and endure with patience those evils of its social condition to which it is not in human power to apply an instant remedy. (52)

By focusing on O'Connell and averting its gaze from other nationalist organizations such as Young Ireland, the translation can represent the Repeal movement as parochial rather than liberal, as the agenda of the "Catholic party" and not of the Irish people as a nation. The threat of a disenfranchised Anglo-Irish Protestant minority hovers too on the edges of the argument in *Considerations*: "It is evident that if Repeal took place, it would be due to the successful efforts of the popular and Catholic party, and consequently that the first independent legislature would be almost exclusively composed of members of that party" (90). The *Considerations* is no flat-footed piece of propaganda, but it nevertheless relies rhetorically on the view that O'Connell, the Catholic party, and insurgents in general are inconsistent, dithering, and short-sighted, unable to see the grand march of history in which Britain leads and Ireland may follow (a variation on Leslie's claims in *Killarney*).

While maintaining this universal history as the only means of social progress as well as the arbiter of which political struggles are significant, the essay also situates Ireland and England, as a synecdoche for Britain, within three geopolitical arenas and historically located epochs. First, Ireland and Britain together form a colonial dyad in which Ireland is clearly the past victim of an unconscionable (and even incompetent) brutal regime—but that is firmly in the past. Second, in the present, Ireland and Britain within Europe are entangled in European views of Britain: as the flagship of a liberalism that balances democracy with aristocracy, the essay suggests, Britain draws the ire of both conservatives and radicals on the Continent, who thus join together as well in their support of the Irish nationalist cause because Irish agitation challenges the efficacy and power of British liberal moderation. Third, Britain is an imperial power whose "foreign affairs . . . are numerous, important, and complicated" (83), making it important to a global future, whereas Ireland is insignificant in this sphere. Thus, the translation of Cavour's essay supports British interests by discounting European support for Irish nationalism and making the empire itself the paramount concern of the international community because of its role in global stability and liberal progress. The only means of achieving Irish independence, the essay insists, is through an insurrection after "an unsuccessful foreign war, exhausting the resources of England. . . . If Repeal were purchased at the price of the humiliation of England, it would cost too much to the cause of humanity; and no one who is sincere would have it on such terms" (141). In *Considerations*, Britain is the liberal gear that will drive world history forward.

Yet to accomplish this move Britain's gear needs to be freed of the brake that threatens to grind it to a halt—Ireland. Hence, the essay grasps the relationship between Britain and Ireland in myriad terms in which it is consistently to Ireland's civil and economic benefit to accept British rule. For instance, Cavour both calculates Ireland's share of Britain's national debt and surveys the brutality of English colonial domination before 1800, while apologizing for the latter as an effect of a barbarity that the British have now transcended. Geographically, however, the focus is precise. The essay repeatedly invokes St. George's Channel, the body of water that separates the south of Ireland from Wales and links the Irish Sea to the Atlantic. The channel is a geographical feature that both registers and facilitates political relations. Early in the essay, for instance, Ireland's resistance to conquest is geographically situated: "powerful Norman barons, whose sway had extended throughout England, and who had obliterated even the shadow of Saxon nationality, were unable to establish their authority upon the same foundation on the other side of St. George's Channel. The vast bogs with which Ireland was covered, its extensive heaths which stretch towards the west, especially in Connaught, offered for ages a safe refuge to the unsubdued Celts, and enabled them to preserve, at the price of poverty and every kind of suffering, a savage independence" (7). Ireland is thus not only geographically divided, but also geographically distinctive from Britain, so distinctive that it cannot be assimilated politically. And, as in so much eighteenth- and nineteenth-century writing about Ireland, the bog is a symbol of both recalcitrance and barbarity—just as the bog is not transformed into arable land, so "the unsubdued Celts" will not be absorbed into a productive social order.[19]

Later in the essay, Pitt is represented as the brave diplomat who sought to elide the channel in the unification of the islands through the Act of Union: "The end which Pitt had in view was great and noble. In uniting under the same government the two islands, separated by St. George's Channel, he hoped to strengthen and consolidate British power, which was, at that time, the butt of formidable attacks" (25). St. George's Channel is now a hurdle to be overleaped in the fortification of the islands against France. This is the very argument upon which Drennan builds—indeed, both Drennan and the "Friend to Ireland" use the word *consolidate* to describe the strategic impetus behind the Act of Union (*Letter*, 8; *Considerations*, 25). Later, in outlining the benefits to Ireland of continuing participation in rather than separation from a unified British Isles, the *Considerations* suggests that "[s]ome persons may, perhaps, think that by adopting a system of protection, and closing its ports to England, several branches of manufactures might be able to flourish in Ireland. But this is absurd. A custom-house war between two islands separated by St. George's Channel would be fatal to both, although England would suffer much the least of the two. Ireland, from its essentially agricultural character, finds in Great Britain the most favourable outlet for its produce" (98–99). Ireland is represented as a merely agricultural nation, and its neighbor as a fully fledged commercial state, thus following not only the "four-stages theory" in which societies progress from hunting to herding to farming and finally to commerce, but also what Adam Smith defined as the relationship between town and country: "The great commerce of every civilized society, is that carried on between the inhabitants of the town and those of the country," in which surplus raw materials flow to the town, and "a part of the manufactured produce" flows to the country.[20] Ireland is rendered both backward (agricultural rather than commercial) and provincial, the rural adjunct of a fully commercialized Britain—as in Leslie's *Killarney* seventy years earlier. Ireland is thus inevitably economically reliant on its more advanced neighbor, and the reinstatement of St. George's Channel as a boundary for taxation will forestall Ireland's economic advancement out of the agricultural stage.[21] So, in these three moves, spread across ninety pages of a substantial essay, the *Considerations* establishes Ireland's geographical distinctness from Britain, the importance to British security of politically absorbing a (pacified) Ireland,[22] and Ireland's economic reliance on continuing trade with Britain across St. George's Channel. Although the first point might seem at odds with the other two in establishing a reason for separation instead of a basis for close communication, it is in fact essential: geographical distinctness defines Ireland as an agricultural nation and hence politically backward, providing the preconditions for both its economic reliance on Britain and the short-sightedness of its political aspirations. Britain offers Ireland what it offers the world—access to modernity. Without it, all Ireland can hope for is "savage independence."

The final reference to St. George's Channel is especially resonant. The *Considerations* suggests that Ireland's transatlantic position makes it an ideal focal point for the global network emerging through the Victorian British Empire: "railroads would bestow great commercial importance upon Ireland. If one of those miraculous means of communication traversed the island from east to west, and placed St. George's Channel in immediate communication with the western coast, washed by the Atlantic, . . . Ireland would become, as a matter of necessity, the high road between the two hemispheres, and its future prospects would be glorious. The consequences arising from such an undertaking would be incalculable, not only for her, but for the whole world" (103). *Considerations* here erases both Irish sovereignty and Irish land at once. The "miraculous" "railroads" can place "St. George's Channel in immediate communication with the western coast, washed by the Atlantic": Ireland, not even rhetorically the possessor of this "western coast," disappears with the speed of modern technology. It has no ports, no cities, no national infrastructure—it is only a space to be traversed by the rails. This was indeed happening as, in some senses, technology was already eliding St. George's Channel itself. In 1843, Samuel Carter Hall and Anna Maria Hall wrote, in one of their tourist guidebooks, "Steam-boats have done more than either Time or Legislation to unite England and Ireland: they facilitate intercourse almost as much as a bridge across St. George's Channel; and render the voyage, in summer time, little else than a pleasure excursion. Formerly, it was serious business,—of so uncertain a duration, that not unfrequently weeks were spent between the opposite Ports."[23] But my greater interest here is in the rhetorical moves that Cavour makes to further such erasure. For Cavour, technology creates the means through which Ireland's position on the cusp of the transatlantic space as well as on the periphery of the British metropole can be turned to considerable economic advantage as well as make Ireland at last significant on the world stage as a tool of British empire. No longer just drawing off French forces from the English countryside, as Drennan argued it did in the 1790s, Ireland is now imagined as a means of increasing the speed and profitability of imperial trade. No longer subordinated as a part of the transatlantic colonial sphere, it is now in a unique geographical position to take advantage of its peripheral position in relation to the British Isles and so become "commercially importan[t]" rather than a merely agricultural state dependent on a commercial neighbor, fulfilling the promise of Leslie's *Killarney* (see chapter 1). But in outlining this hopeful future, the *Considerations* virtually elides the island as a geographical entity with "sun" and "soil," mountains and rivers, transforming Ireland into a simple extension of St. George's Channel—the transport interface between Britain and its empire.

Geopolitics versus Universal History: From Drennan to Cavour

I have been using the term *geopolitical* somewhat anachronistically here because it was not coined until 1904 and was theorized by such turn-of-the-century thinkers as Sir Halford John Mackinder. Christopher GoGwilt suggests that geopolitics emerged from a break with "nineteenth-century ideas of culture,"[24] but similar concepts were in play from at least the late eighteenth century forward, particularly in geographical complications of universal history as a key eighteenth- and nineteenth-century concept broadly founded on the historiographic premise that human history progresses according to a developmental model that is governed by a uniform set of principles, a kind of secular Providence, and therefore differences among societies are attributable to their different locations on that developmental track (variously theorized by such thinkers as George Sale, Immanuel Kant, G. W. F. Hegel, and of course Karl Marx). GoGwilt's view of nineteenth-century "cosmopolitical" discourse (which he opposes to the "geopolitical") is tacitly rooted in universal history: "the European hypothesis of culture as cosmopolitan" is "conceived in terms of the educational ideal of 'Bildung,' with its cosmopolitan narrative imperative to unfold the individual's story in harmony with the development of human history as a whole."[25] David Lloyd has a different perspective on this "educational ideal," however: for him, "the term 'culture' . . . impl[ies] its relationship to a general idealist conception of aesthetics and of aesthetic education or *Bildung*: aesthetic culture is not to be understood merely as the cultivation of a taste for the beautiful, but as invoking a concept of man in general as producer of form. . . . That is to say, aesthetics posits the universal formal identity of the human."[26] This framing of "aesthetic education" facilitates Lloyd's analysis of the ways in which such theories of culture were used to reinforce the value of the metropole within a universal history in which the colonial subject is always trailing behind: "Predicated on the notion of universality, this aesthetic both legitimates and transmits the ethnocentric ideology of imperialism. In its very postulation of an eventual reassimilation of the racial or sexual other through historical development, the canon of culture permits and enacts the exclusion of that other as being a not yet fully realized form of humanity. Culture, moreover, gives the law for the form in which that humanity must—always asymptotically—approach realization."[27] GoGwilt, focusing on the transition from the nineteenth to the twentieth centuries, makes an interesting case for a discursive shift from a temporal view of world relations—the *Bildung* of the individual and "the development of human history as a whole"—to a spatial model in which geography, rather than history, is the key explanatory discipline; conversely, Lloyd, addressing earlier decades, argues for resistance to the *Bildung* model taking place through a "refusal to constitute the narrative as productive" and offers as an example a character who is a "land surveyor."[28] Both Lloyd and GoGwilt oppose the spatial (and local) and the temporal (and universal) even though they diametrically disagree on the value of one over the other. Drawing on Lloyd, who moves from the eighteenth to the nineteenth centuries in this argument, we can understand geopolitics not only as a conservative nationalist attempt in the early twentieth century to scientifically reinforce European hegemony, as GoGwilt suggests,[29] but also as part of an older, ideologically varied reaction against hegemonic ideas of universal history—an anti-imperial geopolitics.

Geopolitics, particularly as a means of insisting on the effects of the local (who borders whom, where the ports are, what the distribution of arable lands is, where mineral and water resources are),[30] provides the materials for a challenge to the universalisms that reinforce imperial hegemony. The universal subject parallels universal history in annihilating the difference on which more local claims can be asserted or, in the vivid words of *The Nation* in 1843, on the attitude of their imperial "tyrants," "They would attach to the physiognomy of nations the mask of a slavish uniformity, lest the brotherhood of freemen should recognise their kin—lest we should remember that Italians cannot be Germans, Flemings Dutch, nor Celts Saxons. They would drive the ponderous rolling-stone, as it were, over the different families of man, to render more facile their own regal tread over prostrate human nature."[31] The category of the "cosmopolitan" invoked by GoGwilt is founded upon an elision of geographical distinctions to imagine a uniform world through which the universal imperial subject moves and develops in the *Bildung* discussed by both GoGwilt and Lloyd. Consider, for instance, James Howell's "The Vote, Or Poem Royal" appended to Howell's *Epistolæ Hoelianæ: Familiar Letters, Domestick and Foreign* (1645–55), republished throughout the late seventeenth and eighteenth centuries:

> *Earth* is our common Mother, every ground
> May be one's Country, for by birth each man
> Is in this world a *Cosmopolitan*,
> A free-born Burgess.[32]

Written by an Oxford-educated English Royalist imprisoned by a Parliament asserting its constitutional rights, this passage defines the individual's sovereignty on terms that not only anticipate John Locke by a few decades but concomitantly rely upon the nonspecificity of the world of which this subject is a citizen. There are no borders, indigenous populations, rivers, mountains, or deserts in Howell's "every ground." It is a space that is defined through the cosmopolitan's freedom to move—just as Ireland is defined at the end of the *Considerations* in terms of the freedom of England's trains to move across it.[33] Conversely, *The Citizen of the World*, first published serially in 1760–61 by Irish author Oliver Goldsmith, troubles such a cosmopolitanism by making its "Citizen of the World," Lien Chi, neither universal nor free: Lien Chi is rendered culturally specific through the emphasis on his Chinese nationality and his incomprehensibility to the English orientalists he meets, and he is subject to tyranny at home and abuse in England.[34] By attending to the specificities of place, geopolitics as such provides a different view of geography in relation to politics than is possible with postcolonial ideas of alterity, as in Simon Gikandi's useful *Maps of Englishness*, or with more ethnographic views in which place serves as a metonym for cultural, historical, or social differences, as in the treatments of Victorian London from Peter Stallybrass and Allon White forward to Simon Joyce.[35] The ambivalence of the prefix *geo-* (Greek for "earth") allows geopolitics to tie together two concepts—geography as a source of politics and politics as a global dynamic—while retaining the materiality of geography as a discipline concerned with natural resources and local particulars as well as spatial relationships. It allows us, like the speaker of MacCarthy's "Walk," both to organize the history of international relations through "here" and to see "here" as a material space (see chapter 5).

Long before the word *geopolitical* was coined in 1904, Drennan used the phrase "the policy of geography" to grasp such concerns. In his first *Letter*, Drennan argues against the Act of Union, suggesting, "if the cruel alternative be proposed to me, unite for ever with England, or separate for ever, I would say—*separate*, in the name of God and nature. If such be the alternative, let no little pert pre-eminence say to me, 'look at the map,' and attempt to reconcile the perfidy of policy to the policy of geography" (44). The "policy of geography," for Drennan, leads to cooperation among independent nations rather than to domination:

> The true system of the world was long a paradox to philosophers as well as to the people, and when the Genoese pilot, in pursuit of the East Indies, steered due *west*, he steered most paradoxically, but, while he was losing one world, he made another. I will venture the paradox, and, steering due *west*, I will assert that the interest of *Britain* lies in the real and absolute independence of Ireland, on the immediate renunciation of all governmental connexion, a just compensation for past treatment, but also the truest wisdom, by securing our friendship in a *solitary* world. The stranger, the foreigner, the supposed foe would then become fellow countrymen and fellow citizens and brothers; and our greater population and capacity to purchase would produce to Britain a better market, (to

> *her* supreme felicity,) for there is not a country, which grows and increases, that does not, in its collateral consequences, augment the industry of the whole world. (44–45)

As independent nations in a "solitary world," Ireland and Britain shall, with all other nations, benefit with "the whole world." Drennan invokes the French Revolutionary principles of *liberté* ("absolute independence") and *fraternité* ("fellow citizens and brothers") through an *equality* between Britain and Ireland that facilitates economic ties. He argues similarly in his *Second Letter to the Right Honorable William Pitt* (1799) that "nature designed" Ireland to be "a Free Port for the world" (36). Instead of "citizens of the world," they are "fellow citizens," defined socially and through trade rather than as sovereign subjects roving through an undifferentiated global space. Drennan imagines an international body that would regulate and protect the independence of the world's nations on such relational terms: "I do assert that the great perfection of this sublunary system would be such a law of nations, recognized and supported, as might cover the universality of *independent* countries, fulfilling their duties and asserting their rights, with its tutelary authority, defending the weakest from the most ambitious, and guaranteeing to all the full possession of their independence, under the ægis of a common power" (*Letter*, 46). In using the phrase "the law of nations," as we saw in the introduction, Drennan locates his argument within the legal discourse that led Jeremy Bentham to coin the word *international* in a work first published in 1789: "The word *international*, it must be acknowledged, is a new one; though, it is hoped, sufficiently analogous and intelligible. It is calculated to express, in a more significant way, the branch of law which goes commonly under the name of the *law of nations*," the phrase used to translate the title of Emer de Vattel's *Le droit des gens* (1758).[36] Such a "policy of geography" moves us away from the binaries of metropole/periphery, east/west, first world/third world that are tacitly organized by the narrative pull of universal history. Instead, Drennan argues strenuously (and at length) for the value of a "universality" that protects individuality and autonomy at the level of the national, setting aside the ideal of the free Enlightenment subject who roams at will over the globe and so can function as an imperial agent, while also redefining a universality that has room for the colonized in ways that the discourse analyzed by Lloyd does not.

❧

Geopolitics offered writers such as Drennan a framework within which to imagine international relations outside of a universal history that reifies metropolitan values, but Cavour's essay reveals the ways in which a localized geopolitics could also serve the interests of the metropole under another guise. In broad terms, the *Considerations* uses geopolitics locally and universal history globally. The essentializing, even fascist, impetus that GoGwilt finds in twentieth-century geopolitics is deployed in *Considerations* to render Irish concerns local and particular, "minor" in Lloyd's terms, while Britain remains both universal and geographically diffused over an undefined empire and a generalized "globe." Or, put another way, Ireland is rendered provincial while Britain is imagined as cosmopolitan—"Earth is our common Mother, every ground / May be one's Country"—and so as rising above local interests that are expressed through the international realm where law, treaty, and geography must be addressed. Romantic-era geopolitics could function, as in Drennan's writing, to support the local and the national against the universalizing and the imperial by using the materials of geography to contest the idealized abstractions of "aesthetic education" and universal history. Cavour's *Considerations*, implicitly soliciting both British support in the rising European crisis over Italy and continental support for Britain as a liberalizing player on the world stage, meets this local politics on its own ground in order to set it aside and hence reinstate, on securer terms, a universal history centered on London. The *Considerations* thus reveals the ways in which universal history and geopolitics, though theoretically opposed, could make strange bedfellows in the pursuit of a pragmatic policy of buttressing British imperial power in order to challenge more reactionary European regimes.

Conclusion

The Case of the Love Elegy

> The English have had their Collections; so have the Scotch; and both have enriched their publications with Gems from *Ireland*. We know of nothing before, of this nature, undertaken amongst us; and, in the latter respect, we have been rather more delicate than our neighbours, cautiously avoiding to insert any thing which was not properly of native growth.
>
> —"Prefatory Epistle," in *The Shamrock* (1772)

As we have seen in the preceding chapters, Irish literature is often concertedly international in concern, from John Leslie's interest in the transatlantic to William Drennan's in Western geopolitics, to the poetry of Irish migrants and literary depictions of such figures, to national tales set outside of the British Isles, and to the broader corpus of even romantic nationalists, such as *The Nation* poets. The epigraph to this chapter points to the codependence of such nationalism and internationalism: even this early, preromantic collection of poetry only "of native growth," *The Shamrock*, frames its project in terms of the nation's "neighbours." Count Camille de Cavour's analysis of the "problem of Ireland" schematizes what Irish writers had often struggled with in the preceding seven decades: the multiple, and strategic, positionings of Ireland geographically and (most directly through applications of the "four stages theory") narratively. Part of the literary history of this struggle has been sketched in the preceding chapters: Leslie's *Killarney* helps to found a poetic tradition that is in turn taken up by the national tale and then the national tale's critics; Edward Ledwich blends topographical and antiquarian description with the Burke-inspired gothic, feeding into Drennan's "Glendalloch" and thence into depictions of Glendalough across the nineteenth century; Irish poetry of exile revisits the ideological conundrum of the antebellum United States as the "land of Liberty" from the exiles of 1798 to those of 1848, reshaping the century-old figure of the "wild geese" and countering the dominant tradition of grieving nostalgia for the homeland; the Irish gothic contributes to the development of the detective genre in the Anglo-American tradition and comments on English society and European empire; the national tale has a wider interest in European nation building and, in its domestic symbolism, is part of the prehistory of midcentury gothic and sensation fiction as a counterweight to the masculinist lyricism of Young Ireland's national martyr. Throughout, national tales and gothic fiction and topographical verse—all engaged with questions of land and territory as well as of mobility and migration—weave in and out of the larger fabric of romantic-era Irish literature.

The question of nationality—of who does and who does not count as an "Irish" writer—has not been addressed here explicitly, though it has long haunted Irish literary studies, as the epigraph attests. Nearly two centuries after *The Shamrock* was published, Flann O'Brien complained, "I know of no civilisation to which anything so self-conscious could be indigenous. Why go to the trouble of proving that you are Irish? Who has questioned this notorious fact? If, after all, you are not Irish, who is?"[1] Alicia Lefanu, whose work is discussed in two chapters here, lived in England, perhaps for her whole life. She was the niece of Lady Morgan's Dublin mentor, Alicia Sheridan Lefanu, and of Irish dramatist Richard Brinsley Sheridan, who read and admired her early poetic work; she worked with Thomas Moore on his biography of Richard Brinsley Sheridan, and he worked on her behalf with publishers. But she is included in this study not because of what we might term her ethnic background and diasporic connections. She is relevant because she engaged with the same literary tradition as the writers discussed here: her novel *Henry the Fourth of France* clearly builds on Lady Morgan's second novel, *The Novice of Saint Dominick*, and *The Outlaw* alludes to Moore, Mary Tighe, and Morgan's third novel, *The Wild Irish Girl*; her biography of her grandmother, Frances Sheridan, a key figure in eighteenth-century Irish literature, is still a staple of scholarship on that novelist and playwright. Alicia Lefanu is thus an interesting case in point. Is she Irish in literary terms rather than political terms? Is she an Irish writer ethnically, in nationalism studies' sense of "the collective acceptance of a shared self-image,"[2] through her participation in a literary tradition and collaborative group of writers strongly connected to Ireland, but not in the terms of more biologically determined Herderian nationalism because she lived with her Ireland-born parents in England? Does she, in other words, belong to the narrative of Irish literary history, if not to the space of Irish land? She, like the emigrants discussed in chapter 3 and the more typically expatriate Morgan and Moore (both of whom left Ireland to live in the publishing center of the British Isles—London), wrote from outside of Ireland's borders, but her work helps to define the contours of its literary landscape. And that, ultimately, is what I have hoped to chart here—not in its entirety by any means, but at least some of its relatively unmapped territories, such as the larger genealogy of the national tale, the place of the transatlantic in the national imaginary before the Famine, and the textual genealogies through which sites such as Glendalloch become fixed in the cultural mind's eye. More broadly, I would suggest, we need to take the time to chart a complex Irish literary tradition that is grounded in but not bound by insular notions of geography or politics.

The love elegy is an illustrative genre in this context and thus constitutes my final example of Irish modes and genres of this era. A recurring form across the history of Irish literature, from Irish-language verse in the Middle Ages to the twentieth century, it was a common form of poetry in Irish writing in English long before William Butler Yeats. As I suggest here, it underwent a resurgence in the late eighteenth century and then seems to have more or less disappeared in the first decade of the nineteenth, a period closely coincident with the "early Irish romantic period" I define in the introduction. It was chosen by writers of various regions, classes, political affiliations, and linguistic backgrounds, and it draws on Latin, English, and Irish-language literary precedents. It is neither overtly political nor nationalist, being, by its nature, more private in its themes,[3] but it is nevertheless a register of the ways in which Irish literature can be both distinctively Irish and richly international.

The love elegy also brings us back to 1772, the year of *Killarney*'s publication. In Dublin that year, Samuel Whyte, a member of the extended Sheridan family and a well-regarded Dublin schoolmaster who counted Moore and Richard Brinsley Sheridan among his students, published an anthology of poetry under the title *The Shamrock: Or, Hibernian Cresses.*[4] As with much eighteenth-century work of this sort, its authorship is uncertain. Whyte is not explicitly named as editor of the work—his name appears only on the title page as the author of an appended essay on school reform—but the editor's "Prefatory Epistle" is dated "Grafton-Street," where Whyte lived. J. N. Hook suggests that Whyte is not only the editor, but also "probably author of a considerable part of its contents," and Andrew Carpenter proposes that it collected the work of Whyte's pupils, but Bill Overton has noted that it reproduces some material published nearly twenty years earlier.[5] The volume's lack of concern with identifying authorial literary property is counterweighted by its insistence on identifying *national* literary property:

> The English have had their Collections; so have the Scotch; and both have enriched their publications with Gems from *Ireland*. We know of nothing before, of this nature, undertaken amongst us; and, in the latter respect, we have been rather more delicate than our neighbours, cautiously avoiding to insert any thing which was not properly of native growth. If it should in any instance appear otherwise, it must be imputed to inadvertency, not intention. We could prove an indubitable claim to many things which they have appropriated; but have resumed only two or three pieces at the special direction of their author, who asserted his property, and thought it no robbery to make free with his own. (*Shamrock*, iv–v)

The editor not only draws on the rhetoric of natural resources ("Gems," "enriched") and property rights ("claim," "property," "robbery") seen in earlier chapters, from Drennan's "Erin" to Leslie's *Killarney, The Exile of Erin!*, and Cavour's *Considerations*, but also justifies his title, "abstracted from any religious allusion," as a reference to the "principal and most favourite food" of the Irish in the time of St. Patrick (vii) and forward to Edmund Spenser, as a title-page epigraph indicates. *The Shamrock* is a (cultural) resource—analogous to food, gems, and property—but as a resource it must exclude the political:

> Very few political pieces, or such as are professedly satirical, have gained admittance here: for, in both cases, 'tis to be feared, they are too often the ebullutions of private pique, and unwarrantable prejudices, dictated by an irritable rancourous spirit, rather than a sincere desire of correcting abuses, and benefiting mankind. The love of honest praise is natural, and inherent in the human soul; 'tis authorized by the Deity; and whoever pretends to ridicule or despise it, tacitly arraigns himself, and confesses his own unworthiness. We have made this ennobling quality the basis, on which to recommend and establish the principles of virtue, and generous emulation, and, agreeably to the observation, that example confirms and gives influence to precept. (*Shamrock*, v)

This is what we might expect from an Enlightenment schoolmaster: instruct by positive example, he insists. But in doing so, the author of the "Prefatory Epistle" draws a distinction between (personal) partisan politics and (universal) civic virtue, just as the volume as a whole obscures individual authorship and stresses national literary property. And this cultural resource that is both "native" and universalist in its capacity to foster virtue is, according to the full title, "a Collection of Poems, Songs, Epigrams, &c., Latin as well as English, the Original Production of Ireland." The exclusion of Irish-language verse is noticeable but not very remarkable in 1772, before the work of Joseph Cooper Walker and Charlotte Brooke as translators and historians of Irish-language culture began to educate English speakers on Irish letters. It does, however, stress the Latinate literary tradition that, in the Irish context, is not merely a matter of elite education, but also of a long tradition of church-related Latin education. The volume's classical debts are readily apparent and arguably little different from many English productions in the same period. But the volume is remarkable for the number of poems written in a particular Latin tradition—the love elegy.

The love elegy does not fit the Irish elegiac traditions of national grief and remembrance traced by such scholars as Katie Trumpener in pastoral elegies of the second half of the eighteenth century and Norman Vance in similar elegies in the middle of the nineteenth.[6] Pastoral elegy follows Greek precedent and was given new impetus by Thomas Gray's influential "Elegy Written in a Country Churchyard" (1751): mourning the dead in a natural setting consonant with grief, often with some political content, as in John Milton's critique of the Church of England in *Lycidas* (1637), the pastoral elegy worked well for Irish poets mourning national decline and the loss of national leaders, with major examples from Oliver Goldsmith's *Deserted Village* to Samuel Ferguson's powerful elegy for Thomas Davis (1847). In the love elegy, however, the beloved is generally apart from the speaker but not dead (though some Irish elegies draw on both traditions through a deceased love object), putting the genre on a lesser level of seriousness than the pastoral elegy. The love elegy, moreover, is derived from Latin, not Greek, precedents and is perhaps most strongly associated with Ovid, especially his *Amores*, as well as with such poets as Tibullus, Catullus, and Propertius.[7] John Donne's love elegies, written in the 1590s, helped to launch the genre in the English tradition and to set their poetic form, elegiac couplets, by drawing on Latin conventions. One of Donne's more famous love elegies thus begins, "Come, Madam, come, all rest my powers defy / Until I labour, I in labour lie," and more than a century later George Lyttelton, in a translation of Tibullus dated 1729–30, declares, "With thee, my love, to pass my tranquil days, / How would I slight ambition's painful praise!"[8] But then the English poet James Hammond established, in place of the elegiac couplet, what would become known as the elegiac quatrain in his volume *Love Elegies*, published in 1743; this popular volume was republished for decades, including a 1762 Dublin edition.[9] Using four-line groups of iambic pentameter rhyming *abab*, Hammond set the metrical form that Gray followed a few years later in his highly influential "Elegy Written in a Country Churchyard," and the elegiac quatrain, rather than couplets, would become standard for elegies of all stripes in British verse.

The love elegy in post-1770 Ireland is also complicated by literary sensibility, creating a tension between neoclassicism's emphasis on learning and sensibility's privileging of authenticity and passion. *The Shamrock* includes five poems explicitly identified as love elegies: "Love Elegy" and two pairs, each of the latter placed under the heading "Two Love Elegies." Epigraphs in the *Shamrock*'s love elegies signal the genre's Latinate roots, being drawn from mostly Latin authors—Virgil, Martial, Propertius. The first love elegy begins typically:

> Whither, ye bright-ey'd Train, immortal Maids,
> With whom, in tuneful Ease, I wont to rove,
> Through smiling Fancy's ever blooming Shades,
> Oh whither are ye fled?—To what fam'd Grove? (*Shamrock*, 78)

The beloved is Daphne, a name prominent in Ovid's *Metamorphoses*. Elegy I of the first "Two Love Elegies," however, is sensitive to the complications of neoclassicism during the heyday of sensibility. Its epigraph is taken from Propertius, and its second stanza insists, "Nor did I learn this Skill by *Ovid*'s Rule . . . I never study'd but in *Myra*'s School" (134). But Myra, whom the speaker of Elegy II asks to "plant a Myrtle o'er his Tomb" (140), suggests Myrrha, transformed into a myrtle tree in Ovid's *Metamorphoses*, and a line in Elegy I is footnoted as a translation of Ovid (135). The elegiac speaker presents himself on the terms of sensibility as artless, knowing the human heart rather than the lettered book and praising the "sympathetic Tear" (135), while the elegist everywhere demonstrates his learning, footnoting lines translated from Propertius and Tibullus as well as

Ovid. This sort of virtuoso performance of both heartfelt sensibility and Latin education is common in such elegies and crucial to their value in Irish letters in the late eighteenth century. The second pair of love elegies extends the concern with sensibility into the bleak, almost gothic, tone of Gray's elegy. The five poems explicitly designated "love elegies" in *The Shamrock* illustrate the range of influences in evidence in Irish love elegies, from the lighter pastoral of the Latin love elegy to the melancholy of the post-Gray elegy. We can add at least one more poem to the list. "To Lisetta," designated an elegy in the table of contents, fits the thematic requirements of a love elegy and explicitly invokes the sentimental tradition: "With Tenderness, exciting soft Desire, / And Sensibility, the Ground of Taste" (*Shamrock*, 128).

"To Lisetta" and the first three poems titled "Love Elegy" are all in elegiac quatrains. But the second pair of love elegies, though recalling Gray in their tone, offer the earliest instances I have found of what would become a regular Irish form—that is, the love elegy in long meter quatrains:

'Tis Night, dead Night; and o'er the Plain
  Darkness extends her ebon Ray,
While wide along the gloomy Scene
  Deep Silence holds her solemn Sway:

. . . .

The World has, now, no Joy for me;
  Nor can Life now one Pleasure boast;
Since all my Eyes desir'd to see,
  My Wish, my Hope, my All, is lost;

Since she, so form'd to please, and bless,
  So wise, so innocent, so fair,
Whose Converse sweet made Sorrow less,
  And brighten'd all the Gloom of Care,

Since SHE is lost:—Ye Powers divine!
  What have I done, or thought, or said?

O say! what horrid Act of mine,
Has drawn this Vengeance on my Head? (*Shamrock*, 169, 170–71)

Other poems designated elegies in *The Shamrock* eschew elegiac quatrains: for instance, "Elegiac Stanzas, to the Memory of a Young Gentleman" is in common meter, a form associated with hymns; "An Elegy," on the Battle of the Boyne, is in long meter quatrains; and "An Elegy, on the Death of Two Goldfinches" is in eight-line stanzas that follow the form of two common meter quatrains. There are occasional examples of elegies in long meter quatrains that are not attributable to Irish writers: the anonymous author of *The Prince of Peace, and Other Poems* (1779), for instance, uses long meter for a love elegy but elegiac quatrains for "Elegy, on the Death of a Friend" and "Elegy, to Mr. Gray."[10] Generic innovation was not unusual in the late eighteenth century, and neither the English nor the Irish are exceptional on any metrical variant. But the elegiac stanza of Gray and Hammond that dominates English elegies was regularly not chosen by Irish authors, of both sexes, in this period, who demonstrate a preference for the tetrameter line (especially in long meter quatrains) and the older form of elegiac couplets.

The second part of Anna Maria Edwards's *Poems on Various Subjects* (1787), for instance, begins with four love elegies between Damon and Delia, perhaps responding in part to George Lyttelton's four neoclassical eclogues in "The Progress of Love," which also focuses on lovers of those names.[11] The first three of Edwards's elegies are in couplets, with the more plaintive Elegy II in elegiac couplets and the last in long meter quatrains; unusually, the first three are tacitly written in the female voice, presumably Delia's: "Young Damon tried each winning art, / To captivate my Virgin heart."[12] The fourth, in elegiac quatrains, in Damon's voice, addresses Delia as the lovers are reunited amidst images of spring, somewhat matching the resolution of Lyttelton's fourth eclogue, "Possession."

In the Irish-language rather than neoclassical tradition of elegy, Charlotte Brooke's *Reliques of Irish Poetry* (1789) stresses the love elegy over what Brooke terms the "funeral elegy" precisely because of its value in sentimental terms, recalling *The Shamrock* elegies' investment in authentic feeling: "Of the . . . *Funeral Elegy*, I have been able to procure but few good originals. The Irish language, perhaps beyond all others, is peculiarly suited to every subject of Elegy; and, accordingly, we find it excel in plaintive and sentimental poetry. The *Love Elegies* of the Irish are exquisitely pathetic, and breathe an artless tenderness, that is infinitely more affecting than the laboured pomp of declamatory woe."[13] Brooke translates one of her Irish-language love elegies into mostly elegiac couplets and the other two, at least roughly, into long meter quatrains: she apparently struggled to adapt Irish verse to English forms and seems to shorten by a half-foot a number of lines in both translations (in general, the second and fourth of each quatrain in the first, and the first and third of each quatrain in the second). She includes translations of only two "funeral elegies," one in elegiac quatrains and one in elegiac couplets. One love elegy translation, for instance, begins,

When oaths confirm a lover's vow,
    He thinks I believe him true:—
Nor oaths, nor lovers heed I now,
    For memory dwells on you![14]

Another opens with praise of the beloved and relies heavily on alliteration as well as roughly on the long meter quatrain:

Bright her locks of beauty grew,
    Curling fair, and sweetly flowing;
And her eyes of smiling blue,
    Oh how soft! how heav'nly glowing!

Ah! poor plunder'd heart of pain!
    When wilt thou have end of mourning?[15]

Brooke's translations of love elegies are not overtly neoclassical—indeed, she may well be dismissing neoclassical verse with her remark about "laboured pomp"—but, like the elegies in *The Shamrock*, they rely on the value of authentic sentiment even as they demonstrate literary expertise. And Brooke's translations of love elegies, like the final pair of love elegies in *The Shamrock*, do not use the pentameter line favored by English poets.[16]

In the late eighteenth century, love elegies continued to appear in anthologies and volumes by single poets, but often without the overtly classicist apparatus of the *Shamrock* love elegies, instead further developing Brooke's rejection of "laboured pomp" in favour of "artless tenderness." Thomas Dermody's "Elegy to Florelia" appeared in his juvenile volume *Poems, Consisting of Essays, Lyric, Elegiac, &c., . . . Written between the 13th and 16th year of his age* (1792), and "Love-Elegy, Written on the First of May" is included in his later volume *Poems on Various Subjects* (1802), both in elegiac quatrains of the stricter sort. Edward Athenry Whyte's *Collection of Poems, on Various Subjects*, first published in 1791, includes a love elegy in elegiac quatrains, "Expostulation, to an Unfaithful Mistress."[17] John Corry included fourteen poems entitled "Elegy" in his 1797 volume *Odes and Elegies*, a number of which are love elegies, including "Elegy, to Maria M.," which ends morally, "Woo and win the tender maid / Whose virtues shall thy social moments bless,"[18] again raising the connection between love elegy and Enlightenment notions of virtue. Samuel Whyte's *Shamrock* seeks "to recommend and establish the principles of virtue, and generous emulation," as noted earlier, and William Preston's 1803 essay on love elegy for the Royal Irish Academy begins, "The history of poetry ancient and modern, shews us, that *erotic* compositions are not the growth of rude manners, and early ages of society. That such is the case, cannot be denied."[19] Later in the essay, Preston makes clear that he has an Enlightenment sense of social advancement, writing of "*Alcaeus*, the illustrious poet of *Lesbos*," who would "unbend himself, with the erotic muse," "that the island of which he was a native, flourished, in commerce and wealth. It had a number of famous and opulent cities, and was the abode of pleasure."[20] He effusively praises Sappho, too, another inhabitant of Lesbos, for "the most lively and affecting descriptions of the emotions of love."[21] In love elegies that appear after the publication of *The Shamrock*, then, neoclassicist performance fades as the sentimental rises even further in an emphasis on authentic and elevating emotion and the virtues that Enlightenment sensibility contended accompanied such emotion—the social virtues that undergird civil society in eighteenth-century thought.[22]

In 1801, *A Collection of Poems, by Several Hands* was published in Dublin and with nationalist aims similar to that of *The Shamrock*: "the compiler [Joshua Edkins] has endeavoured to erect a monument to the honour of his native country; by combining a number of specimens of the poetical talent of IRISH WRITERS. . . . [I]t is solely, and exclusively, the GROWTH of IRELAND."[23] This volume includes a number of poems by William Drennan, including "Love-Elegy" and "Love-Elegy, Imitated from Tibullus" as well as "Verses to a Young Lady"—the latter two, along with a number of other poems in *Collection*, were later included in Drennan's *Fugitive Pieces* (1815). "Verses" is in common meter quatrains and deals with a lost love. It also draws heavily on sentiment and the authenticity of the "artless":

> while you read, and melting feel
> Soft Pity's artless stile,
> I'll watch the woe you half conceal,
> Beneath a weeping smile.[24]

Drennan's most explicitly neoclassical love elegy is "Love-Elegy, Imitated from Tibullus," in which the serious Dr. Drennan turns to sex and elegiac couplets:

> Yes—'twas the vow that clos'd the happy night—
> "None of thy sex shall taste such dear delight!"
> Still as that night thou wert, the same thou art,
> Light to my eyes, and rapture to my heart. . . .
> Again do I attest that mystic pow'r,
> Who mark'd our transports in the silent hour![25]

The second line is in quotation marks because it translates Drennan's epigraph from Tibullus, putting this poem closer to the neoclassical love elegies of *The Shamrock* than to those of Corry or Dermody and making it a rare post-1780 instance of an Irish love elegy that explicitly acknowledges Latin debts. But it and Drennan's other "Love-Elegy" are in elegiac couplets—the form closest to the Latin originals and widely in use in English-language elegies before Hammond and Gray. Corry generally used elegiac quatrains for his elegies on a plethora of subjects but turned to elegiac couplets for three elegies—two commemorating deceased but virtuous women and one with the odd title "Pleasure, an Elegy." "Elegy, to the Memory of Miss H—tt, of Belfast" warns the addressee, "Once, beautiful, like you, she danc'd along, / And was the loveliest of the lively throng; / But, now she sleeps, unconscious, in the tomb."[26] All three poems end in the grave and praise the pursuit of virtue, inverting the values of the classical love elegies imitated and translated from Donne forward.

In general, across these various volumes, as neoclassicist referencing faded before sensibility's insistence on "artless" expressions of feeling, the more traditional classical form of the couplet was resurrected in Ireland while poets continued to turn to common and long meter quatrains rather than to Hammond's and Gray's elegiac quatrains. At the same time, Gray's authority was roundly challenged: Edward Athenry Whyte's *Collection* includes an advertisement that charges Gray with plagiarizing his famous "Elegy," going far beyond conventional claims that the poem is a patchwork of quotation,[27] on the authority of "Mr. Giffard," who "in turning over some books at Watson the bookseller's, who then lived in Dame-street [in Dublin], dipped into an old Collection of Poems, and, to his great surprise, popped upon one, in an obsolete style, from which Gray had copied almost the whole of his Elegy."[28] But this movement away from elegiac quatrains also takes us back to Preston, the author of the 1803 essay on elegy, quoted earlier. Born and educated in Dublin, Preston was a lawyer and a published poet from the 1770s. He was a man of political contradictions: he was a member of the nationalist but not radical

Monks of the Screw (an elite drinking club, named for a corkscrew) and a contributor to United Irishmen publications,[29] but also the author of the popular play *Democratic Rage* (1793), which inveighs against the leaders of the French Revolution, praises British law, and warns of the dangers of the mob. He deplores women's licentiousness in the poem *The Female Congress* and identifies Methodism with it ("The fury *Methodism* deserts her bow'r; / Queen of the holy leer"), but he is also mentioned in *Memoirs of Mrs. Margaret Leeson* (1797), by a prominent Dublin brothel owner, as "my friend P—n."[30] And he was one of the leading contributors to Edkins's *Collection.*

Preston has received scant attention in Irish literary studies,[31] and he is precisely the sort of poet that goes missing if we focus on overtly nation-themed work. Like Dermody and Corry, who are also underexamined, he wrote neoclassical imitations, poems on sensibility, and occasional addresses, such as "To a Lady, on her saying Poetry is but Fiction" (the speaker disagrees, of course),[32] as well as a number of plays and essays. He was a leading figure in the early years of the Royal Irish Academy, working as its first secretary,[33] and his collected *Poetical Works* (1793) was published in his lifetime, the same year the tragedy *Democratic Rage* was published in Dublin and London, later followed by *Posthumous Poems* (1809) soon after his death. Preston is not a minor writer, and Vance suggests that in 1790s Ireland "the most important writers . . . are William Drennan and (perhaps) the literary barrister William Preston."[34]

Edkins notes, "a large number of [Preston's] poems are included in" *A Collection of Poems, by Several Hands*, before conveying Preston's apology for them as juvenalia.[35] Preston was born in 1750, so this would suggest that the poems are the work of the mid- to late 1760s, about the time of *The Shamrock*'s compositions. A number of Preston's poems in Edkins's *Collection* are love elegies, including "Maria, an Elegy" and "Love Elegies," one "in the manner of Tibullus" and the other "imitated from Tibullus"—all in elegiac quatrains. Preston's first collection of poems under his name, *Poems, On Several Occasions*, appeared in 1781 and includes a section entitled "Love Elegies," with six elegies, all in elegiac couplets.[36]

Poetical Works of 1793 includes an expanded series of love elegies, along with a number of Anacreontics and other neoclassical poems. The 1793 series begins with a love elegy "In the Manner of Hammond"—that is, elegiac quatrains;[37] the next five are the first five of the 1781 set of six, with the last omitted from the 1793 series (it is subtitled "Written by a Friend," so it may have been deleted for authorship reasons); then follow five more. All but the first, "In the Manner of Hammond," are in elegiac couplets. "Elegy the Tenth" begins, for instance,

Where dost thou rove, Lavinia?—be the ground,
Where'er you tread, with greenest herbiage crown'd.
May nature there thy gladden'd senses greet,
Mild as thy looks, and as thy temper sweet.
May guardian spirits there their wings extend,
May choicest blessings on thy head descend.
And say, Lavinia, loveliest, best belov'd,
Canst thou forget the happiness we prov'd.[38]

Preston's love elegies are diverse in tone and device, but the adult poet almost always used the elegiac couplet. In 1809, *Posthumous Poems* appeared. Eschewing the designation "love elegy," it does not include the love elegies of the 1781 volume, but it does include the two elegiac quatrain poems "in the manner" or "imitated from Tibullus" and some of Preston's couplet love elegies, though the elegiac quatrain form predominates.[39] Preston's verse, then, synecdochally registers the shift we have seen from *The Shamrock* to Drennan—away from elegiac quatrains as defined by the English poets Hammond and Gray in the mid-1700s. Moreover, the downplaying of "love elegy" as a form in *Posthumous Poems* adds to evidence that the genre began to lose status in the early 1800s.

Indeed, it is suggestive that the love elegy starts to fade from view about the time that Thomas Moore published his influential series "Love-Songs to Nea" (1806), also called the "Odes to Nea." The thirteen poems have subject matter consistent with love elegies and draw on the same Latin tradition: the second poem in the series, for instance, takes its epigraph from Propertius.[40] Moore was familiar with the tradition of Latin love elegy invoked by *The Shamrock*: the preface to his early volume *The Poetical Works of the Late Thomas Little* (1801) includes a discussion of "the poetry of love," assessing the major Latin authors of love elegies with the quips, "Ovid made love like a rake, and Propertius like a schoolmaster," but "Tibullus abounds with touches of fine and natural feeling."[41] The "Love-Songs to Nea," like late eighteenth-century Irish love elegies, also draw on both the couplet and long meter quatrain: Ode V is in iambic pentameter couplets (which we might call elegiac couplets, given the theme), for instance, and Ode VI in long meter quatrains. The series addresses Nea, a lost love:

> Dear absent girl! whose eyes of light,
> Though little priz'd when all my own,
> Now float before me, soft and bright,
> As when they first enamouring shone![42]

These four lines are from the first poem in the series and set the theme of the larger work, but most of the poem is in couplets, and at no point is a quatrain marked off in it. The first verse paragraph follows the pattern of two long meter quatrains; the next verse paragraph is four iambic tetrameter couplets; and the next verse paragraph after that follows the metrical pattern of a long meter quatrain and then five iambic tetrameter couplets. The poem's mixed structure is not incompatible with the irregular ode, given the license implied by the term, but it is rather unlike most eighteenth-century odes and certainly differs from Moore's most famous odes before this, in *Odes of Anacreon* (1800)—and in couplets.[43] The "Love-Songs" instead clearly draw on the long meter quatrain used by Irish love elegists, pushing still further Irish formal innovations on the love elegy while continuing to draw on established metrical and thematic conventions for that genre.

Moreover, as we have seen, Preston's love elegies were republished for decades, and Preston was a major literary figure in Dublin during Moore's youth. Indeed, Moore's 1806 volume does not look very different from Preston's 1781 volume: both include epistles, odes (including poems specified as "dithyrambic odes"), and Anacreontics, and both address love, travel, classical material, and occasional subjects. Moore's neoclassicist verse, from his important volume *Odes of Anacreon* to his scathing political satires from 1808 on, makes much more sense when placed alongside Preston's body of work and alongside Drennan's early published verse as well.

In Ireland, neoclassicism survived into the early 1800s through the Latinate love elegy and on terms in which formal experimentation and both elegiac meters (quatrains and couplets) were in play. Conversely, in England up to about 1810, love elegies seem rarer, especially among major poets, and fairly consistently use the strict English elegiac quatrain—the comic "Love Elegies" by "Abel Shufflebottom" (1799), for instance, and Amelia Opie's love elegies in *The Warrior's Return* (1808).[44] The literary history of romantic-era Ireland is too sketchy as yet to determine the degree to which Preston followed or set the trend, but it is clear that Irish poets regularly innovated on the elegiac quatrain so de rigueur with English poets by using long meter quatrains and returning to the older form of elegiac couplets as well. Moreover, the love elegy, though superficially erotic and even sometimes frivolous in tone, was associated with national progress, especially through sensibility's emphasis on "artless" expressions of what Enlightenment thinkers termed the social affections.

Moreover, this brief survey of Irish love elegies has dealt with authors from various class, regional, religious, and political categories: Dermody was the son of a schoolmaster from the south who tutored Lady Morgan and her sister when they were young Owensons, and then he became a British soldier; Brooke was the daughter of an established author and connected to Dublin literati; Preston was a Church of Ireland, Dublin-educated lawyer who worked for the judicial system in Ireland and partied, from the brothel to the drinking club, with the reformist elite; Corry was a self-educated poet from the north who left Ireland in the late 1790s and counted a number of United Irishmen among his 1797 volume's subscribers but seems to have had no other involvement; Drennan, from Belfast, was an Edinburgh-educated physician and son of a Presbyterian minister who joined the United Irishmen in Dublin and left the organization shortly before the Uprising; even basic details of Edwards's life are unknown,[45] but there are numerous members of the Church of Ireland on the subscription list for her *Poems*; and Moore was a Trinity-educated Catholic from Dublin and the son of a grocer. They cross linguistic divides as well: Brooke wrote translations of Irish-language material; Dermody, Preston, and Moore were classicist scholars fluent in Greek and Latin; Drennan wrote translations of Irish material and imitations of Latin verse; the others' linguistic range is unknown. There are some clear coterie connections among this group: Drennan, Preston, and two editors of collections discussed here, Samuel Whyte and Edkins, were all members of the Dublin Literary Society,[46] for instance, and Corry, Moore, Drennan, and Preston had some affiliation with nationalist groups in the 1790s.

While Latin in romantic-era England was largely the province of the well-educated man, in Ireland it was taught in Hedge schools and village schools, and it is not unusual to find Latin phrases in popular texts directed at the lower classes, such as James Porter's *Billy Bluff and 'Squire Firebrand*. In Morgan's *The O'Briens and the O'Flahertys*, three characters speak Latin well: the well-educated man, the convent-educated heroine, and their devoted, illiterate servant, who is more comfortable with religious Latin than with English. Love elegies thus formally, and often allusively, draw on a broader Latinate culture than was imaginable in England as well as on an Irish-language tradition of some centuries' standing that was, in this period, becoming available through translation as well. The love elegy is nationally specific, in other words, in a genealogical sense, but not nationalist in theme, while at the same time there are clear connections between these elegies and the pan-archipelago sentimental tradition that heavily influenced romantic-era political thought in Ireland. If we are to develop a fuller picture of Irish literature of this period (and the prehistory of such poets as Yeats), then, we need to consider Irish writing outside of the domain of romantic nationalism and start to map the distinctive literary traditions to emerge from the various literary circles and literary languages of Ireland in this period.

The transmutation of topographical verse into the novel of the Big House, of the gothic into sensation fiction, of love elegies in Irish and Latin into a distinctive Irish English-language corpus, of the interplay between the national tale and gothic and verse traditions—we are only just beginning to trace these lines of Irish literary history. We know a great deal about canonical English poets' influences, reading, allusions—and virtually nothing about their Irish counterparts' debts, allusions, and references to each other. Without that context, we risk naturalizing the continuities that are apparent—explorations of national identity, anti-imperial critique, interest in the gothic—as the psychological effects of the colonial dispensation, making Irish literature inescapably and fundamentally secondary, a reflex kick against the colonial rather than the willed and creative exploration of ideas, feelings, and material circumstances through broad experience and wide reading, often across multiple languages and nations and historical eras. If we attend, however, to the more international concerns and to the ways in which writers responded to each other, another picture emerges in which the colonial dispensation still looms large but does not solely define a rich literary landscape. Irish literature in the late eighteenth and early nineteenth centuries is shaped by regional, national, and international literary traditions as well as by regional, national, and international concerns, including not only the affective relationship of people to the land, but also the rich variety of resources that can be drawn from and pass over it.

Notes

Bibliography

Index

Notes

Note: Poetry is cited by line number where available in the edition used and by page number otherwise. Julia M. Wright, ed., *Irish Literature, 1750–1900: An Anthology* (Oxford: Wiley-Blackwell, 2008), is hereafter abbreviated as *IL*.

Introduction

1. William Drennan, "Erin," in *IL*, 1–4.

2. William Drennan, "Note on Erin," in *Fugitive Pieces in Verse and Prose* (Belfast: F. D. Finlay, 1815), 4, and in *IL*, 137n.

3. See, for instance, Seamus Deane, "The Production of Cultural Space in Irish Writing," *boundary 2* 21 (1994): 117–44, and *Strange Country: Modernity and Nationhood in Irish Writing since 1790* (Oxford: Clarendon Press, 1997); Luke Gibbons, "Topographies of Terror: Killarney and the Politics of the Sublime," *South Atlantic Quarterly* 95 (1996): 23–44; John Wilson Foster, "The Topographical Tradition in Anglo-Irish Poetry," *Irish University Review* 4–5 (1974–75): 169–87, reprinted in *Colonial Consequences: Essays in Irish Literature and Culture*, 9–29 (Dublin: Lilliput Press, 1991); John Waters, "Topographical Poetry and the Politics of Culture in Ireland, 1772–1820," in *Romantic Generations: Essays in Honor of Robert F. Gleckner*, edited by Ghislaine McDayter, Guinn Batten, and Barry Milligan, 221–44 (Lewisburg, PA: Bucknell Univ. Press, 2001); Glenn Hooper, *Travel Writing and Ireland, 1760–1860: Culture, History, Politics* (New York: Palgrave Macmillan, 2005); Úna Ní Bhroiméil and Glenn Hooper, eds., *Land and Landscape in Nineteenth-Century Ireland* (Dublin: Four Courts Press, 2008); and, most recently, Claire Connolly, *A Cultural History of the Irish Novel, 1790–1829* (Cambridge: Cambridge Univ. Press, 2012).

4. Pedro I, "Manifesto of the Prince Regent of Brazil to Friendly Governments and Nations," *London Times*, Oct. 16, 1822.

5. Úna Ní Bhroiméil and Glenn Hooper, "Introduction," in Ní Bhroiméil and Hooper, eds., *Land and Landscape in Nineteenth-Century Ireland*, 9.

6. Deane, "The Production of Cultural Space in Irish Writing," 127.

7. For a useful overview of this historical scholarship, see Andrew Murphy, "Revising Criticism: Ireland and the British Model," in *British Identities and English Renaissance Literature*, edited by David J. Baker and Willy Maley, 24–33 (Cambridge: Cambridge Univ. Press, 2002).

8. Connolly, *Cultural History*, 47–84.

9. Benedict Anderson, *The Spectre of Comparisons: Nationalism, Southeast Asia, and the World* (London: Verso, 1998), 66.

10. Anthony D. Smith, *Nationalism* (Oxford: Blackwell, 2004), 22, 23.

11. William Drennan, *A Letter to the Right Honorable William Pitt* (Dublin: James Moore, 1799), 46.

12. Jeremy Bentham, *An Introduction to the Principles of Morals and Legislation* (1789), edited by J. H. Burns and H. L. A. Hart (Oxford: Clarendon Press, 1996), 296n.

13. Lady Morgan, *O'Donnel: A National Tale*, 3 vols. (London: Henry Coburn, 1814), 1:235.

14. *The Exile of Ireland! Or, The Wonderful Adventures, and Extraordinary Escapes, of an Irish Rebel Officer* (London: printed for the author, n.d.); *The Life, Voyages, Travels, and Wonderful Adventures of Captain Winterfield . . . a Distinguished Rebel Chief in Ireland* (London: J. Bailey, n.d.), which the Corvey Project attributes to James Harrison and is not to be confused with the novel *Exile of Erin* (1808) by Irish novelist Elizabeth Gunning Plunkett. Neither of these pamphlets is dated, though the British Library suggests they were published around 1800–1805, and *Exile* includes a poem attributed to Thomas Campbell and published in the *Morning Chronicle* in 1801 (on Campbell's poem, see Frank Molloy, "Thomas Campbell's 'Exile of Erin': English Poem, Irish Reactions," in *Back to the Present, Forward to the Past: Irish Writing and History since 1798*, 2 vols., edited by Patricia A. Lynch, Joachim Fischer, and Brian Coates, 1:43–52 [New York: Rodopi, 2006]). The *Winterfield* text seems likely to be the later publication, including significantly truncated versions of *Exile*'s Canadian and Irish narratives and in an order that makes less sense (in the Canadian narrative, the protagonist is a young man about to be battle tested for the first time; in the *Winterfield* text, this narrative appears after the Exile has already had significant military experience, making less sense than the *Exile* version, in which the Canadian narrative is an account of his first military posting).

15. *The Exile of Ireland!* 35.

16. The foundational work in "four nations" considerations of British Isles history (as opposed to a metropole- and Anglo-centric view) is J. G. A. Pocock, "British History: A Plea for a New Subject," *Journal of Modern History* 47 (1975): 601–28. See also, for example, Linda Colley, *Britons: Forging the Nation, 1707–1837* (New Haven, CT: Yale Univ. Press, 1992); J. G. A. Pocock, *The Discovery of*

Islands: Essays in British History (Cambridge: Cambridge Univ. Press, 2005); and Alexander Murdoch, *British History, 1660–1832: National Identity and Local Culture* (London: Macmillan, 1998).

17. *The Exile of Ireland!* 35.

18. The Exile's love interest in Spain has the same name, Elvira, as "Pizarro's mistress" in Richard Brinsley Sheridan's play *Pizarro* (1799).

19. Colley, *Britons.*

20. Chenxi Tang, *The Geographic Imagination of Modernity: Geography, Literature, and Philosophy in German Romanticism* (Stanford, CA: Stanford Univ. Press, 2008), 4.

21. Anderson, *Spectre of Comparisons*, 62.

22. John Godfrey Herder [Johann Gottfried von Herder], *Outlines of a Philosophy of the History of Man*, translated by T. Churchill (London: J. Johnson, 1800), 166.

23. Ibid., 185, emphasis in original.

24. Ernest Renan, "What Is a Nation?" in *The Poetry of the Celtic Races, and Other Studies by Ernest Renan*, translated by William G. Hutchison, 61–83 (London: Walter Scott, 1896).

25. David Hume, "Of National Characters," in *Political Essays*, edited by Knud Haakonssen (Cambridge: Cambridge Univ. Press, 1994), 85.

26. Ibid., 84; Herder, *Outlines of a Philosophy of the History of Man*, 185, emphasis in original.

27. Herder, *Outlines of a Philosophy of the History of Man*, 187.

28. Hume, "Of National Characters," 84.

29. J. Th. Leerssen, *National Thought in Europe: A Cultural History* (Amsterdam: Amsterdam Univ. Press, 2006), 16.

30. Ibid., 17, emphasis added.

31. Anthony D. Smith, "Neo-classicist and Romantic Elements in the Emergence of Nationalist Conceptions," in *Nationalist Movements*, edited by Anthony D. Smith (London: Macmillan, 1976), 81, emphasis added.

32. Ibid. See also Ernest Gellner, *Nations and Nationalism* (Ithaca, NY: Cornell Univ. Press, 1983).

33. Anthony D. Smith, *The Nation in History: Historiographical Debates about Ethnicity and Nationalism* (Hanover, NH: Univ. Press of New England, 2000), 53, 62, 71.

34. Ibid., 77.

35. Benedict Anderson, *Imagined Communities: Reflections on the Origin and Spread of Nationalism*, rev. ed. (New York: Verso, 1991).

36. See Julia M. Wright, *Ireland, India, and Nationalism in Nineteenth-Century Literature* (Cambridge: Cambridge Univ. Press, 2007), esp. chap. 1.

37. Smith, *The Nation in History*, 76–77.

38. Leerssen, *National Thought in Europe*, 17.

39. Ibid.

40. "National Character," *The Nation*, Sept. 9, 1843.

41. Hume, "Of National Characters," 85.

42. Murray Pittock, *Scottish and Irish Romanticism* (Oxford: Oxford Univ. Press, 2008); David Duff and Catherine Jones, eds., *Scotland, Ireland, and the Romantic Aesthetic* (Lewisburg, PA: Bucknell Univ. Press, 2007); Katie Trumpener, *Bardic Nationalism: The Romantic Novel and the British Empire* (Princeton, NJ: Princeton Univ. Press, 1997); Ina Ferris, *The Romantic National Tale and the Question of Ireland* (Cambridge: Cambridge Univ. Press, 2002). For more on this body of writing, see J. Th. Leerssen, *Remembrance and Imagination: Patterns in the Historical and Literary Representation of Ireland in the Nineteenth Century* (Notre Dame, IN: Univ. of Notre Dame Press, 1997); Norman Vance, *Irish Literature, a Social History: Tradition, Identity, and Difference* (Oxford: Blackwell, 1990); and Patrick Rafroidi's long-invaluable resource *Irish Literature in English: The Romantic Period, 1789–1850* (Gerrards Cross, UK: Colin Smythe, 1980). For a useful overview of some of the scholarship, see Laurence M. Geary and Margaret Kelleher, eds., *Nineteenth-Century Ireland: A Guide to Recent Research* (Dublin: Univ. College Dublin Press, 2005).

43. Stephen C. Behrendt, "Placing 'Irish' and 'Romanticism' in the Same Frame," in *Ireland and Romanticism: Publics, Nations, and Scenes of Cultural Production*, edited by Jim Kelly (New York: Palgrave Macmillan, 2011), 212.

44. Terence Brown, *Northern Voices: Poets from Ulster* (Dublin: Gill and Macmillan, 1975). A few examples in the series published by Colin Smythe include Robert Welch's *Irish Poetry from Moore to Yeats* (1980), Barbara Hayley's *Carleton's Traits and Stories and the 19th Century Anglo-Irish Tradition* (1983), Barry Sloan's *Pioneers of Anglo-Irish Fiction, 1800–1850* (1986) and, with early essays influenced by postcolonial theory and written by Seamus Deane and Tom Paulin, the volume *Critical Approaches to Anglo-Irish Literature*, edited by Michael Allen and Angela Wilcox (1989).

45. The volume's contributors cite Connolly's 2006 essay at least three times (Kelly, ed., *Ireland and Romanticism*, 2, 116, 208). With the name "Big M's," I allude to the longstanding ironic use of "Big Six" to refer to the New Critics' canon of British romantic poets: William Blake, William Wordsworth, Samuel Taylor Coleridge, John Keats, P. B. Shelley, and Byron.

46. A study of northern Irish romantic-era verse building on the foundational work of Irish studies scholars such as Terence Brown (*Northern Voices*) and John Hewitt would have rich bodies of poetry on which to draw, including volumes by James Porter, James Corry, William Drennan, William Hamilton Drummond,

Mary Balfour, weaver poets such as James Orr, and, toward the end of the era, the early poetry of Samuel Ferguson.

47. See, for instance, the important work of the *Field Day Anthology of Irish Writing*, general editor Seamus Deane (Derry: Field Day, 1991), especially in its full five-volume version, but also specific efforts to define regional traditions, such as Brown, *Northern Voices*.

48. Claire Connolly, "Irish Romanticism, 1800–1830," in *The Cambridge History of Irish Literature*, 2 vols., edited by Margaret Kelleher and Philip O'Leary, 1:407–48 (Cambridge: Cambridge Univ. Press, 2006); Rafroidi, *Irish Literature in English*; Norman Vance, "Irish Literary Traditions and the Act of Union," *Canadian Journal of Irish Studies* 12, no. 2 (1986): 41.

49. This key conundrum in romanticism studies goes as far back as A. O. Lovejoy's "On the Discrimination of Romanticisms" (1924).

50. Pittock, *Scottish and Irish Romanticism*, 12.

51. Smith, "Neo-classicist and Romantic Elements," 83.

52. On Young Ireland and the emergence of cultural nationalism in Ireland, see David Dwan, *The Great Community: Culture and Nationalism in Ireland* (Dublin: Field Day, 2008); Leerssen, *Remembrance and Imagination*; and especially David Lloyd, *Nationalism and Minor Literature: James Clarence Mangan and the Emergence of Irish Cultural Nationalism* (Berkeley: Univ. of California Press, 1987). Dwan suggests that Young Ireland's ideas emerged from "a basic opposition between a historically grounded nationalism and a more general or universal language of legitimization" (32), roughly corresponding to what I have traced elsewhere as antiquarian and inaugural nationalist discourses in United Irishmen writings and Lady Morgan's novel about the movement (Julia M. Wright, "'The Nation Begins to Form': Competing Nationalisms in Morgan's *The O'Briens and the O'Flahertys*," *ELH* 66 [1999]: 939–63).

53. On Famine literature, see, for instance, Patrick Brantlinger, *Dark Vanishings: Discourse of the Extinction of Primitive Races, 1800–1930* (Ithaca, NY: Cornell Univ. Press, 2003); Hooper, *Travel Writing and Ireland*; Margaret Kelleher, *The Feminization of Famine: Expressions of the Inexpressible?* (Durham, NC: Duke Univ. Press, 1997); Melissa Fegan, *Literature and the Irish Famine, 1845–1919* (Oxford: Oxford Univ. Press, 2002); and especially the crucial study by Christopher Morash, *Writing the Irish Famine* (Oxford: Clarendon Press, 1995).

54. See especially Foster, "The Topographical Tradition," and Waters, "Topographical Poetry."

55. Jane Austen, *Northanger Abbey*, in *Northanger Abbey, Lady Susan, The Watsons, and Sanditon*, edited by John Davie (Oxford: Oxford Univ. Press, 1990), 159.

1. The Maids of Killarney: Transatlantic Circulation and the Origins of the National Tale

1. Recent discussions of this tradition include Kevis Goodman, *Georgic Modernity and British Romanticism* (Cambridge: Cambridge Univ. Press, 2008); Frans De Bruyn, "From Georgic Poetry to Statistics and Graphs: Eighteenth-Century Representations and the 'State' of British Society," *Yale Journal of Criticism* 17 (2004): 103–39.

2. Karen O'Brien, "Imperial Georgic, 1660–1789," in *The Country and the City Revisited: England and the Politics of Culture, 1550–1850*, edited by Gerald MacLean, Donna Landry, and Joseph P. Ward (Cambridge: Cambridge Univ. Press, 1999), 161.

3. Raymond Williams, *The Country and the City* (Oxford: Oxford Univ. Press, 1975).

4. Denis Florence MacCarthy, "A Walk by the Bay of Dublin," in *IL*, 17–21.

5. Foster, "The Topographical Tradition." John Waters also notes Denham's significance in "Topographical Poetry."

6. Foster, "The Topographical Tradition," 11, 12; Andrew Carpenter, ed., *Verse in English from Eighteenth-Century Ireland* (Cork: Cork Univ. Press, 1998), 77.

7. Rev. James Ward, "Phoenix Park," in *Miscellaneous Poems, Original and Translated, by Several Hands* (London, 1724), 379. The poem is excerpted in Carpenter, ed., *Verse in English*, 77–79.

8. Alexander Pope, "Windsor-Forest," in *Pope: Poetical Works*, edited by Herbert Davis (London: Oxford Univ. Press, 1966), 431, 36–42.

9. Roland Barthes, *Mythologies*, translated by Annette Lavers (New York: Hill and Wang, 1972).

10. See Marjorie Levinson, *Wordsworth's Great Period Poems* (Cambridge: Cambridge Univ. Press, 1986), and the summary of her argument about "Tintern Abbey" in Jerome McGann, *The Romantic Ideology: A Critical Investigation* (Chicago: Univ. of Chicago Press, 1983), 86. For an overview of more recent discussions of the poem in this vein, see David S. Miall, "Locating Wordsworth: 'Tintern Abbey' and the Community with Nature," *Romanticism on the Net* 20 (Nov. 2000), http://www.erudit.org/revue/ron/2000/v/n20/005949ar.html.

11. Williams, *Country and the City*, 75, 285.

12. Carole Fabricant, "The Garden as City: Swift's Landscape of Alienation," *ELH* 42 (1975): 531. Fabricant is referring to Maynard Mack, *The Garden and the City: Retirement and Politics in the Later Poetry of Pope, 1731–1743* (Toronto: Univ. of Toronto Press, 1969).

13. Andrew Marvell, "Upon Appleton House," in *Andrew Marvell: The Complete Poems*, edited by Elizabeth Story Donno (New York: Penguin, 1972), 761–68.

14. De Bruyn, "From Georgic Poetry," 118.

15. See ibid., 118–19.

16. Ben Jonson, "To Penshurst," in *Ben Jonson: The Complete Poems*, edited by George Parfitt (New York: Penguin, 1975), 22–25.

17. John Wilson Foster, "The Measure of Paradise: Topography in Eighteenth-Century Poetry," *Eighteenth-Century Studies* 9 (1975–76): 233.

18. Foster, "The Topographical Tradition," 19–20; Waters, "Topographical Poetry," 224–32.

19. Gibbons, "Topographies of Terror," 24.

20. Sir James Ware, *The Antiquities of Ireland*, in *The Whole Works of Sir James Ware Concerning Ireland Revised and Improved*, 3 vols. (Dublin: printed for the author, 1739–46), 2:170.

21. See, for instance, Foster, "The Topographical Tradition," 19; John Wilson Foster, "Encountering Traditions," in *Nature in Ireland: A Scientific and Cultural History* (Montreal: McGill-Queen's Univ. Press, 1997), 61; and Carpenter, ed., *Verse in English*, 539.

22. *Killarny. A Poem* (Dublin: printed for Thomas Ewing, n.d.).

23. Joseph Atkinson, *Killarney: A Poem* (Dublin: William Porter, 1798), iv.

24. Anna Maria Edwards, "The Princess of Killarney," in *Poems on Various Subjects, by the Author of the Enchantress*, part 2, 120–40 (Dublin: H. Colbert, 1787); Mary Tighe, "Written at the Eagle's Nest, Killarney," "Written at Killarney," and "On Leaving Killarney," in *The Collected Poems and Journals of Mary Tighe*, edited by Harriet Kramer Linkin, 45–46 (Lexington: Univ. Press of Kentucky, 2005); Charles Hoyle, *Three Days at Killarney, with Other Poems* (London: Longman, Rees, Orme, Brown, and Green, 1828); Hannah Maria Bourke, *O'Donoghue, Prince of Killarney: A Poem* (Dublin: William Curry Jr., 1830); "Killarney," *Dublin University Review, and Quarterly Magazine* (later *Dublin University Magazine*) 1, no. 1 (Jan. 1833): 147–50; Patrick O'Kelly, *Killarney: A Descriptive Poem* (Dublin, 1791); and Michael MacCarthy, *Lacus Delectabilis: A Descriptive and Historical Poem on the Lakes of Killarney* (Cork, 1816). Waters also mentions a poem by W. A. Bryson, "Moonlight Scenes at Killarney" ("Topographical Poetry," 235), and the popular "Kate Kearney" ballad offers a passing reference to Killarney.

25. Robert Torrens, *The Victim of Intolerance; Or, The Hermit of Killarney: A Catholic Tale*, 4 vols. (London, 1814); [Patrick Brontë], *The Maid of Killarney; Or, Albion and Flora: A Modern Tale; in which are interwoven some cursory remarks on Religion and Politics* (London: Baldwin, Cradock, and Joy, 1818); Regina Maria Roche, *The Tradition of the Castle; Or, Scenes in the Emerald Isle*, 4 vols. (London: A. K. Newman, 1824).

26. Roche, *The Tradition of the Castle*, 1:35.

27. John Leslie, *Phoenix Park* (London: George Robinson, 1772), 15.

28. Foster, "The Topographical Tradition," 19.

29. O'Brien, "Imperial Georgic," 168.

30. Waters, "Topographical Poetry," 226.

31. *Mount Leinster; Or, The Prospect, A Poem* (London: Longman, Hurst, Rees, Orme, and Browne; Dublin: R. Milliken, 1819), iv.

32. John Leslie, *Killarney*, in *IL*, hereafter cited parenthetically in the text by line number for verse and page number for Leslie's footnotes.

33. Leslie, *Phoenix Park*, 6–7.

34. Ibid., 7.

35. Ward, "Phoenix Park," 385.

36. Pope, "Windsor-Forest," 385–87.

37. See Paul Gilroy's useful articulation of black "double consciousness" in an Atlantic frame as one that pivots on these homonyms: "modern black political culture has always been more interested in the relationship of identity to roots and rootedness than in seeing identity as a process of movement and mediation that is more appropriately approached via the homonym routes" (*The Black Atlantic: Modernity and Double Consciousness* [London: Verso, 1993], 19). This idea of identity "as a process of movement and mediation" has been widely taken up in transatlantic studies, and it is in that sense that it is used here rather than to suggest that Leslie is invoking a more broadly subaltern "double consciousness."

38. Kevin Whelan, "The Green Atlantic: Radical Reciprocities between Ireland and America in the Long Eighteenth Century," in *A New Imperial History: Culture, Identity, and Modernity in Britain and the Empire, 1660–1840*, edited by Kathleen Wilson, 216–38 (Cambridge: Cambridge Univ. Press, 2004). On the Irish in America in the nineteenth century, see, for instance, Kerby A. Miller, *Ireland and Irish America: Culture, Class, and Transatlantic Migration* (Dublin: Field Day, 2008); Charles Fanning, ed., *The Exiles of Erin: Nineteenth-Century Irish-American Fiction*, 2nd ed. (Chester Springs, PA: Dufour Editions, 1997). On the transatlantic and more recent Irish literature, see, for example, Brian G. Caraher and Robert Mahony, eds., *Ireland and Transatlantic Poetics: Essays in Honor of Denis Donoghue* (Newark: Univ. of Delaware Press, 2007).

39. Laurence Whyte, "The Parting Cup," in *Poems on Various Subjects, Serious and Diverting, Never Before Published* (Dublin: S. Powell, 1740), 70, 92.

40. Thomas Sheridan, *Brave Irishman*, in *IL*, 9. Esther K. Sheldon notes that the play first appeared on stage in 1743 and was a regular offering from 1745 to 1758 (*Thomas Sheridan of Smock-Alley* [Princeton, NJ: Princeton Univ. Press, 1967], 20, 402); editions appeared in Ireland, Scotland, and England between 1755 and 1791. On this military reference, see Julia M. Wright, "'Wel gelun a gud?': Thomas Sheridan's *Brave Irishman* and the Failure of English," *Irish Studies Review* 16

(2008): 451. Manuscript versions of the play, which predate the war, of course do not include such a reference; for an edition based on manuscript evidence, see Christopher Wheatley and Kevin Donovan, *Irish Drama of the Seventeenth and Eighteenth Centuries*, 2 vols., 1:421–62 (Bristol, UK: Thoemmes Press, 2003). The manuscript versions are significantly different from the published versions, which were based on performances at the major national theaters and, as was conventional, include embellishments for topical and comical effect.

41. *An Account of the Present State of Nova-Scotia in Two Letters to a Noble Lord* (London, 1756), 10, 11.

42. Carol Watts, *The Cultural Work of Empire: The Seven Years' War and the Imagining of the Shandean State* (Edinburgh: Edinburgh Univ. Press, 2007), 11.

43. Foster, "The Topographical Tradition," 20; Waters, "Topographical Poetry," 227.

44. Atkinson, *Killarney*, 11.

45. Waters, "Topographical Poetry," 229–30.

46. Charles J. Withers, "Where Was the Atlantic Enlightenment? Questions of Geography," in *The Atlantic Enlightenment*, edited by Susan Manning and Francis D. Cogliano (Burlington, VT: Ashgate, 2008), 47.

47. *Killarny* (c. 1769), 4.

48. Maureen Harkin, "Adam Smith's Missing History: Primitives, Progress, and Problems of Genre," *ELH* 72, no. 2 (2005): 433–34.

49. Leslie, *Phoenix Park*, 8n., 11.

50. See Helen O'Connell, "Improved English, and the Silence of Irish," *Canadian Journal of Irish Studies* 30 (2004): 13–20, and *Ireland and the Fiction of Improvement* (Oxford: Oxford Univ. Press, 2006), which includes another version of this 2004 journal article. For recent discussions of Lawrence's text in this context, see David Armitage, "The Political Economy of Britain and Ireland after the Glorious Revolution," in *Political Thought in Seventeenth-Century Ireland*, edited by Jane Ohlmeyer (Cambridge: Cambridge Univ. Press, 2000), 227–28; Deana Rankin, *Between Spenser and Swift: English Writing in Seventeenth-Century Ireland* (Cambridge: Cambridge Univ. Press, 2005), 63–74.

51. On Irish exports to overseas British imperial possessions, see, for instance, Thomas Bartlett, "'This Famous Island Set in a Virginian Sea': Ireland in the British Empire, 1690–1801," in *The Oxford History of the British Empire: The Eighteenth Century*, edited by P. J. Marshall (Oxford: Oxford Univ. Press, 1998), esp. 255–58.

52. Waters, "Topographical Poetry," 228.

53. David Hume, "Of the Origin of Government," in *Political Essays*, 21, 20.

54. Ibid., 22–23.

55. *Oxford English Dictionary Online* (Oxford: Oxford Univ. Press, 2010), http://www.oed.com.

56. In contrast, Leslie's *Phoenix Park* positions Ireland in a European context: "I compar'd her [Ireland's] state, her bustling times, / With all the miseries of distant climes, / The wild disorder of the Dane and Swede, . . . What pangs dismember'd Poland now must feel" (12).

57. Isaac Weld, *Illustrations of the Scenery of Killarney and the Surrounding Country* (London: Longman, Hurst, Rees, and Orme, 1807), 82–83.

58. Leslie, *Phoenix Park*, 14.

59. In Thomas Moore's account, the Volunteers were formed after "the town of Belfast . . . applied to government for protection, and received the memorable answer, 'We have not the means;—you must defend yourselves'" (*The Life and Death of Lord Edward Fitzgerald*, 2nd ed., 2 vols. [London: Longman, Rees, Orme, Brown, and Green, 1831], 1:186–87).

60. Gibbons, "Topographies of Terror," 31.

61. See ibid., 32–33.

62. Waters, "Topographical Poetry," 230.

63. See Robert Tracy, "Maria Edgeworth and Lady Morgan: Legality versus Legitimacy," *Nineteenth-Century Fiction* 40 (1985): 1–22; Mary Louise Pratt, *Imperial Eyes: Travel Writing and Transculturation* (New York: Routledge, 1992); Ina Ferris, *The Achievement of Literary Authority: Gender, History, and the Waverley Novels* (Ithaca, NY: Cornell Univ. Press, 1991) and *The Romantic National Tale*; Trumpener, *Bardic Nationalism*. See also, for example, Mary Jean Corbett, *Allegories of Union in Irish and English Writing, 1790–1870: Politics, History, and the Family from Edgeworth to Arnold* (Cambridge: Cambridge Univ. Press, 2000); Francesca Lacaita, "The Journey of the Encounter: The Politics of the National Tale in Sydney Owenson's *The Wild Irish Girl* and Maria Edgeworth's *Ennui*," in *Critical Ireland: New Essays in Literature and Culture*, edited by Alan A. Gillis and Aaron Kelly, 148–54 (Dublin: Four Courts Press, 2001); Thomas Tracy, "The Mild Irish Girl: Domesticating the National Tale," *Éire-Ireland* 39 (2004): 81–109; and Wright, *Ireland, India, and Nationalism in Nineteenth-Century Literature*. For a valuable recent overview of some scholarship on the national tale, see Miranda Burgess, "The National Tale and Allied Genres, 1770s–1840s," in *The Cambridge Companion to the Irish Novel*, edited by John Wilson Foster, 39–59 (Cambridge: Cambridge Univ. Press, 2006).

64. Leslie, *Phoenix Park*, 13, 13n.

65. This is Leslie's term for political resistance in *Phoenix Park* (15n.).

66. See Gibbons, "Topographies of Terror," for a useful discussion of this aristocrat's place in contemporary sectarian politics.

67. James Thomson, "Summer," *The Seasons*, in *James Thomson: The Poetical Works*, edited by J. Logie Robertson (London: Oxford Univ. Press, 1965), 649–52.

68. Wright, *Ireland, India, and Nationalism*, 72.

69. Lady Morgan (Sydney Owenson), *The Wild Irish Girl* (1806), edited by Kathryn Kirkpatrick (Oxford: Oxford Univ. Press, 1999), 249. On the uneasy marital solution in Owenson's novel, see, for example, Julia Anne Miller, "Acts of Union: Family Violence and National Courtship in Maria Edgeworth's *Absentee* and Sydney Owenson's *The Wild Irish Girl*," in *Border Crossings: Irish Women Writers and National Identities*, edited by Kathryn Kirkpatrick (Tuscaloosa: Univ. of Alabama Press, 2000), 28–29; and Wright, *Ireland, India, and Nationalism*, 71–72.

70. Morgan, *The Wild Irish Girl*, 240, emphasis added.

71. Waters, "Topographical Poetry," 231.

72. Edwards, "The Princess of Killarney," 121, hereafter cited parenthetically in the text.

73. Morgan, *The Wild Irish Girl*, 120, 216.

74. Sharon Murphy suggests that we read the poem as "cautionary" in "causing Britons to have a more perfect understanding of the complexities—and original inequities—of the Anglo-Irish relationship" ("Anna Maria Edwards," in *Irish Women Poets of the Romantic Period*, edited by Stephen C. Behrendt [Alexandria, VA: Alexander Street Press, 2008]), but this reading raises the same dilemma as that posed by the end of Moore's "Oh! Blame Not the Bard": the British can learn the lesson only after the abjection, and in this case even the obliteration, of the Irish.

75. Gibbons, "Topographies of Terror," 29.

76. Ibid., 31.

77. Brontë, *Maid of Killarney*, 83, hereafter cited parenthetically in the text.

78. Wright, *Ireland, India, and Nationalism*, 64.

79. See ibid., 71–72.

80. On Torrens's significance in Irish thought on political economy, see Lionel Robbins's foundational study *Robert Torrens and the Evolution of Classical Economics* (London: Macmillan, 1958). Torrens is unfortunately absent from the important discussion of Irish political economy in Thomas A. Boylan and Timothy P. Foley's *Political Economy and Colonial Ireland: The Propagation and Ideological Function of Economic Discourse in the Nineteenth Century* (New York: Routledge, 1992), which stresses the Victorian era. For a brief account of his life that stresses his nonfiction, see the *Oxford Dictionary of National Biography* (Oxford: Oxford Univ. Press, 2004–12), http://www.oxforddnb.com, though the entry gives the wrong date for *The Victim of Intolerance* and omits the first part of its title.

81. See Robert Torrens, *Thoughts on the Catholic Question*, 2nd ed. (London: Gale, Curtis, and Fenner, 1813).

82. I am deeply grateful to the Princeton University Library for lending me its exceedingly rare copy of the fourth volume as I was working on this project; it has since been digitized and is available via Google Books and Nineteenth Century Collections Online (Corvey Collection).

83. Torrens, *Victim of Intolerance*, 4:265–66, hereafter cited parenthetically in the text by volume and page number.

84. *Exile of Ireland!* 27; Charles Hamilton Teeling, *Personal Narrative of the Irish Rebellion of 1798* (London: Henry Colburn, 1828), 43n.

2. "This Vale of Tears": Glendalough and the Gothic

1. Gibbons, "Topographies of Terror," 25.

2. John Carr, *The Stranger in Ireland; Or, A Tour in Southern and Western Parts of that Country, in the Year 1805* (London: Richard Phillips, 1806), 175. On Killarney and insurgency, see Gibbons, "Topographies of Terror."

3. Gibbons, "Topographies of Terror," 25–26.

4. Drennan, *Fugitive Pieces in Verse and Prose*; William Drennan, *Glendalloch, and Other Poems, with Additional Verses by his Sons*, 2nd ed. (Dublin: William Robertson, 1859); William Drennan, "Glendalloch," in *The Poetical Register, and Repository of Fugitive Poetry, for 1804*, 19–31 (London: F. and C. Rivington, 1806); William Drennan, "Glendalloch," *Belfast Monthly Magazine* 6, no. 33 (Apr. 30, 1811): 308–12. The *Belfast Monthly Magazine*, which regularly included articles under the title "Discoveries and Improvements in Arts, Manufactures" and on education as well as on foreign literature and politics, published an article on "modernizing" that argued for dispensing with the classical languages in higher education and as qualification for office ("Modernizing," *Belfast Monthly Magazine* 6, no. 32 [Mar. 31, 1811]: 218–19).

5. For early publications of this material, see Thomas Moore, "By that Lake Whose Gloomy Shore," 4th number of *Irish Melodies* (London, 1811); Samuel Lover, *Saint Kevin: A Legend of Glendalough, sung by the Author in his Irish Evenings* (London: Duff & Hodgson, n.d. [c. 1846]); *Glendalough, or The Seven Churches: A Didactic Poem, by an Ex-Moderator, T. C. D.* (Dublin: Hodges and Smith, 1848); Edmund John Armstrong, "Glandalough: A Story of Wicklow," in *The Poetical Works of Edmund J. Armstrong*, edited by George Francis Armstrong, 101–26 (London: Longman, Green, 1877); Dora Sigerson, "The Deer-Stone: A Legend of Glendalough," in *A Legend of Glendalough and Other Ballads*, 7–14 (Dublin: Maunsel, 1919).

6. The painting is held at the Ulster Museum and is reproduced on the cover of this book.

7. Sigerson, "The Deer-Stone," 12.

8. Siobhán Kilfeather, "Terrific Register: The Gothicization of Atrocity in Irish Romanticism," *boundary 2* 31 (2004): 49–71; Jarlath Killeen, *Gothic Ireland: Horror and the Irish Anglican Imagination in the Eighteenth Century* (Dublin: Four Courts Press, 2005).

9. Robert Miles, *Gothic Writing, 1750–1820: A Genealogy* (New York: Routledge, 1993), 33–35.

10. David B. Morris, "Gothic Sublimity," *New Literary History* 16 (1985): 306.

11. For a valuable survey of the elevating sublime, see James Kirwan, *Sublimity: The Non-rational and the Irrational in the History of Aesthetics* (New York: Routledge, 2005), esp. 6–7.

12. See Richard Haslam, "Irish Gothic: A Rhetorical Hermeneutics Approach," *Irish Journal of Gothic and Horror Studies* 2 (2007), at http://irishgothichorror journal.homestead.com/IrishGothicHaslam.html.

13. David Dwan contests "questionable genealogies of influence in which German romanticism plays a disproportionately large role in Irish letters" by challenging Thomas Davis's "mythic visit" to "Germany in 1839–40" (*The Great Community*, 15, 15n.). Folkloric exchanges in the 1820s, particularly given Herder's significance to German folkloric studies, offer a much firmer foundation for the significance of German romanticism in Irish literature from the 1820s forward.

14. *Glendalough, or The Seven Churches*, 25.

15. Ibid., 25–26.

16. Morris, "Gothic Sublimity," 302, 303.

17. Ibid., 311–12. This of course is somewhat anticipated by the final part of Burke's *Enquiry*.

18. Charles O'Conor, "Advertisement," in *Seasonable Thoughts Relating to Our Civil and Ecclesiastical Constitution* (Dublin, 1753), n.p. This volume is a substantially revised edition of the anonymously published *Some Seasonable Thoughts, Relating to Our Civil and Ecclesiastical Constitution: Wherein is Occasionally Consider'd, The Case of the Professors of Popery* (Dublin, 1751).

19. On unproductive terror, see especially Steven Bruhm, *Gothic Bodies: The Politics of Pain in Romantic Fiction* (Philadelphia: Univ. of Pennsylvania Press, 1994).

20. Edmund Burke, *A Philosophical Enquiry into the Origins of Our Ideas of the Sublime and Beautiful*, edited by Adam Phillips (Oxford: Oxford Univ. Press, 1990), 53, 60.

21. Ibid., 54.

22. Weld, *Illustrations of the Scenery of Killarney*, i.

23. Ware, "Of the Bishops of Glendaloch," in *The Whole Works of Sir James Ware*, 1:372.

24. William Camden, *Britannia: Or, A Chorographical Description of the Flourishing Kingdoms of England, Scotland, and Ireland, and the Islands Adjacent*, 3 vols., translated and enlarged by Richard Gough (London: John Nichols, 1789), 1:vi, 3:552.

25. Ibid., 3:553.

26. Quoted in Gibbons, "Topographies of Terror," 25.

27. Jonathan Fisher, *The Scenery of Ireland* (Dublin: printed for the author, 1795); Jonathan Fisher, *A Description of the Lake of Killarney . . . Being an Appendix to His "Scenery of Ireland"* (Dublin: W. Chambers, 1796).

28. Fisher, *Description*, 2.

29. Fisher, "Description of the Valley of Glendalough," in *Scenery of Ireland*, 1 (this volume is largely unpaginated, pairing one page of prose description with an engraving of the scene; this chapter, although it is the last one, is separately paginated). Of the five and a half pages of prose, four pages are devoted to a detailed description of the ruins, and three of the five engravings focus on ruins as well.

30. Phrases such as "agreeably surprized" abound in discussions of landscape aesthetics. Daniel Defoe's *Tour Thro' the Whole Island of Great Britain* (1742), for instance, uses the same phrase: "When we had gained the Top, we were agreeably surprised to see a smooth and pleasant Plain" (*A Tour Thro' the Whole Island of Great Britain*, 4 vols. [London, 1742], 3:206). It also appears, for instance, in Thomas West's *Guide to the Lakes* (1780) as well as in William Guthrie's *A New System of Modern Geography* in a description of the Wicklow mountains: "A stranger, upon entering the bay of Dublin, . . . is agreeably surprised with the beautiful prospect on each side, and the distant view of the Wicklow mountains" (Thomas West, *Guide to the Lakes*, 2nd ed. [London, 1780], 126; William Guthrie, *A New System of Modern Geography*, 3rd ed. [London, 1786], 415).

31. Fisher, "Description of the Valley of Glendalough," 1–3.

32. Gibbons, "Topographies of Terror," 25, Gibbons's ellipsis.

33. Ferris, *Romantic National Tale*, 108–9.

34. Ibid., 110; Sean Ryder, "Ireland in Ruins: The Figure of Ruin in Early Nineteenth-Century Irish Poetry," in *Landscape and Empire, 1770–2000*, edited by Glenn Hooper (Burlington, VT: Ashgate, 2005), 82.

35. Kevin Whelan, "Reading the Ruins: The Presence of Absence in the Irish Landscape," in *Surveying Ireland's Past: Multidisciplinary Essays in Honour of Anngret Simms*, edited by Howard B. Clarke, Jacinta Prunty, and Mark Hennessy (Dublin: Geography Publications, 2004), 298, 299.

36. Fisher, "Description of the Valley of Glendalough," 1.

37. Ferris, *Romantic National Tale*, 111.

38. For a discussion of landscape in relation to the gothic, see, for instance, Jayne Lewis, "'No Colour of Language': Radcliffe's Aesthetic Unbound," *Eighteenth-Century Studies* 39 (2006): 377–90. Ryder suggests, provocatively, that Irish ruin poems, in distinction to their English counterparts, are more amenable to the gothic devices of "ghosts and spirits" ("Ireland in Ruins," 85). My interest here is the gothic aesthetic rather than such supernatural devices.

39. Fisher, "Description of the Valley of Glendalough," 2. The most substantial recent scholarly discussion of Ledwich is in Clare O'Halloran, *Golden Ages and Barbarous Nations: Antiquarian Debate and Cultural Politics in Ireland, c. 1750–1800* (Notre Dame, IN: Univ. of Notre Dame Press, 2005).

40. Edward Ledwich, *Antiquities of Ireland* (Dublin: Edward Grueber, 1790), 159.

41. Oliver MacDonagh, *States of Mind: A Study of Anglo-Irish Conflict, 1780–1980* (London: Allen & Unwin, 1983), 1.

42. O'Halloran, *Golden Ages and Barbarous Nations*, esp. 86–91 and 135–40; Leith Davis, *Music, Postcolonialism, and Gender: The Construction of Irish National Identity, 1724–1874* (Notre Dame, IN: Univ. of Notre Dame Press, 2006), 68; Joseph Lennon, *Irish Orientalism: A Literary and Intellectual History* (Syracuse, NY: Syracuse Univ. Press, 2004), 133–34; Leerssen, *Remembrance and Imagination*, 100, 314.

43. Ledwich, *Antiquities of Ireland*, iii–iv, 259.

44. Ibid., iv.

45. Ibid., 31.

46. Morris, "Gothic Sublimity," 300–301.

47. Horace Walpole's *Castle of Otranto* similarly promises a tale in which "the mind is kept up in a constant vicissitude of interesting passions," including "pity" and "terror" (*Castle of Otranto*, edited by W. S. Lewis [Oxford: Oxford Univ. Press, 1998], 6).

48. William Drennan, "Glendalloch," in *IL*, 142–54; hereafter for this poem, verse is cited parenthetically in the text by line number and footnotes by page number.

49. Ledwich, *Antiquities of Ireland*, 47–48.

50. Ibid., 33.

51. Carr, *Stranger in Ireland*, 178. Just after this duplication, Carr invokes "the profound and amiable Ledwich" in promising to provide an excerpt of Ledwich's work later on (178); this excerpt ends the chapter on Glendalough (see 188–97).

52. Armstrong, "Glandalough," 108.

53. Mary Helen Thuente, *The Harp Re-strung: The United Irishmen and the Rise of Irish Literary Nationalism* (Syracuse, NY: Syracuse Univ. Press, 1994), 111; Brown, *Northern Voices*, 25.

54. Waters, "Topographical Poetry," 237–38, 238.

55. The 1806 publication may be the first because the *Register* invited contributions of original verse in the opening advertisement of its volumes, and Drennan published verse in four volumes of the eight-volume *Register* (these poems later appeared, with some revision, in *Fugitive Pieces*). Among the 1806, 1811, and 1815 versions of "Glendalloch," most variations are in spelling ("havoc" versus

"havock," for instance) and punctuation, and in Drennan's addition of a lengthy footnote in 1811, kept in the 1815 text. The 1811 version departs from the 1806 and 1815 texts in the reversal of two lines and some rephrased passages (including the strange switching of the gender of the "adult'rer" to female), but the most significant variation among these three publications during Drennan's lifetime is in the third-last verse paragraph. Drennan drafted two versions of a section on a deceitful courtier (1806, 1811) but removed it from the 1815 text.

56. Drennan's poem postdates the now famous *Lyrical Ballads* (1798), with its influential place poem "Tintern Abbey," but Wordsworth and Coleridge's volume was not instantly successful. In 1800, Wordsworth was still substantially outshone by Mary Robinson, for instance (see Stuart Curran, "Mary Robinson's *Lyrical Tales* in Context," in *Re-visioning Romanticism: British Women Writers, 1776–1837*, edited by Carol Shiner Wilson and Joel Haefner, 17–35 [Philadelphia: Univ. of Pennsylvania Press, 1994], esp. 19–22).

57. Vance, *Irish Literature*, 94–95.

58. Foster, "Topographical Tradition," 10.

59. Luke Gibbons, *Transformations in Irish Culture* (Notre Dame, IN: Univ. of Notre Dame Press, 1996), 159. The chapter cited here is a version of an earlier essay, "Race against Time: Racial Discourse and Irish History," *Oxford Literary Review* 13, nos. 1–2 (1991): 95–117.

60. Ryder, "Ireland in Ruins," 82.

61. Leslie, *Killarney*, in *IL*, 23–28.

62. Waters, "Topographical Poetry," 237–38.

63. Compare, for instance, Goldsmith's *Deserted Village* (in *IL*, 36–42, hereafter cited parenthetically in the text) and Drennan's "Glendalloch" (135–40).

64. Vance, *Irish Literature*, 94–95; Drennan, *Letter to the Right Honorable William Pitt*, 43.

65. John Locke, *An Essay Concerning Human Understanding*, edited by Peter H. Nidditch (Oxford: Clarendon Press, 1975), 248 (chap. 21, sec. 26), emphasis in original.

66. O'Conor, *Seasonable Thoughts*, n.p.

67. Burke, *A Philosophical Enquiry*, 53.

68. Vance, *Irish Literature*, 95.

69. Thomas Gray, "Elegy Written in a Country Church Yard," in *The Complete Poems of Thomas Gray*, edited by H. W. Starr and J. R. Hendrickson (Oxford: Clarendon Press, 1966), 13–17.

70. Vance, *Irish Literature*, 95.

71. Vance suggests this passage is "derived perhaps from Pope's *Essay on Man*," representing "Nature" as "the mirror of the eternal mind imperfectly perceived (ibid., 95).

72. O'Halloran, *Golden Ages and Barbarous Nations*, 86.

73. Ibid., 90.

74. O'Conor, *Seasonable Thoughts*, n.p.

75. Review of William Drennan's *A Letter to the Right Hon. William Pitt*, *Analytical Review*, new series, 1 (Feb. 1799): 154.

76. Burke, *A Philosopical Enquiry*, 42.

77. Ibid., 158.

78. James Orr, "Lambert: An Elegaic Ode," in *Poems, On Various Subjects* (Belfast: Smith and Lyrons, 1804), 25. Drennan is not on the list of subscribers for Orr's volume but was connected to the family through his famous elegy for James Orr's brother William, "Wake."

79. Erasmus Darwin, *The Botanic Garden; A Poem, in Two Parts* (London: J. Johnson, 1791), part II, canto III, 237–38.

80. Ibid., part II, 115n. For a useful overview of the Upas tree myth in eighteenth- and nineteenth-century literature, see Richard F. Gustafson, "The Upas Tree: Pushkin and Erasmus Darwin," *PMLA* 75 (1960): 101–3.

81. Critics have widely associated the trees in Blake's "The Human Abstract" and "A Poison-Tree," both from *Songs of Experience*, with the Upas (and with Darwin's verse). For a recent discussion, see Ashton Nichols, "An Empire of Exotic Nature: Blake's Botanic and Zoomorphic Imagery," in *The Reception of Blake in the Orient*, edited by Steve Clark and Masashi Suzuki (New York: Continuum, 2006), 125–26.

82. Smith, "Neo-classicist and Romantic Elements," 83.

83. [Lady Morgan], "Absenteeism, Part I," *New Monthly Magazine* 10 (1824): 482. The three-part series (1824–25) was collected under Morgan's name in *Absenteeism* (London: Henry Colburn, 1825).

84. Whelan, "Reading the Ruins," 320.

85. MacDonagh, *States of Mind*, 2.

86. Vance, *Irish Literature*, 88, 90–91.

87. Waters, "Topographical Poetry," 238.

88. Leith Davis notes that Ledwich, in an appendix to Joseph Cooper Walker's *Historical Memoirs of the Irish Bards*, argues that it was the English who invented the Irish national symbol of the harp, so that "the symbol of music is given to the Irish by the English, who 'allowed us eminence in nothing but music.' The identity of the colonized is limited to that which is recognized by the colonizing nation and, further, becomes involved in 'the ornament and support' of that colonizing nation" (*Music, Postcolonialism, and Gender*, 68).

89. Ledwich, *Antiquities of Ireland*, 44.

90. Ibid., 47. Lennon notes that Ledwich elsewhere also attributes the round towers to the Danes (*Irish Orientalism*, 109–10).

91. Lennon, *Irish Orientalism*, 84–85.

92. Thuente, *The Harp Re-strung*, 111; Waters, "Topographical Poetry," 239.

93. Ledwich, *Antiquities of Ireland*, 34.

94. See Geoffrey Keating's "Table of the Kings of Ireland," in *General History of Ireland* (London, 1723). The 1723 edition is the first published English translation of his early seventeenth-century Irish-language history, a text that circulated in manuscript. There were other kings named Tuathal, including one contemporary with Saint Kevin, according to Keating's "Table."

95. Carr, *Stranger in Ireland*, 174–75.

96. Ibid., 175.

97. Ibid.

98. Ibid.

99. Alicia Lefanu, *The Outlaw*, in *Tales of a Tourist, Containing The Outlaw and Fashionable Connexions*, 4 vols. (London: A. K. Newman, 1823), 2:130–32. Similar imagery also marks the conclusion of William Carleton's "Wildgoose Lodge" (originally published in 1830 under another title).

100. Whelan, "Reading the Ruins," 307.

101. *Glendalough, or The Seven Churches*, iv.

102. Dion Boucicault, *Arrah-na-Pogue*, in *IL*, 438, 439.

103. Ibid., 440.

104. Ibid., 440, 464.

105. Noah Heringman, *Romantic Rocks, Aesthetic Geology* (Ithaca, NY: Cornell Univ. Press, 2004), 243. Heringman valuably discusses Drummond's poetic treatment of geology at length; see also Foster, "Encountering Traditions," 63–65.

106. William Hamilton Drummond, *The Giants' Causeway: A Poem* (London: Longman, Rees, Orme, and Brown, 1811), 9.

107. Ibid., 102.

108. Brown, *Northern Voices*, 23. For a nearly contemporary prose representation of the same scenery that evinces scientific interest but also involves landscape aesthetics and challenges conventional representations of the Irish, see the first volume of Lady Morgan's *O'Donnel* (1814).

109. Thomas Moore, "By that Lake Whose Gloomy Shore," in *IL*, 1–2.

110. Ibid., 19–20,

111. Ibid., 30–32.

112. Ibid., 38–40.

113. Leslie, *Killarney*, in *IL*, 318, 309–10, 335–36.

114. Thomas Moore, "O'Donohue's Mistress," in *Irish Melodies*, 8th ed. (London: Longman, Rees, Orme, Brown, and Green, 1827), 184n.

115. Ibid., 184n.

116. Armstrong, "Glandalough," 124–25.

117. See Goodman, *Georgic Modernity.*

118. For a discussion of *Mount Leinster* as well as of its possible attribution to either Anna Liddiard or William Liddiard, see Julia M. Wright, "Introduction: Anna Liddiard," in Behrendt, ed., *Irish Women Poets of the Romantic Period.*

119. Alan Liu, *Wordsworth: The Sense of History* (Stanford, CA: Stanford Univ. Press, 1989), 18. See Goodman, *Georgic Modernity*, for a valuable overview of the georgic in English romanticist scholarship.

3. Transatlantic Movements: Exile and Migration

1. Anderson, *Spectre of Comparisons*, 58–74.

2. Thomas Campbell published the poem as his own in 1801, but charges of plagiarism began to appear soon thereafter, attributing the poem to Irish poet George Nugent Reynolds; see, for example, W. H. Grattan-Flood, "Authorship of 'The Exile of Erin': A Vindication of Thomas Campbell," *Irish Monthly* 49 (1921): 229–34; Molloy, "Thomas Campbell's 'Exile of Erin.'"

3. William Allingham, "The Winding Banks of Erne: Or, The Emigrant's Adieu to Ballyshanny," in *IL*, 501–3, 1–8.

4. John Locke, *Two Treatises of Government*, edited by Peter Laslett (Cambridge: Cambridge Univ. Press, 1988), 325.

5. Henry Grattan, "Declaration of Right," in *Speeches of the Right Honourable Henry Grattan in the Irish, and in the Imperial Parliament*, 4 vols., edited by his Son [Henry Grattan] (London: Longman, Hurst, Rees, Orme, and Brown, 1822), 1:41.

6. See J. L. Austin, *How to Do Things with Words*, 2nd ed., edited by J. O. Urmson and Marina Sbisà (Cambridge, MA: Harvard Univ. Press, 1975).

7. Dwan suggests, "Grattan's republican defense of Irish freedoms . . . was initially aimed at securing no more than free trade" (*Great Community*, 73), but I would add that we need to take fuller account of the significance of trade to conceptualizations of national sovereignty in the era and particularly in the wake of Adam Smith's *Wealth of Nations* (1776).

8. Grattan, *Speeches of the Right Honourable Henry Grattan*, 1:232.

9. In their headnote to Barbauld's poem, editors William McCarthy and Elizabeth Kraft associate it more broadly with "the passing of empire from east to west" (Anna Letitia Barbauld, "Eighteen Hundred and Eleven," in *Anna Letitia Barbauld: Selected Poetry and Prose*, edited by William McCarthy and Elizabeth Kraft [Peterborough: Broadview Press, 2002], 160–61). But, partly a critique of imperial aggression as a sign of Britain's moral collapse, "Eighteen Hundred and Eleven" depicts the New World as the site of scientific, cultural, and economic progress: "Thy Lockes, thy Paleys shall instruct their [American] youth" (l. 89).

10. Drennan, "Erin," in *IL*, 5–8.

11. James Porter, *Billy Bluff and 'Squire Firebrand* (Belfast, 1797), 9; the letters were originally published serially in 1796.

12. See, for instance, Martin Burke, "Piecing Together a Shattered Past: The Historical Writings of the United Irish Exiles in America," in *The United Irishmen: Republicanism, Radicalism, and Rebellion*, edited by David Dickson, Dáire Keough, and Kevin Whelan, 297–306 (Dublin: Lilliput Press, 1993); Stephen Small, *Political Thought in Ireland, 1776–1798: Republicanism, Patriotism, and Radicalism* (Oxford: Oxford Univ. Press, 2003); David A. Wilson, *United Irishmen, United States: Immigrant Radicals in the Early Republic* (Ithaca, NY: Cornell Univ. Press, 1998); and, on shared political symbolism, Mary Helen Thuente, "Liberty, Hibernia, and Mary Le More: United Irish Images of Women," in *Women of 1798*, edited by Dáire Keough and Nicholas Furlong, 9–25 (Dublin: Four Courts Press, 1998). For recent discussions of race and the United Irishmen, see, for instance, Luke Gibbons, "'The Return of the Native': The United Irishmen, Culture, and Colonialism," in *1798: A Bicentenary Perspective*, edited by Thomas Bartlett, David Dickson, Dáire Keogh, and Kevin Whelan, 52–74 (Dublin: Four Courts Press, 2003); David A. Wilson, "Comment: Whiteness and Irish Experience in North America," *Journal of British Studies* 44 (2005): 153–60.

13. Quoted in Wilson, *United Irishmen, United States*, 58.

14. *The Exile of Ireland!* 5.

15. "To a Red-Breast, My Daily Visitor," *Belfast Monthly Magazine* 6, no. 30 (Jan. 31, 1811): 54.

16. In *Local Poets and Social History: James Orr, Bard of Ballycarry* (Belfast: Public Record Office of Northern Ireland, 1977), Donald Harmon Akenson and W. H. Crawford suggest such a direct representation in pairing "The Passengers" with "Extracts from 'A Journal of a Voyage from Belfast to Boston'" (by John Cunningham). For further discussion of Orr's work, see in particular Carol Baraniuk, "James Orr: Ulster-Scot and Poet of the 1798 Rebellion," *Scottish Studies Review* 6 (2005): 22–32, but also John Hewitt, *Rhyming Weavers and Other Poets of Antrim and Down* (Belfast: Blackstaff Press, 1971); Brown, *Northern Voices*, 10–13; Linde Connoly Lunney, "Attitudes to Life and Death in the Poetry of James Orr," *Ulster Folklife* 31 (1985): 1–12; and Philip Robinson, "The Historical Presence of Ulster-Scots in Ireland," in *The Languages of Ireland*, edited by Michael Cronin and Cormac Ó Cuilleanáin, 112–26 (Dublin: Four Courts Press, 2005).

17. James Orr, "Song Composed on the Banks of Newfoundland," in Carpenter, ed., *Verse in English*, 542–43, 11–16, 17–24.

18. James Orr, "The Passengers" (1804), in *IL*, 73–74; hereafter cited by line number for verse and page number for footnotes.

19. Brown, *Northern Voices*, 11.

20. James Orr, "Song," in *Poems, on Various Subjects*, 142.

21. Ibid.

22. Ibid.

23. Morgan, *Wild Irish Girl*, 94–95.

24. See Gilroy, *Black Atlantic*.

25. Andrew M. Kaye, *The Pussycat of Prizefighting: Tiger Flowers and the Politics of Black Celebrity* (Athens: Univ. of Georgia Press, 2004), 21–25.

26. Ibid., 23.

27. Ibid., 22, 21. This history includes the more famous case of Tom Molineaux in the early 1800s, but Kaye notes that there may have been much earlier precedents, such as Bill Richmond, who traveled to England in 1777 (22). Thomas Moore's satire *Tom Crib's Memorial to Congress* (1819) refers to African American boxer Sam Robinson's fights in England.

28. David Roediger, *Working towards Whiteness: How America's Immigrants Became White* (New York: Basic Books, 2005), 119.

29. See especially ibid. and Wilson, "Comment."

30. *Exile of Erin!*, 6.

31. Quoted in Bruce Nelson, "'Come Out of Such a Land, You Irishmen': Daniel O'Connell, American Slavery, and the Making of the 'Irish Race,'" *Éire-Ireland* 42, nos. 1–2 (2007): 70.

32. "A Voice from America," in *IL*, 3–4.

33. This political contradiction, of course, is a major issue in historical studies of the United Irishmen in transatlantic exile. For a particularly deft and thorough piece on this subject and on key works of scholarship about it to date, see Wilson, "Comment."

34. See Thomas Moore, *Epistles, Odes, and Other Poems* (London: J. Carpenter, 1806); in his preface to this volume, Moore traces his disillusionment with the postrevolutionary United States, and several poems address the subject. For a recent discussion of this part of Moore's early work and life, see Jane Moore, "'Transatlantic Tom': Thomas Moore in North America," in Kelly, ed., *Ireland and Romanticism*, 77–93. Moore's representation of his American travels has long been a staple of Moore studies. See, for instance, Herbert G. Eldridge, "Anacreon Moore and America," *PMLA* 83 (1968): 54–62; the chapter on Moore in D. M. R. Bentley, *Mimic Fires: Accounts of Early Long Poems on Canada* (Montreal: McGill-Queen's Univ. Press, 1994); and Jeffrey W. Vail, "Thomas Moore in Ireland and America," *Romanticism* 10 (2004): 41–62.

35. On McGee's early life in Ireland and the United States, see David A. Wilson, *Thomas D'Arcy McGee*, vol. 1: *Passion, Reason, and Politics, 1825–1857* (Montreal: McGill-Queen's Univ. Press, 2008).

36. Ibid., 1:21.

37. For further biographical information on Adam Kidd, see the entry on him in *Dictionary of Canadian Biography Online*, http://www.biographia.ca.

38. Thomas D'Arcy McGee, "Freedom's Journey," in *IL*, 7–12.

39. Adam Kidd, preface to *The Huron Chief, and Other Poems* (Montreal: Printed at the Office of the Herald and New Gazette, 1830), x–xi. Critical discussion of Kidd to date has focused on *The Huron Chief* in the context of the Canadian long poem (assisted greatly by the invaluable critical edition of Kidd's work, *The Huron Chief*, edited by D. M. R. Bentley, with contributions and appendices by Charles R. Steele [London, Ontario: Canadian Poetry Press, 1987]) and on the significance of the poem as a major representation of native Canadians. See, for instance, Bentley, *Mimic Fires*; Chaim David Mazoff, *Anxious Allegiances: Legitimizing Identity in the Early Canadian Long Poem* (Montreal: McGill-Queen's Univ. Press, 1998); Leslie Monkman, *A Native Heritage: Images of the Indian in English–Canadian Literature* (Toronto: Univ. of Toronto Press, 1981).

40. Emigrant quoted in Wilson, *United Irishmen, United States*, 58.

41. Charles Gavan Duffy, *Letter to John Mitchel* (Supplement to the Nation) (Dublin: Printed at the Nation Office, 1854), 6.

42. Ibid., 2.

43. Ibid., 16.

44. Thomas D'Arcy McGee, *Poems by Thomas D'Arcy McGee, Chiefly Written in America* (Dublin: Published at the Nation Office, 1854).

45. McGee, "Hail to the Land," in *IL*, 27–29.

46. "A Voice from America," in *IL*, 5–7.

47. McGee, "Hail to the Land," 51–60.

48. McGee, "A Salutation," in *Poems by Thomas D'Arcy McGee*, 16. The poem was anthologized in W. B. Yeats's *Book of Irish Verse* (1899).

49. Ibid.

50. McGee, "St. Patrick's of the Woods," in *IL*, 26, 28.

51. Thomas D'Arcy McGee, *Canadian Ballads, and Occasional Verses* (Montreal: John Lovell, 1858), dedication.

52. Duffy, *Letter to John Mitchel*, 4.

53. McGee, preface to *Canadian Ballads*, n.p.

54. McGee, "Hail to the Land," 1–2, 14, 19.

55. McGee, "Home-Sick Stanzas," *Canadian Ballads*, 67, 68.

56. Ibid., 68.

57. McGee, "To a Friend in Australia," in *Canadian Ballads*, 53.

58. Kidd, "My Irish Home," in *Huron Chief, and Other Poems*, 134–35.

59. Kidd, "The Hibernian Solitary," in *Huron Chief, and Other Poems*, 211, 212.

60. Kidd, "Cathleen," in *Huron Chief, and Other Poems*, 172, hereafter cited parenthetically in the text.

61. See Smith, "Neo-classicist and Romantic Elements."

62. Ibid., 83.

63. As Terry Eagleton puts it more broadly, "For romantic nationalism, the hyphen in the phrase nation-state suggests a unity of culture and politics, a realm in which the latter luminously expresses the former" ("Nationalism and the Case of Ireland," *New Left Review* 234 [Mar.–Apr. 1999]: 47, http://www.newleftreview.org/?page=article&view=1984.

64. Thomas Wyse, *Historical Sketch of the Late Catholic Association of Ireland*, 2 vols. (London: Henry Colburn, 1829), 94.

65. [Lady Morgan], "Absenteeism, Part III," *New Monthly Magazine* 11 (1825), 164.

66. See Tracy, "Maria Edgeworth and Lady Morgan."

67. Lefanu, *The Outlaw*, 1:219, hereafter cited parenthetically in the text by volume and page number.

68. Moore, *Life and Death of Lord Edward Fitzgerald*, 1:5, 1:21.

69. Ibid., 1:304.

70. See Julia M. Wright, "'All the Fire-Side Circle': Irish Women Writers and the Sheridan–Lefanu Coterie," *Keats–Shelley Journal* 55 (2006): 63–72. Frances Sheridan was the elder Lefanu's mother and the younger's grandmother.

71. Lady [Sydney] Morgan, *The O'Briens and the O'Flahertys: A National Tale* (1827), edited by Julia M. Wright (Peterborough, Canada: Broadview Press, 2013), 109, 221, hereafter cited parenthetically in the text by page number.

4. From Terror to Terrorism: Gothic Movements in England

1. Kilfeather, "Terrific Register," 60. For other key discussions of Irish gothic, see, for instance, Deane, *Strange Country*; Julian T. Moynahan, *Anglo-Irish: The Literary Imagination in a Hyphenated Culture* (Princeton, NJ: Princeton Univ. Press, 1995); W. J. McCormack, "Irish Gothic and After," in Deane, gen. ed., *Field Day Anthology of Irish Writing*, 2:831–54; Margot Gayle Backus, *The Gothic Family Romance: Heterosexuality, Child Sacrifice, and the Anglo-Irish Colonial Order* (Durham, NC: Duke Univ. Press, 1999); Killeen, *Gothic Ireland*; Haslam, "Irish Gothic"; Richard Haslam, "'Broad Farce and Thrilling Tragedy': Mangan's Fiction and Irish Gothic," *Éire-Ireland* 41 (2007): 215–44.

2. See Lloyd, "Introduction," in *Nationalism and Minor Literature*; and Wright, "'All the Fire-Side Circle.'"

3. See Haslam, "Irish Gothic."

4. See McCormack, "Irish Gothic and After," 833–36.

5. Ibid., 836–37, 832.

6. Moynahan, *Anglo-Irish*, 5.

7. McCormack, "Irish Gothic and After," 832, 833.

8. Nicholas Rance, *Wilkie Collins and Other Sensation Novelists* (Cranbury, NJ: Associated Univ. Presses, 1991), 157. For more recent work on LeFanu and sensation fiction, see, for example, Devin P. Zuber, "Swedenborg and the Disintegration of Language in Sheridan Le Fanu's Sensation Fiction," in *Victorian Sensations: Essays on a Scandalous Genre*, edited by Kimberley Harrison and Richard Fantina, 74–84 (Columbus: Ohio State Univ. Press, 2006); Lyn Pykett, "Sensation and the Fantastic in the Victorian Novel," in *The Cambridge Companion to the Victorian Novel*, edited by Deirdre David, 192–211 (Cambridge: Cambridge Univ. Press, 2001). For a foundational work, see Patrick Brantlinger, "What Is 'Sensational' about the 'Sensation Novel'?" *Nineteenth-Century Fiction* 37 (1982): 1–28.

9. See Emer Nolan, *Catholic Emancipations: Irish Fiction from Thomas Moore to James Joyce* (Syracuse, NY: Syracuse Univ. Press, 2007), and note 33 for this chapter.

10. Sir Walter Scott, *Ivanhoe*, edited by Ian Duncan (Oxford: Oxford Univ. Press, 1996), 16.

11. See Bill Ashcroft, Gareth Griffiths, and Helen Tiffin, *The Empire Writes Back* (New York: Routledge, 1989).

12. On the gothic as a response to emergent anxieties about modernity, see the important work of Jerrold Hogle, esp. "'Frankenstein' as Neo-Gothic: From the Ghost of the Counterfeit to the Monster of Abjection," in *Romanticism, History, and the Possibilities of Genre*, edited by Tilottama Rajan and Julia M. Wright, 176–210 (Cambridge: Cambridge Univ. Press, 1998). http://users.ox.ac.uk/~scat0385/ghost.html.

13. Louis Perry Curtis, *Apes and Angels: The Irishman in Victorian Caricature* (Washington, DC: Smithsonian Institution Press, 1971).

14. Thomas Carlyle, *Chartism* (London: James Fraser, 1840), 28–29.

15. Corbett, *Allegories of Union*, 94.

16. Michael de Nie, "Britannia's Sick Sister: Irish Identity and the British Press, 1798–1882," in *Writing Irishness in Nineteenth-Century British Culture*, edited by Neil McCaw (Burlington VT: Ashgate, 2004), 181.

17. On Irish migration in early-eighteenth-century Irish drama, see Helen Burke, "Crossing Acts: Irish Drama from George Farquhar to Thomas Sheridan," in *Companion to Irish Literature*, 2 vols., edited by Julia M. Wright, 1:127–41 (Oxford: Wiley-Blackwell, 2010).

18. Carr, *Stranger in Ireland*, 318.

19. Caroline Reitz, "Bad Cop/Good Cop: Godwin, Mill, and the Imperial Origins of the English Detective," *Novel: A Forum on Fiction* 33 (2000): 175–95.

20. Kerby A. Miller, "Belfast's First Bomb, 28 February 1816: Class Conflict and the Origins of Ulster Unionist Hegenomy," *Éire-Ireland* 39 (2004): 262–80.

21. On conspiracy fears in late-eighteenth-century Ireland, see, for example, Jim Smyth, "Anti-Catholicism, Conservatism, and Conspiracy: Sir Richard Musgrave's *Memoirs of the Different Rebellions in Ireland*," *Eighteenth-Century Life* 22 (1998): 62–73. For a nonreligious, if satiric, example, see *The House of Peeresses: Or, Female Oratory, Containing the Debates of several Peeresses on the Bishop of Landaff's Bill For the more effectual Discouragement of the Crime of Adultery*, 2nd ed. (London, 1779), objecting to a bill that would have curtailed the right of those named as adulterers in divorce cases to remarry: the lady president declares, "in case of any indirect or covert opposition made by the Male-Estates of this realm, such females as shall be declared capable to serve the High Court of Parl—t now assembled, are . . . commanded . . . to take, burn, or in any other wise destroy such of the enemies garrisons or other places of defence as shall impede the progress of such forces" (n.p.).

22. [William Preston], *The Female Congress; Or, The Temple of Cotytto: A Mock-Heroic Poem, in Four Cantos* (London: T. Davies, 1779), canto 4, 321–28. The poem was published anonymously, but Preston includes it in his own collection of his verse, listing it by its subtitle in the contents but leaving these lines unchanged; see William Preston, *The Poetical Works of William Preston, Esq.*, 2 vols. (Dublin, 1793), 1:87–148.

23. James Whitlark, "Heresy Hunting: *The Monk* and the French Revolution," *Romanticism on the Net* 8 (Nov. 1997), http://users.ox.ac.uk/~scat0385/heresy .html.

24. [J. J. Stockdale], *The History of the Inquisitions, Including the Secret Transactions of Those Horrific Tribunals* (London: J. J. Stockdale, 1810), xvi, emphasis in original.

25. Maria Edgeworth, "Limerick Gloves," in *IL*, 192, hereafter cited parenthetically in the text by page number.

26. [Patrick Colquhoun], *A Treatise on the Police of the Metropolis, Explaining the Various Crimes and Misdemeanours Which at Present Are Felt as a Pressure upon the Community, and Suggesting Remedies for Their Prevention, by a Magistrate* (London: C. Dilly, 1796), 180, emphasis in original.

27. Ibid., 140, emphasis in original.

28. Ria Omasreiter, "Maria Edgeworth's Tales: A Contribution to the Science of Happiness," in *Functions of Literature: Essays Presented to Erwin Wolff on His Sixtieth Birthday*, edited by Ulrich Broich, Theo Stemmler, and Gerd Stratmann (Tübingen, Germany: Max Niemeyer, 1984), 196.

29. On the publication and circulation of Edgeworth's *Popular Tales*, see *British Fiction, 1800–1829: A Database of Production, Circulation, and Reception*, at http://www.british-fiction.cf.ac.uk/.

30. Friedrich Schiller, *On the Naive and Sentimental in Literature* (1795), translated by H. Watanabe-O'Kelly (Manchester, UK: Carcanet New Press, 1981), 22.

31. O'Connell, *Ireland and the Fiction of Improvement.*

32. William Wordsworth, preface to *Lyrical Ballads* (1802), in *William Wordsworth*, edited by Stephen Gill (New York: Oxford Univ. Press, 1989), 597.

33. Ferris, *Romantic National Tale*, 151. Moynahan also considers the negative portrayal of the Anglo-Irish in this novel (*Anglo-Irish*, 106–8). Other novels by the Banims have been aligned with the national tale. As Barton R. Friedman notes, Robert Lee Wolff argues for Michael Banim's debts to Scott's *Redgauntlet* in his 1826 novel *The Boyne Water*, and "Thomas Flanagan more reasonably proposes *Waverley* (1814) as Banim's model" (Barton R. Friedman, "Fabricating History, or John Banim Refights the Boyne," *Éire-Ireland* 17 [1982]: 41). Because *Waverley* is indebted to the originary national tale, Morgan's *The Wild Irish Girl* (1806), it is clear that the Banims are participating in the ongoing development of the national tale—Morgan's final national tale, *The O'Briens and the O'Flahertys* was published a year after *The Boyne Water*. See Helen O'Connell, "Reconciliation and Emancipation: The Banims and Carleton," in Wright, ed., *Companion to Irish Literature*, 1:411–26. For an important discussion of the complexity of the Banims' representation of Ireland in their novels, see Nolan, *Catholic Emancipations*, chap. 2.

34. Headnote on John Banim and Michael Banim in *Library of the World's Best Literature, Ancient and Modern*, 31 vols., edited by Charles Dudley Warner (New York: J. A. Hill, 1902), 3:1459. *Library* was first published in 1896.

35. Review of *The Ghost-Hunter and His Family*, *Dublin University Review, and Quarterly Magazine* (*Dublin University Magazine*) 1, no. 2 (Apr. 1833): 218, 220.

36. [John Banim], *Revelations of the Dead-Alive* (London: W. Simpkin and R. Marshall, 1824), 73, 69, 83–85, 106.

37. Ibid., 96.

38. See "The Church-Yard Watch, A True Tale, by the Author of 'Tales of the O'Hara Family'," in *Republic of Letters*, 4 vols., edited by A. Whitelaw, 1:297–305 (Glasgow: Blackie and Son, 1833); the story previously appeared in *Friendship's Offering* for 1832 (Whitelaw, 1:297n.) and was favorably noticed in reviews of that annual (see, for instance, article 5 in *The Monthly Review* 3, new series [Nov. 1831]: 381–84). The story is also in the Banims' collection *The Bit o' Writin' and Other Tales*, "By the O'Hara Family," 3 vols. (London: Saunders and Otley, 1838). All quotations here are taken from the edition in *IL*, hereafter cited parenthetically in the text by page number.

39. Haslam, "Irish Gothic."

40. William Wordsworth, "Nutting," in *William Wordsworth*, 41–46.

41. Ibid., 31, 33–34, 36.

42. Ibid., 36, 37.

43. William Wordsworth, "We Are Seven," in *William Wordsworth*, 30–36, 43–44.

44. Tom Dunne, "Haunted by History: Irish Romantic Writing, 1800–1850," in *Romanticism in National Context*, edited by Roy Porter and Mikuláš Teich, 68–91 (New York: Cambridge Univ. Press, 1988).

45. See, for instance, the "Paddy" ballads in Mary O'Brien's *Political Monitor* (1790), but especially the United Irishmen ballads collected in various versions of the book *Paddy's Resource* (c. 1795). Moore's *Irish Melodies* are part of this tradition but tend to be more complicated metrically and more formal in language than the 1790s ballads, where a conversational tone is standard, both in the mode of address in the poems and in the use of colloquialisms and other elements of everyday language.

46. John Banim and Michael Banim, *Chaunt of the Cholera: Songs for Ireland* (London: James Cochrane, 1831), 21.

47. John Banim and Michael Banim, "Chaunt of the Cholera," in "Writing Ireland into Europe: An Edition of Three Nineteenth-Century Poems," edited by Julia M. Wright, *Canadian Journal of Irish Studies* 30 (2004): 55–65, 160–68, hereafter cited parenthetically in the text.

48. Alan Bewell, *Romanticism and Colonial Disease* (Baltimore: Johns Hopkins Univ. Press, 1999), 246.

49. Ibid., 247.

50. Banim and Banim, "Song," in *Chaunt*, 25; all Banim poems, except "Chaunt," are cited from *Chaunt*.

51. Ibid., 23.

52. Banim and Banim, "The Irish Soldier," 29.

53. Banim and Banim, "The Irish Mother to Her Child," 30–31.

54. Banim and Banim, "Song," 34, 34n.

55. Ibid., 33n.

56. Banim and Banim, "Song," 56.

57. Banim and Banim, "The Irish Mother to Her Child," the "Song" that appears on pages 51–52, and "The Irish Priests' Song," 41–42.

58. See Banim and Banim, "Song," 37–38.

59. See Banim and Banim, *Chaunt*, 62, 64, 66, 71, 79, 84.

60. Banim and Banim, "Song," 61.

61. Banim and Banim, "The Clare Election," 74.

62. Banim and Banim, "The Irish Soldier," 28, 29; "Song," 34.

63. Banim and Banim, "Song," 37.

64. Banim and Banim, "Song," 62.

65. Ibid., 63.

66. Banim and Banim, "Song," 37; "Song," 25; "The Irish Maiden's Song," 40; "The Irish Priests' Song," 41.

67. Banim and Banim, "Song," 61; "The Clare Election," 74; "The Peasants' Armed Police," 82; "The New Reformation," 85.

68. Deane, "Production of Cultural Space in Irish Writing."

69. Haslam, "Irish Gothic."

70. [John Banim], "The Fetches," in *Peter of the Castle; and the Fetches*, a new edition by John Banim (Dublin: James Duffy, 1866), 211, hereafter cited parenthetically in the text by page number. The story appeared in the first series of *Tales by the O'Hara Family* (1825).

71. A key exception is Jarlath Killeen's *Gothic Ireland*, where Early Modern gothic texts written in and about Ireland are brought into Ireland's gothic genealogy, but this is not much different from studies of English gothic where Shakespeare's plays and other pre-1764 texts are understood to form part of the prehistory of the mode; see Hogle, "'Frankenstein' as Neo-gothic," for instance, on the significance of *Hamlet* to English gothic.

72. See Luke Gibbons, *Gaelic Gothic: Race, Colonization, and Irish Culture* (Dublin: Arlen House, 2004).

5. Foreign Landscapes and the Domestication of the National Subject

1. Anderson, *Spectre of Comparisons*, 62.

2. William Maginn, "On Irish Songs," in *Miscellanies: Prose and Verse*, 2 vols., edited by R. W. Montagu (London: Sampson Low, Marston, Searle, and Rivington, 1885), 1:306, 308. The essay appeared under the pseudonym "Odoherty" in *Blackwood's Edinburgh Magazine* in 1825; biographical details taken from the entry on Maginn in the *Oxford Dictionary of National Biography.*

3. Maginn, "On Irish Songs," 1:313.

4. "National Character."

5. Thomas Davis, "Ballad Poetry of Ireland," in *Literary and Historical Essays, 1846* (Washington, DC: Woodstock Books, 1998), 230–31.

6. David Lloyd, *Anomalous States: Irish Writing and the Post-colonial Moment* (Durham, NC: Duke Univ. Press, 1993), 91.

7. Herder, *Outlines of a Philosophy of the History of Man*, 185, under the heading "Too sudden, too precipitate transitions to an opposite hemisphere and climate are seldom salutary to a nation."

8. Lloyd, *Nationalism and Minor Literature*, 50.

9. Ibid., 72, 71; Lloyd, *Anomalous States*, 91.

10. Burgess, "The National Tale and Allied Genres," 50, 51.

11. Ian Duncan, "Ireland, Scotland, and the Materials of Romanticism," in Duff and Jones, eds., *Scotland, Ireland, and the Romantic Aesthetic*, 258.

12. Mary Tighe, "Bryan Byrne, of Glenmalure," in *IL*, 157–58.

13. Sydney Owenson (later Lady Morgan), *The Novice of Saint Dominick*, 4 vols. (London: Richard Phillips, 1806), 2:154–55, hereafter cited parenthetically in the text by volume and page number. Although early editions date the novel 1806, its publication was announced in the press in September 1805.

14. Morgan in her early years as a writer was mentored by Alicia Lefanu's aunt Alicia Sheridan Lefanu; Morgan was also friends with Thomas Moore, who worked with Alicia Lefanu on his 1825 biography of her uncle, Richard Brinsley Sheridan.

15. Anthony D. Smith, *National Identity* (Reno: Univ. of Nevada Press, 1991), 79.

16. The maniac woman-survivor is a recurring figure in treatments of civil disturbance in Ireland. Tighe's Ellen is, like Morgan's "maniac," a mother, and Mary Le More, in a ballad that appears in various versions across the first half of the nineteenth century, is left a "maniac" after she is raped and her father killed; see Thuente, "Liberty, Hibernia, and Mary Le More," 20–25.

17. Smith, *National Identity*, 79.

18. Drennan, "Glendalloch," in *IL*, 314.

19. Edmund Burke, *Reflections on the Revolution in France*, edited by Conor Cruise O'Brien (Markham, Ontario: Penguin, 1986), 123.

20. Marlon B. Ross, "Romancing the Nation State: The Poetics of Romantic Nationalism," in *Macropolitics of Nineteenth-Century Literature: Nationalism, Exoticism, Imperialism*, edited by Jonathan Arac and Harriet Ritvo, 56–85 (Philadelphia: Univ. of Pennsylvania Press, 1991).

21. Alicia Lefanu, *Henry the Fourth of France: A Romance*, 4 vols. (London: A. K. Newman, 1826), 1:39, hereafter cited parenthetically in the text by volume and page number.

22. Smith, *National Identity*, 79.

23. Morgan, *The O'Briens and the O'Flahertys*, 86, 88.

24. Ibid., 86.

25. Ibid., 86, 87–88.

26. *The Wild Irish Girl* and *Castle Rackrent* have even been packaged together in a volume, James M. Smith, ed., *Two Irish National Tales* (Boston: Houghton Mifflin, 2005).

27. Burgess, "The National Tale and Allied Genres," 41.

28. *The Missionary* is included in Gary Kelly, ed., *Varieties of Female Gothic*, 6 vols. (London: Pickering and Chatto, 2002).

29. Ferris, *Romantic National Tale*; Burgess, "The National Tale and Allied Genres."

30. W. J. McCormack, *Sheridan LeFanu and Victorian Ireland* (Oxford: Clarendon Press, 1980), 82.

31. The only LeFanu text discussed by Backus is the much later "Carmilla" (1871–72); see Backus, *Gothic Family Romance.*

32. Alison Milbank, *Daughters of the House: Modes of the Gothic in Victorian Fiction* (New York: St. Martin's Press, 1992); McCormack, *Sheridan LeFanu and Victorian Ireland*, 79.

33. J. Sheridan LeFanu, "A Chapter in the History of a Tyrone Family" (1839), in *IL*, 413, and "Passage in the Secret History of an Irish Countess," *Dublin University Magazine* 12 (Nov. 1838), 518, 511; both are hereafter cited parenthetically in the text by page number.

34. Victor Sage, *LeFanu's Gothic: The Rhetoric of Darkness* (New York: Macmillan Palgrave, 2004), 21.

35. McCormack, *Sheridan LeFanu and Victorian Ireland*, 79, 80.

36. Ibid., 80.

37. Haslam, "Irish Gothic."

38. Moynahan, *Anglo-Irish.*

39. I allude here to Lee Edelman's phrase "reproductive futurism" in *No Future: Queer Theory and the Death Drive* (Durham, NC: Duke Univ. Press, 2004).

40. Lloyd, *Nationalism and Minor Literature*, 74. As Gregory Schirmer notes, MacCarthy's publishing career began in the periodical press in the 1830s (*Out of What Began: A History of Irish Poetry in English* [Ithaca, NY: Cornell Univ. Press, 1998], 143). Schirmer also refers to MacCarthy's interest in "the spiritual quality of nationhood" (144).

41. "Poetry—Matthew Arnold and Mac Carthy," *Dublin University Magazine* 51, no. 303 (Mar. 1858): 331–44. For a brief discussion of MacCarthy's contributions to the *DUM*, see Wayne E. Hall, *Dialogues in the Margin: A Study of the Dublin University Magazine* (Washington, DC: Catholic Univ. of America Press, 1999), 140.

42. Advertisement appended to the end of volume 2 of Denis Florence MacCarthy, trans., *Dramas of Calderon, Tragic, Comic, and Legendary*, 2 vols. (London: Charles Dolman, 1853).

43. Samuel Taylor Coleridge, "Fears in Solitude," in *Coleridge: Poems*, edited by John Beer (London: J. M. Dent, 1982), 2, 12, 176, 229–31.

44. MacCarthy, "A Walk by the Bay of Dublin," 96–99, hereafter cited parenthetically by line number in the text.

45. Coleridge, "Fears in Solitude," 176; William Wordsworth, "Lines Written a Few Miles above Tintern Abbey," in *William Wordsworth*, 123.

46. James Clarence Mangan, "The Lovely Land," in *IL*, 33–40.

47. Lloyd, *Nationalism and Minor Literature*, 98.

48. *Mount Leinster*, 2.

49. Denis Florence MacCarthy, "The Living Land," in *IL*, 39–40.

50. Morash, *Writing the Irish Famine*, 16, 102–3.

51. Herder, *Outlines of a Philosophy of the History of Man*, 168.

52. Ibid., 349.

53. Elizabeth Fay, *Becoming Wordsworthian: A Performative Aesthetics* (Amherst: Univ. of Massachusetts Press, 1995), 8.

54. Ibid., 11.

55. Ibid., 50.

56. Ibid., 50.

57. Even in "Fears in Solitude," Coleridge personalizes the recent national past by focusing on the "humble man" who is grieved by national events.

58. Ferris, *Romantic National Tale*; Ryder, "Ireland in Ruins"; see also chapter 2.

59. See Wright, *Ireland, India, and Nationalism*, chap. 2.

60. Drennan, "Erin," in *IL*, 29–32, 37.

61. Anonymous, "Edward," in *IL*, 1–7.

62. MacCarthy, "The Living Land," 31–32, 37–38.

63. MacCarthy, "The Sick Youth" and "Contentment," in *Ballads, Poems, and Lyrics, Original and Translated* (Dublin: James McGlashan, 1850), 231, 267.

64. On Wordsworth as a "masculinist" poet, see, for instance, Fay, *Becoming Wordsworthian*; Gillen D'Arcy Wood, "Crying Game: Operatic Strains in Wordsworth's *Lyrical Ballads*," *ELH* 71 (2004): 969–1000; Anne K. Mellor, *Romanticism and Gender* (New York: Routledge, 1993).

6. Geopolitics from Drennan to Cavour: Locating Ireland in a Changing Europe

1. *Mount Leinster*, iv. See also chapters 1 and 2.

2. Drennan, *Letter to the Right Honorable William Pitt*, hereafter cited parenthetically in the text by page number.

3. William Drennan, *A Second Letter to the Right Honorable William Pitt* (Dublin: George Folingsby, 1799), 6, hereafter cited parenthetically in the text by page number.

4. Paul W. Schroeder, "Did the Vienna Settlement Rest on a Balance of Power?" *American Historical Review* 97 (1992): 686–87.

5. "How Long Will Russia Be Permitted . . . ," *London Times*, July 20, 1831.

6. I discuss this context at greater length in "'A Wicked Whisper': Censorship, Affect, and Coleridge's 'Rime of the Ancient Mariner,'" in *The Public Intellectual and the Culture of Hope*, edited by Joel Faflak and Jason Haslam, 51–71 (Toronto: Univ. of Toronto Press, 2013).

7. "The Nation," *The Nation* Oct. 15, 1842.

8. R. F. Foster, *Modern Ireland, 1600–1972* (Markham, Canada: Penguin, 1989), 311.

9. For the argument that Young England was influential on Young Ireland, see Dwan, *Great Community.*

10. (Count) Camille de Cavour, *Considerations on the Present State and Future Prospects of Ireland*, translated from the French by a Friend to Ireland (London: Longman, Brown, Green, and Longmans, 1845), hereafter cited parenthetically in the text by page number.

11. Hodgson seems unaware of the earlier translation, despite its publication by a leading London publisher, and suggests that Cavour's essay is "little known beyond, or even within, the bounds of Italy" (W. B. Hodgson, preface to Camille de Cavour, *Thoughts on Ireland: Its Present and Its Future*, translated by W. B. Hodgson [London: Trübner, 1868], vii). The translations are quite similar, sentence by sentence, but vary regularly from each other in the precise wording: for instance, for the first sentence of the essay, the 1845 translation reads, "The singular state of Ireland has attracted throughout Europe the attention of all who take any interest in politics" (1), and Hodgson's translation reads, "The present singular condition of Ireland has excited the attention of all Europe who are interested in politics" (1).

12. Nicholas Mansergh, *The Irish Question, 1840–1921*, 3rd ed. (Toronto: Univ. of Toronto Press, 1975), 89–95; Harry W. Rudman, *Italian Nationalism and English Letters: Figures of the Risorgimento and Victorian Men of Letters* (1940; reprint, New York: AMS Press, 1966), 274.

13. A. J. Whyte, *The Early Life and Letters of Cavour, 1810–1848* (Oxford: Oxford Univ. Press, 1925), 291. Other scholars make the same point in similar language: see, for example, Mansergh, *The Irish Question*, 89, and Rudman, *Italian Nationalism and English Letters*, 274.

14. Justice O'Connor, "Ireland's Money Claim against Great Britain," *Journal of Comparative Legislation and International Law*, 3rd ser., 6 (1924): 15–16.

15. For a useful discussion of Carlyle's work in this context, see Roger Swift, "Thomas Carlyle, *Chartism*, and the Irish in Early Victorian England," *Victorian Literature and Culture* 29 (2001): 67–83.

16. Hodgson, preface to Cavour, *Thoughts on Ireland*, ix.

17. Rudman refers to Cavour's "Anglophile leanings" and notes Cavour's wide reading in English history and other aspects of English culture, including the works of Adam Smith and Jeremy Bentham (*Italian Nationalism*, 272). Mansergh attends to the politics of these leanings: "The majority of the great Italian patriots of the Risorgimento were 'anglophile' in sentiment. In the long years of exile Italian nationalists found in London a welcome, such as they could find in no other capital in Europe. Cavour, that most practical of statesmen, dreamed for one brief moment

that English troops might fight on the plains of Lombardy for the independence of Italy" (*Irish Question*, 87).

18. Whyte, *Early Life and Letters of Cavour*, 292.

19. Draining bogs was a recurring theme of English travel writing about Ireland, and several parliamentary commissions in the early nineteenth century were charged with investigating the possibility. On this topic, see, for example, Patrick J. Duffy, *Exploring the History and Heritage of Irish Landscapes* (Dublin: Four Courts Press, 2007), 32–33 and, for a seventeenth-century example, 219.

20. Adam Smith, *An Inquiry into the Nature and Causes of the Wealth of Nations*, edited by Edwin Cannan (New York: Modern Library, 1994), sec. III.1, p. 407.

21. Ireland's excessive reliance on agriculture was of concern to nationalists before the Famine as well. See, for instance, Young Irelander Thomas D'Arcy McGee's *Historical Sketches of O'Connell and His Friends, with a Glance at the Future Destiny of Ireland* (1845).

22. On the trope of absorption in relation to the Union (1800), see Ferris, *The Romantic National Tale*.

23. Anna Maria Hall and Samuel Carter Hall (Mr. & Mrs. S. C. Hall), *A Week at Killarney* (London: Jeremiah How, 1843), 3.

24. Christopher GoGwilt, *The Fiction of Geopolitics: Afterimages of Culture, from Wilkie Collins to Alfred Hitchcock* (Stanford, CA: Stanford Univ. Press, 2000), 3.

25. Ibid., 5.

26. Lloyd, *Nationalism and Minor Literature*, 6.

27. Ibid., 20.

28. GoGwilt, *Fiction of Geopolitics*, 5; Lloyd, *Nationalism and Minor Literature*, 21.

29. GoGwilt, *Fiction of Geopolitics*, 23–24.

30. Important here, particularly for United Irishmen writers such as Drennan—who was educated partly in Scotland and frequently invokes Scottish Enlightenment thinkers (see Pittock, *Scottish and Irish Romanticism*, 100–101)—is the emphasis in Hume's "Of National Characters" not on the physical effects of the landscape on the people, as in a more "romantic" nationalism (Herder), but on the cultural effects of different economic structures, government, the governments and economies of neighboring countries, and so forth.

31. "National Character," 763.

32. James Howell, *Epistolæ Ho-elianæ: Familiar Letters, Domestick and Foreign* (London, 1650), unpaginated.

33. For a suggestive analysis of the ways in which cosmopolitanism works as a limited emancipatory project, see Walter D. Mignolo: "Narratives of cosmopolitan

orientation could be either managerial (what I call *global designs*—as in Christianity, nineteenth-century imperialism, or late-twentieth-century neoliberal globalization) or emancipatory (what I call *cosmopolitanism*—as in Vitoria, Kant, or Karl Marx, leaving aside the differences in each of these projects), even if they are oblivious to the saying of the people that are supposed to be emancipated" ("The Many Faces of Cosmo-polis: Border Thinking and Critical Cosmopolitanism," *Public Culture* 12 [2000]: 722–23).

34. For an important discussion of Goldsmith's larger engagement with "cosmopolitanism," see James Watt, "Goldsmith's Cosmopolitanism," *Eighteenth-Century Life* 30 (2006): 56–76.

35. Simon Gikandi, *Maps of Englishness: Writing Identity in the Culture of Colonialism* (New York: Columbia Univ. Press, 1996); Peter Stallybrass and Allon White, *The Politics and Poetics of Transgression* (Ithaca, NY: Cornell Univ. Press, 1986); Simon Joyce, *Capital Offenses: Geographies of Class and Crime in Victorian London* (Charlottesville: Univ. of Virginia Press, 2003).

36. Bentham, *An Introduction to the Principles of Morals and Legislation*, 296n.

Conclusion: The Case of the Love Elegy

1. Flann O'Brien, *Flann O'Brien at War*, quoted in Joseph Brooker, "Irish Mimes: Flann O'Brien," in Wright, ed., *Companion to Irish Literature*, 2:188.

2. Leerssen, *National Thought in Europe*, 16.

3. In his foundational work on the genre, Georg Luck stresses the "personal" nature of Latin love elegies; see Georg Luck, *The Latin Love Elegy* (1959; London: Methuen, 1969), 32.

4. *The Shamrock: Or, Hibernian Cresses* (Dublin, 1772), hereafter cited parenthetically in the text as *Shamrock* and by page number.

5. J. N. Hook, "Three Imitations of Spenser," *Modern Language Notes* 55, no. 6 (1940): 431; Carpenter, ed., *Verse in English*, 320; Bill Overton notes that *The Shamrock*'s *Peruvian Letters* were "first published under a different title in 1753" ("The Verse Epistle," in *A Companion to Eighteenth-Century Poetry*, edited by Christine Gerrard [Oxford: Wiley-Blackwell, 2006], 421).

6. Trumpener, *Bardic Nationalism*, 43–44; Vance, *Irish Literature*, 158. On the nineteenth-century elegy, see also, for example, Schirmer, *Out of What Began*, 135–36.

7. For an interesting contemporary overview of the genre, see William Preston, "Some Considerations on the History of Ancient Amatory Writers, and the three great ROMAN Elegiac Poets, OVID, TIBULLUS, and PROPERTIUS," *Transactions of the Royal Irish Academy* 9 (1803): "Polite Literature," 139–72.

8. John Donne, Elegy 19: "To his Mistress Going to Bed," in *Complete English Poems*, edited by A. J. Smith (New York: Penguin, 1986), 1–2; [George Lyttelton], "Part of an Elegy of Tibullus, Translated," in *A Collection of Poems, by Several Hands*, 3 vols. (London: R. Dodsley, 1748) 2:55 (the first poem in the post-1748 continuation of the collection, volume 4, published in 1755, is Gray's "Elegy").

9. See J. Fisher, "James Hammond and the Quatrain of Gray's 'Elegy,'" *Modern Philology* 32 (1935): 301–10. Hammond's collection was published posthumously and includes a quatrain addressed to a "Lyttleton" (James Hammond, *Love Elegies, Written in the Year 1732* [London, 1743], 19). Of the fifteen elegies, only the last, which addresses Mr. George Grenville and uses elegiac couplets, is not in elegiac quatrains.

10. *The Prince of Peace and Other Poems* (London, 1779).

11. [George Lyttelton], "The Progress of Love in Four Eclogues," in *Collection of Poems*, 2:3–18. Lyttelton returns to the characters in "Damon and Delia, in Imitation of Horace and Lydia," included in the same volume (51–52). The structure of four poems and their trajectory, however, are more suggestive than the names, which are common in love elegies.

12. Anna Maria Edwards, "Elegy I," part 2, in *Poems on Various Subjects*, 3. Edwards's preferred forms in the rest of the volume are common meter and long meter, with only a few poems in pentameter lines or couplets.

13. Charlotte Brooke, *Reliques of Irish Poetry* (1789; reprint, Gainesville, FL: Scholars' Facsimiles and Reprints, 1970), 189.

14. Ibid., 200.

15. Ibid., 208.

16. Although Yeats is beyond the purview of this study, it is worth noting that his poem "He Wishes his Beloved were Dead" (1898), often termed a sonnet, continues the use of adapted quatrain forms in Irish love elegy: it is composed of three quatrains, with an extra line added to the last, and the first and third quatrains are in alternating couplets like the elegiac quatrain, but riffing on the shorter line often found in romantic-era Irish love elegies rather than using the strict pentameter of the English form. Jahan Ramazani includes the poem as an "elegiac love poem" in *Yeats and the Poetry of Death: Elegy, Self-Elegy, and the Sublime* (New Haven, CT: Yale Univ. Press, 1990), 17; and Elizabeth Butler Cullingford terms it a "love-elegy" in *Gender and History in Yeats's Love Poetry* (Syracuse, NY: Syracuse Univ. Press, 1996), 283.

17. "Expostulation, to an Unfaithful Mistress," in *A Collection of Poems, on Various Subjects, Including The Theatre, a Didactic Essay . . . by Samuel Whyte*, 2nd ed., edited by Edward Athenry Whyte, 122–25 (Dublin, 1792).

18. John Corry, "Elegy, to Maria M.," in *Odes and Elegies, Descriptive and Sentimental, with The Patriot, A Poem* (Newry, 1797), 94. This kind of pedantic

moral twist is typical of Corry's writing: "Sensuality, an Elegy" warns, for instance, "When Sensuality the passions sways, / Then sacred Reason's voice is heard no more" (in *Odes and Elegies*, 102).

19. Preston, "Some Considerations," 139.

20. Ibid., 141.

21. Ibid.

22. For further discussion of the social virtues in late eighteenth- and nineteenth-century Irish writing, see Wright, *Ireland, India, and Nationalism.*

23. Joshua Edkins, "Advertisement," in *A Collection of Poems, by Several Hands*, edited by Joshua Edkins (Dublin, 1801), vi, vii. Vance notes this collection briefly in *Irish Literature*, 98.

24. William Drennan, "Verses to a Young Lady," in Edkins, ed., *Collection of Poems, by Several Hands*, 59. Drennan seems to follow the stricter form of the English elegiac quatrain only in his elegy "Thomas Drennan," on the death of a child and published in *Fugitive Pieces.*

25. William Drennan, "Love-Elegy, Imitated from Tibullus," in Edkins, ed., *Collection of Poems, by Several Hands*, 80–81.

26. Corry, "Elegy, to the Memory of Miss H—tt, of Belfast," in *Odes and Elegies*, 108.

27. For an excellent discussion of allusiveness and Gray's poem, see John Guillory, "Literary Capital: Gray's 'Elegy,' Anna Laetitia Barbauld, and the Vernacular Canon," in *Early Modern Conceptions of Property*, edited by John Brewer and Susan Staves (New York: Routledge, 1995), 394–95.

28. Advertisement in Whyte, ed., *Collection of Poems, on Various Subjects*, xiv. The paragraphs making this claim also appeared in "Progress of Plagiarism," no. III, *Monthly Mirror* (Oct. 1796): 336–38. The volume remains unidentified in this account because Giffard did not buy the book, but the charge, if it is based on an authentic account, may derive from irregular anthologization practices; a 1762 anthology, for instance, includes a poem titled "Evening" (no author indicated) that combines the first three quatrains of Gray's "Elegy" as a single verse paragraph and follows them with a second verse paragraph of three couplets from John Gay's *Dione* (see *A Collection of Poems for Reading and Repetition, Selected from the Most Celebrated British Poets* [Edinburgh, 1762], 30–31).

29. See the entry on Preston in the *Oxford Dictionary of National Biography.*

30. [Preston], *The Female Congress*, 2:10–11; Margaret Leeson (a.k.a. Peg Plunkett), *Memoirs of Mrs. Margaret Leeson* (1797), vol. 6 of *Whore Biographies, 1700–1825*, 8 vols., edited by Julie Peakman (London: Pickering and Chatto, 2007), 6:184 (see also 6:157). Leeson complains that "*Democratic Rage* . . . was cramm'd down the throats of all his Majesty's dutiful and loyal subjects,—in order to impress the *Canaille* with horror against the *Sans Culottes*" (6:184, referring to William

Preston, *Democratic Rage; or, Louis the Unfortunate* [London, 1793]). Preston's play is discussed briefly in some accounts of British responses to the French Revolution; see, for example, John Barrell, "Sad Stories: Louix XVI, George III, and the Language of Sentiment," in *Refiguring Revolutions: Aesthetics and Politics from the English Revolution to the Romantic Revolution*, edited by Kevin Sharpe and Steven N. Zwicker (Berkeley: Univ. of California Press, 1998), 81.

31. In rare references to Preston, both Carpenter and Leerssen note Preston's significance as a satirist and his 1770s attacks on Richard Twiss in particular (Carpenter, ed., *Verse in English*, 369; J. Th. Leerssen, *Mere Irish and the Fíor-Ghael: Studies in the Idea of Irish Nationality, Its Development, and Literary Expression prior to the Nineteenth Century* [Philadelphia: John Benjamins, 1986], 353). Vance discusses him briefly as a leading poet of the neoclassicist school ("Irish Literary Traditions," 41–42); and he is included, very slightly, in Patrick Fagan, ed., *A Georgian Celebration: Irish Poets of the Eighteenth Century* (Dublin: Branar, 1989), 147–49.

32. William Preston, "To a Lady, On her Saying Poetry is But Fiction," in *Poetical Works of William Preston*, 1:381.

33. Vance, "Irish Literary Traditions," 41.

34. Ibid.

35. Edkins, "Advertisement," viii.

36. According to the *Oxford Dictionary of National Biography*, "a collection of [Preston's] verse in 1781 proved abortive when the printer went bankrupt," but the British Library has a copy of this 1781 edition, which I use here: William Preston, *Poems, On Several Occasions* (Dublin: printed by William Halthead, 1781).

37. Preston, "Elegy the First: In the Manner of Hammond," in *Poetical Works*, 1:297.

38. Preston, "Elegy the Tenth," in *Poetical Works*, 1:339.

39. William Preston, *The Posthumous Poems of William Preston, Esq. (Late One of the Judges of Appeals)* (Dublin: Wilkinson and Courtney, 1809). The first edition of *Posthumous Poems* includes a list of subscribers that, though often vague (for instance, "Dr. Teeling, M.D." or "Miss Lyons," neither with an address), likely has some authors who are mentioned in preceding chapters in the preceding chapters, including Rev. Dr. Ledwich and J. C. Walker, Esq., as well as Lefanus, probably related to the literary Lefanus, particularly because they have the family names "Joseph" and "William." It also includes a number of subscribers in Jamaica, speaking to the transatlantic reach of Preston's literary influence.

40. See Moore, *Epistles, Odes, and Other Poems*, 84; the poems appear under the heading "Love Songs to Nea; Written at Bermuda" (79) in the text and as "Odes to Nea" in the table of contents. Also, suggestively, the name of the beloved in Moore's poems echoes somewhat that of Hammond's: Neæra.

41. [Thomas Moore], "Preface by the Editor," in *The Poetical Works of the Late Thomas Little*, 2nd ed. (London: J. & T. Carpenter, 1802), vii, viii. Moore's volume betrays a preference for long meter quatrains, including in three poems titled "Elegiac Stanzas" (not love elegies, however).

42. Moore, "Ode I," in *Epistles*, 82.

43. In his essay "Thoughts on Lyric Poetry," predominantly on the ode, which first appeared in the *Transaction of the Royal Irish Academy*, Preston argues extensively for poetic license with form, enumerating a number of reasons: "First, it leaves the poet at liberty to follow the order and connexion of his ideas, and to express them in the most apt and forcible manner. He is not obliged to sacrifice strength and energy to stanza, to become a literary Procrustes" (in *Poetical Works*, 2:12). For a discussion of the essay in terms of its Enlightenment sensibilities, see Michael Brown, "Configuring the Irish Enlightenment: Reading the *Transactions of the Royal Irish Academy*," in *Clubs and Societies in Eighteenth-Century Ireland*, edited by James Kelly and Martyn J. Powell (Dublin: Four Courts Press, 2010), 170–72.

44. See Abel Shufflebottom, "Love Elegies," in *The Annual Anthology*, vol. 1, 218–26 (London, 1799); Amelia Opie, "Love Elegy, to Laura" and "Love Elegy, to Henry," in *The Warrior's Return and Other Poems* (London: Longman, Hurst, Rees, and Orme, 1808), 105–13.

45. See Murphy, "Anna Maria Edwards."

46. Joseph Cooper Walker and Edward Ledwich were also members. See Johanna Archbold, "Book Clubs and Reading Societies in the Late Eighteenth Century," in Kelly and Powell, eds., *Clubs and Societies in Eighteenth-Century Ireland*, 156–57.

Bibliography

An Account of the Present State of Nova-Scotia in Two Letters to a Noble Lord. London, 1756.

Akenson, Donald Harman, and W. H. Crawford. *Local Poets and Social History: James Orr, Bard of Ballycarry*. Belfast: Public Record Office of Northern Ireland, 1977.

Allingham, William. "The Winding Banks of Erne: Or, The Emigrant's Adieu to Ballyshanny." In Wright, *Irish Literature*, 501–3.

Anderson, Benedict. *Imagined Communities: Reflections on the Origin and Spread of Nationalism*. Rev. ed. New York: Verso, 1991.

———. *The Spectre of Comparisons: Nationalism, Southeast Asia, and the World*. London: Verso, 1998.

Archbold, Johanna. "Book Clubs and Reading Societies in the Late Eighteenth Century." In *Clubs and Societies in Eighteenth-Century Ireland*, edited by James Kelly and Martyn J. Powell, 138–62. Dublin: Four Courts Press, 2010.

Armitage, David. "The Political Economy of Britain and Ireland after the Glorious Revolution." In *Political Thought in Seventeenth-Century Ireland*, edited by Jane Ohlmeyer, 221–43. Cambridge: Cambridge Univ. Press, 2000.

Armstrong, Edmund John. "Glandalough: A Story of Wicklow." In *The Poetical Works of Edmund J. Armstrong*, edited by George Francis Armstrong, 101–26. London: Longman, Green, 1877.

Ashcroft, Bill, Gareth Griffiths, and Helen Tiffin. *The Empire Writes Back*. New York: Routledge, 1989.

Atkinson, Joseph. *Killarney: A Poem*. Dublin: William Porter, 1798.

Austen, Jane. *Northanger Abbey, Lady Susan, The Watsons, and Sanditon*. Edited by John Davie. Oxford: Oxford Univ. Press, 1990.

Austin, J. L. *How to Do Things with Words.* 2nd ed. Edited by J. O. Urmson and Marina Sbisà. Cambridge, MA: Harvard Univ. Press, 1975.

Backus, Margot Gayle. *The Gothic Family Romance: Heterosexuality, Child Sacrifice, and the Anglo-Irish Colonial Order.* Durham, NC: Duke Univ. Press, 1999.

[Banim, John.] *Revelations of the Dead-Alive.* London: W. Simpkin and R. Marshall, 1824.

——. "The Fetches." In *Peter of the Castle; and the Fetches*, by the O'Hara Family, new edition by John Banim, 195–323. Dublin: James Duffy, 1866.

[Banim, John, and Michael Banim]. *The Bit o' Writin' and Other Tales.* "By the O'Hara Family." 3 vols. London: Saunders and Otley, 1838.

———. "Chaunt of the Cholera." In "Writing Ireland into Europe: An Edition of Three Nineteenth-Century Poems," edited by Julia M. Wright. *Canadian Journal of Irish Studies* 30 (2004): 55–65.

———. *Chaunt of the Cholera: Songs for Ireland.* London: James Cochrane, 1831.

———. "The Church-Yard Watch." In Wright, *Irish Literature*, 317–22.

———. "The Church-Yard Watch, a True Tale, by the Author of 'Tales of the O'Hara Family.'" In *Republic of Letters*, edited by A. Whitelaw, 4 vols., 1:297–305. Glasgow: Blackie and Son, 1833.

Baraniuk, Carol. "James Orr: Ulster-Scot and Poet of the 1798 Rebellion." *Scottish Studies Review* 6 (2005): 22–32.

Barbauld, Anna Letitia. "Eighteen Hundred and Eleven." In *Anna Letitia Barbauld: Selected Poetry and Prose*, edited by William McCarthy and Elizabeth Kraft. Peterborough, Canada: Broadview Press, 2002.

Barnard, F. M. "National Culture and Political Legitimacy: Herder and Rousseau." *Journal of the History of Ideas* 44 (1983): 231–53.

Barrell, John. "Sad Stories: Louix XVI, George III, and the Language of Sentiment." In *Refiguring Revolutions: Aesthetics and Politics from the English Revolution to the Romantic Revolution*, edited by Kevin Sharpe and Steven N. Zwicker, 75–98. Berkeley: Univ. of California Press, 1998.

Barthes, Roland. *Mythologies.* Translated by Annette Lavers. New York: Hill and Wang, 1972.

Bartlett, Thomas. "'This Famous Island Set in a Virginian Sea': Ireland in the British Empire, 1690–1801." In *The Oxford History of the British Empire: The Eighteenth Century*, edited by P. J. Marshall, 253–75. Oxford: Oxford Univ. Press, 1998.

Behrendt, Stephen. "Placing 'Irish' and 'Romanticism' in the Same Frame: Prospects." In *Ireland and Romanticism: Publics, Nations, and Scenes of Cultural Production*, edited by Jim Kelly, 207–20. New York: Palgrave Macmillan, 2011.

Bell, David A. *The Cult of the Nation in France: Inventing Nationalism, 1680–1800*. Cambridge, MA: Harvard Univ. Press, 2001.

Bentham, Jeremy. *An Introduction to the Principles of Morals and Legislation*. 1789. Edited by J. H. Burns and H. L. A. Hart. Oxford: Clarendon Press, 1996.

Bentley, D. M. R., ed. *The Huron Chief*. By Adam Kidd. With contributions and appendices by Charles R. Steele. London, Ontario: Canadian Poetry Press, 1987.

———. *Mimic Fires: Accounts of Early Long Poems on Canada*. Montreal: McGill-Queen's Univ. Press, 1994.

Bewell, Alan. *Romanticism and Colonial Disease*. Baltimore: Johns Hopkins Univ. Press, 1999.

Boucicault, Dion. *Arrah-na-Pogue*. In Wright, *Irish Literature*, 438–76.

Bourke, Hannah Maria. *O'Donahue, Prince of Killarney: A Poem*. Dublin: William Curry Jr., 1830.

Boylan, Thomas A., and Timothy P. Foley. *Political Economy and Colonial Ireland: The Propagation and Ideological Function of Economic Discourse in the Nineteenth Century*. New York: Routledge, 1992.

Brantlinger, Patrick. *Dark Vanishings: Discourse of the Extinction of Primitive Races, 1800–1930*. Ithaca, NY: Cornell Univ. Press, 2003.

———. "What Is 'Sensational' about the 'Sensation Novel'?" *Nineteenth-Century Fiction* 37 (1982): 1–28

British Fiction, 1800–1829: A Database of Production, Circulation, and Reception. At http://www.british-fiction.cf.ac.uk/.

[Brontë, Patrick]. *The Maid of Killarney; Or, Albion and Flora: A Modern Tale; in which are interwoven some cursory remarks on Religion and Politics*. London: Baldwin, Cradock, and Joy, 1818.

Brooke, Charlotte. *Reliques of Irish Poetry*. 1789. Reprint. Gainesville, FL: Scholars' Facsimiles and Reprints, 1970.

Brooker, Joseph. "Irish Mimes: Flann O'Brien." In *Companion to Irish Literature*, 2 vols., edited by Julia M. Wright, 2:176–91. Oxford: Wiley-Blackwell, 2010.

Brown, Michael. "Configuring the Irish Enlightenment: Reading the *Transactions of the Royal Irish Academy*." In *Clubs and Societies in Eighteenth-Century Ireland*, edited by James Kelly and Martyn J. Powell, 163–78. Dublin: Four Courts Press, 2010.

Brown, Terence. *Northern Voices: Poets from Ulster.* Dublin: Gill and Macmillan, 1975.

Bruhm, Steven. *Gothic Bodies: The Politics of Pain in Romantic Fiction.* Philadelphia: Univ. of Pennsylvania Press, 1994.

Burgess, Miranda. "The National Tale and Allied Genres, 1770s–1840s." In *The Cambridge Companion to the Irish Novel*, edited by John Wilson Foster, 39–59. Cambridge: Cambridge Univ. Press, 2006.

Burke, Edmund. *A Philosophical Enquiry into the Origins of Our Ideas of the Sublime and Beautiful.* Edited by Adam Phillips. Oxford: Oxford Univ. Press, 1990.

———. *Reflections on the Revolution in France.* Edited by Conor Cruise O'Brien. Markham, Ontario: Penguin, 1986.

Burke, Helen. "Crossing Acts: Irish Drama from George Farquhar to Thomas Sheridan." In *Companion to Irish Literature*, 2 vols., edited by Julia M. Wright, 1:127–41. Oxford: Wiley-Blackwell, 2010.

Burke, Martin. "Piecing Together a Shattered Past: The Historical Writings of the United Irish Exiles in America." In *The United Irishmen: Republicanism, Radicalism, and Rebellion*, edited by David Dickson, Dáire Keough, and Kevin Whelan, 297–306. Dublin: Lilliput Press, 1993.

Butler, Marilyn. *Maria Edgeworth: A Literary Biography.* Oxford: Oxford Univ. Press, 1990.

Camden, William. *Britannia: Or, A Chorographical Description of the Flourishing Kingdoms of England, Scotland, and Ireland, and the Islands Adjacent.* 3 vols. Translated and enlarged by Richard Gough. London: John Nichols, 1789.

Campbell, Matthew. "Lyrical Unions: Mangan, O'Hussey, and Ferguson." *Irish Studies Review* 8 (2000): 325–38.

Caraher, Brian G., and Robert Mahony, eds. *Ireland and Transatlantic Poetics: Essays in Honor of Denis Donoghue.* Newark: Univ. of Delaware Press, 2007.

Carlyle, Thomas. *Chartism.* London: James Fraser, 1840.

Carpenter, Andrew, ed. *Verse in English from Eighteenth-Century Ireland.* Cork: Cork Univ. Press, 1998.

Carr, John. *The Stranger in Ireland; Or, A Tour in Southern and Western Parts of That Country, in the Year 1805.* London: Richard Phillips, 1806.

Cavour, (Count) Camille de. *Considerations on the Present State and Future Prospects of Ireland.* Translated from the French by a Friend to Ireland. London: Longman, Brown, Green, and Longmans, 1845.

———. *Thoughts on Ireland: Its Present and Its Future.* Translated by W. B. Hodgson. London: Trübner, 1868.

Channing, William Ellery. *The Importance and Means of a National Literature.* London: Edward Rainford, 1830.

Coleridge, Samuel Taylor. *Coleridge: Poems.* Edited by John Beer. London: J. M. Dent, 1982.

A Collection of Poems, by Several Hands. 2nd ed. 6 vols. London: R. Dodsley, 1748–58.

A Collection of Poems for Reading and Repetition, Selected from the Most Celebrated British Poets. Edinburgh, 1762.

Colley, Linda. *Britons: Forging the Nation, 1707–1837.* New Haven, CT: Yale Univ. Press, 1992.

———. *Captives: Britain, Empire, and the World, 1600–1850.* London: Jonathan Cape, 2002.

[Colquhoun, Patrick.] *A Treatise on the Police of the Metropolis, Explaining the Various Crimes and Misdemeanours Which at Present Are Felt as a Pressure upon the Community, and Suggesting Remedies for Their Prevention, by a Magistrate.* London: C. Dilly, 1796.

Comitini, Patrica. *Vocational Philanthropy and British Women's Writing, 1790–1810.* Burlington, VT: Ashgate, 2005.

Connolly, Claire. *A Cultural History of the Irish Novel, 1790–1829.* Cambridge: Cambridge Univ. Press, 2012.

———. "Irish Romanticism, 1800–1830." In *The Cambridge History of Irish Literature*, 2 vols., edited by Margaret Kelleher and Philip O'Leary, 1:407–48. Cambridge: Cambridge Univ. Press, 2006.

Corbett, Mary Jean. *Allegories of Union in Irish and English Writing, 1790–1870: Politics, History, and the Family from Edgeworth to Arnold.* Cambridge: Cambridge Univ. Press, 2000.

Corry, John. *Odes and Elegies, Descriptive and Sentimental, with The Patriot, A Poem.* Newry, 1797.

Cullingford, Elizabeth Butler. *Gender and History in Yeats's Love Poetry.* Syracuse, NY: Syracuse Univ. Press, 1996.

Curran, Stuart. "Mary Robinson's *Lyrical Tales* in Context." In *Re-visioning Romanticism: British Women Writers, 1776–1837*, edited by Carol

Shiner Wilson and Joel Haefner, 17–35. Philadelphia: Univ. of Pennsylvania Press, 1994.

Curtis, Louis Perry. *Apes and Angels: The Irishman in Victorian Caricature*. Washington, DC: Smithsonian Institution Press, 1971.

Darwin, Erasmus. *The Botanic Garden; A Poem, in Two Parts*. London: J. Johnson, 1791.

Davis, Leith. *Music, Postcolonialism, and Gender: The Construction of Irish National Identity, 1724–1874*. Notre Dame, IN: Univ. of Notre Dame Press, 2005.

Davis, Richard. *The Young Ireland Movement*. Dublin: Gill and Macmillan, 1987.

Davis, Thomas. *Literary and Historical Essays, 1846*. Washington, DC: Woodstock Books, 1998.

———. *Thomas Davis: Selections from His Prose and Poetry*. Edited by T. W. Rolleston. New York: AMS Press, 1982.

Deane, Seamus, gen. ed. *The Field Day Anthology of Irish Writing*. 3 vols. Derry: Field Day, 1991.

Deane, Seamus. "The Production of Cultural Space in Irish Writing." *boundary 2* 21 (1994): 117–44.

———. *Strange Country: Modernity and Nationhood in Irish Writing Since 1790*. Oxford: Oxford Univ. Press, 1997.

De Bruyn, Frans. "From Georgic Poetry to Statistics and Graphs: Eighteenth-Century Representations and the 'State' of British Society." *Yale Journal of Criticism* 17 (2004): 103–39.

Defoe, Daniel. *A Tour Thro' the Whole Island of Great Britain*. 3 vols. London, 1742.

De Nie, Michael. "Britannia's Sick Sister: Irish Identity and the British Press, 1798–1882." In *Writing Irishness in Nineteenth-Century British Culture*, edited by Neil McCaw, 173–93. Burlington, VT: Ashgate, 2004.

Dermody, Thomas. *Poems, Consisting of Essays, Lyric, Elegiac, &c., . . . Written between the 13th and 16th Year of His Age*. Dublin, 1792.

———. *Poems on Various Subjects*. London, 1802.

Donne, John. *Complete English Poems*. Edited by A. J. Smith. New York: Penguin, 1986.

Drennan, William. "Erin." In Wright, *Irish Literature*, 136–37.

———. *Fugitive Pieces in Verse and Prose*. Belfast: F. D. Finlay, 1815.

———. "Glendalloch." *Belfast Monthly Magazine* 6, no. 33 (Apr. 30, 1811): 308–12.

———. "Glendalloch." In *The Poetical Register, and Repository of Fugitive Poetry, for 1804*, 19–31. London: F. and C. Rivington, 1806.

———. "Glendalloch." In Wright, *Irish Literature*, 139–48.

———. *Glendalloch, and Other Poems, with Additional Verses by his Sons*. 2nd ed. Dublin: William Robertson, 1859.

———. *A Letter to the Right Honorable William Pitt*. Dublin: James Moore, 1799.

———. *A Second Letter to the Right Honorable William Pitt*. Dublin: George Folingsby, 1799.

Drummond, William Hamilton. *The Giants' Causeway: A Poem*. London: Longman, Rees, Orme, and Brown, 1811.

Duff, David, and Catherine Jones, eds. *Scotland, Ireland, and the Romantic Aesthetic*. Lewisburg, PA: Bucknell Univ. Press, 2007.

Duffy, Charles Gavan. *Letter to John Mitchel*. Supplement to *The Nation*. Dublin: Printed at the Nation Office, 1854.

Duffy, Patrick J. *Exploring the History and Heritage of Irish Landscapes*. Dublin: Four Courts Press, 2007.

Duncan, Ian. "Ireland, Scotland, and the Materials of Romanticism." In *Scotland, Ireland, and the Romantic Aesthetic*, edited by David Duff and Catherine Jones, 258–78. Lewisburg, PA: Bucknell Univ. Press, 2007.

Dunne, Tom. "Haunted by History: Irish Romantic Writing, 1800–1850." In *Romanticism in National Context*, edited by Roy Porter and Mikuláš Teich, 68–91. New York: Cambridge Univ. Press, 1988.

Dwan, David. *The Great Community: Culture and Nationalism in Ireland*. Dublin: Field Day, 2008.

Eagleton, Terry. "Nationalism and the Case of Ireland." *New Left Review* 234 (Mar.–Apr. 1999): 44–61. At http://www.newleftreview.org/?page=article&view=1984.

Edelman, Lee. *No Future: Queer Theory and the Death Drive*. Durham, NC: Duke Univ. Press, 2004.

Edgeworth, Maria. "Limerick Gloves." In Wright, *Irish Literature*, 187–203.

Edkins, Joshua. "Advertisement." In *A Collection of Poems, by Several Hands*, v–x. Dublin, 1801.

———, ed. *A Collection of Poems, by Several Hands*. Dublin, 1801.

"Edward." In Wright, *Irish Literature*, 133–34.

Edwards, Anna Maria. *Poems on Various Subjects, by the Author of The Enchantress*. Dublin: H. Colbert, 1787.

Eldridge, Herbert G. "Anacreon Moore and America." *PMLA* 83 (1968): 54–62.

The Exile of Ireland! Or, The Wonderful Adventures, and Extraordinary Escapes, of An Irish Rebel Officer. London: printed for the author, n.d.

Fabricant, Carole. "Colonial Sublimities and Sublimations: Swift, Burke, and Ireland." *ELH* 72 (2005): 309–37.

———. "The Garden as City: Swift's Landscape of Alienation." *ELH* 42 (1975): 531–55.

Fagan, Patrick, ed. *A Georgian Celebration: Irish Poets of the Eighteenth Century*. Dublin: Branar, 1989.

Fanning, Charles, ed. *The Exiles of Erin: Nineteenth-Century Irish-American Fiction*. 2nd ed. Chester Springs, PA: Dufour Editions, 1997.

Fay, Elizabeth. *Becoming Wordsworthian: A Performative Aesthetics*. Amherst: Univ. of Massachusetts Press, 1995.

Fegan, Melissa. *Literature and the Irish Famine, 1845–1919*. Oxford: Oxford Univ. Press, 2002.

Ferris, Ina. *The Achievement of Literary Authority: Gender, History, and the Waverley Novels*. Ithaca, NY: Cornell Univ. Press, 1991.

———. *The Romantic National Tale and the Question of Ireland*. Cambridge: Cambridge Univ. Press, 2002.

Fisher, J. "James Hammond and the Quatrain of Gray's 'Elegy.'" *Modern Philology* 32 (1935): 301–10.

Fisher, Jonathan. *A Description of the Lake of Killarney . . . Being an Appendix to His "Scenery of Ireland."* Dublin: W. Chambers, 1796.

———. *The Scenery of Ireland*. Dublin, 1795.

Foster, John Wilson. "Encountering Traditions." In *Nature in Ireland: A Scientific and Cultural History*, 23–70. Montreal: McGill-Queen's Univ. Press, 1997.

———. "The Measure of Paradise: Topography in Eighteenth-Century Poetry." *Eighteenth-Century Studies* 9 (1975–76): 232–56.

———. "The Topographical Tradition in Anglo-Irish Poetry." *Irish University Review* 4–5 (1974–75): 169–87. Reprinted in *Colonial*

Consequences: Essays in Irish Literature and Culture, 9–29. Dublin: Lilliput Press, 1991.

Foster, R. F. *Modern Ireland, 1600–1972*. Markham, Canada: Penguin, 1989.

Friedman, Barton R. "Fabricating History, or John Banim Refights the Boyne." *Éire-Ireland* 17 (1982): 39–56.

Geary, Laurence M., and Margaret Kelleher, eds. *Nineteenth-Century Ireland: A Guide to Recent Research*. Dublin: Univ. College Dublin Press, 2005.

Gellner, Ernest. *Nations and Nationalism*. Ithaca, NY: Cornell Univ. Press, 1983.

Gibbons, Luke. *Gaelic Gothic: Race, Colonization, and Irish Culture*. Dublin: Arlen House, 2004.

———. "Ireland, America, and Gothic Memory: Transatlantic Terror in the Early Republic." *boundary 2* 31 (2004): 25–47.

———. "Race against Time: Racial Discourse and Irish History." *Oxford Literary Review* 13, nos. 1–2 (1991): 95–117.

———. "'The Return of the Native': The United Irishmen, Culture, and Colonialism." In *1798: A Bicentenary Perspective*, edited by Thomas Bartlett, David Dickson, Dáire Keogh, and Kevin Whelan, 52–74. Dublin: Four Courts Press, 2003.

———. "Topographies of Terror: Killarney and the Politics of the Sublime." *South Atlantic Quarterly* 95 (1996): 23–44.

———. *Transformations in Irish Culture*. Notre Dame, IN: Univ. of Notre Dame Press, 1996.

Gikandi, Simon. *Maps of Englishness: Writing Identity in the Culture of Colonialism*. New York: Columbia Univ. Press, 1996.

Gilroy, Paul. *The Black Atlantic: Modernity and Double Consciousness*. London: Verso, 1993.

Glendalough, or The Seven Churches: A Didactic Poem, by an Ex-Moderator, T. C. D. Dublin: Hodges and Smith, 1848.

GoGwilt, Christopher. *The Fiction of Geopolitics: Afterimages of Culture, from Wilkie Collins to Alfred Hitchcock*. Stanford, CA: Stanford Univ. Press, 2000.

Goldsmith, Oliver. *Collected Works of Oliver Goldsmith*. Edited by Arthur Friedman. 5 vols. Oxford: Clarendon Press, 1966.

———. *The Deserted Village*. In Wright, *Irish Literature*, 26–35.

Goodman, Kevis. *Georgic Modernity and British Romanticism*. Cambridge: Cambridge Univ. Press, 2008.

Grant, Ruth W. *John Locke's Liberalism*. Chicago: Univ. of Chicago Press, 1987.

Grattan, Henry. *Speeches of the Right Honourable Henry Grattan in the Irish, and in the Imperial Parliament*. 4 vols. Edited by his Son [Henry Grattan]. London: Longman, Hurst, Rees, Orme, and Brown, 1822.

Grattan-Flood, W. H. "Authorship of 'The Exile of Erin': A Vindication of Thomas Campbell." *Irish Monthly* 49 (1921): 229–34.

Gray, Thomas. *The Complete Poems of Thomas Gray*. Edited by H. W. Starr and J. R. Hendrickson. Oxford: Clarendon Press, 1966.

Guillory, John. "Literary Capital: Gray's 'Elegy,' Anna Laetitia Barbauld, and the Vernacular Canon." In *Early Modern Conceptions of Property*, edited by John Brewer and Susan Staves, 389–410. New York: Routledge, 1995.

Gustafson, Richard F. "The Upas Tree: Pushkin and Erasmus Darwin." *PMLA* 75 (1960): 101–9.

Guthrie, William. *A New System of Modern Geography*. 3rd ed. London, 1786.

Hall, Anna Maria, and Samuel Carter Hall (Mr. & Mrs. S. C. Hall). *A Week at Killarney*. London: Jeremiah How, 1843.

Hall, Wayne E. *Dialogues in the Margin: A Study of the Dublin University Magazine*. Washington, DC: Catholic Univ. of America Press, 1999.

Hammond, James. *Love Elegies, Written in the Year 1732*. London, 1743.

Harkin, Maureen. "Adam Smith's Missing History: Primitives, Progress, and Problems of Genre." *ELH* 72, no. 2 (2005): 429–51.

Haslam, Richard. "'Broad Farce and Thrilling Tragedy': Mangan's Fiction and Irish Gothic." *Éire-Ireland* 41 (2007): 215–44.

———. "Irish Gothic: A Rhetorical Hermeneutics Approach." *Irish Journal of Gothic and Horror Studies* 2 (2007). At http://irishgothichorrorjournal.homestead.com/IrishGothicHaslam.html.

Herder, Johann Gottfried. *Outlines of a Philosophy of the History of Man*. Translated by T. Churchill. London: J. Johnson, 1800.

Heringman, Noah. *Romantic Rocks, Aesthetic Geology*. Ithaca, NY: Cornell Univ. Press, 2004.

Hewitt, John. *Rhyming Weavers and Other Poets of Antrim and Down*. Belfast: Blackstaff Press, 1971.

Hogle, Jerrold E. "'Frankenstein' as Neo-gothic: From the Ghost of the Counterfeit to the Monster of Abjection." In *Romanticism, History, and the Possibilities of Genre*, edited by Tilottama Rajan and Julia M. Wright, 176–210. Cambridge: Cambridge Univ. Press, 1998.

———. "The Ghost of the Counterfeit—and the Closet—in *The Monk*." *Romanticism on the Net* 8 (Nov. 1997). At http://www.erudit.org/revue/ron/1997/v/n8/005770ar.html.

———. "Stoker's Counterfeit Gothic: *Dracula* and Theatricality at the Dawn of Simulation." In *Bram Stoker: History, Psychoanalysis, and the Gothic*, edited by William Hughes and Andrew Smith, 205–24. New York: St. Martin's Press, 1998.

Hook, J. N. "Three Imitations of Spenser." *Modern Language Notes* 55, no. 6 (1940): 431–32.

Hooper, Glenn. *Travel Writing and Ireland, 1760–1860: Culture, History, Politics*. New York: Palgrave Macmillan, 2005.

The House of Peeresses: Or, Female Oratory, Containing the Debates of several Peeresses on the Bishop of Landaff's Bill For the more effectual Discouragement of the Crime of Adultery. 2nd ed. London, 1779.

Howell, James. *Epistolæ Ho-elianæ: Familiar Letters, Domestick and Foreign*. London, 1650.

"How Long Will Russia Be Permitted. . . ." *London Times*, July 20, 1831.

Hoyle, Charles. *Three Days at Killarney, with Other Poems*. London: Longman, Rees, Orme, Brown, and Green, 1828.

Hume, David. *Political Essays*. Edited by Knud Haakonssen. Cambridge: Cambridge Univ. Press, 1994.

Jonson, Ben. *Ben Jonson: The Complete Poems*. Edited by George Parfitt. New York: Penguin, 1975.

Joyce, Simon. *Capital Offenses: Geographies of Class and Crime in Victorian London*. Charlottesville: Univ. of Virginia Press, 2003.

Kaye, Andrew M. *The Pussycat of Prizefighting: Tiger Flowers and the Politics of Black Celebrity*. Athens: Univ. of Georgia Press, 2004.

Keating, Geoffrey. *General History of Ireland*. London, 1723.

Kelleher, Margaret. *The Feminization of Famine: Expressions of the Inexpressible?* Durham, NC: Duke Univ. Press, 1997.

Kelly, Gary, ed. *Varieties of Female Gothic*. 6 vols. London: Pickering and Chatto, 2002.

Kelly, Jim, ed. *Ireland and Romanticism: Publics, Nations, and Scenes of Cultural Production*. New York: Palgrave Macmillan, 2011.

Kidd, Adam. *The Huron Chief, and Other Poems*. Montreal: Printed at the Office of the Herald and New Gazette, 1830.

Kilfeather, Siobhán. "Terrific Register: The Gothicization of Atrocity in Irish Romanticism." *boundary 2* 31 (2004): 49–71.

"Killarney." *Dublin University Review, and Quarterly Magazine* 1, no. 1 (Jan. 1833): 147–50.

Killarny. A Poem. Dublin: printed for Thomas Ewing, n.d.

Killeen, Jarlath. *Gothic Ireland: Horror and the Irish Anglican Imagination in the Eighteenth Century*. Dublin: Four Courts Press, 2005.

Kirwan, James. *Sublimity: The Non-rational and the Irrational in the History of Aesthetics*. New York: Routledge, 2005.

Lacaita, Francesca. "The Journey of the Encounter: The Politics of the National Tale in Sydney Owenson's *The Wild Irish Girl* and Maria Edgeworth's *Ennui*." In *Critical Ireland: New Essays in Literature and Culture*, edited by Alan A. Gillis and Aaron Kelly, 148–54. Dublin: Four Courts Press, 2001.

Ledwich, Edward. *Antiquities of Ireland*. Dublin: Edward Grueber, 1790.

Leerssen, J. Th. *Mere Irish and Fíor-Ghael: Studies in the Idea of Irish Nationality, Its Development, and Literary Expression prior to the Nineteenth Century*. Philadelphia: John Benjamins, 1986.

———. *National Thought in Europe: A Cultural History*. Amsterdam: Amsterdam Univ. Press, 2006.

———. "On the Edge of Europe: Ireland in Search of Oriental Roots, 1650–1850." *Comparative Criticism* 8 (1986): 91–112.

———. *Remembrance and Imagination: Patterns in the Historical and Literary Representation of Ireland in the Nineteenth Century*. Notre Dame, IN: Univ. of Notre Dame Press, 1997.

Leeson, Margaret (a.k.a. Peg Plunkett). *Memoirs of Mrs. Margaret Leeson*. 1797. Vol. 6 of *Whore Biographies, 1700–1825*, 8 vols., edited by Julie Peakman. London: Pickering and Chatto, 2007.

Lefanu, Alicia. *Henry the Fourth of France: A Romance*. 4 vols. London: A. K. Newman, 1826.

———. *The Outlaw.* In *Tales of a Tourist, Containing The Outlaw and Fashionable Connexions*, 4 vols. 1:23–3:88. London: A. K. Newman, 1823.

LeFanu, J. Sheridan. "A Chapter in the History of a Tyrone Family." 1839. In Wright, *Irish Literature*, 400–20.

———. "Passage in the Secret History of an Irish Countess." *Dublin University Magazine* 12 (Nov. 1838): 502–19.

Lennon, Joseph. *Irish Orientalism: A Literary and Intellectual History.* Syracuse, NY: Syracuse Univ. Press, 2004.

Leslie, John. *Killarney.* In Wright, *Irish Literature*, 62–79.

———. *Phoenix Park.* London: George Robinson, 1772.

Levinson, Marjorie. *Wordsworth's Great Period Poems.* Cambridge: Cambridge Univ. Press, 1986.

Lewis, Jayne. "'No Colour of Language': Radcliffe's Aesthetic Unbound." *Eighteenth-Century Studies* 39 (2006): 377–90.

The Life and Adventures of Bampfylde-Moore Carew, the Noted Devonshire Stroller and Dog-Stealer. Exon, 1745. Later, *An Apology for the Life of Bampfylde-Moore Carew*, with editions from 1749 forward.

The Life, Voyages, Travels, and Wonderful Adventures of Captain Winterfield . . . a Distinguished Rebel Chief in Ireland. London: Printed by J. Bailey, n.d.

Liu, Alan. *Wordsworth: The Sense of History.* Stanford, CA: Stanford Univ. Press, 1989.

Lloyd, David. *Anomalous States: Irish Writing and the Post-colonial Moment.* Durham, NC: Duke Univ. Press, 1993.

———. *Nationalism and Minor Literature: James Clarence Mangan and the Emergence of Irish Cultural Nationalism.* Berkeley: Univ. of California Press, 1987.

Locke, John. *An Essay Concerning Human Understanding.* Edited by Peter H. Nidditch. Oxford: Clarendon Press, 1975.

———. *Two Treatises of Government.* Edited by Peter Laslett. Cambridge: Cambridge Univ. Press, 1988.

Lover, Samuel. *Saint Kevin: A Legend of Glendalough, sung by the Author in his Irish Evenings.* London: Duff & Hodgson, n.d. (c. 1846).

Luck, Georg. *The Latin Love Elegy.* 1959. London: Methuen, 1969.

Lunney, Linde Connoly. "Attitudes to Life and Death in the Poetry of James Orr." *Ulster Folklife* 31 (1985): 1–12.

[Lyttleton, George]. "Damon and Delia, in Imitation of Horace and Lydia." In *A Collection of Poems, by Several Hands*, 3 vols., 2:51–52. London: R. Dodsley, 1748.

———. "Part of an Elegy of Tibullus, Translated." In *A Collection of Poems, by Several Hands*, 3 vols., 2:54–56. London: R. Dodsley, 1748.

———. "The Progress of Love in Four Eclogues." In *A Collection of Poems, by Several Hands*, 3 vols., 2:3–18. London: R. Dodsley, 1748.

MacCarthy, Denis Florence. *Ballads, Poems, and Lyrics, Original and Translated*. Dublin: James McGlashan, 1850.

———, trans. *Dramas of Calderon, Tragic, Comic, and Legendary*. 2 vols. London: Charles Dolman, 1853.

———. "The Living Land." In Wright, *Irish Literature*, 423–24.

———. "A Walk by the Bay of Dublin." In Wright, *Irish Literature*, 433–35.

MacCarthy, Michael. *Lacus Delectabilis: A Descriptive and Historical Poem on the Lakes of Killarney*. Cork, 1816.

MacDonagh, Oliver. *States of Mind: A Study of Anglo-Irish Conflict, 1780–1980*. London: Allen & Unwin, 1983.

Mack, Maynard. *The Garden and the City: Retirement and Politics in the Later Poetry of Pope, 1731–1743*. Toronto: Univ. of Toronto Press, 1969.

Maginn, William. *Miscellanies: Prose and Verse*. 2 vols. Edited by R. W. Montagu. London: Sampson Low, Marston, Searle, and Rivington, 1885.

Mangan, James Clarence. "The Lovely Land." In Wright, *Irish Literature*, 350–51.

———. *Poems of James Clarence Mangan*. Edited by D. J. O'Donoghue. Dublin: M. H. Gill, 1922.

Mansergh, Nicholas. *The Irish Question, 1840–1921*. 3rd ed. Toronto: Univ. of Toronto Press, 1975.

Marvell, Andrew. *Andrew Marvell: The Complete Poems*. Edited by Elizabeth Story Donno. New York: Penguin, 1972.

Mazoff, Chaim David. *Anxious Allegiances: Legitimizing Identity in the Early Canadian Long Poem*. Montreal: McGill-Queen's Univ. Press, 1998.

McCarthy, William, and Elizabeth Kraft, eds. *Anna Letitia Barbauld: Selected Poetry and Prose*. Peterborough, Ontario: Broadview Press, 2001.

McCormack, W. J. "Irish Gothic and After." In *The Field Day Anthology of Irish Writing*, 3 vols., gen. ed. Seamus Deane, 2:831–54. Derry: Field Day, 1991.

———. *Sheridan Le Fanu and Victorian Ireland*. Oxford: Clarendon Press, 1980.

McGann, Jerome. *The Romantic Ideology: A Critical Investigation*. Chicago: Univ. of Chicago Press, 1983.

McGee, Thomas D'Arcy. *Canadian Ballads, and Occasional Verses*. Montreal: John Lovell, 1858.

———. "Freedom's Journey." In Wright, *Irish Literature*, 516–17.

———. "Hail to the Land." In Wright, *Irish Literature*, 512–14.

———. *Poems by Thomas D'Arcy McGee, Chiefly Written in America*. Dublin: Published at the Nation Office, 1854.

———. "St. Patrick's of the Woods." In Wright, *Irish Literature*, 515–16.

Mellor, Anne K. *Romanticism and Gender*. New York: Routledge, 1993.

Miall, David S. "Locating Wordsworth: 'Tintern Abbey' and the Community with Nature." *Romanticism on the Net* 20 (Nov. 2000). At http://www.erudit.org/revue/ron/2000/v/n20/005949ar.html.

Mignolo, Walter D. "The Many Faces of Cosmo-polis: Border Thinking and Critical Cosmopolitanism." *Public Culture* 12 (2000): 721–48.

Milbank, Allison. *Daughters of the House: Modes of the Gothic in Victorian Fiction*. New York: St. Martin's Press, 1992.

Miles, Robert. *Gothic Writing, 1750–1820: A Genealogy*. New York: Routledge, 1993.

Miller, Julia Anne. "Acts of Union: Family Violence and National Courtship in Maria Edgeworth's *Absentee* and Sydney Owenson's *The Wild Irish Girl*." In *Border Crossings: Irish Women Writers and National Identities*, edited by Kathryn Kirkpatrick, 13–37. Tuscaloosa: Univ. of Alabama Press, 2000.

Miller, Kerby A. "Belfast's First Bomb, 28 February 1816: Class Conflict and the Origins of Unionist Hegemony." *Éire-Ireland* 39 (2004): 262–80.

———. *Ireland and Irish America: Culture, Class, and Transatlantic Migration*. Dublin: Field Day, 2008.

"Modernizing." *Belfast Monthly Magazine* 6, no. 32 (Mar. 31, 1811): 218–19.

Molloy, Frank. "Thomas Campbell's 'Exile of Erin': English Poem, Irish Reactions." In *Back to the Present, Forward to the Past: Irish Writing and History since 1798*, 2 vols., edited by Patricia A. Lynch, Joachim Fischer, and Brian Coates, 1:43–52. New York: Rodopi, 2006.

Monkman, Leslie. *A Native Heritage: Images of the Indian in English-Canadian Literature.* Toronto: Univ. of Toronto Press, 1981.

Moore, Jane. "'Transatlantic Tom': Thomas Moore in North America." In *Ireland and Romanticism: Publics, Nations, and Scenes of Cultural Production*, edited by Jim Kelly, 77–93. New York: Macmillan Palgrave, 2011.

Moore, Thomas. *Epistles, Odes, and Other Poems.* London: J. Carpenter, 1806.

———. *Irish Melodies.* 4th number. London, 1811.

———. *Irish Melodies.* 8th ed. London: Longman, Rees, Orme, Brown, and Green, 1827.

———. *The Life and Death of Lord Edward Fitzgerald.* 2nd ed. 2 vols. London: Longman, Rees, Orme, Brown, and Green, 1831.

———. *The Poetical Works of the Late Thomas Little*, 2nd ed. London: J. & T. Carpenter, 1802.

Morash, Christopher. *Writing the Irish Famine.* Oxford: Clarendon Press, 1995.

Morgan, Lady [Sydney Owenson]. *Absenteeism.* London: Henry Colbourn, 1825.

———. "Absenteeism, Part I." *New Monthly Magazine* 10 (1824): 481–95.

———. "Absenteeism, Part III." *New Monthly Magazine* 11 (1825): 162–76.

———. *The Novice of Saint Dominick.* 4 vols. London: Richard Phillips, 1806.

———. *The O'Briens and the O'Flahertys: A National Tale.* 1827. Edited by Julia M. Wright. Peterborough, Ontario: Broadview Press, 2013.

———. *O'Donnel: A National Tale.* 3 vols. London: Henry Coburn, 1814.

———. *The Wild Irish Girl.* 1806. Edited by Kathryn Kirkpatrick. Oxford: Oxford Univ. Press, 1999.

Morris, David B. "Gothic Sublimity." *New Literary History* 16 (1985): 299–319.

Mount Leinster; Or, The Prospect, A Poem. London: Longman, Hurst, Rees, Orme, and Browne; Dublin: R. Milliken, 1819.

Moynahan, Julian T. *Anglo-Irish: The Literary Imagination in a Hyphenated Culture.* Princeton, NJ: Princeton Univ. Press, 1995.

Murdoch, Alexander. *British History, 1660–1832: National Identity and Local Culture.* London: Macmillan, 1998.

Murphy, Andrew. "Revising Criticism: Ireland and the British Model." In *British Identities and English Renaissance Literature*, edited by David J. Baker and Willy Maley, 24–33. Cambridge: Cambridge Univ. Press, 2002.

Murphy, Sharon. "Anna Maria Edwards." In *Irish Women Poets of the Romantic Period*, edited by Stephen C. Behrendt. Alexandria, VA: Alexander Street Press, 2008.

"The Nation." *The Nation*, Oct. 15, 1842.

"National Character." *The Nation*, Sept. 9, 1843.

Nelson, Bruce. "'Come Out of Such a Land, You Irishmen': Daniel O'Connell, American Slavery, and the Making of the 'Irish Race.'" *Éire-Ireland* 42, nos. 1–2 (2007): 58–81.

Ní Bhroiméil, Úna, and Glenn Hooper. "Introduction." In *Land and Landscape in Nineteenth-Century Ireland*, edited by Glenn Hooper and Úna Ní Bhroiméil, 9–12. Dublin: Four Courts Press, 2008.

Nichols, Ashton. "An Empire of Exotic Nature: Blake's Botanic and Zoomorphic Imagery." In *The Reception of Blake in the Orient*, edited by Steve Clark and Masashi Suzuki, 121–33. New York: Continuum, 2006.

Nolan, Emer. *Catholic Emancipations: Irish Fiction from Thomas Moore to James Joyce.* Syracuse, NY: Syracuse Univ. Press, 2007.

O'Brien, Karen. "Imperial Georgic, 1660–1789." In *The Country and the City Revisited: England and the Politics of Culture, 1550–1850*, edited by Gerald MacLean, Donna Landry, and Joseph P. Ward, 160–79. Cambridge: Cambridge Univ. Press, 1999.

O'Connell, Helen. "Improved English, and the Silence of Irish." *Canadian Journal of Irish Studies* 30 (2004): 13–20.

———. *Ireland and the Fiction of Improvement.* Oxford: Oxford Univ. Press, 2006.

———. "Reconciliation and Emancipation: The Banims and Carleton." In *Companion to Irish Literature*, 2 vols., edited by Julia M. Wright, 1:411–26. Oxford: Wiley-Blackwell, 2010.

O'Connor, Justice. "Ireland's Money Claim against Great Britain." *Journal of Comparative Legislation and International Law*, 3rd ser., 6 (1924): 1–18.

O'Conor, Charles. *Seasonable Thoughts Relating to Our Civil and Ecclesiastical Constitution*. Dublin, 1753.

———. *Some Seasonable Thoughts, Relating to Our Civil and Ecclesiastical Constitution: Wherein is Occasionally Consider'd, The Case of the Professors of Popery*. Dublin, 1751.

Ó Gallchoir, Clióna. *Maria Edgeworth: Women, Enlightenment, and Nation*. Dublin: Univ. College Dublin Press, 2006.

O'Halloran, Clare. *Golden Ages and Barbarous Nations: Antiquarian Debate and Cultural Politics in Ireland, c. 1750–1800*. Notre Dame, IN: Univ. of Notre Dame Press, 2005.

O'Kelly, Patrick. *Killarney: A Descriptive Poem*. Dublin, 1791.

Omasreiter, Ria. "Maria Edgeworth's Tales: A Contribution to the Science of Happiness." In *Functions of Literature: Essays Presented to Erwin Wolff on His Sixtieth Birthday*, edited by Ulrich Broich, Theo Stemmler, and Gerd Stratmann, 195–208. Tübingen, Germany: Max Niemeyer, 1984.

Opie, Amelia. *The Warrior's Return and Other Poems*. London: Longman, Hurst, Rees, and Orme, 1808.

Orr, James. "The Passengers." 1804. In Wright, *Irish Literature*, 211–15.

———. *Poems, On Various Subjects*. Belfast: Smith and Lyrons, 1804.

———. "Song Composed on the Banks of Newfoundland." 1804. In *Verse in English from Eighteenth-Century Ireland*, edited by Andrew Carpenter, 542–43. Cork: Cork Univ. Press, 1998.

Overton, Bill. "The Verse Epistle." In *A Companion to Eighteenth-Century Poetry*, edited by Christine Gerrard, 417–28. Oxford: Wiley-Blackwell, 2006.

Pedro I. "Manifesto of the Prince Regent of Brazil to Friendly Governments and Nations." *London Times*, Oct. 16, 1822.

Pittock, Murray. *Scottish and Irish Romanticism*. Oxford: Oxford Univ. Press, 2008.

Pocock, J. G. A. "British History: A Plea for a New Subject." *Journal of Modern History* 47 (1975): 601–28.

———. *The Discovery of Islands: Essays in British History*. Cambridge: Cambridge Univ. Press, 2005.

"Poetry—Matthew Arnold and Mac Carthy." *Dublin University Magazine* 51, no. 303 (Mar. 1858): 331–44.

Pope, Alexander. *Pope: Poetical Works.* Edited by Herbert Davis. London: Oxford Univ. Press, 1966.

Porter, James. *Billy Bluff and 'Squire Firebrand.* Belfast, 1797.

Pratt, Mary Louise. *Imperial Eyes: Travel Writing and Transculturation.* New York: Routledge, 1992.

Preston, William. *Democratic Rage; Or, Louis the Unfortunate.* London, 1793.

———. *The Female Congress; Or, The Temple of Cotytto: A Mock-Heroic Poem, in Four Cantos.* London, 1779.

———. *Poems, On Several Occasions.* Dublin, 1781.

———. *The Poetical Works of William Preston, Esq.* 2 vols. Dublin, 1793.

———. *The Posthumous Poems of William Preston, Esq. (Late One of the Judges of Appeals).* Dublin: Wilkinson and Courtney, 1809.

———. "Some Considerations on the History of Ancient Amatory Writers, and the three great ROMAN Elegiac Poets, OVID, TIBULLUS, and PROPERTIUS." *Transactions of the Royal Irish Academy* 9 (1803): "Polite Literature," 139–72.

Priestman, Martin, ed. *The Cambridge Companion to Crime Fiction.* Cambridge: Cambridge Univ. Press, 2003.

The Prince of Peace and Other Poems. London, 1779.

"Progress of Plagiarism," no. III. *Monthly Mirror* (Oct. 1796): 336–38.

Pykett, Lyn. "Sensation and the Fantastic in the Victorian Novel." In *The Cambridge Companion to the Victorian Novel*, edited by Deirdre David, 192–211. Cambridge: Cambridge Univ. Press, 2001.

Rafroidi, Patrick. *Irish Literature in English: The Romantic Period, 1789–1850.* Gerrards Cross, UK: Colin Smythe, 1980.

Ramazani, Jahan. *Yeats and the Poetry of Death: Elegy, Self-Elegy, and the Sublime.* New Haven, CT: Yale Univ. Press, 1990.

Rance, Nicholas. *Wilkie Collins and Other Sensation Novelists.* Cranbury, NJ: Associated Univ. Presses, 1991.

Rankin, Deana. *Between Spenser and Swift: English Writing in Seventeenth-Century Ireland.* Cambridge: Cambridge Univ. Press, 2005.

Reitz, Caroline. "Bad Cop/Good Cop: Godwin, Mill, and the Imperial Origins of the English Detective." *Novel: A Forum on Fiction* 33 (2000): 175–95.

Renan, Ernest. "What Is a Nation?" In *The Poetry of the Celtic Races, and Other Studies by Ernest Renan*, translated by William G. Hutchison, 61–83. London: Walter Scott, 1896.

Resnick, David. "John Locke and Liberal Nationalism." *History of European Ideas* 15 (1992): 511–17.

Review of *The Ghost-Hunter and His Family. Dublin University Review, and Quarterly Magazine* 1, no. 2 (Apr. 1833): 214–29.

Review of William Drennan's *A Letter to the Right Hon. William Pitt. Analytical Review*, new series, 1 (Feb. 1799): 154–58.

Robbins, Lionel. *Robert Torrens and the Evolution of Classical Economics.* London: Macmillan, 1958.

Robinson, Philip. "The Historical Presence of Ulster-Scots in Ireland." In *The Languages of Ireland*, edited by Michael Cronin and Cormac Ó Cuilleanáin, 112–26. Dublin: Four Courts Press, 2005.

Roche, Regina Maria. *The Tradition of the Castle; Or, Scenes in the Emerald Isle.* 4 vols. London: A. K. Newman, 1824.

Roediger, David R. *Working towards Whiteness: How America's Immigrants Became White.* New York: Basic Books, 2005.

Ross, Marlon B. "Romancing the Nation State: The Poetics of Romantic Nationalism." In *Macropolitics of Nineteenth-Century Literature: Nationalism, Exoticism, Imperialism*, edited by Jonathan Arac and Harriet Ritvo, 56–85. Philadelphia: Univ. of Pennsylvania Press, 1991.

Rudman, Harry W. *Italian Nationalism and English Letters: Figures of the Risorgimento and Victorian Men of Letters.* 1940. Reprint. New York: AMS Press, 1966.

Ryder, Sean. "Ireland in Ruins: The Figure of Ruin in Early Nineteenth-Century Irish Poetry." In *Landscape and Empire, 1770–2000*, edited by Glenn Hooper, 79–91. Burlington, VT: Ashgate, 2005.

Sage, Victor. *LeFanu's Gothic: The Rhetoric of Darkness.* New York: Macmillan Palgrave, 2004.

Schiller, Friedrich. *On the Naive and Sentimental in Literature.* 1795. Translated by H. Watanabe-O'Kelly. Manchester, UK: Carcanet New Press, 1981.

Schirmer, Gregory. *Out of What Began: A History of Irish Poetry in English.* Ithaca, NY: Cornell Univ. Press, 1998.

Schroeder, Paul W. "Did the Vienna Settlement Rest on a Balance of Power?" *American Historical Review* 97 (1992): 683–706.

———. *Transformation of European Politics, 1763–1848*. New York: Oxford Univ. Press, 1994.

Scott, Sir Walter. *Ivanhoe*. Edited by Ian Duncan. Oxford: Oxford Univ. Press, 1996.

The Shamrock: Or, Hibernian Cresses. [Edited by Samuel Whyte.] Dublin, 1772.

Sheldon, Esther K. *Thomas Sheridan of Smock-Alley*. Princeton, NJ: Princeton Univ. Press, 1967.

Sheridan, Richard Brinsley. *Speeches of the Late Right Honourable Richard Brinsley Sheridan*. Edited by "A Constitutional Friend." 5 vols. London: Patrick Martin, 1816.

Sheridan, Thomas. *The Brave Irishman*. In Wright, *Irish Literature*, 5–18.

Shufflebottom, Abel. "Love Elegies." In *The Annual Anthology*, vol. 1, 218–26. London, 1799.

Sigerson, Dora. *A Legend of Glendalough and Other Ballads*. Dublin: Maunsel, 1919.

Small, Stephen. *Political Thought in Ireland, 1776–1798: Republicanism, Patriotism, and Radicalism*. Oxford: Oxford Univ. Press, 2003.

Smith, Adam. *An Inquiry into the Nature and Causes of the Wealth of Nations*. Edited by Edwin Cannan. New York: Modern Library, 1994.

Smith, Anthony D. *National Identity*. Reno: Univ. of Nevada Press, 1991.

———. *Nationalism*. Oxford: Blackwell, 2004.

———. *The Nation in History: Historiographical Debates about Ethnicity and Nationalism*. Hanover, NH: Univ. Press of New England, 2000.

———. "Neo-classicist and Romantic Elements in the Emergence of Nationalist Conceptions." In *Nationalist Movements*, edited by Anthony D. Smith, 74–87. London: Macmillan, 1976.

Smith, James M., ed. *Two Irish National Tales*. Boston: Houghton Mifflin, 2005.

Smyth, Jim. "Anti-Catholicism, Conservatism, and Conspiracy: Sir Richard Musgrave's *Memoirs of the Different Rebellions in Ireland*." *Eighteenth-Century Life* 22 (1998): 62–73.

Spivak, Gayatri. "Can the Subaltern Speak?" In *Marxism and the Interpretation of Culture*, edited by Cary Nelson and Lawrence Grossberg, 271–313. Chicago: Univ. of Illinois Press, 1988.

Stallybrass, Peter, and Allon White. *The Politics and Poetics of Transgression*. Ithaca, NY: Cornell Univ. Press, 1986.

[Stockdale, J. J.]. *The History of the Inquisitions, Including the Secret Transactions of Those Horrific Tribunals.* London: J. J. Stockdale, 1810.

Suleri, Sara. *The Rhetoric of British India.* Chicago: Univ. of Chicago Press, 1992.

Swift, Roger. "Thomas Carlyle, *Chartism*, and the Irish in Early Victorian England." *Victorian Literature and Culture* 29 (2001): 67–83.

Tang, Chenxi. *The Geographic Imagination of Modernity: Geography, Literature, and Philosophy in German Romanticism.* Stanford, CA: Stanford Univ. Press, 2008.

Teeling, Charles Hamilton. *Personal Narrative of the Irish Rebellion of 1798.* London: Henry Colburn, 1828.

Thomson, James. *James Thomson: The Poetical Works.* Edited by J. Logie Robertson. London: Oxford Univ. Press, 1965.

Thuente, Mary Helen. *The Harp Re-strung: The United Irishmen and the Rise of Irish Literary Nationalism.* Syracuse, NY: Syracuse Univ. Press, 1994.

———. "Liberty, Hibernia, and Mary Le More: United Irish Images of Women." In *Women of 1798*, edited by Dáire Keough and Nicholas Furlong, 9–25. Dublin: Four Courts Press, 1998.

Tibullus. *Tibullus: Elegies.* Edited and translated by Guy Lee. 2nd ed. Liverpool: Francis Cairns, 1982.

Tighe, Mary. "Bryan Byrne, of Glenmalure." In Wright, *Irish Literature*, 219–24.

———. *The Collected Poems and Journals of Mary Tighe.* Edited by Harriet Kramer Linkin. Lexington: Univ. Press of Kentucky, 2005.

"To a Red-Breast, My Daily Visitor." *Belfast Monthly Magazine* 6, no. 30 (Jan. 31, 1811): 54.

Torrens, Robert. *Thoughts on the Catholic Question.* 2nd ed. London: Gale, Curtis, and Fenner, 1813.

———. *The Victim of Intolerance; Or, The Hermit of Killarney: A Catholic Tale.* 4 vols. London, 1814.

Tracy, Robert. "Maria Edgeworth and Lady Morgan: Legality versus Legitimacy." *Nineteenth-Century Fiction* 40 (1985): 1–22.

Tracy, Thomas. "The Mild Irish Girl: Domesticating the National Tale." *Éire-Ireland* 39 (2004): 81–109.

Trumpener, Katie. *Bardic Nationalism: The Romantic Novel and the British Empire*. Princeton, NJ: Princeton Univ. Press, 1997.

Vail, Jeffrey W. "Thomas Moore in Ireland and America." *Romanticism* 10 (2004): 41–62.

Vance, Norman. "Irish Literary Traditions and the Act of Union." *Canadian Journal of Irish Studies* 12, no. 2 (1986): 29–47.

———. *Irish Literature, a Social History: Tradition, Identity, and Difference*. Oxford: Blackwell, 1990.

Virgil. *The Georgics of Virgil*. Translated by Thomas Neville. Cambridge: Cambridge Univ. Press, 1767.

"A Voice from America." In Wright, *Irish Literature*, 336.

Walpole, Horace. *Castle of Otranto*. Edited by W. S. Lewis. Oxford: Oxford Univ. Press, 1998.

Ward, Rev. James. "Phoenix Park." In *Miscellaneous Poems, Original and Translated, by Several Hands*, 379–91. London, 1724.

Ware, Sir James. *The Whole Works of Sir James Ware Concerning Ireland Revised and Improved*. 3 vols. Dublin, 1739–46.

Warner, Charles Dudley, ed. *Library of the World's Best Literature, Ancient and Modern*. Vol. 3 of 31. New York: J. A. Hill, 1902.

Waters, John. "Topographical Poetry and the Politics of Culture in Ireland, 1772–1820." In *Romantic Generations: Essays in Honor of Robert F. Gleckner*, edited by Ghislaine McDayter, Guinn Batten, and Barry Milligan, 221–44. Lewisburg: Bucknell Univ. Press, 2001.

Watt, James. "Goldsmith's Cosmopolitanism." *Eighteenth-Century Life* 30 (2006): 56–76.

Watts, Carol. *The Cultural Work of Empire: The Seven Years' War and the Imagining of the Shandean State*. Edinburgh: Edinburgh Univ. Press, 2007.

Weld, Isaac. *Illustrations of the Scenery of Killarney and the Surrounding Country*. London: Longman, Hurst, Rees, and Orme, 1807.

West, Thomas. *Guide to the Lakes*. 2nd ed. London, 1780.

Wheatley, Christopher, and Kevin Donovan, eds. *Irish Drama of the Seventeenth and Eighteenth Centuries*. 2 vols. Bristol, UK: Thoemmes Press, 2003.

Whelan, Kevin. "The Green Atlantic: Radical Reciprocities between Ireland and America in the Long Eighteenth Century." In *A New Imperial*

History: Culture, Identity, and Modernity in Britain and the Empire, 1660–1840, edited by Kathleen Wilson, 216–38. Cambridge: Cambridge Univ. Press, 2004.

———. "Reading the Ruins: The Presence of Absence in the Irish Landscape." In *Surveying Ireland's Past: Multidisciplinary Essays in Honour of Anngret Simms*, edited by Howard B. Clarke, Jacinta Prunty, and Mark Hennessy, 297–328. Dublin: Geography Publications, 2004.

Whitlark, James. "Heresy Hunting: *The Monk* and the French Revolution." *Romanticism on the Net* 8 (Nov. 1997). At http://users.ox.ac.uk/~scat0385/heresy.html.

Whyte, A. J. *The Early Life and Letters of Cavour, 1810–1848*. Oxford: Oxford Univ. Press, 1925.

Whyte, Edward Athenry, ed. *A Collection of Poems, on Various Subjects, Including The Theatre, a Didactic Essay . . . by Samuel Whyte*. 2nd ed. Dublin, 1792.

Whyte, Laurence. *Poems on Various Subjects, Serious and Diverting, Never before Published*. Dublin: S. Powell, 1740.

Williams, Raymond. *The Country and the City*. Oxford: Oxford Univ. Press, 1975.

Wilson, David A. "Comment: Whiteness and Irish Experience in North America." *Journal of British Studies* 44 (2005): 153–60.

———. *Thomas D'Arcy McGee*. Vol. 1: *Passion, Reason, and Politics, 1825–1857*. Montreal: McGill-Queen's Univ. Press, 2008.

———. *United Irishmen, United States: Immigrant Radicals in the Early Republic*. Ithaca, NY: Cornell Univ. Press, 1998.

Withers, Charles J. "Where Was the Atlantic Enlightenment? Questions of Geography." In *The Atlantic Enlightenment*, edited by Susan Manning and Francis D. Cogliano, 37–60. Burlington, VT: Ashgate, 2008.

Wood, Gillen D'Arcy. "Crying Game: Operatic Strains in Wordsworth's *Lyrical Ballads*." *ELH* 71 (2004): 969–1000.

Wordsworth, William. *William Wordsworth*. Edited by Stephen Gill. New York: Oxford Univ. Press, 1989.

Wright, Julia M. "'All the Fire-Side Circle': Irish Women Writers and the Sheridan–Lefanu Coterie." *Keats–Shelley Journal* 55 (2006): 63–72.

———. "Introduction: Anna Liddiard." In *Irish Women Poets of the Romantic Period*, edited by Stephen C. Behrendt. Alexandria, VA: Alexander Street Press, 2008.

———. *Ireland, India, and Nationalism in Nineteenth-Century Literature*. Cambridge: Cambridge Univ. Press, 2007.

———, ed. *Irish Literature, 1750–1900: An Anthology*. Oxford: Wiley-Blackwell, 2008.

———. "'The Nation Begins to Form': Competing Nationalisms in Morgan's *The O'Briens and the O'Flahertys*." *ELH* 66 (1999): 939–63.

———. "'The Order of Time': Nationalism and Literary Anthologies, 1774–1831." *Papers on Language and Literature* 33 (1997): 339–65.

———. "'Wel gelun a gud?': Thomas Sheridan's *Brave Irishman* and the Failure of English." *Irish Studies Review* 16 (2008): 445–60.

———. "'A Wicked Whisper': Censorship, Affect, and Coleridge's 'Rime of the Ancient Mariner.'" In *The Public Intellectual and the Culture of Hope*, edited by Joel Faflak and Jason Haslam, 51–71. Toronto: Univ. of Toronto Press, 2013.

Wyse, Thomas. *Historical Sketch of the Late Catholic Association of Ireland*. 2 vols. London: Henry Colburn, 1829.

Zuber, Devin P. "Swedenborg and the Disintegration of Language in Sheridan Le Fanu's Sensation Fiction." In *Victorian Sensations: Essays on a Scandalous Genre*, edited by Kimberley Harrison and Richard Fantina, 74–84. Columbus: Ohio State Univ. Press, 2006.

Index

Julia M. Wright is professor of English at Dalhousie University. She was a Canada Research Chair (2002–2012) and is the author of *Blake, Nationalism, and the Politics of Alienation* (2004) and *Ireland, India, and Nationalism in Nineteenth-Century Literature* (2007). She is also the editor of *Irish Literature, 1750–1900: An Anthology* (2008), Lady Morgan's *The Missionary* (2002) and *The O'Briens and the O'Flahertys* (2013), and the two-volume *Companion to Irish Literature* (2010). She has also coedited a number of other volumes, most recently *Handbook to Romanticism Studies* (2012).